A WORLD FULL OF GODS

The Strange Triumph of Christianity

KEITH HOPKINS

THE FREE PRESS

NEW YORK   LONDON   TORONTO   SYDNEY   SINGAPORE

*f*P

THE FREE PRESS
A Division of Simon & Schuster Inc.
1230 Avenue of the Americas
New York, NY 10020

First Free Press Edition 2000
Originally published in the UK in 1999 by Weidenfeld & Nicolson
Published by arrangement with Orion Publishing.

THE FREE PRESS and colophon are trademarks
of Simon & Schuster Inc.

Designed by Karolina Harris

Manufactured in the United States of America

1   3   5   7   9   10   8   6   4   2

Library of Congress Cataloging-in-Publication Data
Hopkins, Keith, date.
A world full of gods : the strange triumph of Christianity / Keith Hopkins.
p.   cm.
Includes bibliographical references and indexes.
1. Christianity—Origin—Miscellanea. 2. Rome—Religion—Miscellanea. I. Title.

BR129 H67 2000
270.1—dc 21   00-032127
ISBN 0-7432-0010-1

Acknowledgments

Five friends in particular have helped me enormously in writing this book, by their generosity of time and acumen: Mary Beard, Christopher Kelly, Henry Hurst, Winrich Löhr, and Seth Schwartz. James Carleton-Paget, Catherine Hezser, and William Horbury jovially tolerated and relieved some of my ignorance of Judaism and Christianity; Graham Burton, as often before, skillfully helped me at a critical time. Oisin Timoney and Caroline Vout deftly criticized and encouraged. Wolfram Kinzig, Christoph Markschies; and Markus Vinzent at different stages discussed, read, or disputed my thoughts. The provost, fellows, and managers of the Research Centre at King's College, Cambridge, provided invaluably stimulating support.

Outside Cambridge, Ryoji Motomura and Atsuko Gotoh at the University of Tokyo, Takashi Minimikawa at the University of Kyoto, Glen Bowersock, Peter Brown, and Josh Ober at Princeton, Roger Bagnall, Alan Cameron, and William Harris at Columbia, Susan Kane at Oberlin, Liz Clark at Duke, and Jan Bremmer, Wim Jongman, and Hank Versnel at Leiden and Groningen organized seminars to discuss early drafts of chapters and/or made critical comments of their own, which were vital in the process of composition and completion.

Ben Hopkins taught me about writing a film script; my other children showed more tolerance than I deserve. Rebecca Wilson cleverly persuaded me that I would finish this book. Above all, I'd like to thank the hundreds of excellent scholars, classical and biblical, whose writings it has been such a continuous pleasure to read and contemplate.

Keith Hopkins
Finchingfield
July 1999

Jennifer
Uxori dilectissimae

Contents

Illustrations

(Between pages 308 and 309)

1. Jokey fresco and graffito from lavatory (Pompeii).
2. Sexual intercourse on a tightrope. Pompeian pub scene.
3. The priests of Isis perform their rites in front of the faithful (Pompeii).
4. Fancy wall decoration in the House of the Gilded Cupids (Pompeii).
5. Jolly man weighs his erect penis against a bag of money. Entrance hall to the House of the Vettii (Pompeii).
6. Family portrait from Roman Syria (third-century mosaic).
7. The beautiful Goddess Artemis (Diana), multibreasted statue (second century, Ephesus).
8. The emperor Commodus as Demigod Hercules: inside a slaughtered lion's head (second century, Rome).
9. Christ, naked and uncircumcised, being baptized (sixth century, Ravenna).
10. The gospel writer Mark as demonic lion (fifth century, Naples).
11. Christ as lamb with halo (fifth century, Rome).
12. Christ the teacher enthroned in gold (fifth century, Rome).
13. Street scene (Pompeii).
14. Caricature of Rome's founding hero (Pompeii).
15. Household altar with statuettes of Gods (Pompeii).
16. Household Gods, bronze statuettes (Pompeii).
17. Garden made to look like a temple courtyard (Pompeii).
18. Phallus as fountain (Pompeii).
19. A grand bronze mirror back, with erotic images (first century, Rome).
20. Priests carrying a mummified crocodile in a sacred procession (first to second century, Theadelphia, Egypt).

A World
Full
of Gods

Introduction

This is a tale of passion, illusion, and controversy. It retells the magnificent though troubling story of the growth and triumph of Christianity in the Roman empire during the first three centuries after Jesus' birth. Christianity triumphed, but only after prolonged struggles with the Roman state, with competing religions, and with internal dissidents. So in order to understand the growth of early Christianity—perhaps "Christianities" would reflect its diversity better—we have to set it in its Jewish and pagan contexts, and we have to trace its fierce internal controversies.

The real Jesus was a Jew, the leader of a radical revisionist movement within Judaism. It seems improbable that he had any intention of founding a new religion. But after his execution, ordered by a combination of Jewish priests and Roman officials, the Jesus movement rapidly evolved into an independent religion, persecuted and protected by the Roman state. Three centuries later, against all the odds, the Roman emperor Constantine (306–37 CE) converted to Christianity. All his successors (except briefly Julian the Apostate, 361–63) were Christian. By the end of the fourth century, pagan rites had been banned and Christianity had become the official religion of the Roman state. Within four more centuries, the heartlands of early Christianity—Palestine, Syria, Egypt, and north Africa—had all become predominantly Muslim. Religious allegiance followed political power.

Religions create, and thrive on, passionate commitment and passionate conflicts. Jesus is a symbol both of devotion and of disagreement. Pagans and most Jews thought that it was absurd to claim that Jesus was the Son of God. And early Christians disagreed fervently among themselves as to whether Jesus was wholly divine, or wholly human, or a subtle mixture of human and divine. Modern believers have tried to forget these ancient

debates, and have largely succeeded. But these were only some of the beliefs which early Christians died and later killed for. They help to remind
us that there were then, as there still are today, many Christianities. And
it was by no means predictable which orthodoxies would win.

This book is an experiment in how to write religious history. It started
with a research project on early Christianity at King's College, Cambridge, comprising five scholars of different nationalities, religious out-
looks, and academic specialties (American, British, German; Jewish,
Protestant, Catholic, agnostic, atheist; Jewish history, Roman history,
New Testament, church history, rabbinics, patristics, theology). Unsurprisingly (in retrospect), we couldn't work together. We disagreed about
almost everything, although (as we now claim) we all learned a huge
amount from one another.

So what did I learn? Primarily that I didn't know enough, and sometimes didn't want to learn, about other faiths. Beneath the liberal veneer,
there was a reluctance, a deep resistance, to be open minded, to unlearn
the half-unconscious absorptions of childhood and adolescence. Put another way, my atheism was indelibly Protestant. And religious history is
inevitably affected by what writers, and their readers, believe. But history
is, or should be, a subtle combination of empathetic imagination and
critical analysis.

This history plays on several irreconcilable tensions. What was it like
to be there? We don't and cannot know. And yet surely empathetic imagination should play its part. We have to imagine what Romans, pagans,
Jews, and Christians thought, felt, experienced, believed. But, as with
baroque music played on ancient instruments, we listen with twentieth-
century ears. We read ancient sources with modern minds. And if we report what we do know in quasiobjective, analytical terms, then inevitably
our whole language of understanding and interpretation is deeply influenced by the modern world, and who we are in it. We cannot reproduce
antiquity. And religious history is necessarily subjective. We know from
experience that other writers, and readers, are very likely and fully entitled to disagree.

So why, then, don't we incorporate this empathetic wonder, knowledge, pseudo-objective analysis, ignorance, competing assumptions, and
disagreements into the text of the book? That's what I've tried to do.

Successive chapters explore Roman paganism, Judaism, and early Christianity in their variety and interactions. But they also explore different methods of historical reportage, description, and analysis, and some of my colleagues' objections.

We start in ancient Pompeii. Two modern time travelers report what they've seen during a brief stay, timed just before the eruption of Vesuvius. By this tactic, I wanted to share the liveliness, pervasiveness, and passion of paganism through texts and artifacts. But inevitably, we see the Roman world only through modern eyes; the alien culture of ancient Rome has to be interpreted by us. Time travelers stand for one version of history, fictionalized in order to expose the difficulties which all historians face in recreating the past. But time travelers have a restricted view; they can report only what we already know. I'm far too inhibited an academic to make things up. This is not a novel, even if it has a few novel-like characteristics. And in a letter incorporated into the text of the book, one of my liberal colleagues roundly criticizes the whole experiment: innovative perhaps, rambunctious, but from an intellectual standpoint fatally flawed. Even the endnotes, which cautiously document every step and most words, can't fend off her criticism.

The second chapter tries to go one better. But the problem is slightly different: how to evoke the flavor of an obsessional sect of fervently committed Jews from Qumran, the site of the Dead Sea Scrolls, discovered in 1947? The tiny Qumran sect of ascetic males opens a small window on the religious ferment in Roman Palestine in the first century, before the Jewish rebellion of 66–73 CE. These Jews were not proto-Christians— far from it, though they shared with Jewish Christians both religious passion and hopes about the Messiah(s). They highlight the intense religiosity in Palestine during the period in which Christianity first arose. But the Dead Sea Scrolls are repetitive and difficult to understand. So here I try to capture both the intensity of their religious passion and the difficulty of reporting it now, by using a quintessentially modern idiom, a TV drama, in which all that we see/read is mediated by a simplifying process of (mis)interpretation. This TV play is set partly in ancient Rome, partly in the modern world. The Qumran myth is replayed, as all old myths should be, with ancient and modern players, and with authentic words. But in the modern medium, much is also changed; there are, for example, slippages of time and character. That too is unlikely to please my critical colleagues. So they too are given a voice, though only after the show is over. For me, the hero of this play is the TV camera itself, which, like a historical source, arbitrarily selects what it chooses to show, never lies, and never understands.

The third chapter, on the evolution of early Christianity as a revolutionary movement, is a conventional, objective analysis. This "objectivity" is the product of my unbeliever's distance from the Christian sources; but then, this unbeliever stance might not seem "objective" to believers. Indeed, what would an objective account of early Christianity look like? This chapter concentrates on the evolution of the New Testament, on the growth of an orthodox tradition of belief, on orthodox Christians' increasing efforts to impose a unity of faith through a hierarchy of priests and the canonical New Testament. It finishes with a study of persecutions and martyrs, which partly subverts convention by arguing that the Roman state largely protected Christians. And it argues that Christian Martyr Acts, which are dramatic accounts of Christians' trials and sufferings, functioned more as an alternative than as a stimulus to martyrdom. Reading about martyrs' bravery and faith recreated the performance, with only vicarious suffering.

The fourth chapter, called "Jesus and His Twin Brother," retells some of the religious stories from the secret (apocryphal), nonorthodox writings which from the second century onward supplemented the New Testament. And Jesus' twin brother is an icon for Christian religious inventiveness. Some Christians, at least, thought they needed to pursue salvation by enlarging the divine within themselves. They needed an intermediary between their own inadequate humanity and the transcendently divine Jesus. Jesus' twin brother is a symbol of believers' need to search for God within themselves. The chapter is split round a letter from a German academic who trenchantly objects to the infantilization produced in the reader by these stories. Stories, he claims, are no substitute for rigorous intellectual analysis. Religious history, if not religion, is too serious for stories. But in the Roman world, stories, not analysis, were the stuff of religious persuasion. And storytelling used to be the stuff of history.

The second half of the book has a similar structure. We begin again with our two time travelers, Martha and James. But this time they visit Egypt, Syria, and Asia Minor (Turkey) to see something of the variety of pagan practice and religious passion. It's a radically different world, of disease, dirt, and animal sacrifice, of temples, professional priests, magic, blood, violence, short lives, and long stories. Romantically, we often imagine Greece and Rome as our cultural ancestors. We tend to forget that the strangely alien cultures of Egypt and Syria were important parts of the Roman empire and cradles of early Christianity. Suitably, in a story about religion, at the end of the chapter James is unjustly arrested, thrown into prison, summarily tried by a Roman judge, and strung up to be tortured. But in the nick of time he is saved by a miracle of modern science. This naive fiction invites the reader to reflect on the difference between the unbelievable, the believable, and the believed. Some early Christians believed that Jesus too did not actually suffer on the cross, but escaped by a magical illusion.

Chapter Six comprises a "previously unpublished" letter written by a recent convert to Christianity in the early third century seeking advice from a more experienced believer. The new Christian, Macarius, has (unwisely) accepted a dinner party invitation from an old friend, still pagan. At dinner they all discuss religion, and the pagans take the opportunity to offload all their pent-up criticisms of upstart Christianity. Ancients were not as kindly as modern liberals. Much of what they say is probably untrue, but that did not necessarily reduce its force; besides, Macarius probably exaggerates Christian virtues. Even so, he doesn't manage to say all that he wanted to, and subsequently thinks of. To add insult to injury, at dinner he is seated next to a Jew (as though there were no difference) who comforts him by giving his scurrilous account of Jesus' life: all pure invention. Long before the evening ends, most of the guests have turned from serious discussion to ghost stories and dancing girls. Macarius leaves bruised, but with his convictions undiminished.

Chapter Seven recreates the rival, semi-Christian universes of Gnostics and Manichees by retelling their versions of creation. In creation, we see the nature of God(s) and of the humans they made. Stories of creation set the stage for the first interaction between God and humans. They allow believers to explore the nature(s) of God(s) and humanity. And since practically no one nowadays is either Gnostic or Manichee, they provide us with an ideal template for perceiving how believers construct God(s) and their religion's foundation myths. For Gnostics and Manichees, one basic problem was, why did a good and omnipotent God allow evil into the world? The Gnostics' typical answer was that it was a tragic and stupid mistake, committed by God's youngest daughter, Sophia-Wisdom. Manichees saw world history as a continuous struggle between the forces of Light and Dark, good and evil. Orthodox Christians eventually followed Augustine in considering evil as humans' fatal flaw, inherited by all of us from Adam and Eve. The chapter ends with Augustine's deathbed nightmare, previously unrecorded, in which he dreams scarily that some of his beliefs were ill founded.

The final chapter is a study of Jesus, not so much of the historical Jesus as of the many and varied Jesuses of history, constructed over time. Jesus, I argue, is not just, nor even primarily, a historical person. Rather, like the sacred heroes of other great religions, he is a mirage, an image in believers' minds, shaped but not confined by the images projected in the canonical gospels. To be sure, his canonical historicity is part, but only part, of the image. But as with all beliefs, most is imagination and inspiration. History here is a history of representations, not of facts. So, ancient Christians constructed many Jesuses, as modern believers still do. Fixation on any particular version as the true Jesus is more a matter of believer choice than of historical truth or falsity.

The structure of the book is like a triple helix of multicolored and interwoven strands. The three major strands—Judaism, paganism, and Christianity—were each in themselves diverse, complex, and changing. They continually interacted, both inside themselves and with their own variants, and externally with one another. Patterns of identity and fusion are visible much more in the illusory calm of retrospection than they ever were to contemporaries. And so to reexperience the thoughts, feelings, practices, and images of religious life in the Roman empire, in which orthodox Christianity emerged in all its vibrant variety, we have to combine ancient perceptions, however partial, with modern understandings, however misleading. That is the tension and the excitement of recreating and reading a history of a vanished world which was once full of harsh realities, dreams, demons, and gods.

ONE

A World Full of Gods

INTRODUCTION

I could see no other way. Hesitantly, I placed the following advertisement in London's *Time Out:*

Wanted Urgently: two intrepid Time Travelers
Destination: Ancient Rome
Qualifications: Applicants should be in good health, nonsmokers; at least one of the successful pair will be male. Travel experience in third world essential; medical or anthropological skills an advantage. Academic knowledge of ancient Roman literature, art, or history an advantage.
　　We provide round trip, choice of status (slave, merchant, etc.), appropriate retinue, language skills (Latin and Greek), impenetrable disguise, all inoculations, substantial out-of-purse expenses (by kind gift of the Royal Netherlands Coin Cabinet), free transport between towns, life insurance, and comprehensive health insurance.
Duration of trip: 2–3 weeks. Successful applicants must keep detailed travelogue. Handsome bonus on completion.
Preliminary enquiries and further details from Sarah or Charlotte, on 0207 493 4876. Serious applicants only.

I didn't have many decent applicants, just your usual stream of dropouts and obsessives. And to be frank, at first sight neither James nor Martha (that's what they said their names were) seemed ideal, but it's a wonder what a toga can disguise. Yet they both turned out to be a fantastic success: resourceful, intelligent, and fairly knowledgeable about things Roman.

I didn't enquire too closely about their personal relations, especially when they passed the aptitude tests with flying colors and took to Latin like ducks to water. They said they wanted a break, needed the money, and had always wondered what ancient Rome was really like. Of course,

I stressed the need for absolute secrecy. I didn't want others reaping the reward of our inventions. Anyhow, to my relief, they signed the exclusive publishing contract without demur. In fact, I think they wanted to keep their trip together secret every bit as much as I did.

In due course, when the plans and technical tests were finalized, I wrote them a brief letter of confirmation.

King's College
Cambridge CB2 1ST
June 21, 1997

Dear Martha, Dear James,

Just to confirm our arrangements. Your trip is planned for July 1, 1997, at 4 A.M. Please be at the Sidgwick site steps at 11 P.M. Transport, medical, final briefing will take place then. As a precaution, please do not eat after 2 P.M. on June 30. You should both arrive at the Sidgwick site by midnight. Return will be in the late evening, July 21. We'll arrange transport home for you by taxi.

A bonus of $10,000–$15,000 will be paid to each of you on receipt of a detailed written report covering your trip. Your primary objective is to recover as much information as you can about Roman religious practices among pagans in the first three centuries CE. You have both signed a contract giving KH Inc. sole publishing, film, and TV rights. Complete confidentiality about the techniques of time travel is strictly required. But you may use any information gained about the Roman world in your scholarly lives and writings after January 1, 2000.

Itinerary: Pompeii (Italy), Tebtunis (Egypt), Hierapolis (Syria), Ephesus (Turkey), Rome. Transport by holographic time machine between locations will be provided. This will allow you a short respite for recuperation, minor recalibrations of time period, readjustments of your interactive language implant if necessary, opportunity to change persona and disguise, briefings on new site and entourage.

Status and Durations: In order to optimize your range of information, it would be best if you could change status and persona in each location, though final adjustments can be made in the light of your experiences.

Congratulations on being selected for this chance-of-a-lifetime and record-breaking experience.

From all the team, our fervent best wishes.

Keith Hopkins (Academic coordinator)

The contract with our technical backers specified that absolutely no details about the techniques of time travel should be included in the historical reportage. They would release preliminary analyses in scientific journals, and in fact the *New Scientist* has already carried articles which attracted widespread attention. What follows are extracts from Martha's and James' individual accounts.

To my surprise, their final reports were exhilarating, though a bit patchy. It was not their fault, or not completely. They came back emotionally drained and quite exhausted. The imprisonment and James' trial had been traumatizing. Each novel experience crowded into the other, and they had found it very hard to find the privacy, time, and even the light to write up as they went along. So the stories they came back with—conflicting of course—needed some drastic editing. But they always do, don't they? And besides, you know what publishers are like: they pretend to be easygoing, but in the end they want it all in one coherent style.

THE TRIP (MARTHA)

We were scared shitless. The thought of going away on vacation together was fine, rather romantic actually, though of course James wouldn't admit it, even to himself. But we really didn't know if we'd get home again, and rather stupidly we didn't realize beforehand that we couldn't talk much about what had happened. Not because of the contract, which we'd signed without reading all the details, like car rental insurance, but because no one ever believed that we had actually broken through time barriers and had gone to ancient Rome and back. Some friends did ask us about it all, with a sort of amused tolerance, but their staying power was five minutes max, as though we were talking about a package tour on the Costa Brava.

Technically, the arrangements worked out fine. We'd go to Pompeii first, partly because we thought it would be easier to find our way round a small town, not such a culture shock as Rome itself, and we had a map of the place in our minds. We weren't allowed to take any twentieth-century artifacts, though I smuggled a pack of paracetamol, antiseptic ointment, and some Tampax. Besides, no one knew how accurately the time calibrator worked, and we thought it would be inconvenient to postpone our visit to Pompeii and then arrive just after, or worse, just when, Vesuvius erupted.

We'd agreed on status and disguises with Keith before we left. In Pompeii James was to be a teacher of Greek from Ephesus, Caius Stertinius Aquila, with me (a bit against the grain) as his tagalong wife, Stertinia Eirene. But we could change status between destinations. We agreed with him that variety of perspectives would make the total trip more interesting. In Pompeii we would be ambitious Greek-speaking immigrants, semiforeigners so to speak, whose oddities would be overlooked, while we learned the ropes. That would give our interactive language implants time to improve; they were designed (like teach-yourself-typing chips) to become more competent with use. The more we heard, the better we'd speak. That was the theory anyhow.

Then we'd be rich foreign tourists in Tebtunis and Hierapolis, young provincial grandees in Rome, and for the sake of variety, skilled slaves in Ephesus. Keith promised to find us a kind owner. His promises proved as misleading as a vacation brochure. But more of that later.

POMPEII (MARTHA)

We landed outside the town just before dawn, while it was still dark. Luckily there was no one around, and once we were on the road, there was nothing (we hoped) to make us conspicuous. If anything, it was a relief to see real peasants trudging along toward their fields with baskets on their backs. James seemed anxious, but he said *"Ave"* more or less distinctly, and with increasing confidence as we went along. Soon we saw the Villa of the Mysteries on the left, and the line of grand tombs which stretch outside the town. Some are like miniature houses, with stone dining rooms outside for banquets to feast the dead. One of the grandest tombs had vivid pictures of men killing wild beasts and of gladiators fighting and killing one another, probably at games held to commemorate the dead man. Charming.

We got to the city of the living through the city of the dead, with a pyre still smoldering from a funeral the night before. Human bodies burning, I thought, must smell like roast pork, enough to turn one vegetarian. Anyhow, we had made it to Pompeii—to judge from the telltale signs of damage and renovation, sometime after the earthquake of 62 CE.

A peasant with a cartload of vegetables had blocked the central arch of the gate; he was arguing vociferously with a tax collector levying a small percentage on goods coming into the town. We sidled through the smaller gate for pedestrians. No one paid any attention to us. So I turned around to see the outcome of the peasant's argument; of course, he was paying up, and cursing feebly. But I didn't look where I was going and almost bumped into a couple of men we had been following. They had stopped to say a brief prayer at the altar and statue of Minerva tucked into a niche just inside the gate. They were probably praying for a good day in town. So were we.

We went along with a gentle stream of others, toward the Forum—first street left, third right, I remembered from our briefing. The streets were paved with large stone blocks and had high curbs protecting the sidewalks, with occasional stepping-stones across the road, in case of rain and to avoid the horrendous litter—no plastic bags or Coke bottles, but general garbage, vegetable peelings, donkey droppings, the occasional carcass of a cat. We saw a few live ones around, skin and bones. The dogs, wolfish-looking hounds, looked better fed but ferocious; luckily they were usually chained. Some houses had a warning mosaic of a dog just inside the door with the motto *Cave Canem* (Beware of the Dog) written below.

It all looked much more lived in than it does now, which is hardly surprising, and much more crowded (plate 13). Thinking back, what I remember most are the noises (people hammering, shouting, selling, arguing), the bright colors, especially on stone columns and marble statues (which are now white, but most of them weren't then), the enormous gap between rich and poor (much more visible, once we'd actually been inside a few houses), the smells and flies everywhere. No wonder some rich guys went round in litters holding roses to their noses.[1]

Our first job was to find an inn and buy some slaves (without them we'd get no respect on the street and be an easy target for thieves). But before anything else, we needed breakfast. We hadn't eaten since yesterday. "I'd kill for a coffee," I muttered to James.

"By the look of it, you'll have to do with some bread and goat's milk from that shop over there," he replied laconically, in hesitant Greek, "unless you're feeling more adventurous." James had some greasy-looking grilled sausage, which I thought risky. I just had bread and milk; at least dieting was going to be easy here.

When we turned into Mercury Street, we both stood stock-still, like old-style Europeans amazed on first seeing Manhattan. The street was broader now, and swept relatively clean. Over the street, crowded with people between its boldly colored walls, was a tall triumphal marble arch, with another arch echoing it farther along, marking the grand entrance to the Forum. Astride the arch was an emperor on horseback, in shining bronze; and by each arch, the grandiose marble pediment and bronze roof tiles of two temples, one, as we found out, dedicated to the Good Fortune of the emperor Augustus, jutting into the street, and the other to Jupiter, which filled a whole side of the Forum. Of course, none of these buildings was tall like a skyscraper, but in the Roman scale of things, temples and emperor lorded it together, towering over us humble citizens who walked underneath.[2]

At our level, the house walls were windowless on the ground floor, I assume to minimize risks of robbery, but they were plastered and painted. And on the paint were dozens of slogans, graffiti of every type, so that the whole surface within reach was covered, like an old-style New York subway car. There were new and old election posters for town magistrates: "The fruit sellers want M. Cerinius as *aedile*." "All the fruit sellers want M. Holconius Priscus as *duovir*." There were painted advertisements for a tavern, and then just your normal clutter of scribbles: "Down with Nucerians" (a local rival town), "Up Pompeii" *(sic)*, "Vespa[sian]" (the new emperor's name), "Aphrodite," "Romulus," various people's names, and "Martial is a cunt licker."[3] These Romans seem to have a sexual fixation. Well, now I think of it, perhaps we all do. But they express it, or the men do, with phalli everywhere. But more of that later.

A couple of minutes later, through the second arch, we went into the Forum. Actually, James, who was watching a pretty young girl bending over to fill a bucket with water at a fountain, fell into the Forum, down two steps, right into the lap of a ragged beggar, sensibly squatting at the bottom. James apologized in what I thought was impressively vernacular Latin, but a guy saying a quick prayer at an altar tucked against the wall gave him a very odd stare. In his embarrassment, James reached for his purse and gave the beggar, to judge from his reaction, an absurdly generous tip. Anyhow, the beggar thanked him effusively, and said that Good Fortune must have tripped him up.

My initial impression of Pompeii (and the whole trip confirmed it) was that there were temples and Gods, and humans praying to them, all over the place: at the entrance to the town, at the entrance to the Forum; there were altars at crossroads, Gods in niches as you went along, with passersby just casually blowing a kiss with their hands to the statue of a God set in a wall.[4] And of course, here in the Forum, the ceremonial center of the town, there were temples, altars, Gods, heroes just about everywhere we looked, to say nothing of statues of emperors and of local dignitaries, on horseback or simply standing there, impressively impassive, in marble. Our end of the square was filled by the grand Temple to Jupiter, with Vesuvius magnificently snowcapped behind. And all the rest of the buildings looked as though they could be temples too.[5]

We wandered farther into the Forum, trying to look unself-conscious, but were pestered, inevitably, I suppose, by other beggars, who spotted that we were strangers, and by a sharp-eyed youth who asked us if we wanted an inn. He knew the best. We shook him off with the experience gained in modern Egypt; we could have told him that his numerous descendants still flourished, but he wouldn't have understood. On the left was the Market Hall, filled with vegetable sellers and shouts and, to judge from the smell, with fish. There were lots of stalls in the Forum itself, and under the porticoes around. But they were selling food, cloth, leather, and pots. We wanted something grander.

We thought we'd find a slave trader in the commercial meeting place, the Hall of Eumachia, named after a priestess who had paid for its refurbishment. But that turned out to be a modern misconception. It was decorated rather pretentiously on the outside with statues of Roman heroes—Aeneas and Romulus (Rome's mythical founders) and Anchises (Aeneas' father). Their identification was made easier for us—and for semiliterate Pompeians, we thought—by largish stone plaques telling us who they were. This fashion for glorifying Rome's heroic past had started in the city of Rome, promoted by the emperors there. Smaller Italian towns copied it—as though Pompeii could look like Rome! We even saw an Aeneas picture above a shop in the main street. It was rather like flying the national flag to drum up custom.[6]

In fact, not everyone took this heroization of traditional history so seriously. Inside one private house which we visited later, we saw a small obscene caricature of Aeneas and Anchises, painted with dogs' heads and large drooping penises, and carrying a dice box instead of the sacred household Gods (plate 14).[7] In one sense the official propaganda had obviously worked well enough. For a caricature to succeed, the Aeneas image had to be immediately recognizable; on the other hand, authority here was obviously not so oppressive that antiauthoritarian jokes were banned, at least so long as they were kept inside.

Anyhow, we went through the grand entrance of the Eumachia building, decorated with acanthus leaves. And it wasn't a hive of commerce, after all, more like a social meeting place. But James eventually plucked up courage and asked a group of men where we could buy slaves. Several of them made competing suggestions, but one of them said that a slave trader from Macedonia was in town. He had sold several slaves yesterday at Toranius' auction house. Some might be left over. He called a young boy over, obviously one of his slaves, and told him to guide us there.

BUYING A SLAVE (MARTHA)

God, they looked depressed, and shivering in spite of the spring sunshine. A gang of eight male slaves, chained in a line by their necks, slouched against a wall in the courtyard.[8] "I'm sorry, they're sold," the slave trader Caprilius said, without a hint of apology. "I haven't got much left, or not at your price," he went on. "Of course, if you're feeling extravagant"—he winked at James like a used-car salesman producing a Rolls-Royce, and nodded to his assistant, who brought out two stunningly pretty curly-haired boys, aged about ten.

What I wanted to say is not printable. Of course, I trust James completely, but I didn't know how native he might be induced to go. Besides, it's all very well having an interactive language implant, so that we could speak Greek and Latin increasingly well, but what we really needed was knowledge about the culture. How did Roman wives signal no, I mean NO! to their husbands? Actually, I guessed from the slave dealer's posture that I shouldn't have been there. This was man's business. Anyhow, as soon as I heard the price, I knew James' virtue was safe. Fifty thousand sesterces each (and twenty times what we expected to pay) was more than we had in the kitty. So I just looked demure. Perhaps I *was* learning the culture.

In the end, buying slaves proved harrowing but simple. We found a strapping big youth called Myrmex, who might have been a good buy but for the fact that he was quite obviously simple. He had an iron collar around his neck, not because he was really a runaway but just in case he got lost. Later that day we took him to a blacksmith and had the collar taken off.[9] His back was quite scarred from old whippings, and he seemed understandably anxious about who was going to buy him, but to judge from his answers to James' questions, he seemed basically amenable.

What amazed me was the speed with which James seemed to get used to examining the bodies of the slaves on sale, as though they were animals. "Open your mouth, strip naked, open your legs." The Greek word for slave dealer literally means "body seller." And that's exactly how these slaves were being treated, as bodies, just like used cars, in fact. We bought the other two slaves quickly enough, because effectively there wasn't much choice. Obviously, we paid far too much, to judge from the speed and amiability with which the dealer had the contract drawn up and witnessed, and the sales tax paid. At least the contract told us the date; we had come to Pompeii in the eighth consulship of the emperor Vespasian (77 CE). We knew what these locals didn't; lots of them were about to be wiped out by the volcano.

James bought a slave for me, a very pretty olive-skinned girl called Fotis, in her late teens, from Asia Minor. We were lucky to get her—she'd arrived just too late for yesterday's auction. She'd been put on the market by her previous owner's widow, but not before she'd been branded in revenge for her ex-husband's affections. Poor girl, she kept trying to cover the mark up. And for himself James bought the ugliest fellow you could imagine, thick lipped, potbellied, squinting—his whole body shook when he laughed—but with intelligent eyes and a sharp tongue. You could see that he would be a load of trouble, but he'd be smart enough to help us through the maze of Roman culture—at a price and if he wanted to. At least, he wanted us to buy him, practically begged James. "Buy me," he said, "and by Isis I'll be useful to you."[10] His name was Aesop.

Once we'd got our three slaves, we felt almost like real Romans, able to cut a figure as we went back across the Forum again, off to buy clothes for them as well as for ourselves, and to find a good room at an inn. The Forum was even busier now, perhaps because there was a sacrifice going on in front of the Temple of Jupiter. It was March 1, the birthday of

Mars. A white bull wreathed in flowers stood ready for the chop, at the great altar in front of the temple. A town dignitary, looking proud, stood above our heads on the temple platform, recited a longish prayer, poured a libation, and burned incense on the smaller altar up there, and then solemnly processed down the narrow temple steps, toward the bull, where near-naked slaves brandished hammer and knives, waiting to stun and kill the poor animal.

I realized that worrying about slaughter was mere sentimentality. For poor citizens of Pompeii, the bull meant a rare piece of meat, even a public banquet with free wine, or sometimes, if the meat ran out, just cakes or biscuits in the shape of the emperor.[11] For the richest Pompeians, being a priest was part of the job which every town magistrate did for a year at a time. Public sacrifice gave magistrates an opportunity to show off, win prestige, dramatize their status, and repay to the citizens a small percentage of what they had taken in rents.

A small crowd watched the sacrifice; they had come along as part of the procession. Other people gave a passing glance and went on with their business. I thought it was rather like a modern church service in an ancient cathedral, a core of adherents with lots of tourists milling around. But of course, all this was happening outside, at one end of the Forum, as though it was designed for an ever-fluctuating mixture of participants and spectators. We could be there, without belonging. In the Roman world, only Jews, Christians, and mystery cults kept their private religious rites solely for insiders.

THE BATHS (MARTHA)

We decided to split up. James asked the innkeeper where the best baths for women were. The innkeeper said that if I wanted the women-only baths, he'd heard there was a respectable establishment in town. But everyone said that the new baths for men and women, just outside the town walls toward the sea, were more luxurious, though more expensive than the older baths inside the town. So we walked in that direction together, each now like any prosperous Roman, with our own slave attendant. Well, when I say we went together, I mean that James walked ahead followed by Aesop and Myrmex, and I followed with Fotis behind me, carrying an oil flask, a flesh scraper, towels, and a change of clothes.

When we got to the Sea Gate, James went off to do some more shopping, and I turned off with Fotis to the baths.

It was still only midmorning, more of a time for women to bathe than for men, or for mixed bathing. I paid at the entrance, not a huge sum, but enough to frighten off *hoi polloi*. Just inside the entrance, there was only one changing room. Its decoration was a show stopper.[12] Fotis just giggled. The equipment was ordinary enough: a simple trestle table with wooden boxes on top for us to put our clothes in. And then, above the table, there was a painting of the table with numbered boxes on it (*I, II, III*, and so on); the picture jokily mirrored reality. But above these numbered boxes, above our heads, there was a whole series of sexy pictures. So customers had a double mnemonic. They could remember where they had left their clothes either by number or by type of sexual coupling.

You know how modern textbooks on Roman art or social history tend to leave sex out, as though it wouldn't be right for us to have sexually outrageous Romans as our cultural ancestors.[13] And college students have sex on the brain enough, so there's no need to add stimulus. Besides, it's exploitative to use women as passive images of male desire, and modern scholars claim that Roman men were interested only in conquest by penetration, and thought that mutual gratification was decadent or even diseased. OK. But here in real Pompeii, in the only changing room of these upscale baths, used by women, men, and children, explicit pictures of sexual couplings confront you whether you like it or not. And the women (or their images projected by men) were not uniformly passive. Sure, in *II* the man was having the woman from behind, but number *I* showed the woman on top, and *III* was a picture of a woman fellating a man, interrupted in his reading. These changing rooms were clearly aiming at an educated clientele. Then to balance matters, there was cunnilingus by a man (Roman satirists always sneer at this, as though it was demeaning for a real man to devote himself to a woman's pleasure). The next picture was more conventional, except that the woman had one leg athletically over the man's shoulder.

After all that, the sexual combinations became rather more complicated, and I felt a bit embarrassed at the length of time I'd already spent looking at them, with Fotis standing behind me. Not that she was looking modestly at the floor; far from it. She was taking it all in, probably encouraged by the fact that I couldn't help myself smiling, though I personally didn't find the pictures erotic or arousing. Anyhow, the next two pictures showed a trio of two men and a woman, and then a quartet of two men and two women in a homosexual and heterosexual chain. And the series finished with a solitary man reading a papyrus roll, but with his penis seriously deformed by testicular dropsy, as though to say (at least that's what I thought), all's well above, but not below.[14]

Perhaps collectively the pictures were saying, Here we cater for all tastes (except the prudish). Or more kindly, Here you must undress, but no matter what you expose, we've seen it all before, in pictures. I suppose one stunning aspect of Roman society was this contrast between the staid clothing of public appearances in the Forum outside and the almost daily routine of seeing one another stripped of clothing, naked in the baths.

Well, this was my real baptism into Roman life. So I took the plunge and undressed; Fotis did too. Naked, we went into the first room of the baths proper, the cold room. It was extraordinarily pretty, with marble floors, space for exercising, and a cold bath. Water was tumbling down mosaic steps to produce a wall of water, and below that a large pool, painted blue and decorated with fish. We joined them and a human couple splashing energetically. We soon understood why: the water was freezing.

We decided to leave exercises to another day and hurried into the next room. My commitment to Roman pleasures was dwindling. Besides, I thought that we'd have to follow certain routines or look strange, and I decided I looked strange enough as it was. The next two rooms were increasingly hot, and more crowded. People must stay here longer. And to judge from the gossip levels, most of them were regulars; perhaps they came here every day. Luckily, there was room for us on a bench in the hottest room, near the window in the apse (did Christians building churches borrow apses from Roman baths?), overlooking a small garden and the canal beyond, where ships were tied up. The glass was a bit thick, but the view was still attractive. We could watch the world go by. And while we sweated with lazy pleasure, sailors carted goods up the slope into the city, and slaves doubtless shoveled their sweat into the furnaces beneath us.[15]

Luckily, Fotis knew what to do. She occasionally splattered a bucket of cold water on the hottest stones, to create more steam. And when I found the heat unbearable, all we had to do was to go into the next room for another swim, in a comfortably heated pool. At intervals, Fotis oiled me, gave me a massage, and scraped my skin. I began to see how Romans could get addicted to owning slaves and bathing (incidentally, the Latin word for washed, *lautus*, means "prosperous"). I could get attached to the whole slow ritual of bathing, moving from one room to another, chatting, exercising, contemplating one's own privilege. This was the Roman equivalent of a plush London club. And of course, I'd even got used to my own, though not to everyone else's, nakedness. You could even understand perhaps why Roman guys had so much of a penis fixation; they were always on show. One emperor even chose his ministers by the size of their dicks, a bit unimaginative, and probably a fib.[16]

I haven't said anything about religion and bathing, because in these baths there were no statues of Gods, though there were in other baths we visited. There was a painting of the Goddess Fortune in the toilet, but James will probably tell you more about that than you want to know. One thing did strike me, when we visited the temple of Isis a couple of days later. The paintings in these baths—country scenes, strange animals, sea battles, and mythical figures—were very much like the paintings in the temple. But then, in Roman life baths and temples were complementary, not opposed.

ROOM AT THE INN (JAMES)

I was worried. I don't think Martha ever realized how worried I was. After all, I was the man. I would have to do all the talking for both of us, at least in public. It was my neck sticking out. But the language chip worked well, improved with use. Clever design.

I felt much better after breakfast—well, for a time. Then my stomach turned liquid. Emergency; luckily I remembered there was a large public toilet just behind the Forum. Wizened hag at door took my money, and fumbled for change. I gestured generosity and made for nearest seat, incredibly low, but made of stone and clean. Instant relief and looked around. God! I thought, and saw a Goddess looking down, painted on rough plaster, presiding over her twenty-seater, set around three sides of the wall. No privacy, just functional, and flushed, intermittently. Men and women mixed; just as well it had been an emergency, might have hesitated otherwise and looked for a quiet corner. Some people went in the street, you could tell from the stink and the occasional notices painted on walls: "Piss or shit here, and you'll have all the Gods after you." Strange guys, these Romans, at least different; there's a public toilet at Ostia, I read somewhere, made out of old tombstones.[17] Perhaps they regularly went there for a crap and a chat with chums.

And while I'm on the subject, these large open public toilets, forty- or fifty-seaters even, were quite common. I went to one in Ephesus, but could never quite bring myself to go *with* Martha. And I always thought I was uninhibited. Just in words. I went to a small toilet in a bar in Pompeii, with a large painted Goddess Fortuna in a red dress towering over a naked male shitter, squatting on a pair of entwined snakes, the normal emblem of prosperity (plate 1). Symbolically, he was shitting exactly where the household altar normally would have been. So you squat, just as he does, with the Goddess Fortuna looking down at you. Above him the words are scratched/painted: "Shitter, shun evil" (*Cacator, cave malum*). Is it meant to be scary, or funny? To complete the ensemble, underneath the painting there was a cheap terra-cotta altar. So these guys have Gods in (what we would think of as the strangest places) toilets, baths, bars, make fun of them, and worship them at the same time.[18]

There was room at the inn, just off the main drag, near the amphitheater. I reserved two, upstairs. Saw with relief, latrine for each floor, not private but not superpublic either. Then discovered that slave Aesop expected me to defecate into chamber pot, and him to clear away. He was discreet, stood with water and towel, but I found him standing there unsettling. Romans, I decided after thinking, have a different sense of personal space. I realize that you don't want to hear my personal experiences, but they did feel significant at the time, and the point that Romans are different seemed important.

Most guests were leaving as we arrived. Perhaps we're odd too. The courtyard inside the inn still had some carts and animals. Its back wall had an altar for the landlord or visitors to pray at; detective James deduced, from ashes and half-burned incense sticks, that it was used often. Various small clay statues stood around in niches, little Gods in skirts (Lares), plus your regular snakes painted on the wall underneath, for good luck. There was a large picture on another wall of the landlord pouring wine; that and cartoons in the nearby wine shop illustrate that

Romans have a passion for gambling and fistfights, and make jokes about sex and constipation.[19] *Plus ça change*, but St. Augustine wouldn't have approved.

OK, you want examples. But don't expect high-class humor from inns. The bedroom walls, like the street walls outside, were covered in graffiti. "Vibius Restitutus slept here all alone and missed his Urbana," poor guy; felt more sympathy for him than for "C. Valerius Venustus soldier of the first cohort of the palace guard I fucked mightily [*maxime*]." Actually, the writing was difficult to decipher; could have been "I fucked Maximus" instead.[20]

One local bar had a bronze bell hanging over the counter shaped as a humpbacked pygmy, with several large penises and five bells. To get service, you just yanked on one of the penises. We saw bells like this all over Pompeii, and in grand houses too. Some quite artistically made. Vulgar, you think. Well, that's nothing. Inside taverns, guys quite often played with counters made of bronze or bone. These counters had numbers on one side (*I–XVI* in one series, *I–XXX* in another) and on the other side either explicit sex scenes, rather like what Martha saw in the baths, or the head of an emperor, a God, or a hero. Or they had mottoes for vices or virtue; so Thief scored 2, Adulterer 3, Swindler 4, Queer 8, Impotent 8, Fucker 8, Cunt Licker 12, Lover 30.[21] But I still don't know (I asked, but couldn't understand the answer) whether these were bonus or penalty points. Pity, otherwise you'd have a Roman moral economy by numbers.

Another tavern had an imaginative wall painting of a dining room (plate 2) in which two ropes are stretched taut and secured at one end to the legs of a table, and at the other end offstage. Two dancers balance on the tightropes, a man and a woman, both naked or almost. The woman wears a yellow band which supports but does not cover her naked breasts. She is leaning forward, the man is fucking her from behind, while each of them is holding in one hand a wineglass almost full of red wine, which is clearly shown to be slightly at an angle, off-balance.[22] A male fantasy, a provocative sexual image, but even as a barroom fresco in a tavern, it's more bawdy than anything I ever came across as a sex-crazed adolescent in Manchester. It's the sort of thing you can see in videos, if you want to, but what struck me as strange here was its open visibility on a wall. Christianity demolished such public fantasies; in my subculture at least, you can enjoy them only secretly and guiltily. But here in Pompeii, eroticism (or a male version of it) is public, pervasive, and ostensibly condoned.

Roman inns have a rotten reputation, even among Romans. Inns are dirty, smoky (the open charcoal fires were much worse than cigarettes), filled with thieves, dancing girls who expect to have sex with customers, or vice versa, and bad food.[23] OK. That's a few facts mixed with rumors; but you know how fantasy and reality interweave. We heard lots of stories about inn food, again mostly pure fantasy, like ads for nightmare vacations: how a man ordered pork stew and found human fingers. Another one was about the nightmares you get from eating cheese. One hotel customer ate cheese, fell into a high fever from which no one could wake him. His friends feared for his life. Finally, when he recovered, several days later, he told them where he had been. The treacherous innkeeper's wife, skilled in magic, had drugged him and converted him into a horse to carry supplies to a distant town, and it was only when the convoy of pack animals got back that he had recovered.

The man who told us this story was educated and respectable. He himself (typical!) had heard it from someone completely trustworthy. Both apparently believed it to be absolutely true.[24] No wonder this was a world pervaded with belief in the supernatural. Really sensible hotel customers controlled their fate by getting their own slaves to cook food separately in the courtyard.[25] And that's what we did. The quality of the cooking wasn't great, and Aesop probably ripped us off something terrible, saving up for his freedom, I suppose, but at least we could eat what we wanted and didn't have to put up with the raucous songs in the common dining room.

ISIS IN PROCESSION (MARTHA)

We got up quite early, to get good places from which to watch. The crowd gradually became more excited, and even the sausage sellers gave up shouting their wares and joined in as spectators. I suppose that was one of the main differences between Roman religion and your stereotypical Christianity. Christianity is an insider religion; ceremonies are, or used to be, strictly for believers; nonbelievers, keep out. Pagan religious ceremonies, by contrast, always involved at least two sets: participants and observers.

Anyhow, this procession celebrating the opening of the seas to sailing ships involved dozens of people, rather like a village fair. First came people in costume, one got up as a soldier, another as a huntsman brandishing a hunting knife and spear. Yet another was dressed as a woman, with gold sandals, wig, silk dress, and expensive jewelry. Then came a man got up as a gladiator, and another pretending to be a magistrate, in purple-bordered toga, and yet another as a philosopher, with goatee, cloak, and staff. But what the crowd liked best was a tame bear, dressed as a respectable matron, carried in a sedan chair, and a monkey in a yellow cloak, made up as a caricature of Ganymede, Jupiter's toyboy.[26]

Then came the real procession, led by women dressed in pure white, crowned with garlands of spring flowers, and from the folds of their dresses they scattered even more flowers over the road, in preparation for the Goddess. After them, more women; some with polished bronze mirrors attached to their backs to magnify the oncoming Goddess, others gesturing with ivory combs as though they were combing the Goddess' hair, still others sprinkling costly perfume over the ground. And finally, in this part of the procession, men and women together, calling out the Goddess' name and carrying lamps, candles, and tapers.

Next a whole orchestra of pipes, flutes, and trumpets, and a chorus of carefully chosen boys, all in white and singing a hymn, followed by attendants shouting, "Make way for the Goddess." Then came the initiates of Isis, dressed all alike in white linen. We found out later, when we stayed at Poppaeus' house, that Isis devotees included some of the richest families in Pompeii. The women were gauzily veiled, the men had their heads completely shaven, all of them waving rattles of bronze and silver, some even of gold.

After them came the stars of the procession, the priests of Isis, in tight linen skirts with the top drawn tight around their chests (plate 3). They looked fantastically sexy, I thought, but a bit chilly. They carried the cult's holy symbols, a lantern shaped like a ship, made of gold. The second priest carried the "Altar of Help," or that's what one of our neighbors helpfully told us in his excitement. A third priest carried a palm branch made of fine gold leaf and a staff, making him look like the Roman God Mercury; another carried an incense burner in the shape of a crooked left hand ("That's meant to represent justice," my talkative neighbor said) and a golden jug shaped like a woman's breast, from which he dripped libations of milk. The last two priests in this part of the procession carried a gold sieve and a wine jar, containing not wine but water, as we saw later, with which to purify the chief priest's hands and the image of the Goddess, back at the Temple of Isis in town.

The last part of the formal procession consisted of shaven-headed priests representing Gods, Gods on earth as it were, with human feet. One of them wore a mask of the dog-headed Anubis, who guides souls to hell and the lands of the blessed, while a second carried a statuette of the cow-headed Isis, mother of all. Then came two more priests, one with a box hiding the cult's most sacred mysteries, whose exact character only priests know precisely. Some people say it contains the head of Osiris. When he was murdered, his sister/lover, Isis, searched all over Egypt for the chopped-up bits of his body. Other people say it's his penis in the box.[27] The last priest held a gleaming vase, golden and long spouted, with a snake for a handle, formed like a hooded cobra ready to strike; it also looked just like the vases which Egyptians used for the entrails of the dead, though it actually contained water from the River Nile—at least that's what our credulous neighbor claimed.

I feel I've gone on a bit about the Isis procession, but you did ask me to write all I could about Roman religion, and this is what we saw, or rather what I say we saw. Of course, I have very little idea what the people around me made of the procession. For the most part they looked as though they were enjoying the show, and it was impressive, all that gleaming gold and the pantomime of Gods on earth. It certainly looked as though the cult of Isis here had strong popular support, and the patronage of prosperous people. And the shaven-headed male devotees had made a public statement of their religious commitment, almost like coming out nowadays. As one of the priests told James later: "Once you have begun to serve the Goddess, you will be in a better position to appreciate the rewards of your freedom."[28] Mutatis mutandis, that sounded quite Christian, but perhaps several religions/ideologies, including capitalism, disguise drudgery as freedom.

Throughout our whole trip, religion in the Roman world, as we saw it, was largely a matter of performance. Romans joined in rituals—whether domestic or public, seasonal or life-cycle, personal or institutional, as participants or spectators. This didn't mean that participants had no religious fervor or feelings; only, as I understood it, that there was no particular emphasis on specifying the precise nature of religious beliefs. Of course, we may have got the wrong informants, though once I think about it, I realize that you can't get wrong informants. There is no justification for privileging informants who intellectualize religion. Perhaps that's what I'm doing, and that presumably is your job, Keith, so I'd better get on with describing.

Once the procession was past, we all joined in and went down to the seashore, where a beautifully made model ship was loaded with expensive perfumes and sent on its way, as a harbinger of future safe journeys for sailors. The chief priest said solemn prayers, did a trick or two with egg and sulphur, to judge from the flashes and smell, and the crowd joined in with libations of milk and meal poured into the sea. We knew what it was because we bought some from the vendors, who had magically rematerialized from the crowd of worshipers, like space travelers.

And then everyone, well actually lots of people, wandered off or sat down to picnic on the beach, but the devotees and hangers-on processed with the sacred objects back to the temple in town. There the chief priest stood on the steps of the temple, surrounded by the lesser priests and lines of devotees. Another priest read out more prayers, some about the morning's ritual and others praising the emperor, the Senate, the knights, the entire people of the Roman empire. That was quite important, I thought. Unofficial cults like those of Isis kept their noses clean with the authorities by praising the status quo. And everyone around, well most of them, applauded, brought flowers, and went up to the silver statue of Isis, which had been carried in the parade, and kissed her feet.

Finally, the cult statues and sacred objects were taken inside the temple. It became clear that only initiates were allowed inside, and James had far too much hair to look like a bald devotee of Isis, so I snuck up to one of the under priests (perhaps a *pastophoros?*), flashed a charming smile, and showed him a gold coin. He shook his head firmly, but winked and told me to come back, to the side door of the temple, at dusk. He could show me a thing or two then, he said. He took the coin though—as a contribution to Isis, of course.

The more I thought about it, I wasn't at all sure what this priest guy had in mind. You know the old stories. Credulous woman goes to temple of Isis to stay the night in contemplation of the divine and have communion with the God, and a sneaky priest lets some fellow with a crush on her hide there as well. What's more, this fellow takes advantage of her faith by disguising himself as the god Anubis, complete with dog's head, and then rapes her. She, poor simpleton, still doesn't know she's been duped, until he, the idiot, typical macho male, boasts to her. Outrage, scandal. Even the emperor gets to hear of it, crucifies the guilty priest, and burns down the temple of Isis.[29] But then, perhaps it's just a story.

Ideally, of course, these priests were men of virtue and high standing. Only a few years back, the emperor Vespasian and his son had spent all night at the temple of Isis and Sarapis at Rome, just before they celebrated their triumph over the Jews.[30] So, did I really have reason to worry?

ISIS—A CONVERSION (JAMES)

That evening, after supper, Martha went to bed quite early. She'd decided it was too risky to overnight in the temple of Isis. She had had enough of Romans, and of me, I suspected, for a day. Left to my own devices, I went to one or two taverns to sample local wine, disgusting, and culture. One of them had a sign outside of two erect penises and a cup. It promised more than it delivered. The serving girls inside were quite fetching, but I thought there were limits to what Martha might forgive me for. Besides, you never know what you might catch, even if it was pre-syphilis. Still, the pictures round the walls were quite suggestive; they fluctuated between constipation and erotics.[31]

In the beginning the place was full and rowdy. Then it got a bit quieter, and some of the regulars settled down to gambling on a sort of board-game, called XII Tables. It looked rather like backgammon, with dice made of bone and counters. But even that involved occasional shouting and swearing. I got the sense of imminent violence, bubbling below the surface. On the table next to mine, a hulking, red-faced workman triumphantly shouted, "I'm out!" His opponent, a thin runt dressed in leather apron, objected: "That's not a *III*, it's a *II*." In a flash the table was over, and they were squaring up to each other, charge and counter-charge, with their friends holding them back. Hulk: "You cheat. Mine was a *III*. I won." Runt: "Come off it, you cocksucker. I won." But then the bartender, a diminutive hunchback, got in on the act, and brave guy tugged at the bigger fellow by his clothes, and told them both: "Go and brawl outside."[32]

I got quite drunk, but that helped me pluck up courage to speak to my neighbors, two youngish men, about thirty, who were at least as far gone

as I was. We chatted about this and that, and then one left. He said he
was quite scared of his father; he had given him a terrible time last night,
bawled him out for being drunk and a social disgrace. Couldn't risk it
again.[33] I found it quite dispiriting that grown Roman men still had to be
subservient to their fathers. In our culture, that job falls to wives. Perhaps Roman men had two bosses.

Cnaeus and I got talking, and I paid for another jar of wine. I told him
I'd seen the Isis procession that morning. "Lot of rogues," he said, "just
in it for the money. I was initiated once; cost me a fortune." I murmured
something sympathetic. "It was what I thought I wanted," he said, "so I
deserved what I got, I suppose." He took another slug of the inn's disgusting wine and raised his glass to a small statue of Jupiter in the
corner.[34]

"It was their promise of a new life now, and life after death in the
Elysian fields (paradise), which got to me. You probably know the stuff;
all the mysteries make similar promises. But Isis seemed something special. I had friends who had been initiated, and although they were a bit
secretive, I knew I would survive the fake-death rite, and I did. It was the
salvation and rebirth which I didn't get. But beforehand I was keen (like
a starving dog offered meat), and they made me wait until I was all keyed
up and agreed to everything they demanded. Well, I suppose, they had
the promise of heaven and the threat of hell on their side, so it wasn't a
fair contest.

"I had to pay a large initiation fee, and I spent a small fortune on all
the preparations. The new initiate has to pay for his own celebratory
banquet, you know. So, on the day of my initiation, the priest took me to
the temple and slowly went through the morning ritual with the normal
spiel. Then, from a secret hiding place, he brought out the sacred books
and read me the special instructions for my initiation. It was all written
in that Egyptian sign writing, which is completely illegible and mysterious. Like the *ingénu* I was then, I was very impressed.

"I went to the baths with the priest and a group of initiates—yes, just
to the normal baths—and got thoroughly washed, and then back at the
temple, down in the underground crypt, the priest prayed for the blessing of the Gods on me, and sprinkled water all over me."

I interrupted, and said it sounded just like a Christian initiation ritual,
but Cnaeus hadn't heard of Christians. He just looked blank. I suppose
there weren't many of them around then.

Cnaeus went on (I've clarified his drunkenly disjointed account), "And you know what, when they took me back up to the temple proper, I was solemnly ordered: for the next ten days, no sex, no meat, no wine."

His voice sank to a loud whisper. "You know I'm not meant to tell anyone the secrets of initiation," he said, "but I'll tell you." No one was listening. He belched generously and grabbed another mouthful of olives. "They took me down to their underground chamber again, gave me some drug to drink, so that I felt very drowsy, and of course, I'd been fasting, well not completely, for the last ten days, so I felt quite weak. They stripped me naked ("putting off the old man," they said), and left me drowsily alone in the pitch dark, on what I only saw later was a funeral couch. They told me I was going through the rites of the God Osiris, and as you know, he was chopped in pieces. You can imagine, I was scared to death; well, I was virtually dead, with statues of Gods all around me, and bald priests praying and chanting.[35]

"Then suddenly they woke me with a whole ring of flaming torches. That scared the shit out of me. But they were quite reassuring, and dressed me in fresh new clothes (of course, it was me who paid for them), to mark my "rebirth." And, they said, provided I was attentive in my service to the Goddess (that is, more money for the priests) and constantly chaste (not a hope, mate, but you can buy a few pardons), I'd get a longer life and happy immortality from the Goddess, who favors *you* (that's what they said then).[36]

"The whole ritual lasted three days, with two feasts in the special banqueting rooms they've got behind the temple, and lots of the faithful gorging themselves at my expense. You'd imagine they'd all been fasting, not just me."

"What was the best bit?" I asked.

"If you're into this sort of stuff," Cnaeus replied, "then the high point, I suppose, was the morning after my initiation. They dressed me up like a God—in a wonderful full-length cloak, embroidered with dragons and griffons and magical birds. I wore a crown of palm leaves and held a flaming torch. All this behind closed doors. Then they let the others in, and two of the priests with a dramatic flourish opened the curtains, and there was me for everyone to behold, admire, and congratulate: divine instead of mortal, on this the birthday of my initiation.[37]

"That was the high point. The low point came later, when I discovered that they wanted to initiate me again, and at considerable extra cost.

So I quit. Quite a lot of my friends still do Isis. But next year," Cnaeus said, and got up, much to the relief of the bartender and Aesop, who both looked as though they were asleep on their feet, "I'm going to be one of the town's mayors (*duoviri*), and one of my old slaves (I freed him, of course) is going to be master of the Lares of the emperor Vespasian. You know, I met him once, before he became emperor. One of my family married Nero." And this time, Cnaeus Poppaeus really did whisper. In some circles Nero had been distinctly unpopular, and the crowds in Rome had destroyed every statue of Poppaea in sight.[38] Now, under a new regime, it was obviously better to be cautious. Still, Cnaeus was clearly flourishing. "I'll have my hands full," he said, "organizing processions, sacrifices, feasts. But they'll be for my benefit, not for a set of rascally priests. Good night."

Not before time, you may think. But it all turned out rather well. Cnaeus had found out we were staying at an inn, and as we lurched through the dark streets, with Aesop and Cnaeus' slaves leading the way, he asked me a few questions, and simply insisted we move out of the inn next morning and come to stay at his house. I thought he'd forget all about it, but amazingly, next morning, a slave appeared at our inn and asked us to accompany him to the House of the Gilded Cupids. It was the breakthrough we needed.

A WEDDING IN THE HOUSE OF THE VETTII (MARTHA)

We got there midmorning. The doorkeeper told us that his master was out, but please to come in. And a suave slave, the butler so to speak, soon appeared, and gave Aesop and Fotis directions where to put our clothes. The house was beautiful—light and colorful, tastefully decorated, with paintings covering every wall and cloth hangings which softened the angularity of the walls. There were handsome bronze candelabras, a few comfortable-looking chaise longues, but on the whole much less furniture than we would put into a bourgeois household. The butler didn't seem to mind us gawking like tourists, partly because he was just a slave, and we were his master's guests, but mostly because the public rooms of the house, where we started, were meant to be gawked at. Furnishings were status.[39]

The entrance hall was narrow, painted black below and white above, decorated with birds and fruit. It led into the traditional atrium, open to the skies in the middle, with a pool and fountain in the center. Beyond that there was a gorgeous colonnaded courtyard (white-painted columns, with bases in red and gold, standing out dramatically against black walls), built round a garden stuffed with bushes and statues. Our room, comfortably large, had a vast double bed on a black-and-white mosaic; its walls were painted in a delicious gold-and-red carpet pattern, with a delicate blue-and-white stuccoed cornice. "It used to be the master's room," said the butler, "but they've moved over there near the dining room." Obviously, James had made quite an impression last night. "These are quite rare," said the butler, and pointed to the four gold medallions decorated with Cupids, covered with glass, set into the wall over our bed (plate 4).[40] This was luxury, Roman style. But for us what mattered more—luxury, modern style—there was a toilet almost next door. It was a huge advance on the inn. I almost forgave James for getting drunk, but decided against telling him yet.

On one side of the colonnade there was a shrine, shaped like a small temple, with bronze statuettes of Gods: the household Gods in their flouncy skirts (Lares) and the traditional Roman trio of Jupiter, Juno, and Minerva, plus Mercury on the side (plates 15–16). To judge from his Gods, this guy Poppaeus, James' drunken friend, was clearly a pro-Roman traditionalist.[41] At least, that's what I thought, until we got round to the other side of the colonnade, where, filling a corner, there was another shrine, dedicated to Isis, complete with Egyptian-style dog-headed God, Isis, and Sarapis. There's the advantage of polytheism; you don't have to put all your eggs in one basket, and in Roman Italy you didn't have to jettison the traditional Gods—which would have been unwise because they were the allies of the upper classes (or vice versa)—you just added an extra God or two. Anyhow, however critical of Isis Poppaeus had been yesterday evening in his cups, at one time he or some other occupier of the house had been an Isis devotee.

I mentioned the two shrines first because we were sent here to find out primarily about religion, and almost automatically we associate religion with specific acts of worship. But actually the total setting of the colonnaded garden was, in some sense, equally religious. It was adorned throughout with reliefs, marble statues, herms topped with Gods' heads, dramatically arranged, and with marble mobiles hanging between the columns and twisting in the breeze. What's more, as we stood outside our bedroom and looked across, we realized that the far end of the garden was built to look exactly like the entrance to a temple, with wide steps, podium, high columns, and triangular front (plate 17). The garden itself had been carefully designed to look like a sacred grove in the countryside, and of course, like a rich man's villa, but on a diminished scale.[42]

So we had a miniature rural landscape in the center of town, and a temple inside a house—sure, not a real temple, but the image of a temple. The garden, screened from the busy colonnade by a garlanded pergola, was a separate world, peopled with, or rather, watched over by dozens of country Gods, primarily Dionysus/Bacchus, the God of drama, wine, and mysteries, and his minions (satyrs, Silenus, centaurs), and of course, Priapus. But in this modest garden (so different from the house of the Vettii, right next door), Priapus was remarkably nonphallic, though on one herm, water was spouting out of a pussy's mouth, just where you would expect a penis. The butler came up quietly behind us. "The collection was started by the master's father, but tragically, lots of the pieces were damaged in the terrible earthquake we had a few years ago," he said, "and when the master had them repaired, many of the marbles were set into the walls as reliefs, for safety."

A few minutes later Cnaeus Poppaeus came back. I was introduced to him and his wife, pretty, old money, but charming with it, and about my age. I took to her at once. Apparently they'd been out at the first part of a wedding. The girl next door, from the Vettii family, was getting married. They had made an early-morning sacrifice of a pig and a sheep at the Temple of Venus. I said I didn't know how they celebrated weddings in Italy (hint, hint), and Lucretia said I would know quite a lot soon enough, because we were invited to the wedding feast. James made polite noises of the "Are you sure?' kind, and we accepted. I asked Lucretia what I should wear, and she said she'd be glad to advise. She suggested Fotis bring some of my clothes to her room so we could look at them together. I was glad that Fotis had learned a lot with her former mistress.[43]

Apparently there had been lots of people at the wedding sacrifice. The brothers Vettii were stinking rich; one of them was marrying his lovely but very young daughter, barely thirteen, into an old, established family, and whatever you could say about the Vettii, old was not it, even if they were beginning to be influential in the town. "They're freed slaves really," Lucretia said, but then she looked slightly abashed, because of course James had told Cnaeus that we were freed slaves too—respectable, educated, apparently well off, but still first-generation freed slaves. I suppose we didn't really behave in character. How could we?

"So, it's rather a splashy affair, this wedding, with a grand donation to the various clubs of local tradesmen to have feasts to celebrate. It'll pay off at the next election," Lucretia laughed, "but it must have cost him a lot—thirty thousand sesterces, I heard some people say, and that's just for the plebs to get fat on. At least they all came to the sacrifice at the temple, and not just to the feasts.[44] And they'll be there again for the bridal procession, when we take her from her father's house to the groom's, so it all helps in the end to make the marriage a grand occasion."

Lucretia had spent the previous evening helping with the bride's preparations. They had wanted everything done just right. "You know what sticklers nouveaux riches are for tradition, though sticklers would hardly hold a wedding at the beginning of March; but then, perhaps nowadays some people would think that worrying about dates is just superstition. We put her hair into six braids, parted with a spearhead dipped in the blood of a dying gladiator.[45] Don't ask me why, no one knows why most of these customs persist; but there was a gladiator show just a few days ago, so Vettius fixed things up." I said that James had been at the games too.

"And needless to say the bride wanted to see how her veil fitted, and try out her dress and headdress, go through the ritual—you know, go through the words she has to say when she gets to her husband's house, and the things she has to do, like putting a coin on the altar of her new household Gods tomorrow. There's quite a lot to remember in all the excitement. And of course, her mother wanted us to know how many clothes and jewels the girl was taking in her trousseau. In fact, they are all listed in the marriage contract, with their value. Do you do it like that in Ephesus?" I said we did, and prayed I was right. "You'll look stunning in this," Lucretia said, fingering a fine flimsy linen in pale blue. "By Venus, it's almost time we went."

The Vettii house was right next door, just across a small street. In this house, phalli everywhere. As soon as you go into the entrance hall, what greets you, eye height, is a bearded God, painted on a wall, negligently leaning on a pillar. He is effeminately dressed, or rather half dressed, in yellow and green, wearing gold earrings and a Phrygian cap, like a freed slave (I wondered to myself whether the painter had put the hat there as a risqué joke about his employer's slave origins). One hand delicately lifts his robe to reveal—how could he hide?—a drooping penis as long as, or just longer than, his forearm, while the other hand holds a pair of scales, which humorously balances the penis against a bag stuffed with money. Underneath, as a sign of the luxury we are about to encounter, is a lavish basket of fruit (plate 5). And in the center of the garden, directly in view from the front entrance, there was a fine marble statue of a slender male, with a long erect penis, from which spouts a gush of water (plate 18). What a setting for a wedding![46]

The atrium was crowded with relatives, friends, guests. Luckily Fotis had shyly reminded me that we needed to take a present. Panic! James suggested I give the bride that nice silver engraved mirror he had given me, just the day before. I looked sulky, so he promised he'd buy me an even better one; and to do him credit he really did try when we got to Ephesus, and gave me a striking bronze mirror surrounded by signs of the zodiac (these Romans are crazy about star signs), showing on its reverse a couple athletically making out on a comfortable bed, cheered on by a picture hanging on the wall behind them, of a couple making love (plate 19). Perhaps it had originally been made as a wedding present; it was certainly meant to be used by a woman of taste. We hung it on the wall behind our bed. It's the sort of thing later Christians disapproved of. But at least, some pagans thought sex was fun. Anyhow, the bride clearly didn't think much of the silver mirror we gave her (or at least she left it behind in her father's house, where it was found nineteen hundred years later), while my bronze mirror, a rather grand piece of work, is now on public display in a small museum in Rome, amusing gleeful adolescents on otherwise boring school visits.[47]

But back to the wedding. The principal relatives and guests, looking suitably impressive and pleased with themselves, witnessed and then sealed the marriage contract. Of course, since we're among Romans, it was only males who could act as witnesses. The groom and bride (again, we're in Roman culture here) sat garlanded with flowers, side by side, on chairs tied together with skeins of wool and covered with the skin of the sheep they'd slaughtered, I mean sacrificed, that morning. You don't get far from blood in Roman rituals. The mistress of ceremonies (the *pronuba*) was a handsome woman in her late thirties, still married (as custom demanded) to her first husband. "Difficult to find in Rome," Lucretia whispered to me. "Everyone there plays fast and loose, men and women. It's fashionable to divorce every year—only the ugly stay married, and husbands are useful only for riling lovers. But here in the provinces women are still faithful, well, except for—"[48]

The main ceremony was about to begin, and Lucretia had to stop before she could take the assembled company apart. Everyone crowded together, and we got squashed in toward the back, at the entrance to a side room. Several young boys opposite us perched (I couldn't help noticing during the ceremony that most of them wore a bronze penis on a chain around the neck) on one of the Vettii's impressively shiny bronze-studded strongboxes, right next to a painting of someone sacrificing adoringly to the golden Goddess Fortune. No difficulty in guessing who was the Vettii's favorite God. But in spite of the crowd, because we were a bit taller than your average Roman, we had a good view of the atrium, lavishly painted in a gorgeous mixture of yellow, black, and expensive cinnabar red, with candelabra and Cupids as repeated motifs, and decorated for this occasion, like most of the guests, with shiny green garlands.

The majordomo hit a large gong and called for silence. An oldish relative, the bride's uncle, announced that the auspices were propitious: the Gods approved of the marriage. The mistress of ceremonies asked the groom and bride in turn if they consented to the wedding, and the bride rather touchingly repeated the age-old formula: *Ubi tu Gaius, ego Gaia*— impossible to translate and corny, but quite emotional in the context. I suppose it means: "Wherever you are, I am your wife." I smiled and looked at James, but he was looking at somebody else.

And then the crowning moment, the *pronuba* joined the couple's right hands together.[49] The groom put his arm affectionately round his new wife's shoulder, and she toyed with her red veil, pulling it over and away from her face, glancing excitedly at him and the floor, until he, sensible guy, kissed her. Everyone cheered and wished them good luck *(Feliciter)*, and the slaves brought round silver goblets of wine. James got one beautifully decorated with peasants boozing, but I got one decorated with emaciated corpses.[50]

After that it was a bit of an anticlimax, except that James and I had a major row. He had never wanted to marry me. Just wanted me as a lover. All my old resentments surfaced, and festered all the more because I had no real opportunity to express them. I sounded off at him briefly in the small side room behind us, which was decorated with pictures of Ariadne and Leander, both failed mythical lovers. So I didn't enjoy the banquet and didn't really notice, didn't really care, what happened. It wasn't my wedding, that's what mattered to me. OK. We had a large dinner, we all poured a libation to and toasted the emperor ("To Augustus, Father of the Fatherland, hail"—*Feliciter*), and followed the family to the household altar to see them worship the household Gods with a bit of incense and a libation; it was the bride's symbolic good-bye to her household Gods.[51]

And then, in the peristyle, which was filled with statues gushing water caught in marble basins, some boring old fart made a wedding speech, celebrating the married couple and the God of marriage, and calling attention to the bride's prettiness ("He is like a rose, and she is like an olive"), alluding to her family's wealth, the good match she had made, and the Cupids flying around the atrium, etc., etc.[52] But in the room where we ate, if your eyes wandered to the pictures on the walls, they nearly all portrayed women killing men, or men torturing women, or men and women being tortured.[53] Of course, I wondered if these myths expressed, reinforced, or ventilated Roman subconscious aggression, but I didn't see how to ask Lucretia about it. So instead I asked her if all grand Roman weddings were like this one. "Oh no," she said, "they are all different."[54]

I began to feel better only when we left the Vettii house toward dusk to accompany the groom and bride on their way to her new home. By now, a crowd of well-fed and tipsy tradesmen had gathered outside with pine flares dipped in pitch, and the local orchestra of flutes, trumpets, and cymbals—same guys actually as for Isis, but without the boy/girl choirs. As we left, the groom ceremonially snatched his bride from the arms of her mother: she wasn't meant to be going willingly. Then everyone followed, not all together in a formal procession but in dribs and drabs, festive and mildly drunk.

Our general direction, apparently, was the Forum, because groom and bride wanted to pay their respects there to the emperor, at the Temple of the Genius of Augustus, with a libation and prayer. The bride's uncle had just held office there, as *augustalis*, so I suppose they wanted to do the right thing.[55] Then to the groom's house, on the south side of town, by the theater and the Temple of Isis, but on the way we stopped at numerous crossroads, for more libations at the altars, and sang bawdy songs, which I didn't understand precisely, but the accompanying gestures spoke for themselves. The groom, who had been more purposeful than we had, was waiting for the bride. Slaves handed us nuts to sprinkle over the bride, like confetti. The bride anointed the doorposts of her new home with wool and oil, and was lifted over the threshold not by the groom, but by her attendants, and after that we all trooped into Marcus Lucretius' house for more ceremonies and drinks. I felt exhausted. But you don't get to a Roman wedding every day, so I stayed.

M. Lucretius, *père*, was a priest of Mars and a senior town councilor. He had probably been there officiating at the sacrifice James and I had witnessed in the Forum, on our first day in Pompeii. He was obviously prosperous; these well-off local families intermarried and grew wealthier. His house had been completely refurbished, and luxuriously, since the earthquake of 62—a profusion of marble, gilded stucco, silvered couches, painted walls, and painted terra-cotta statuettes of Gods and Goddesses. The garden was raised like a theater stage, and was packed (like the garden in the House of the Gilded Cupids, where we were staying) with herms, miniature marble animals and satyrs, and the inevitable marble mobiles, and all this grandly lit for the occasion by dozens of pine flares.[56]

All very impressive, but what struck us most forcibly was the centerpiece in the atrium, the traditional marriage bed, covered with a spotlessly white toga. While most of the guests were, like us, wandering around the house, admiring, sniping, chatting, and smiling, the groom had offered his bride fire and water as symbols of her acceptance into the sacred rites of her new household, burned more incense, and poured a libation on the large and rather vulgar mock-marble household shrine. But then we all drifted back to the atrium and gathered round the traditional marriage bed, the bride looking very young and understandably modest, with the mistress of ceremonies fussing over her dress and reassuringly holding her hand. Poor girl—very pretty though.

"Now we get the bedding speech," Lucretia whispered. "Pity, it's my uncle; he's a lousy public speaker, and fancies himself." By our standards, his speech was extremely alien and alienating in its attitudes, not helped by the stilted delivery, as though the guy had learned it by heart from a textbook on speech making.[57] It was short enough, and had none of the straight vulgarity of the bawdy songs which the men sang to accompany the bride to her house. Of course, it mentioned the luxury and expense of the wedding (old Vettius looked suitably delighted), the distinction of the guests (not us, we thought), the youth and beauty of the bride (right on—she looked stunning), and the groom's strength and prowess. That startled us. You'd think he was talking about an athletics competition. But it got worse, or better, depending what you wanted.

"What is the purpose of this occasion?" our speaker asked. "The young man's initiation in love. The first night of the marriage," he said, "is like an athletic contest"—yes, he really said that—"with the God Love as umpire, and Hymen as herald, and the bedroom like a race-course. Hymen the herald shouted: 'Go, fight in a manner worthy of your fathers.' Now is not the time for cowardice. Remember your skills in hunting and wrestling. Demonstrate your prowess, but beware lest your bride seeks to divert you with guileful chatter. Beware of the disgrace, when there will be so many witnesses tomorrow, after the initiation. Pray to the Gods for help and be brave, so that men of the future will speak well of you." And he himself ended, after too much else, with a longish prayer for happiness and children.

His concentration on the husband, his needs, anxieties, and pleasures, and the pressures on him to perform vigorously as a virile male, stuck out like a sore thumb. The bride, sitting there demurely (what else could the poor girl do?), figured only briefly as a potential beguilement who might divert the groom from penetration and victory. What on earth was she thinking? Being there unfortunately didn't help us understand Roman emotions. Her father's house, with its pervasive erect phalli and pictures of violent conflict between men and women, must have had an influence. But how? Perhaps she was used to it all. I felt sympathetic. Only last night, she had dedicated her girlish clothes and childhood toys at the Temple of Venus, but what sort of love was this?[58]

With a lot of laughter, the groom and bride were escorted to the door of their bedroom. At least, in spite of appearances, the bedding was private. It used to be public, Lucretia told us, but long ago. The band had reappeared, and the party looked set for a long bout of drinking and dancing. I was done for; hearing and speaking Latin was absolutely exhausting. I dragged James (delicately) away, but he was reluctant—he was obviously enjoying himself. I hated him for it. Why was he always so insensitive to my needs? Weddings stir feelings. I told Lucretia we had to get up early tomorrow. She expressed polite and kind regret. But for her too, explaining what she took for granted to strangers had probably been exhausting. I didn't tell her we were off to Egypt tomorrow morning. I don't think she would have understood.

BLOODY GAMES (JAMES)

I woke up screaming, shouting for blood. In the end, I had become just like the rest of them, my civilization a thin veneer over seeping cruelty. "Kill him," we all shouted. Not a voice in his defense. And he hadn't fought badly; he was just unevenly matched against a local hero, Crescens the Netman ("Netter of young girls by night," the graffiti boasted). And now, sunk on one knee in the sand, bleeding, his shield fallen at his feet, exhausted, dejected, all he could do was wait and pray—Nemesis, the Goddess of Fortune, whom he'd trusted, had let him down.[59]

All eyes switched from victim to plump, balding mayor, visibly sweating in his seat of honor in the front row. He had paid for the entire show, a small fortune, 150,000 sesterces, people said. But the expense went with the job. Now it was *his* day of glory, his to decide who survived, who died. The crowd wanted death—they always did. They didn't have to pay the greedy trainer. But it was only a small extra expense: luckily rookies cost so much less than experts like Crescens. And who was he to resist the crowd? Only his young son by his side looked close to tears. He had sat next to the fresh young gladiator last night at dinner. Military service, killing Jews or Britons, will soon toughen him up, thought Marcus Popidius, and with a grandiose gesture so that everyone in the amphitheater could see, he gave the signal for execution.[60]

Crescens, the victor, punched the sky in triumph. One more scalp to his credit. With Good Fortune, he'd soon notch up XX. "Don't hurry, now," said the master of ceremonies, holding him back with his long cane. "Keep them waiting. Don't forget, we've got all day out here." An attendant, dressed in the mask of Pluto, God of the underworld, handed Crescens a specially sharpened dagger of execution. The trumpets blared. With a flourish, a dramatic pause, and a professional display of controlled strength, Crescens the all-Roman star with one hand bent

back the young gladiator's head, and with the other gently slit his throat. The crowd, for a moment silent, sighed and then cheered. A single human sacrifice could not assuage its insatiable lust for blood. The water organ ground out a funeral march, while attendants masked as Charon (the ferryman to Hades) loaded the corpse onto a stretcher and took it out by the Gate of Death.

No market here for snuff movies, I thought; they make their own—and decided I'd had enough of murder to last a lifetime. Martha had refused to come, partly on principle—she hated blood sports—and besides, women could only sit separately in the worst seats at the top of the amphitheater. She hadn't brought her contacts, and wouldn't be able to see much from up there. She would have hated it anyhow, and she'll hate having missed it.

The evening before had been quite jolly, lively with expectations. Posters freshly painted on street walls encouraged people to come; tomorrow there would be "what the whole world wants": games in honor of the emperor Vespasian, a wild-beast show in the morning, gladiators fighting after lunch, and as an extra temptation, gift tokens scattered to the crowd. Graffiti, old and new, proclaimed rival idols, past victories. These were the local film stars—Crescens, billed as Lord of the Dolls; Hercules; Crowd's Roar, who had quite a following: "Young girls' delight." "Girls sigh for him." Whose fantasy was that? we wondered. At the wedding, Martha saw a baby sucking from a bottle stamped with the design of a gladiator fighting, and local shops had dozens of gladiator oil lamps for sale, as well as bronze bells attached to gladiators posing. The

whole town was fight mad, mad not for real war, but for war games. I
suppose it diverts more riots than it causes, I thought, but your real heroes of the tough old republic, like Brutus and Fabius, would have wept
at the decadence. In the Italian homeland, Roman virtue was now de-
fended by paid hacks, while the real soldiers, nearly all of them provincials, were stuck on the frontiers.[61]

We saw the procession first, on its way back from the Forum. What
really gets these people going, obviously, is a procession and a public
banquet. Music, pomp, Gods, a bit of sentiment and symbol, plus food
and wine—an unbeatable combination. They had sacrificed a bull and
some pigs (to judge from the menu at the feast) at the Temple to the Genius of Augustus. Some people call it the Temple of Vespasian, but in
Italy it's really not OK to have a temple to a living emperor. They do that
sort of thing in the provinces.

First came the inevitable town band, then the lictors bearing rods and
cudgels, as a symbol of office and as a threat to hooligans: brush with Roman power and you'll get thrashed. For all its civility, Roman power was
based on face-to-back violence. The two mayors came next, stuffed with
importance, then the other officials, town councilors, priests of Augustus, district officers; many of these were freed slaves, but prosperous in
spite of their origins, and well worth tapping for their contributions to
the town. How did ex-slaves get so wealthy so quickly? OK, I know you
want me to get on with the show. Next came the statuettes and busts of

the twelve great Gods, carried by horse and cart, or by porters in what looked like sedan chairs, garlanded and perfumed with incense, so that you could both see and smell them coming. The Gods were going to dine too on couches among their people. Games were held in honor of, and in the presence of, the Gods, or as ancient Christians polemically put it, "The whole amphitheater is a temple of demons." But I can't just describe the procession; if you'd been there, among your own people, you'd cheer it, laugh at it, question it, join it. This was the whole town on display, watching themselves being watched, officials, priests, Gods, artisans in guilds, wives, girls all eyes and giggles, relatives, lovers, ghosts.[62]

And of course, I almost forgot, right in the center of the procession, after the Gods, came tomorrow's heroes, on their way to be stiffed, I mean stuffed, with the banquet of their lives. They were all there, garlanded Hector, Hercules, Crowd's Roar, and Crescens the Netman, the young rookies looking aggressively anxious, the broken-nosed retainers retired from the ring, lucky still to be hanging in, trainers, masseurs, armor bearers, attendants, all the metal of armor and arms gleaming with promise. Then came a few reluctant wild animals, two zebras, a wild boar in its cage, a bear, some criminals in chains, all tomorrow's certain victims.

We joined in the procession too, at the end; Martha hadn't yet mustered all her scruples. You could think it was just a street banquet: the well-oiled gladiators wrapped like generals in purple cloaks, the magistrates and their chosen guests feasting at long trestle tables, the Gods nearby on banquettes. But above us all loomed the amphitheater, like a cathedral of death. The populace, fobbed off with sweetened wine and cake *(crustum et mulsum)*, toasted the donor of the games *(Principi munerariorum feliciter)* and milled around, gaping, sighing, laughing, admiring the combatants, and if they were brave enough, teasingly feeling the gladiators' muscles, while some, tomorrow's program in hand, weighed the chances and calculated the odds that Crescens and Crowd's Roar would win again.[63] And who knows, perhaps some poor folk thought all that meat and good food heaped on the gladiators' plates was worth dying for.

We went to bed. The next day was almost inevitably an anticlimax. Of course, there were moments of excitement. Just being there was a thrill, wedged in the crowd; the whole of Pompeii city, it seemed, tiered in

ranks around me. This was democracy, Roman style; people power diverted, exorcised, manipulated, indulged, divided, occasionally turning
ugly to boo a local worthy (had he been too hard on his tenants? too
stingy with his games?) or the mayor's decisions. But he knew where his
bread was buttered, and so did the crowd, as he potlatched another small
fortune on small bone tokens (*missilia*), each dated and with a number,
scattered discriminately (this was Roman Italy) into the crowd. Even the
togad (well, how would you spell it?) respectables in the front rows
scrabbled frantically to grab their share, in the hope of winning a fancy
favor (*I* was for wine, *II* for incense, *III* for a sausage, and so on). "It's not
like Rome," grumbled my neighbor. "There you get real gifts, worth a
fortune." "And you get a chance of being executed, or so I've heard," said
the man behind.[64]

I really don't want to describe in detail the mindless killing of animals
which went on in the morning. Not that I'm squeamish, but splattered
blood doesn't excite me. Most of the Romans around me, to judge by the
oohs, hadn't seen the wild animals often before, except perhaps in pictures and mosaics in temples, or in a few rich men's houses. And to be
honest, there is something dramatic, as well as repulsive, in the violence
of killing, in the sudden slaughter of a powerful animal. I suppose I could
add something intellectually fashionable, such as that killing zebras symbolized Roman conquest of the exotic. But I'm not sure that having
archers shoot a mangy bear full of arrows is symbolically edifying, nor is
watching wild dogs take ages to tear a bull to pieces. But then I wasn't
brought up thinking of sacrificing a bull with stun hammer and sharp
knife as a central moment in religious life. The central ritual in my house
was watching TV violence, seen through a screen lightly.

And I did watch, horrified but fixated, the public execution of criminals at midday, one burned screaming in a fanciful recreation of a Roman
myth. If you need to be convinced that Romans were different, turn up
on gladiator day. But then, you don't get to control a huge empire with
cups of tea; or rather, cups of tea are the symbolic veneer which hide the
latent violence. Sorry, I'm getting morbidly philosophical. What's certain is that next night, and for several nights afterward, I had nightmares.

ACADEMIC EPILOGUE

King's College
Cambridge CB2 1ST
August 7, 1997

Dear Mary,

I'm a bit scared to send you this. I'm afraid you may think I've gone off my rocker. But I really want to know whether you think it works, or how it could be made better.

I want to describe what it was like to be pagan in the Roman world. I want to stress how very strange Roman culture was, how diverse, and very different from modern western cultures. And I need to show that religion pervaded every aspect of political and social life, from emperor to pauper, and from cradle to grave. Basically I need to show the context in which Christianity grew. At the same time, I don't think it makes sense (do you?) to describe religion in the Roman world as a separate entity. To understand the world in which Christianity grew, you have to go both inside and outside religion.

Anyhow, I hit upon this idea of sending a couple of academics back into the past. OK, it's obviously a risky tactic (especially for them). But I hoped it would give an immediacy and an informality to the tension between our *now* and their *then*. They can describe what struck them as strange, and yet what the Romans took for granted. That way, they can benefit from the sources, and in their interpretations even go beyond them. Of course, they don't get at the truth; no one does that. And they rapidly realize the limitations of autopsy—you can't understand a complex foreign culture on a two-week vacation.

But they do have some advantages over armchair historians. They can combine the visual with the heard and the read. They can compare what they see with what they already know, or I can supplement their perceptions. Sure, they get mixed signals. But the virtue of the genre is that they don't have to impose an artificial order on a confusing culture.

And they themselves learn a lot, in what turns out to be an intellectual pilgrimage. They confront their informants' unreliability and partiality, and they gradually get to realize that multistranded incompatibilities offer an attractive alternative to pseudo-objective history. Of course, their informants are my versions of surviving ancient sources, and archaeological materials. So perhaps the net result is closer to conventional history than its disguise suggests.

Could we talk about it over a boozy lunch?

Love,

Keith

New Hall
Cambridge
September 23, 1997

Dear Keith,

Thank you for sending me your boisterous piece. You probably feel pleased with the idea of sending time travellers to Pompeii. And of course, eventually adding Egypt, Syria, and Ephesus and Rome in the next sections will drive home the point that Roman religion was extremely varied, as well as odd. But at this rate, won't it get a bit long, even if there needn't be the same degree of detail? At the level of liveliness, your piece works well, but as always it's difficult to mix intellectual analysis with colourful description.

One trouble is that your time travellers only see what they see, and what they see is inevitably selective. Their eyes lack historical depth and analytical framework. You hint at but never seriously discuss the underlying problems: for example, that religious ceremony stands for and negotiates the political and social order, or that myth supplements ritual by explaining and mystifying the complex relations of humans and gods. OK, you do mention that the magistrate is both priest and magistrate, but only in passing. There's no serious theoretical discussion.

But the main difficulty is that your scholarly (sic!) inhibitions prevent you from allowing your time travellers to see/hear significantly more than what modern scholars already know, while your style of presentation allows you to present only a small fraction of that knowledge.

For example, you describe, but you do not explain, the intricacies and multiple meanings of ritual, because that would hold up the dynamics of your narrative. By contrast, a traditional analysis would show how real Romans, as opposed to your pseudo visiting observers, inevitably had a wide range of different experiences and understandings. Real Romans, or at least some of them, even understood, perhaps unconsciously, the principles, if not the theory, behind their rituals. And they have left in their writings (from Varro to Plotinus) sophisticated traces of these understandings. Your dramatic tactic of the quick visit can't do justice to that complexity. But the modern intellectual analyst writing about ancient religion draws his salary precisely because he/she goes beyond the merely visible, to try to understand the logic of Roman ritual construction and performance, their religiosity, piety, ethics.

Your account is halfway between the pure Roman and modern scholarship, and has the advantages of neither. Sure, it has superficial immediacy, and I'd be the last person to knock that, but here it is at the cost of omitting a penetrating analysis of what constituted "paganism." Admittedly, your day-trippers do see quite a lot, but they cannot possibly understand the subtle evolution of Roman religion through its various stages.

I think it would have been helpful if your analysis had included some sense of both persistence and change in Roman religion, to say nothing of the Romans' own religious mythmaking—not as inventive, people say, as the Greeks', and often borrowed from them, but nevertheless substantial and important. Think for example of Romulus, Rome's founder and the first king; Brutus the king slayer; Mucius Scaevola, the suffering hero; Augustus, god and emperor; Seneca, moralist, satirist, tragedian, forced to commit suicide by the tyrant Nero; all ?historical figures, and yet also symbolic figments in Roman myths. These myths form a set of interpretative stories/texts which make sense of and yet mystify the relations between humans and gods, and tell the Romans who read/heard them how they too should behave. It's our job to deconstruct the Roman myths about their own history, but we can set about deconstructing them only after telling people what they were. Your account of paganism, because it relies so much on the visible, is too static, and undermythed.

One particular set of Roman myths about their own religion does seem fundamental (perhaps you could deal with it in a brief appendix?). Roughly speaking, Roman myths envisage a simple evolution from primitive and rustic beginnings, through the gradual accretion of foreign cults as Rome absorbed elements of conquered cultures, until with Augustus and his successors we get to the all-powerful, empire-governing, worldwide (as they saw it) state, integrated by the cult of the divine emperors, yet corrupted by Oriental innovations. The final stage, represented for example by Porphyry and Julian the Apostate, is the self-conscious construction of paganism in its battle with Christianity. These late pagan thinkers (building on earlier Stoicism and Middle Platonism) believed that there was a single underlying divine principle in the universe, and therefore that paganism, in spite of its variety, constituted a religion.

But then, I suppose, you're writing a chapter, not a book. As long as your readers aren't misled into thinking they've had a comprehensive account of paganism, I think this is an innovative introduction. I particularly liked the sense that Roman boundaries between sacred and secular were differently drawn (goddess in the john), that raunchy Roman sexuality (a bit overdone?) backgrounded strict Christian antisexual morality, that our sources are intrinsically unreliable (implicit in Lucretia's stunning/probably untrue answer that all wedding rituals are different), and above all that pagan religion was pervasive, just everywhere (what about demons?).

Sure, you're on for lunch. I hope you're paying.

Love,

Mary

P.S. There are a couple of books you could read, which might help.[65]

TWO

Jews and Christians, or, How the Dead Sea Scrolls Were Found and Lost

CONTEXT

Jesus was a Jew, and remained a Jew for the whole of his life. His first followers, and those who believed him to have been the Messiah and the son of God, apparently continued to attend the temple. They thought of themselves primarily as a special group within, not outside, Judaism, even though some of them, like Paul, angered the Jews who noticed his activities by recruiting some non-Jews as full members of his tiny and scattered cult groups. But Paul was probably atypical among the earliest Christians. James the brother of Jesus, who became the acknowledged leader of the Jesus movement at Jerusalem until 62, twenty-five years after Jesus' death, was admired by Pharisees, who objected vociferously to his execution by a Sadducee high priest.[1]

The Jesus movement started as a small and radical revisionist movement within Judaism. This chapter explores another small Jewish cult group, the Qumran Covenanters, who wrote and preserved the Dead Sea Scrolls. Their commune was much older than the Jesus movement, and it persisted until its annihilation by the Roman army during the massively destructive Jewish rebellion against Rome (66–73). The Qumran community and the associated Essenes were quintessentially Jewish, and in interesting ways were both different from and similar to early Christians. At the very least, they show the religious fervor of committed Jews in the period when the Jesus movement began.

HOW THE DEAD SEA SCROLLS WERE FOUND AND LOST

In 1947 a young Arab shepherd found the first of the Dead Sea Scrolls, carefully hidden in a sealed jar in a cave near Qumran, on the borders of the Judaean desert.[2] These newly discovered manuscripts (of which there are now more than eight hundred), scattered in various caves in the same area, were written mostly in Hebrew and Aramaic, and came from the library of a pious Jewish ascetic sect, closely related to a larger and better known observant sect, the Essenes.[3] Pious Essene communities of men, women, and children were to be found in towns all over Judaea. But the breakaway Qumran commune, founded in the second century BCE, consisted exclusively of celibate males. It flourished with about 150 to 200 members, until their settlement was destroyed by Roman soldiers in 68, in the middle of the Jewish war of liberation/rebellion.[4]

These manuscripts reveal the Qumran commune as ultraconservative, rule bound, and rigorist in its daily religious observance, but at the same time as inventively apocalyptic in imagination and as spiritually sensitive and inspired. Its leaders were ostensibly concerned not only with what the faithful ritually did, but also with what they thought and felt.[5] Of course, we have to be cautious. Religious texts which prescribe rigorous practice and sensitive thought are inevitably idealist. But several ancient observers, Jewish, Greek, and Roman, had been very favorably impressed by the exceptional piety of the Essenes.[6] The Qumran sectarians by their own reckoning were super Essenes.

The founder-hero of the Qumran cult was the Teacher of Righteousness. He had himself been a priest in the temple at Jerusalem. But when his mythical antitype, the Wicked Priest, misled the corrupt establishment of the Jerusalem temple away from the true traditions and teachings of Israel, the Teacher of Righteousness joined the faithful in the desert, where they, like John the Baptist later, pursued salvation. For God had said: "In the wilderness, prepare the way of the Lord, make level in the desert a way for our God."[7] The Qumran sectarians, like Christians later, used sacred writings as objects of study, as pious inspiration, and in order to legitimate their own behavior.

Fortunately, God had revealed to the Teacher of Righteousness, and through him to successive generations of the faithful, two great secrets: the only key to the true understanding of Jewish sacred writings, and the imminence of the world's end—though of course only at the appointed time.[8] The Dead Sea Scrolls reveal in detail what no one had previously known or suspected: the wide range of texts which the Qumran sectarians regarded as sacred and so used as objects of study, and as legitimators of their actions. Even more important, they show the methods which the Covenanters used to interpret and explain the meaning of the holy writings, and so to create for themselves a mythic history, which was also a charter for their daily lives as well as an inspiration for their hopes that the virtuous would in the end be rewarded with a glorious immortality. Past, present, and future were all reinforcing images of one another.

Several of the Dead Sea Scrolls are the earliest surviving detailed commentaries on books of the Bible, which in their methods foreshadow the exegetical practices of the rabbis. So we have line-by-line commentaries which explain what the sacred writings really mean, and (even more significant for Christian history) thematic collections of selected texts, predicting, for example, the eventual arrival of the savior Messiah(s).[9] Such collections imply that when the earliest Christian missionaries wanted to authenticate their view of Jesus as the Messiah, they had available both the idea and actual exemplars of messianic proof texts, selected from the Hebrew Bible.

The Dead Sea Scrolls show both the basic fixity of the central texts of the Hebrew Bible and, at the same time, their fluidity at the margins. For example, several of the writings which the Qumran sectarians considered sacred are in versions which either were later rejected as inauthentic by normative Judaism or were excluded from the canonical Hebrew Bible. But several of these texts were obviously regarded as sacred by the pious Jews at Qumran (for example, the book of Tobit, and the story of Daniel and Susanna), and had been part of the Septuagint, the oldest Greek translation of the Hebrew scriptures. Several were preserved as canonical in the Christian Old Testament.[10]

Even when the text was constant, its meaning was continually being changed through interpretation, in the light of the commune's traditions and needs. For example, the *Commentary on Psalms* makes a general passage (37.23: "The steps of a man are prepared by the Lord") refer specifically to the sect's founder, the Teacher of Righteousness, whom God chose, "for He established him to build the congregation" at Qumran. As to the end of the world, that will take place only after a final prolonged struggle between the forces of Good and the forces of Evil, between the Sons of Light and the Sons of Darkness. So too, each of us now, according to the Qumran texts, is a struggling mixture of good and evil, of darkness and light. But in the end, the forces of Good, aided by two Messiahs, one a priest and the other a king, will triumph, though only after several dangerous defeats, and they will bring to the chosen elite of the persevering righteous, "the men of holiness," a glorious immortality in the sight of God.[11]

In spite of similarities in messianic hopes and millenarian expectations, the Qumran sectarians were in no sense proto-Christians. As represented in these texts, they were passionately devoted Jews, dedicated to the detailed study and rigorous observance of the Mosaic Law as they interpreted it. For example, according to the *Community Rule*, or *Manual of Discipline* as it is also called, all members of the commune were expected to spend one-third of every night in Torah study. Their priestly leader, who "loves them as a father loves his children, and carries them in their distress as a shepherd [cares for] his sheep," was expected to spend all his time in studying the law, but he was also the commune's spiritual and administrative leader.[12] He was the master, the guardian (the word used was the same as later used by Christians—overseer/*episkopos*/bishop). The Qumran guardian was the living representative of the mythical/historical cult founder, the Teacher of Righteousness. The commune was authoritarian, exclusivist, and hierarchical, though the guardian's supreme power was checked by election and limited tenure, and by the very fact that the brethren repeatedly assembled together.

According to the scrolls, the whole life of the commune was circumscribed by rules. At meetings, members sat in strict order of seniority. Annually, when the covenant was renewed and new members were sworn in, each old member was tested on his understanding of the law and purity, and moved up or down in the hierarchy accordingly.[13] New members were admitted only after a long and testing novitiate, and were required on admission to full membership to surrender all their property to the commune. Becoming a holy man involved cutting all ties with the hated wickedness of the external world ("Everlasting hatred for the men of perdition!"); but in return, the Covenanter in his new life received a fresh religious identity, part of a common purpose: "to seek God with his whole heart and soul," "to love all the sons of Light" in "the covenant of love"; "they shall love each man his brother as himself, they shall succor the poor, the needy and the stranger," and all this in obedience to the laws of Moses.[14]

Once inside, commune members were not allowed to spit, interrupt, dress badly, guffaw foolishly, gesture with the left hand, sleep in communal meetings, reveal a naked body to a fellow Covenanter (the covenant rules were fiercely modest), or defecate on the sabbath (the latrines were placed some way from the main camp, beyond the maximum distance which an observant Jew could walk on the sabbath). For each infraction, a penalty was laid down, ranging from a few days' penance and diminished rations to temporary or permanent exclusion. Permanent exclusion was the price paid for blasphemy during a prayer meeting, for sexual intercourse with a wife renounced on entering the community, for slandering the community, or for rebelling against the community's leadership.[15] Obedience was a key virtue.

But many other virtues also counted: humility, patience, charity, goodness, understanding, intelligence, and appreciation of God's lovingkindness.[16] The Qumran writings show a continuous concern not just with outward observance but also, and in particular, with the inner state of the Covenanter's soul. The whole sect had turned away from normative Judaism to find their own salvation by offering—instead of temple sacrifice—prayers and a holy lifestyle, in the hope that these would be seen by God as an acceptable substitute.[17] To find God, they searched continuously for the circumcised heart, avoiding the "foreskin of evil inclination"; in other words, they urged themselves to supplement overt ritual performance with a reverential state of mind, which they hoped to achieve through communal study, self-control, prayer, and hymn singing.[18]

The Qumran Covenanters were the intense devotee core of a dispersed religious sect. I imagine that the celibate commune drew most of its members from this wider membership of the Essenes. These other Essenes were encouraged to marry (though only once) and to have children. They lived in towns and led "normal" lives, though for them too, contact with other Jews and especially with gentiles was circumscribed by rules. For example, all trading transactions with outsiders had to be in cash, presumably to preclude any relations built on mutual trust; no animals could be sold to gentiles, in case they were used for pagan sacrifice; contributions were to be made by young males to the temple at Jerusalem but only once, when they came of age, while contributions were to be made continuously for the widows and orphans of the sect, at the rate of at least two days' earnings per month.[19] Such regulations helped demarcate and preserve the differences (as the sectarians constructed them) between insiders and outsiders.

The differences between Qumran sectarians and early Christians are obvious. The Qumran Covenanters were searching inside Jewish traditions for the essence of Judaism, and were looking forward to a final struggle at the end of time, when the Messiahs would come to help the forces of good defeat the forces of evil. Meanwhile, their answer was withdrawal, careful observance of the Law, piety, prayer, and continuous struggle not only against the Sons of the Pit, outside in the rest of Israel, but also against the forces of evil, ruled by the Angel of Darkness, which persisted inside each of the faithful. The members of the sect were the only true remnant of Israel, the core elite of the Sons of Light. They had been chosen by God through a new covenant, which effectively supplanted or at least supplemented the old covenant between God and Moses. But even the elect had to struggle to achieve their foreordained perfection.[20]

The Jesus movement also obviously began as a renewal movement within Judaism. But there were several critical differences. And of course, for committed sectarians it was those differences which counted most. First, the Jesus movement was marked by a fervent belief that the Messiah had already come: God had cared enough for suffering humanity to send his Son as a saving messenger for those who believed in him. Christian belief centered on Jesus, both human and divine, both man and Christ, instead of on the shadowy, almost notional founder of the Qumran sect, the anonymous but only human Teacher of Righteousness. Christianity's founding myth was anchored firmly in historical time, though (as with the Qumran sectarians) this sense of the past was buttressed, at least initially, by faith in the imminent end of the world. Second, Christianity was induced by circumstances (I think here what mattered most was the initial persecution by temple Jews, and the movement's constricted growth within the heartland of Judaism, plus the sack of Jerusalem in 70, and the disastrous failure of successive Jewish rebellions in 70, 117, and 135) to search for followers outside Israel. In its new homelands, Christianity gradually abandoned the more demanding rules of Jewish ritual and concentrated instead on belief in its mythical history with its salvific and millenarian implications, on its ethical precepts, and on its new liturgical practices (eucharist and baptism).

All that said, there are some striking similarities between the Qumran Covenanters and the early Jesus movement. Both groups were fervently religious and intensely preoccupied with the sacred; both were characterized by a self-sacrificing, collectivist commitment, which enabled all full members to surrender their private property to the commune. Again, at least in their ideals, and probably in practice, both sects were much more committed than outsiders to the care of the unfortunate, widows, and orphans. They lived, at least in their own ideals, like a family, mixing a sense of egalitarian worth (we are all brothers and sisters) with a rigorous internal sense of hierarchy and authority.

Both sects set themselves up in opposition to and isolation from the surrounding wicked world and rejected the corrupt ethics of outsiders, as sinful and eternally damned. In both sects the faithful will be saved; outsiders are condemned to everlasting damnation. Both groups celebrated their commitment and their difference from everyone else by creating their own separatist calendars (a regular solar, 364-day year for the Qumranites, Sundays for Christians). And both movements created inside themselves an inner core of the supercommitted (apostles, celibate Covenanters) and an outer ring of the less committed or less self-sacrificing faithful. But there was also a fundamental difference: Christianity, at least in its surviving writings, often disguised this distinction between elite and mass with the disarmingly inclusivist illusion, or hope, that all believers are able to achieve perfection, while the Qumran sectarians celebrated their own exceptional and exclusivist virtues. Or put another way, expansionist Christianity maintained an ideally rigorist ethic, but softened it with laxist compromises; the Qumranites (at least in their prescriptive literature) maintained their rigorist standards, and were wiped out by Roman soldiers.

In spite of the obvious differences, both Qumran Covenanters and early Christians were fiercely monotheistic in a polytheistic world. Both sects rejected animal sacrifice and substituted in its place prayer and ethical piety in act and thought. Both sects celebrated the pervasive interest of a transcendental, omnipotent, omniscient God in each individual's acts and virtues. Both were passionately committed to the tension generated between idealistic expectations of how ego should behave, feel, and think, and a penetrating sense of ego's sinfulness and inadequacy. In both sects, if the surviving writings are a trustworthy guide, the faithful felt continuously guilty about their incapacity to live up to their own rigorous ideals. This guilt could be temporarily relieved by a subtle combination of ego's confession of sin and repentance interwoven with God's loving-kindness and mercy. In the end, the faithful would find a permanent solution in immortal bliss. The Qumran sectarians were radically different from the earliest Christians but reveal much of the religious environment in which earliest Christianity arose and survived.

QUMRAN REVISITED: *DIALOGUES WITH THE DEAD**

Background

Basically, the story is that Isaac was a devout Jew and a member of the Qumran sect. He escaped from Qumran (where the Dead Sea Scrolls were found) a year or so before its destruction in 68. Actually, he was expelled from the commune, not for any great sin; rather the opposite, he was a senior member, in line, he secretly thought, for election as the next guardian. But that meant he had enemies; rivalries in these small communities run passionate. Sha'ul, a great friend of his in the commune, had an unexpected visit from his wife, and to cut a short story shorter, they had sex, which wasn't allowed under the rules. The food's not bad, and you can drink a moderate amount of wine; but the rule is quite explicit. No sex, even with your wife. You take the oath on entering, and solemnly repeat it every year. OK, it's only one of the many rules, but everyone knows the score.[21]

So the brethren solemnly gathered in their large meeting hall and in order of seniority unanimously decided to expel Sha'ul. The guardian

*Please adjust your set. Conventional reception may be difficult. Cognoscenti who know it all, or the religiously indifferent who just want to get the atmosphere, may wish to fast-forward.

pronounced sentence, and cursed Sha'ul as a rebel: in contravention of his oath, he had fornicated with his wife: "He shall not be counted with all the Sons of Truth, for his soul has rejected the just instructions."[22] End of problem, apparently. Sha'ul returns to his wife, but finds her with another man, which is quite comprehensible in real life (though rarely mentioned in religious stories), since he'd dumped her to join his celibate commune. Sha'ul is thunderstruck, his life is in ruins, he returns to the commune, desperately wanting readmission, knows it will be difficult to fix, and understandably tries it out first with his pal Isaac.[23]

A couple of Isaac's rivals in the commune spot them talking together and blow the whistle—no, not literally, but you see the commune has a rule that you're not allowed to mix with or help an ex-member once he's been expelled, and still another rule that if you see a brother sinning, you cannot pile up the hatred in your heart, you have to out with it and confront him straightaway.[24] So there's a massive confrontation, a report to the guardian, who's very sad at losing Isaac, because new members willing to give up all their property to the commune don't exactly grow on trees—especially now, during the Jewish war of liberation (66–73/4),

A biblical manuscript in tiny writing, found inside a phylactery (tefillin), which is a leather pouch bound on the forehead by pious male Jews at prayer, except on the sabbath (first century, Qumran).

when quite a few of the brethren think they should be fighting against the oppressive Romans with swords instead of prayers.[25] But rules are rules, and Isaac has to go.

In the event, the destruction of Qumran sort of proved that God was on Isaac's side. All the Covenanters, waiting for the imminent end and dreaming that they were God's chosen agents against wicked Jews, got massacred by Roman soldiers, whereas sinning Isaac escaped in the nick of time.[26] And as luck would have it, he (like a lot of Jews in this period, fleeing anti-Jewish riots in the big eastern cities) emigrated to Rome, where one of his brothers was a glass maker, to live comfortably enough, surrounded by his ex-friends' bloodthirsty murderers, the destroyers of Jerusalem, on whom one day soon God would surely wreak his condign vengeance.

Scenario

Isaac, an old Jew on the point of death, lanky and lean, almost thin from years of careful living, but now dressed up to the nines. For all I care, he can look like an eastern European rabbi out of Chagall, complete with phylacteries (incidentally, they found tens of phylacteries at Qumran, so that at least fits; see page 54). The point here is that we're not looking for documentary accuracy in the public television style; we're dealing with stereotypes, so what matters most is that viewers recognize Isaac as an old-style pious Jew.

Isaac is accompanied by his sprightly young nephew, *Hilary* (which is Greek for Isaac, and so symbolizes his parents' and his own desertion of traditional Judaism). Hilary is a good-hearted lad, ethnically Jewish, dark complexion, curly hair, with glowing black eyes and fine teeth (in the Qumran canon, black eyes and good teeth put him among the saved, though appearances, as we shall see, can be misleading).[27] In the modern fashion, Hilary is smart though narcissistic, and he is simply bored by religion (he has become almost as much Roman as Jewish), and is more interested in birds than in his doddering uncle. But his uncle has promised to give him something valuable, so Hilary is hanging in.

The scene is set in a public garden in Rome in about 85 CE, twenty years after Isaac left Qumran, early one spring morning. At this time, the garden is practically empty, apart from a sleeping beggar thinly wrapped in a mat. Isaac puts a silver coin by the shivering man's head. What a waste, Hilary thinks ungenerously. Isaac begins to pray. In the old days, the whole commune used to pray together, but now, much to Hilary's embarrassment, Isaac prays publicly and alone. He won't go to a synagogue, because he hates all the other Jews in Rome. They're the Sons of the Pit, who have deserted the true traditions of Israel; or even worse, like Hilary and his family, to all practical intents and purposes they've become like Romans and have given up Judaism altogether. The destruction of Jerusalem and the temple delivered Israel to God's enemies. The heart went out of Israel: "Why has the mighty God brought this retribution upon us? At least the good among us could have been spared, and only the wicked perish. But who can understand the ways of the Lord? We have all sinned."[28]

"But one day vengeance will come." Isaac had slipped into autopilot fantasy. "Evil Rome will fall, a victim of its own cunning greed. Its palaces, the impure riches of wickedness, are built on top of sewers and dunghills. This empire is like a pig which pretends to be clean; Rome claims to bring justice and civilization, but all it brings instead is violence and high taxes."[29]

"Shsh, Uncle." Hilary interrupts what he fears will become a loud diatribe, sufficient to attract attention. "Someone will hear you, and we could both be arrested. Think of all the prosperity which living in Rome has brought to our family and friends. No other city in the world matches it for size and wealth. No one is powerful enough to defeat Rome. It is God himself who has made Rome powerful as a punishment for Israel's sins. It's useless to struggle; we just have to live with it. Think of what happened when the Jews in Israel rebelled. And besides, Rome itself is surely where the Messiah will himself come."[30]

Good arguments, young Hilary thinks arrogantly to himself, but their only effect, as he should have known from experience, is to unleash an even louder, longer tirade by Isaac against Rome. Luckily old Isaac's Greek accent is incredibly thick, so that any passerby is more likely to think him mad than subversive. Isaac is now half humming, half singing one of those old hymns he used to sing back in the commune, about the birth of a Messiah and the end of the world: "Amid the throes of death, she shall bring forth a son, and amid the pains of hell and childbearing, there shall spring a marvelous mighty Counselor. And the heavens will roar . . . and the wise men will be swallowed up . . . and the gates of hell will open."[31]

Hilary catches only a few words here and there. They certainly don't make sense to him. In fact, he thinks it's all garbled nonsense. And he feels intensely embarrassed. He'd better calm the old man down, get him to sit in the sun, and ask him about the old days. It never fails. And fortunately Isaac plays along. Today he feels so old and tired; he hates Hilary's smart new ideas; they are like a rain of lies. But the old man senses that death is near, and he has a job to do. It's fate and inescapable. Willy-nilly, he has to give Hilary his patrimony.

What oppresses him most, Isaac realizes as he fingers the treasure he has brought from Judaea, is that no one here cares for what he values most. All those years he spent studying and understanding the holy scriptures, in praying, morning and evening, singing hymns, working every day for the commune, diligently washing, cleansing, purifying himself of sin, eating with his fellows, watching and judging the young novitiates, maneuvering his way up the hierarchy, carefully avoiding the poisonous "children of mischief." All that time and dedication had been wasted.

"But no. Mighty and merciful God, who 'pardons those who repent their sins,' is watching over me, as I 'bow down and confess all my transgressions.' You know that 'I have loved thee freely with all my heart, and soul,' and I know that in the end I shall be saved. My immortal soul will stand in the holy presence. I am fated to be raised and live for ever. All 'men of lies' will be damned without escape, chastised for their idols, tortured by avenging angels. 'Crush the enemy.' In the end, 'the army of God' will win."[32]

Very carefully, old Isaac unwinds the strips of linen in which he had wrapped his most precious scroll. And in the clear light of the early morning sun, he begins to read the rules of the community to which he had once belonged. Of course, he no longer really needs to read the text; he knows all its precious phrases by heart. Half aloud, he prays:

> Seek God with your whole heart and soul, do what is right in accordance with what God commanded through Moses and all the prophets, love all that God chose, and hate all he rejected; abstain from evil and keep to the good, practice truth, righteousness, and justice upon earth, and do not persist in the stubbornness of a sinful heart and lustful eyes. All those who willingly devote themselves to observing God's laws shall be admitted to the covenant of love, so as to live perfectly before God, in accord with his revelations. And they should love the Sons of Light, and hate all the Sons of Darkness, whom God will punish according to their guilt.[33]

In those old days of hope, Isaac remembered, all the devotees of the community had willingly contributed their wealth, their knowledge, and their abilities in furtherance of God's laws. Now they are dead. Can he really bear to give his precious scroll, saved from his commune near the Dead Sea, and kept through all life's dangers, to Hilary? Basically, of course, Isaac knows, he is a good lad; he is, after all, his only young relative, his very own nephew. But then, Hilary can't even read Hebrew, doesn't observe the Law, doesn't study the scriptures. Is there any prospect that Hilary will keep the scrolls, respect them, and pass them on to his children's children, so that they will be saved for posterity? Or will he follow the eyes of his lust, and sell the precious scrolls to some shady secondhand book dealer, just to buy a flashy necklace for his harlot girlfriend? In the old days, Isaac recalled with a grim smile, a girl who lost her virginity before marriage was killed.[34] But I am dying and alone, Isaac thinks. What else can I do? Perhaps God will send a miracle.

At this moment of Isaac's indecision and prayer, enter a TV crew with their sharp-tongued presenter, Jeffrey Axeman, in the lead. Alison, the pretty production assistant, had already smoothed the way with Hilary; the garden venue is a setup. Now all they have to do is to get old Isaac to answer some questions about life in the commune for the program, *Judaism, Then and Now*, reminiscences of an insider. And just for contrast, if all goes according to plan, a Christian preacher called Justin will soon be arriving with his flock on the other side of the garden. It's amazing what you can fix up with a bit of cash. Alison glanced quickly, checking her notes; it makes so much difference, even here, if you greet people by name and smile winningly. Our ratings will zoom, she thinks, and dreams of a better apartment—a bit of atmospheric conversation, a few quick background shots of ancient Rome, and bingo, we'll be out of here in a flash. That's how they'd persuaded Axeman to participate. "I know," she bursts out aloud. "*Dialogues with the Dead*, that's what we'll call it. I'll have a word with Ben [the director]."

N.B. The dialogue now moves on two interconnected levels, the ancient and the modern. It is a play, but also a replay of the Qumran charter myth, in which the main characters have their mythical doubles. They are both human and mythical constructs; Isaac is a refugee from Qumran *and* the new Teacher of Righteousness. Each generation has to have one, and by his very nature he is unrecognized by most people. The cameraman, Mike, is both Mike and an unbelieving, vulgar scoffer. All religions need and construct the scoffer. The myth is, of course, history (believed by the faithful to be true). But as with all myths, its legitimacy and credibility to believers are constantly reinforced by being replayed in the present.

In this version of the Qumran myth, Isaac is the new Teacher of Righteousness, the Christian Justin is his Wicked Priest; from the modern world of continuous reinterpretation, Jeffrey Axeman, the TV anchorman, is the Seeker After Smooth Things, the cameraman, Mike (he of thick pudgy fingers and uneven teeth)[35] is the Scoffer, Isaac's handsome nephew, Hilary, is a Spouter of Lies. Alison, the production assistant who makes everything work, is the token woman, who in the ancient male tale had no counterpart. But then, every generation retells the old stories in a new way, while pretending that they're old. The charismatic (almost godlike) director, Ben, is a suave facilitator, whose influence is felt, more than seen. Meg, the TV moneywoman, represents the Devil.[36]

But perhaps the most important character is the TV camera itself, which symbolizes that common and underrated, but nonetheless invaluable, instrument of history writing, namely simplificatory misunderstanding.[37] Substantively, the purpose of the tale is to recapture the atmosphere and passion of Qumran. The method is designed to underline the impossibility and undesirability of writing an objective history of a religious movement. The inconsequentiality of the story mirrors partly the fragmentary nature of the surviving Qumran texts, partly the willful egocentricities of religious fanatics, and of course, partly my own inability to write better.

Cast

Isaac, *the new Teacher of Righteousness*

Justin, *a Christian preacher, thinker, and martyr (for Isaac, he is also the Wicked Priest)*

Hilary, *Isaac's nephew and heir, a Spouter of Lies*

Ben, *director and God*

Meg, *coordinator of religious programs for her network, devout Christian, and Devil*

Mike, *cameraman and Scoffer*

Axeman, *TV presenter and Pharisaic Seeker After Smooth Things*

Alison, *assistant producer, token ingenue*
Professor Pelikan, *distinguished academic*
TV Camera, *restlessly perceptive, but without understanding*

Scene 1: The Messiah

Location: garden in Ancient Rome
Date: c. 85CE
Characters: Isaac, Hilary, Axeman, Mike (camera), Ben (director), Alison (production)

AXEMAN *(fixing Isaac and the camera with one of his ecumenical and oily smiles):* Is it true that when you first entered the community of truth, you were given a shovel, an apron, and a white robe?

ISAAC *(angrily, and looking at* HILARY *suspiciously):* Who is this man of lying tongue and deceitful lips? And why does he ask me about such things? Long ago, we swore not to reveal our secrets to Men of the Pit, or to the scoffers in Jerusalem.[38]

AXEMAN *(with difficulty disguising his impatience. It is important that the camera show him changing face):* The piety and dedication of the Essenes is world famous, and you were a leader in the most devoted commune. Now that the commune and Jerusalem are destroyed, you are the sole surviving remnant of Israel. I just want to record your memories for posterity.

ISAAC *(impatiently):* Then don't let's dwell on the shovel, the loincloth, and the white robe. They were mere instruments, the shovel to dig a pit for excrement, the loincloth for decency while bathing, and the white robe as a symbol of purity. At least we weren't like these disgusting Romans, who have no modesty, bathe naked, defecate in public together, and strut around, yes, even the men, dressed in silk, with their fancy boys.[39] *(Moving from tirade to nostalgia, with barely a pause)* What mattered most in the commune was that every day we studied the Law, we sang hymns together, we prayed together, we ate together. We made sure we were pure for the Lord, by constant washing. We made ourselves fit for the Lord, to await the day of final judgment.

AXEMAN: But people will be wondering, how do you *know* that you alone will be saved?

BEN *(aside to* ALISON*):* That's one secret of Axeman's success, you know, critical acuteness, disguised as viewer opinion. That's why he's famous and rich.

ALISON *(who clearly fancies* BEN *to bits, puts finger to lips):* Envy, envy. Watch the show.

BEN: We are the show.

ISAAC *(his face glazing over as though in a trance, speaks in powerful but apparently disconnected sentences):* Our Teacher of Righteousness interpreted wonderful mysteries, to guide us in the way of his heart. My eyes have gazed on eternity, on wisdom concealed from other men. God will forgive our sins and pardon our wickedness because he has given the destiny of holiness to his chosen ones, the men of truth, the congregation of the poor. We are destined to see God's salvation and to live forever.[40]

MIKE *(sotto voce):* Oh my Lord, we've got a real nutcase here. *(*ISAAC *glares at him, seeing from uneven teeth and pudgy fingers that he is one of the irredeemably unsaved.)*[41]

AXEMAN *(insistently):* But how can you be sure of salvation?

ISAAC *(taking off like a rocket, fires back):* Not being sure is a blasphemy. Every day, with all our heart and soul, we repented our sins. We shall be saved, sanctified by cleansing water, and purified by the humble submission of our souls to the commandments of God. But the Sons of the Pit *(here he fixes Axeman and Mike with a single glare)*, "cursed of men, wallow in whoredom and wicked wealth, under the dominion of Satan. Defiled by the mud of wickedness, they will be tormented without mercy by the wreakers of revenge. Amen."[42]

AXEMAN *(homes in, not for the kill; he likes leaving his victims alive, but juddering):* You say "we," Isaac, but surely all your brethren were killed, not saved? Doesn't that make you question your convictions?

ISAAC *(replies calmly):* The mysteries of God are astonishing. True, the Romans, who continuously plot evil and devour peoples like an insatiable eagle, caused many of Israel to perish.

HILARY *(tugging anxiously at his uncle's sleeve, wheedlingly):* Uncle, anti-Roman talk is dangerous. *(Isaac shrugs him off.)*

ISAAC: My people brought destruction upon themselves because they followed the lying tongues and deceitful lips of the Pharisees, and obeyed the greedy priests and scoffers in Jerusalem, who despised the

Law of the Lord. They forgot God and his commandments, and he smote them with nakedness. He gave them up into the hands of his enemies to be destroyed. But in the end, God will destroy them and all their generals from the face of the earth.[43]

(HILARY, *previously alternating between sullen and bored, looks at his uncle with new respect.*)

ISAAC (*sharper than you might think, notices the change, wonders after all if there is some good in the boy, quotes dreamily*): "In his youth he will be like a man who knows nothing; then he will acquire wisdom."[44] (*At this point, some flash of memory or some sense of urgency must have got to ISAAC. His black eyes flashing, he stands up stiff as a ramrod, and looks straight into camera, like a prophet from Israel's inspirational past.*) Hear now, my sons. If you know righteousness, I shall uncover your eyes, so that you may see and understand the works of God.[45]

ALISON (*quietly to BEN*): I know it looks as though he's not answering Axeman's questions, but in fact this is exactly what we've come for, the actual words of an ancient Jewish prophet. (*And we see MIKE, the squat scoffer, paying just that extra attention to light and angle. No retakes, he realizes. This is it.*)

ISAAC (*in full flood about the imminent arrival of the Messiah*): "This prophecy is true; this word shall surely come to pass: The Son of God he will be proclaimed, and the Son of the Most High they will call him." The people of God will arise, and there will be peace, and God's kingdom will be eternal. "Heaven and earth shall listen to the Messiah; he will heal the wounded and revive the dead."[46]

AXEMAN (*for once, graciously grateful for this answer to his question*): Thank you, Isaac. (*Pauses to look through his notes.*)

ALISON (*again quietly to BEN*): You know, this oddball Jew is much closer to Jesus than most modern Christians would like to accept. For us, Jews and Christians are completely different. And these Qumran guys seem to believe in resurrection, or something like it.

AXEMAN: When will your Messiah come?

ISAAC (*does not reply directly; it is not his style*): Amid the throes of death and grievous pain she shall bring forth a son, begotten of God, a marvelous and mighty Counselor. When he is conceived, all wombs shall quicken. The conceivers of vanity will suffer terrible anguish. The heavens will roar, the gates of hell will open and swallow the conceivers of wickedness. All their wise men will founder.[47]

AXEMAN *(insistently):* But when will all this happen?

MIKE: Hold it. I've got to the end of this reel. Oh shit—it'll take me a minute. How the hell was I to know he was going to say something interesting? *(Grumbling)* The trouble with this bloke is that one minute he's rambling, and the next sec he's predicting the Messiah. You can't tell when he's going to give you the goods. Actually *(to* ALISON*)*, I didn't know Jews were into Messiahs; I thought the Messiah was a Christian fixation.

ALISON: You jerk! Where on earth did you think the Christians got it all from? *(Mike's ignorance got to her sometimes.)*

*(*BEN *glances at them curiously, and wonders, very briefly, if she fancies Mike too.)*

Scene 2: On the Cutting Room Floor

Location: TV cutting room

Time: New York, 1998, day

Characters: Isaac, Hilary, Axeman, Mike, Ben, Alison, and Meg (the administrative boss), who enters later

ALISON: Trouble was that after that break, we never got back to the same tension and excitement.

BEN: I don't think it matters. We can easily intercut Isaac and Axeman angrily arguing off camera with background shots of Rome, perhaps dissolve into a couple of road rage car drivers facing up to each other. We don't even have to hear what Isaac's saying. *(Switches off sound, so that only his own voice can be heard.)* Effing brilliant, not hearing would be much better. The brightest viewers might get to realize that they too don't understand what the Dead Sea Scrolls mean.

ALISON: I'm not sure Meg will approve. She likes her religious programs to be safe as houses; all tidy, bourgeois, bricks-and-mortar. No subversion, Ben, no speculation, no postmodernist trickery. For her, religion and history are true. What *she'll* like is seeing Isaac sick and exhausted, make the viewers feel smugly satisfied they're living now not then.

BEN *(switches on sound again and flicks through images):* Still, it'd be good if we can squeeze in a bit of Isaac when he went on and on about the two Messiahs at the end of time, one a priest, the other a king in the line of David, and the final mighty battle between the Sons of Darkness and the Sons of Light, followed by a huge conflagration, and immortal peace for the saved.[48]

(ALISON, *who knows what she is doing, takes the mouse from* BEN, *and soon we get* ISAAC *rambling on about the end of the world. The spectators in the cutting room,* BEN, ALISON, MIKE, *plus* MEG *now, who enters carefully dressed in a tailored black suit, in contrast to the others, dressed casually, and on screen* HILARY *and* AXEMAN, *all show perplexed confusion and eventually yawning boredom.*)

ISAAC: And God told Habakkuk to write down what would happen at the end of time, but he did not tell him when time would come to an end. And when he said, "Write it on tablets so that a man may read it speedily," this means that God revealed all the mysteries of the prophets to the Teacher of Righteousness.[49]

AXEMAN: You seem to have a scriptural quotation for everything.

MIKE *(sotto voce):* And interpret it to mean what you want.

ALISON: According to one of our experts, that was a quotation from an obscure bit of the Hebrew Bible. But that's the trouble, even when Isaac cites more familiar texts, like Genesis or Psalms.

MIKE: Sure, familiar; everybody reads Psalms.

ALISON: He interprets them to mean something quite different.[50] *(She flicks through the rushes so that we get rapid glimpses, with no intelligible sound.)* Perhaps we can get something out of that story he told about the origins of evil before the flood, and how angels had sex with the beautiful daughters of men.[51]

BEN: I liked the bits when Isaac had a vision of the new, heavenly Jerusalem, and the eventual triumph of the poor, though I suppose it wasn't so much what he said but how he looked. I liked his sense of being persecuted by the mass of Jews in Israel, his dreams of revenge, his acute sense of sin, and the need for confession and repentance.

MIKE: Yeah, "and God's full of mercy and loving-kindness."[52]

ALISON: But can we use it?

BEN: We have to. It's brilliant. With a few cuts, here and there.

MEG: Use it and I'll hire a new director. They'll change channels in droves.

BEN *(aside to* ALISON*):* She's evil. *(To* MEG*)* But don't you realize, this is a real Roman Jew, captured on film.

(On the monitor we see that MIKE *has panned off* ISAAC, *onto his nephew,* HI-

LARY, *to get a reaction shot.* HILARY *is struggling to listen, but his face shows impatient incomprehension.*)

MEG *(triumphantly)*: And there's another authentic Roman Jew, and he's got absolutely no idea what the maniac's on about.

ALISON *(as ever, the peacemaker)*: Couldn't we use some of it, and intercut with academics, to explain it all?

BEN *(snorting contemptuously)*: Yeah. They're actually the same as Isaac. They squabble over minor details, and then claim that theirs is the only correct interpretation.

(MIKE *takes the mouse from* ALISON *and switches over to the interviews they've shot with various academics.*)

PROFESSOR PELIKAN: The last book of the New Testament opened with the salutation "Grace to you and peace from he who is and he who was and he who is come," leaving those christological titles in the nominative, even though the Greek proposition *apo* was supposed to govern the genitive. That solecism and intentional tour de force has been used to justify the identification of the eternal "one who is" with the theophany to Moses at the burning bush, but also with the metaphysical being of classical Greek ontology.[53]

ALISON: OK. You win. He sounds even more obscure and boring. I suppose they do it to convince themselves that they're living on another planet. But look, everyone, the ending with Isaac and Axeman was quite feisty. *(She fast-forwards.)*

AXEMAN *(snappily, barely disguising his impatience)*: Isaac, why do you think God allowed the angels to bring evil into the world? And incidentally, why do you think that God is interested in what you do?

ISAAC *(standing up to his full height, and with great dignity)*: "Blessed art thou, O God of Israel. You have delivered me from my sins and purified me from my indecency." God through his compassionate mercy has planted the Law in our hearts. Through his covenant, which he has renewed with us, he has revealed the plant of truth to his children of righteousness. If you love and walk in righteousness, you are worthy of God's embrace. Walk in the way of peace, and you shall have eternal life. Woe unto those who build oppression and injustice. Woe unto those who build their houses with sin. Woe unto you, O rich people. (ISAAC *here glares directly at* AXEMAN, *who glares back; this is a confrontation between archetypes, at one level: the devotedly pious poor versus the well-heeled, skeptical man of the world.)* Your money makes you appear righteous, but your heart betrays you as a sinner.[54]

(At this point HILARY *once again tries to stop the flow, tugs* ISAAC'S *sleeve)*

HILARY: Shsh, Uncle!

ISAAC *(far too elated to worry about real-world retaliation):* As to the origins of evil, just as a mountain has never turned into a slave, so neither did God bring evil into the world. It is the people who have invented sin. And those who commit sin shall be under a great curse. I swear to you, sinners, that all your evil deeds are recorded every day in presence of the Most High. Woe unto you, fools, for you shall perish through your folly. "Cursed be Satan in all his dominions, and may the sons of Satan be damned in all their works until their annihilation for ever. Amen, amen."[55]

BEN *(on camera):* Cut and finish. One hour's break. Well done, everyone. *(In the cutting room, with a charming but authoritative smile)* Well, Meg, we should be able to make something of that.

MEG: It's so long-winded; it'll be devilishly difficult. Still, we'll see. Anyhow, most viewers will be more interested in what you got about Christians.

BEN *(a bit evasively):* We haven't worked that scene up yet, Meg; Christians were amazingly difficult to find in Rome—apparently, there were very few of them, and they didn't advertise. Alison, why don't you brief Meg, and bring her up to date? *(As* MEG *exits, dissolve her trim black-suited figure into a devil with horns, laughing.)*

Scene 3: Christian vs. Jew

Location: TV cutting room

Characters: Alison and Meg, drinking coffee; later Ben, Mike, and Anonymous Academic; on screen, Isaac, Justin, Hilary, and Axeman

ALISON: You see, what we were trying to do in Scene 3 was to present one form of early Christianity. We wanted to show the continuities and differences between early Christianity and ancient Judaism. *(MEG scowls; she clearly doesn't like* ALISON, *or what she is saying, one little bit.)* As Ben said, we had quite a job finding a Christian in Rome, but I eventually tracked down the perfect guy, called Justin; Hilary was a great help. He seems to have wide connections, and across religious boundaries. He put me onto Justin, and we fixed up to meet him in the same garden, same day in Rome.

Trouble was, that during the break, after we'd finished filming, Isaac and Hilary went bumbling off together, got caught up with Justin and his crowd, and there was a bit of a wrangle. I saw them in the distance, hurried the crew up, but it took us a little longer to get Axeman to join in. *(Giggles)* He had a sudden bout of diarrhea. According to Hilary, it was Justin's Greek accent which first attracted Isaac's attention. Apparently, they both came from Israel; Justin denies he ever was a Jew, but he seems so extremely knowledgeable about Judaism, I can't help wondering.

MEG *(wryly)*: Up to a point, they share the same history. Show me some rushes.

ALISON *(defensively)*: They're unedited. Ben hasn't had time to go through them yet. We didn't get it all, because I had to hurry back and get the crew to come over, but *(she turns to console and moves mouse)* I warn you, even by Isaac's standards, Justin's incredibly dull.

MEG: That's your opinion. Let me judge for myself. Remember, I'm a practicing Christian.

JUSTIN *(thick-set, graying hair, bearded, talking loudly like a practiced preacher, but not ranting, to a small gathering of committed followers)*: The Jews have rejected the new covenant because as the prophet Jeremiah said, "Your ears are closed and your eyes are blind."[56]

ISAAC: This man doesn't know what he's talking about. *(Snorting loudly to HILARY)* That's not Jeremiah, it's from Isaiah [6.10].

(But JUSTIN was not going to be put off by a mild piece of heckling; he was used to it. In fact, he relished it.)

JUSTIN: As Jeremiah predicted, "Behold the day shall come, says the Lord, and I will make a new covenant with the house of Israel" [Jeremiah 31.31]. Jesus Christ has brought to us that new covenant, and we have been led to God through the crucified Jesus Christ. As Isaiah said, "Hear my words and your soul shall live" [55.3]. But although the new lawgiver has come, you do not see him. The new law demands that *we* observe the sabbath continuously, but *you Jews* think that you are pious if you observe a single sabbath, once a week. Repent, and "circumcise the hardness of your hearts" [Deuteronomy 10.16].[57]

ALISON: At this stage, Isaac was becoming apoplectic with rage. He just hated hearing the very words of his own sacred writings being used to accuse all Jews of impiety. He told me later that he thought Justin's words were directed against him personally, and was horrified that anyone could accuse him, of all people, of being satisfied with pious observance only on the sabbath. Was it for this that he had sacrificed his whole life to righteousness? The children of Satan were surrounding him. This graybeard renegade, like himself a refugee from Israel, but dressed as a pagan philosopher, was clearly outside the pale, an apostate or worse. He was more evil than Axeman, and the Seekers After Smooth Things, with their oily words hiding false doctrines in flattery and derision.[58]

MEG *(dryly):* Have you got all that on film?

ALISON: No, but that's what he told me. *(Defiantly)* You wouldn't believe how difficult filming was in the crowd. *(Returns to the monitor.)*

ISAAC *(shouting):* Beware! This is the Wicked Priest, a Spouter of Lies, who flouts the Law and leads the simple astray. Woe on them who abandon me and choose his abominations. *(Thunders)* "God shall deliver him into the hands of his enemies because of his iniquities, and shall take vengeance upon his body of flesh."[59]

JUSTIN *(counters with emphatic gentleness):* We pray for you and all who hate us. *(Warming to his task, now that he knows that he has an opponent in the crowd. One solitary heckler, especially an old geezer curiously dressed, actually makes his job easier.)* I know that you Jews curse us daily in your synagogues because we believe in Christ. It is only the Romans who stop the Jews from attacking us. The Jews feel guilty because they crucified Jesus Christ, the only righteous one, by whose stripes those who believe in him are healed. Small wonder that Isaiah spoke out: "Because of you, my name is blasphemed among the gentiles" [52.5, inaccurately].[60]

ISAAC *(looks angrily puzzled at this alleged quotation from the scripture, but the Wicked Priest moves too fast for him, and besides keeps skipping from topic to topic):* No wonder the people are being led astray.

JUSTIN *(continues unperturbed):* The Jews persecuted Jesus Christ and they must repent, or they will not be saved. Many of the prophets predicted the Messiah's coming. In the book of Daniel we read a wonderful vision in which "the Son of Man came with the clouds of heaven" and came into the presence of God, and God gave him power and a glorious kingdom, and all the peoples of the earth serve him [Daniel 7].

ISAAC: But all that this shows is that one day the Messiah will come.[61] *(Meanwhile the camera strays from attentive pious Christians to stray passing pagans who flirt, ogle, and spit derisively.* MIKE *has cleverly caught both a pickpocket successfully at work and a small boy pissing into some flowers.)*

MEG: Well, we can cut all that out. This is a religious program.

JUSTIN: On the contrary, what it shows is that you do not understand the scriptures. And because of your incomprehension, they have ceased to be *your* scriptures, they are now *ours*. You read the same scriptures, but you fail to capture their spirit, fail to understand how often the prophets clearly predicted the coming of Jesus as Messiah. The very coming of Jesus as Messiah, his crucifixion and resurrection from the dead, all clearly predicted by the prophets, *prove* that our interpretations are true. It is the Jews' own wickedness which prevents them from discerning the scriptures' inner wisdom.[62]

ISAAC *(mumbling to* HILARY*)*: I should have obeyed my teachers. They repeatedly forbade us to listen to or discuss with teachers of false doctrines. *(Louder to* JUSTIN*)* The very idea that a crucified Jesus ascended into heaven, and should be worshiped, is blasphemy. *(And he turns to leave.)*[63]

JUSTIN *(desperately in need of a visible opponent, shouts)*: Don't leave. You hate us because you realize that it is we Christians who really understand the scriptures.

ISAAC *(drawn back, reluctantly)*: You are out of your mind.

JUSTIN: If you stay, I shall persuade you of greater truths. I shall show you from the scriptures that Christ, the Son of God, existed before the sun and moon, then deigned to become flesh, was born of a virgin, in order to conquer the Devil *(cut to* MEG*)*, who was the first sinner, and then the angels followed his example. *(Grandly)* By his death, Christ defeated death and brought it to an end, and when at the end of time Christ comes again, he will bring immortality to those who believe in him, and eternal suffering to the wicked.[64]

HILARY *(temporarily listening, whispers to his uncle)*: It's easier to believe that Jesus was a man and crucified than that he existed before the sun.

ISAAC: It's incredible and impossible, that God agreed to be born as a human.[65] Let's go. I feel tired and weak.

(In fact, Isaac was so weak that he, gratefully even, allowed Hilary to carry his scrolls.)

ALISON: Hilary told me Isaac collapsed on the way home, and died immediately.

MEG: Fascinating.

ALISON: Hilary came back to ask me for some more money for Isaac's funeral. I offered to buy the scrolls, but the bastard had already sold them.

> Luckily, soon after Isaac and Hilary went off, Axeman came back. God knows what he had been doing meanwhile, but he's his own master. It didn't matter too much. Mike had stopped filming. Justin was still going strong. Axeman just got the same basic message again, with some embroidery: how the Jews had crucified Jesus, how the scriptures repeatedly predicted the coming of the Messiah, which the Jews had willfully misunderstood. Their misunderstanding justified their forfeiture of the scriptures, especially now that the Jews had begun to change the original text, in order to cut out explicit predictions about Jesus. Isaac would have had a heart attack on the spot if he'd been here to hear that.[66] *(She realizes too late what she's said.)*

BEN *(who has just slipped into the room)*: We can't use much of this. It's so rabidly anti-Jewish, it simply won't go down here in the States, and even in England we'd get objections.

MEG *(petulantly)*: But it's all *your* fault for finding a Christian like this. It's not proper Christianity.

BEN: Oh, I don't know; I agree Justin's prejudices and target of attack are different. But his patronizing sense of Christian superiority is still pretty common among evangelists, wouldn't you say, Meg?

(BEN flicks mouse and after a while finds just what he wants: a cheery and for once clearheaded ACADEMIC).

ANONYMOUS ACADEMIC: Justin is one of early Christianity's most influential thinkers and defenders. He died a martyr.

ALISON *(head in hands, sotto voce)*: For God's sake, why doesn't Ben realize he needs Meg? *(Then brightly, trying once again to make peace)* Surprisingly, Axeman did get Justin to admit that it was possible for Jews to obey the Law *and* to believe in Christ.

BEN *(unrepentant)*: Big deal.

(ALISON seizes the mouse before BEN can do further damage to the program's prospects.)

AXEMAN: But can the observant Jew, who also believes in Christ, be saved?

JUSTIN: Yes, I think they too will be saved, just as the Jews before Moses were saved, provided they don't try to get other Christians to practice circumcision, and provided they don't refuse to eat with other Christians—though, admittedly, not all Christians agree with me on this point.[67]

MIKE *(sotto voce):* You mean, provided they don't act like proper Jews.

(ALISON *desperately fast-forwards a bit, and gets fragments of the rushes.)*

JUSTIN *(vituperatively):* Some men *call* themselves Christian, but are godless, impious heretics, who teach foul blasphemy. There are whole groups of them, as was predicted—but far from undermining our faith, they actually help make our faith all the stronger. Some of these pseudo Christians refuse communion with Jews who admit that Jesus Christ is Lord, others completely reject the God of Abraham, still others reject the resurrection of the body and foolishly think that only the soul rises to heaven.[68]

(While JUSTIN *is jabbering on about Christian deviants,* ALISON *passes* AXEMAN *a note telling him to ask* JUSTIN *about Jesus.)*

AXEMAN: What is the power of Jesus?

JUSTIN: You can tell the power of Jesus because all demons are effectively exorcised by very mention of his name. You just say he is "the true Son of God, first-begotten of all creatures, born of a virgin, who suffered and was crucified under Pontius Pilate, who died, was then resurrected from the dead, and ascended into heaven." No other exorcism, with or without amulets and incense, works as well.[69] *(Cut to* MEG; *this is not the Christianity she knows.)*

AXEMAN: What do you mean when you say that Jesus was the first-begotten of all creatures?

JUSTIN: In the beginning, when God said, "Let us make man in our own image" [Genesis 1.26], the "us" in Genesis referred to God *and* Jesus. And this Jesus is really the spiritual Word, or Logos, an emanation of God the Father, who appeared time and time again in the Jewish scriptures as the power of God, as an angel of God, in effect as another God. And it was this Jesus who condescended to become a human by a virgin, in accordance with his Father's wishes, and consented to be crucified and die.[70]

MIKE: This chap is even nuttier than Isaac.

ALISON: Well, according to the academic theologians, he's got a problem. He is trying to make Christianity generally appealing. He's got to prove to the Jews that he's a monotheist, and he's got to prove to educated pagans that he recognizes a general divine force, which he calls Logos, which means sort of Reason more than a literal Word. You know, "In the beginning was the Word" [John 1.1].

MIKE: Wow, I never knew what that meant. *(Said with all the conviction of an unbeliever, who has absolutely no intention of understanding.)*

Afterword

It was easy to see that Justin felt quite satisfied with his morning's work. He'd got his views across with vigor and style. Most of his audience had been pleasingly attentive; only that old Jew had been annoyingly stubborn. But he knew that quite a lot of Jews were converting to Christianity nowadays. And those odd fellows with strange clothes and eyeglasses had asked him interesting questions. He returned to his quarters above the baths of Martin, hungry and thirsty. While he was eating, there was a loud knock on the door downstairs; a few minutes later some soldiers burst into the room, asked him his name, and said he was under arrest, accused of being a Christian. Of course, he replied that he was.[71]

But who had betrayed him? Was it Crescens, his philosophical rival? There were so many possibilities. Was it, Justin wondered, the jealous and aggrieved husband of one of his faithful and admiring followers? Of course, he knew that he had done nothing wrong in that respect—though secretly he also realized only too well, what God already knew, that he had sinned with the lust of his eyes. Perhaps it was that wretched Jew? But how could he have known where Justin lived? Only later, in prison, did Justin find out, rather humiliatingly, that his arrest had nothing to do with Christian doctrine. His landlord's daughter wanted to rent his room, to share with her lover.[72] Revolutionaries have a hard time.

Back in the real world, Alison got fed up with Ben's egocentricity and switched her affections to Mike, after he had made an uncharacteristic but stunningly winsome declaration of passion and love. Axeman, for all his hard exterior, never got over his Roman experience, and entered a strict settlement on the West Bank. That left Meg and Ben alone together. By a process I don't understand, and after ferocious arguments, they eventually decided that they needed each other.[73] Meg even had the fantasy that she would reform Ben, and he would be saved.[74]

FIRST REACTIONS: SOME INTERNAL MEMOS

To: *PM—Controller*
   Fox TV
From: *Meg Stacey, Coordinator, Religious Programs*

I write in some dismay. I have just seen the first cuts from the projected program, *Dialogues with the Dead*, about late-antique Judaism and early Christianity. Wonderful title and great to get Axeman; he trebles the ratings.

But it just cannot be shown in its present form. It is inappropriately vulgar and ridicules religious beliefs. It deals in cheap oppositional stereotypes; its choice of early Christian spokesperson (Justin) is, to say the least, unfortunate and inflammatory of anti-Jewish prejudice. We should support religion, not encourage mockery.

All goes to underline the risks of hiring out-of-house directors. Incidentally, the program contains dating inaccuracies, which will tarnish our image, and should not have slipped past our academic advisers.

Can we redo with better-selected Christians and a different director or closer control?

P.S. I attach a selection of reports I got from trusted academic specialists who also saw a preliminary version of the program. These are their measured comments; informally, they were much more damning.

Report A
As I see it, the basic argument of this program is simply that
1. Some Jews in the first century were passionately committed to their own version of Judaism, in direct opposition to mainstream temple Judaism.
2. The Qumranites' peculiar version of Judaism has some interesting similarities to (and differences from) normative Christianity; for example, they thought the Messiah(s) would come, and that the end of the world was imminent and, as the elect, they would all go to heaven.
3. Some Christians, in interpreting the scriptures, used exactly the same techniques as the Jews, but interpreted them to mean something quite different. Occasionally, they scrapped with one another as to what exactly the scriptures said, and accused one another of fiddling with the texts. Passions were high on both sides. I suppose the program also implies (somewhat awkwardly) that there were as many types of Christianity as of Judaism.
4. Finally (and I suspect this is the main point of the idiosyncratic TV framing—showing the show), the intellectual thrust is that there is no such thing as objective history, or if there is, it isn't interesting. What matters more is the interpretive eye with which we understand, and about that we are all inclined to go on disagreeing.

I find all this acceptable enough, but rather labored for its length, but then I don't really watch much television.

Report B

For a program on late-antique Judaism, there are many important points missing. The drama of the Dead Sea Scrolls has crowded out the normative center of regular Judaism, based on the triple pillars of temple worship, the covenant God made with Israel through Moses (obey the Law and I'll look after you), and regular observance of and knowledge about the Law. Only by implication do we glimpse Israel's collective religious identity.

The dramatic framework precludes any sense of evolution. But Judaism changed from being the religion of a nation-state to being the informally led religion of a dispersed minority. The temple was destroyed in 70. Before that and after, Jews were moving gradually from a collective toward an individualistic religiosity, based not on animal sacrifice but, symbolically, on prayer and piety, felt as well as practiced, and supported by vivid visions of heaven and hell.

The anachronistic meeting between Isaac and Justin is a serious error of history and judgment. They belong to different centuries.

I thought the pictures were wonderful.

Report C

I think the program should give much more background. After all, Christianity expanded from a Judaism which was itself changing, a Judaism which was for a considerable time depressed by successive crushing defeats by the Romans in 70, 117, 135. Most early Christians were probably Jews or ex-Jews (a lot depends on the view taken about the nature and timing of the break of Christianity from Judaism; I see it as continuing negotiated tension lasting well beyond 100 CE, not as a sudden, early, and complete rupture). But most Jews remained Jews, or at least did not become Christian.

I think it would be most helpful if the program dwelt a bit more on the overlap and tensions between Jews and Christians, since most people nowadays understandably think of the two categories as distinctively different, and incompatible. In this century, we don't have Jewish-Christians who go to synagogue and church. But in the first century, Jewish Christians constituted a sizable body within/at the margins of the church.

And of course, much more should be said about the varieties of Christianity, and how Christianity evolved. As the program stands, the variety of Christianity selected for viewing here is completely odd. It would be improved by adding some trustworthy academic talking heads.

A final point of detail: why is Meg represented as the Devil *and* a committed Christian? Was this a mistake?

From: PM—Controller
To: Meg Stacey, Coordinator, Religious Programs

Thanks for your note. You're quite right to express your concern about tone and accuracy.

Finance indicates that, subject to normal procedures, OK to do sequel on similar budget with first-century Christians, next year.

Choice of director and his/her remit, of course, up to you.

But we can't scrap existing program at this late stage. I'm told it comes over very well, and we don't want to offend Axeman. I agree with you, he's brilliant.

Personally, I'd quite like to have Ben H. as director again. His work has flair, and the fifty-year slippage with Justin in two millennia surely doesn't matter too much, at least not on TV.

Perhaps we could sound out reaction to prototype on radio; what do you think? Crumbs for sound.

From: Ben H., Director, Dialogues with the Dead
To: PM—Controller

Thanks for keeping me up to date. Love to do sequel. What about a confrontation between St. Peter and St. Paul?

Meg's hysteria seems overdone. Incidentally, I was quite aware that Justin lived later; that's half the fun with mixed-time TV—you can mix times. Besides, it's a bit naive to imagine that getting dates right is a guarantee of correctness. Time is only one dimension of truth. But *you* know that!

THREE

The Christian Revolution

A revolution is not the same as inviting people to dinner, or writing an essay or painting a picture . . . it cannot be anything so restrained and magnanimous. A revolution is an uprising, an act of violence, by which one class overthrows another.

—*Mao Zedong*[1]

FERVENT BELIEFS

The core of Christian belief was quite extraordinary. It is difficult for us now to recapture how very strange and offensive it must have seemed to pagans in the Roman world. Christians claimed that there was only one true God, who had sent his son, Jesus, the Messiah, both human and divine, into the Roman empire to save humanity from sin. Jesus had died, of his own free will, as a crucified criminal, in Palestine.[2] But Christ had not died. He was bodily resurrected from the dead and is now in heaven, passing just but merciful judgment on the living and the dead. In return for believing this, and for living a life free from sin, in deed and thought, and for meeting weekly to pray, Christianity offered its faithful the hope of salvation and immortality. Christ's undignified suffering and death on the cross became the new symbol of human salvation.[3]

Gloss it as you will, the worship of a crucified criminal as the son of God, the divine exaltation of a humble human, the crucifixion of God, and the ethical message of achieving individual salvation through faith, virtue, and repentance constituted a radical break with pagan polytheism, animal sacrifice, and temple worship. Christianity subverted the whole priestly calendar of civic rituals and public festivals on which Roman rule in the provinces rested. Christianity was a revolutionary movement.

Of course, the Christian revolution was not a complete revolution. Modern political scientists use the word "revolution" to describe rapid and massive changes in twentieth-century Russia and China.[4] The ancient Christian revolution took four centuries, not a decade or two. The Chinese revolution was a complete transformation of political ideology and power relations, which brought about fundamental changes in political structures and, with them, a visible redistribution of property between rich and poor. The Chinese achieved so much because the state had hugely superior armed might, a significant redistributable surplus, mass political support, a conscious ideology of thoroughgoing social change, and realistic prospects of economic growth.

The Christian revolution, by contrast, was a revolution principally in symbolism and ideology. Churches replaced temples, prayers replaced animal sacrifice, sermons slowly displaced gladiatorial games, Sundays replaced the traditional Roman calendar of kalends, nones, and ides.[5] At Rome's stage of social and economic evolution, the redistributable surplus was far too small for widespread changes in standards of living. And the Roman army's firepower was too limited to enforce thoroughgoing changes onto a dispersed population. So the Christian revolution evolved gradually. True, there was embattled conflict. The Roman government tried to wipe out the Christian leadership in the Great Persecution of 303–12. And reciprocally, at the end of the fourth century, the triumphant Christian church with state connivance destroyed and pillaged pagan temples. But by and large gradualism, not violence, was the hallmark of the Christian revolution.[6]

This is not to belittle the scale or even the speed of Christian achievements. Against all the odds and from tiny beginnings, the Jesus movement became the official religion of the Roman state. The key moment was the conversion of the emperor Constantine in 312, confirmed by the Christianity of his imperial successors.[7] Without state support, Christianity could not have triumphed. With state support, the Christian church rapidly claimed a religious monopoly. In 391, worship at pagan temples was outlawed: "No one shall be allowed to perform sacrifices; no one shall go around temples; no one shall revere shrines."[8] By then, millions of pagans had converted from traditional polytheism to nominal monotheism. Overtly, paganism was crushed.

But in spite of the obvious differences, the revolutionary processes in

China and in the Roman empire were in some ways strikingly similar. Both revolutions created a radically new nexus of ethical prescriptions and hope, new symbols, new slogans, new literature, and with it, effectively, a new language of apparent simplicity, new ways of thinking, new heroes, and new villains. The Christian revolution promoted a radical message of love and charity, flaunted the idea that even the foolish and uneducated could be wise, that the virtuous simpleton could outargue learned philosophers, that the rich should be generous to the poor, that the holy should care for the sick. Christianity introduced new styles of theological argument, new literary genres such as gospels and sermons, new heroes such as confessors, martyrs, bishops, monks, and saints, with heretics and pagan persecutors as their antitypes.[9]

Of course, in Rome as in China, the veneer of virtuous prescription disguised a multitude of sins; the church grew steadily richer, and more corrupt; Christian rigorists pursued mad ends with obsessional fervor; bishops borrowed the oppressive powers of the state to bully, exclude, and even execute doctrinal rivals. But for all its very considerable excesses, Christianity fostered ideals of kindness and hope, of personal worth and passionate commitment to belief, which are still central to western cultural traditions.

In this chapter I want to analyze the processes by which Christianity gradually separated from its Jewish background, preached its message of salvation and ethics, and in so doing evolved the three main pillars of orthodoxy: the rule of faith, the apostolic succession of authoritative bishops, and the canon of sacred texts. I want to illustrate how Christians fought bitterly against, and at the same time compromised with, the Roman state, and meanwhile created their own frontier heroes and villains: martyrs, ascetic saints, bishops, and heretics. But before we pursue this considerable task, a few words on the nature of the Christian message, the context of its transmission, and the scale of early Christian communities.

Any brief description of the complexities of the Christian message is bound to be misleading, or thought to be wrong in emphasis or by omission, by different sets of believers. But it is essential to appreciate that the early Christian message was understood differently then and now, if only because the whole context of understanding was different. Modern Christianity in the western world is often liberal, individualistic, and relativist; only some Christians now think they have a monopoly of virtue or truth. Early Christians, as I see them, in their pursuit of salvation and immortality, focused on faith, unity, and obedience. They were sure, or presented themselves as completely sure, that they alone were right.

Christianity started as a tiny and embattled sect surrounded by enemies. The perceived hostility of Jews and pagans to Christians, and the complementary hostility of Christians to their enemies, were fundamental ingredients in early Christian identity.[10] Pagan idol worship was foolish and illusory, pagan myths were immoral, their religious and domestic practices were disgusting. As for Jews, they had misunderstood their own scriptures, and out of malevolent ignorance had killed Jesus, the righteous son of God. Even among Christians, false teachers and perverts threatened the small community's purity and reputation—they were cursed to eternal damnation. The pervasive demonic powers of darkness too often blinded the hearts of potential converts. Early Christianity was not a religion of liberal individualism and kindly tolerance. Early Christians did not live in a comfortable and cozy world. Jesus and Paul were not Episcopalians.

Paul acted, preached, and prayed with passionate zeal, both for his old (preconversion) and for his new faith. On the orders of Jewish leaders, he was severely flogged (thirty-nine lashes) five times for his missionary pains. His suffering was itself proof of his unyielding commitment. To explain his new beliefs, he did not rely on complex reasoning but on blinding revelation from God himself. That revelation alone justified his apostleship, and his imperious demand that his followers believe in Christ, the savior. They must abandon their old ways, repent their sins, embrace the new faith, and live in fear of judgment. They should love their fellow Christians, obey their teachers, trust in God, and through Christ Jesus hope for resurrection, salvation, and the kingdom of God.[11]

This radical Christian message opened up for believers a new path to salvation and immortality. By their faith and their deeds, and through a believing heart, a pious life, prayers, and Jesus' merciful intercession, true Christians could win for themselves God's merciful forgiveness, salvation, and immortality. In imitation of Jesus himself, they could even (so some Christian preachers claimed) become like God.[12] And even if believers sinned, they could still gain forgiveness through confession, repentance, and reform. But nonbelievers and unrepentant sinners are being punished, and will be punished eternally.

This chain of sin, guilt, fear of punishment, repentance, forgiveness, salvation, though obviously of Jewish origin, became an established Christian trademark. But in compensation, Christians (like Jews) saw themselves as special, chosen by God. They were the fervent elect, linked together by their difference from and radical rejection of others, as well as by regular communal worship and by a pressing sense that the Messiah would soon come again and that the end of the world was imminent.[13]

Two points should be quickly made. First, Christianity was a missionary religion aimed at winning new converts. It had to sell itself by stating what it stood for and against. The very existence, from early on in Christian history, of brief statements of Christian beliefs set Christianity apart from Judaism and paganism. Put crudely, the contrast is that Christianity became a religion of belief, whereas Judaism and paganism were religions predominantly of traditional practice, with settled adherents. Judaism was the religion of a nation, with few converts in each generation, and few expulsions.[14] Pagans (as we usually conceptualize them) simply did what they had always done. But during the first three centuries CE, a combination of factors—the integration of diverse cultures within the Roman empire into a single political entity, large-scale migration to cities and the evolution of mystery cults—stimulated religious syncretism, and increased fluidity in religious attachment.[15] For the first time in Mediterranean history, religion had become a matter of choice, not of birth.

In reality, both Judaism and paganism were more varied and fluid than this rough, though broadly correct, stereotype allows. But it follows that the vast majority of pagans and Jews were born into their religions. Many Christians, by contrast, in each generation had made a double decision, both to desert traditional practices and to convert. And ideally a Christian could readily tell fellow believers what he/she believed, whereas a pagan typically could not, and a Jew would not typically think of belief as defining his/her religious commitment.

Second, because it was a religion of belief, Christian leaders prided themselves on knowing precisely what constituted correct belief. The New Testament and other early Christian writings are littered with severe imprecations against false teachers. Quite unlike Christianity, rabbinical Judaism after 70 CE evolved a systemic agreement to disagree about interpretations of the Law. What follows is one seemingly trivial example, which nonetheless illustrates typical rabbinic argument. In a discussion about whether ritually pure foods stored in one corner of a basket were polluted by a dead snake found in another corner of the basket,

> Hezekiah stated that the foods which were previously clean remain clean. Rabbi Yohanan stated that the foods which were previously clean were now regarded retrospectively as unclean. But Shammai and Hillel agree that in the case of a basket, the foods which were previously considered clean are now retrospectively deemed unclean. But Shammai and Hillel concur only in the case of a basket without a bottom. But if the basket has no bottom, what could R. Yohanan's reason be?

And so on. The style of argument and the measured disagreement is idiosyncratically Jewish.

Christianity, by contrast, gradually evolved into a church with a strongly idealized sense of its own unity in orthodoxy. It developed an ideology of unity in faith and tradition. "The tradition of the apostles has been made manifest to every church in the whole world; it is available to all those who wish to perceive the truth. We can list the bishops appointed by the apostles to their churches, and their successors down to the present day. And they neither taught nor acknowledged what these madmen teach."[16] Correct belief was forged in conflict with dissident insiders.

The unity of orthodoxy created its own antitheses: heresy, schism, and excommunication. And so Christianity became both universalistic, that is, ideally open to all who believed, and at the same time exclusivist, in the sense that Christian leaders were overtly determined to reform or expel anyone who believed incorrectly or who behaved immorally.[17] Needless to say, ideals affect, even if they do not describe, practice. But even occasional enforcements are symbolically important, and sufficient to keep the ideals notionally in force. So ideals of uniformity in fact disguised a wide degree of diversity.

Christianity was not only a religion of belief but also a religion of ethical prescription. Early Christianity, by its own report, was a religion which required both fervor of belief and a strict morality of action. Again, in spite of these ideals, diversity and infractions inevitably flourished. Indeed, Christianity's success depended in part on its flexible capacity to maintain, adapt, and propagate its ideals as though they were universally applicable and actually practiced by all believers, while in reality condoning, within the framework of orthodoxy and a strict moral code, diversity of thought and sin.

In the first three centuries, strict enforcement of orthodoxy was impracticable. Communications were slow and uncertain. Ships didn't usually sail during winter; roads were by and large safe, but travelers had to keep an eye out for brigands; writers of letters often didn't know when or whether a message had arrived. Christianity was (or soon became) an illegal religion. So early Christians met covertly in private houses. Numerous small groups were dispersed in towns and villages throughout the eastern and central Mediterranean basin.

Until the third century or later, Christians did not meet in purposely built churches, so the basic Christian units were house groups, typically comprising a few dozen members; or perhaps the term "house cult group" recaptures the fervor and subversive marginality of early Christian meetings. In each town, house cult groups were linked together into a notional community, increasingly, from the end of the second century, under the supervisory leadership of an authoritative bishop. But Christianity's illegality, the incapacity of bishops openly or effectively to impose order, the dispersion of house cult groups, the fragile lines of communication, and the rapid growth in the movement's size all contributed to doctrinal and liturgical variety.

Early Christianity was tiny and scattered. No precise figures survive, but best estimates suggest that there were considerably fewer than ten thousand Christians in 100 CE, and only about two hundred thousand Christians in 200 CE, dispersed among several hundred towns.[18] The late-second-century figure equals only 0.3 percent of the total population of the Roman empire (which was about 60 million). I should emphasize that these figures are guesses, only rough orders of magnitude. Admittedly, size is a single and pedestrian measure of a sect's significance, but the very small numbers of early Christians, both absolute and relative, and the rapidity of its growth are fundamental to our understanding. The rapidity of its growth (at this rate, of over 3 percent per year compounded, two-fifths of adult members would have joined in the previous ten years) helps explain why coded statements of belief, rather than complex rules of practice, were the passport to full membership. The very small size of Christianity helps explain why the Roman state paid so little attention to suppressing it effectively. And the tiny size of early Christianity, relative to the empire's population, helps explain why the central Roman government for so long ignored the potential dangers which Christianity eventually posed to pagan civic religions and to the political system which they supported.

The social composition of early Christian groups probably contributed to their neglect. Roman society was highly stratified. Christians simply did not signify. If they surfaced in elite pagan consciousness, they surfaced only occasionally and sporadically, and as an irritating nuisance. The politically powerful in the city of Rome and in the provinces were a tiny group of the rich and educated. Presumably, a radical religion which promised special benefits to the poor in the hereafter did not appeal particularly to them. The pagan powerful considered themselves already saved; the Gods were on the side of the fortunate and well washed. High state and municipal officials served as pagan priests. So it seems likely that very few members of the tiny ruling elite became Christians, at least in the first two centuries.[19]

Snobbish, well-educated pagan critics accused Christians of targeting ignorant men, women, and slaves as potential converts. But by no means all Christians can have been poverty stricken; Christians met in private houses; some Christians must have been prosperous enough to own or rent houses big enough for such meetings.[20] And the mere existence of Christian writings indicates that some Christians were literate. Admittedly, for the first century after Jesus' death, Christian writings do not show the rhetorical sophistication of court literati like Dio Chrysostom or Seneca. But Paul and the gospel writers must have belonged, however tenuously, to the educated but varied and thin subelites (merchants, middle landowners, teachers, clerks and the like, altogether amounting to less than 2 percent of adult males in the Roman world) who could write and read fluently.

It's worth pursuing this line of thought a little further. In the early stages of Christianity, at any one time, perhaps only a few dozen Christians could read or write fluently. On the numbers which I have just cited, and even if we allow for a significantly higher rate of literacy among Christians than among pagans (outside the ruling elite), by the end of the first century all Christianity is likely to have included, at any one time, less than fifty adult men who could write or read biblical texts fluently.[21] And even by the end of the second century, although there may have been (by the same reckoning) over a thousand fluently literate Christians, that still works out, on average, as only about two literates per community. The vast majority of Christians could not read or probably even understand the texts which we now consider fundamental to reconstructing their history. Written Christianity was initially constructed by a tiny group of socially marginal men.

Religion was not a frontier along which the Roman elite considered it needed to defend itself with vigor, at least not until the middle of the third century. And when the state did attack the Christian church on a massive scale, in three purges beginning in 250, 257, and 303, the number of Christians, in spite of temporary setbacks, apparently continued to grow. "The blood of martyrs is the seed" of the church, as the choleric Christian Tertullian pithily put it. By the end of the third century, perhaps 10 percent of the empire's population—6 million out of 60 million people—were Christian.[22] The emperor Constantine openly converted to Christianity in 312, and the emperors who succeeded him were also Christian. Out of commitment or political self-interest, or both, they favored the Christian church with donations and with privileges for the clergy. They gave state support for synods of bishops to decide matters of doctrine; they also used the church as a supplementary instrument of imperial ideology and social control.[23] It is difficult to decide whether this radical transformation of the role of Christianity, which had so much influence on the future course of western culture, should be called the triumph of the Christian church or the triumph of the Roman state.

But for almost three centuries after Jesus' death, while the Christian church was both illegal and at loggerheads with the Roman state, Christian leaders had no effective mechanism for enforcing uniformity in belief or practice. What is amazing is that in spite of the practical difficulties of size, dispersion, rapid growth, and illegality, and in spite of the startling variety of early Christian beliefs, Christian leaders actively pursued and preserved the ideal of unity and orthodoxy. This *ideal* of unity became enshrined in the image of a single Christian church, buttressed by the emerging tradition of *apostolic succession* legitimating episcopal power, of the *rule of faith*, and of the *canonical scriptures*. These became the three pillars of the institutional Catholic church.

Within this diverse unity, a particular sense of Christian identity and history evolved. Orthodox Christian writers proclaimed Christianity's antiquity and its conservative traditionalism. It is tempting to collude with the winners, and treat the losers as marginal, even absurd, and as deserving defeat. But we should be cautious. Winners need losers, and need to go on reminding the faithful of their victories. The losers helped define and refine the winners' organization and beliefs. And in the long run, perhaps, some second-century losers did not deserve to lose. Nor is the battle yet over.

It was the pious heretic Marcion, after all, who in the mid–second century first created a canon of gospel and epistles and who organized his breakaway church around a single selected sacred text.[24] Orthodox Christians, perhaps in competition or imitation, also adopted a canon of gospels and letters over the next half century. Marcion argued forcibly that God's initial creative act and Jewish history were quite separable, and best separated, from the prospect of salvation through Christ's redemptive self-sacrifice. For Marcion, it was the novelty of the Christian message of faith and hope which mattered much more than its antiquity. And now, at the end of the second millennium, Marcion appears to have won in broad sectors of the Christian church. For many modern Christians, the Old Testament is largely ignored. Even if Marcion's ascetic insistence on asexuality as a qualifying condition for baptism was rejected by the orthodox "Great Church," his ideal of ascetic self-denial survived as a radical driving force among rigorist Christians, to reemerge among ascetics, hermits, monks, and nuns from the late third century onward.

Gnostics, with their chaotic inventiveness, pursued the ideal that divinity was to be found inside each human's soul, by self-knowledge.[25] Their search could not be constricted within the straitjacket of the Jewish ethnic myth or the ethically doubtful thoughts and exploits of the God of the Old Testament. So they set about transforming the Judaeo-Christian creation story beyond recognition. For them, this world was far too imperfect to have been created by a supreme Deity; and the historical Jesus was too terrestrial and corporeal. So they projected their spiritualist God and religious imagination onto a cosmic scale. Complementarily, for Gnostics, spiritual success depended on each individual's mental and emotional striving. It did not depend on the help of a professional clergy or on an organized and hierarchical church. For them, bishops had no privileged line to God.

The Great Church, as it came to be, responded by insisting that the

Old Testament was a fundamental part of the Christian faith. Its prophecies foretold all that had come to pass—and therefore Christian interpretations of all that had come to pass were also true. There was only one God, the Creator God. He was both God and judge. Jesus coexisted with that external Creator but had also been physically born human in historical time. Belief in his corporeality and bodily resurrection provided the only path to truth. The canonical gospels were a sufficient witness to his message. He had passed on his teaching to the apostles, and they in turn had passed their wisdom by direct succession to the bishops of the Catholic church. The canonical scriptures, apostolic succession, and the true faith were the sole and sufficient guarantees of righteous teaching.[26]

Eventually, Christian ideologues set out their faith with remarkable precision and with increasing sophistication. Admittedly, theological niceties and logical consistency do not solve all problems, and may not even be helpful in discussions of an unknowable God. But a lively religion needs internal divisions, if only to express the complementary and rival claims of its believers. And once in alliance with the state, Christian leaders exploited their newfound powers in order to impose single versions of correct belief, through votes by universal councils of bishops.[27] Almost inevitably, once its influence and power was buttressed by the state, the church also became in part a business, distributing charity, patronage, privilege, and immortality.

Early Christianity grew and changed (though leaders often tried to disguise these changes by appeal to tradition) through conflict on all sides. Christians divorced Judaism, battled with the Roman state, gradually controlled unruly if inspired evangelism, borrowed and absorbed the conceptual sophistication of pagan intellectual culture, and tried vainly to suppress highly inventive variants of Christian beliefs. Of course, not all changes were the result of conflict. The Christian churches had internal dialectic dynamics of their own. During the second and third centuries, church leaders gradually increased their status and authority. They created the tradition of apostolic succession and the ideal of authoritative bishops, they effectively closed the canon of the New Testament, and they specified with greater care what they considered the rule of faith. They created a new genre of Christian hero and literature, the martyr and the Martyr Acts, and continued to exhort their followers to greater virtue while inventing laxer modes of repentance and forgiveness.

DIVORCE FROM JUDAISM

Jesus was a Jew, and so were most early Christians.[28] James the brother of Jesus, for example, who after Jesus' death was the widely acknowledged leader of the Jesus movement, worshiped at the temple in Jerusalem until his death in 62, thirty years after Jesus' death. To be sure, he was then executed by order of the Sadducee high priest, but against the objections of friendly Pharisees. And later, when Luke wrote the Acts of the Apostles, he pictured Paul as worshiping in the temple long after he had had his miraculous revelation on the Damascus road that Jesus was the Christ, the anointed of God, the Messiah.[29] At that stage, some Christians and Jews clearly still thought it admissible to regard Judaism and belief in Christ as compatible.

Most early believers in Christ as the Son of God were Jews, because the Jesus movement started as yet another radical renewal movement within Judaism, and in Palestine. Strange as it may now seem, these early Jewish Christians both followed the Law and believed that Jesus was Christ. Eventually, because leaders on both sides came to think of Judaism and Christianity as incompatible, Jewish Christianity survived only as a fringe sect, and as a troubling symptom of a buried past, though as such it persisted well into the fourth century.[30]

When the early Christian missionaries began to spread their message outside Palestine, they used synagogues as a natural starting point. True—as Paul, for example, found to his cost—Jews sometimes objected violently to the new Christian message. But even so, in spite of the risks, Jews were early Christianity's potential best customers in the marketplace of competing religions. Jews also already knew most of the Christian story, because then it was based primarily on proof texts selected from Jewish scriptures. So initially Jews were much more likely converts than pagans. Many Jews shared the expectation that one day the Messiah(s) would come, and that the end of the world was imminent.[31] Christians dramatically built on, and subverted, these expectations by asserting that the Messiah had actually already arrived, had died, had been resurrected, and offered salvation to believers at the end of days.

Gradually, as Christians and Christian missionaries increasingly succeeded in converting pagans/gentiles, Jewish Christians and Christians of Jewish origin and their descendants who had deserted the Law became a minority. This switch in Christian membership from being primarily Jewish and ex-Jewish in origin to being primarily ex-pagan and descended from ex-pagans probably did not take place until the early to mid–second century.[32]

Christianity's origins within Judaism left an indelible heritage of similarities: prayers, communal weekly worship inside a building, hymns, baptism, fasts, angels, martyrs, heaven, hell, a sense of being God's chosen people. But most important, Christians—like Jews, but unlike pagans—believed in a single, omnipotent, and omniscient God who had purposefully created this universe and who was deeply interested in all that humans did and thought. Ideally, Christians were convinced that God saw into human hearts; each individual had a recording angel who after death read out to God, the judge, all that a believer had done, thought, or desired, even unconsciously.[33]

The idea of the omniscient and interested God was closely tied to early Christians' magnification of guilt. Pagans found the idea of a supreme God who cared intensely about individual actions incredible, and even some Christians thought it unlikely. The anti-Jewish heretical Christian Marcion, for example, believed that God was not interested in individual human acts. Marcion reduced God's charity to the single salvific act of having sent Jesus (of course, not his son—much too fleshly a concept) to open up for humans a possible path toward redemption. Gnostic Christians thought creation far too flawed to have been the work of the supreme God, and attributed it instead to an inferior Creator God, whom the Jews and orthodox Christians foolishly worshiped. For Gnostic Christians, salvation came primarily through self-knowledge (gnosis). But for orthodox Christians the chain of purposeful creation, Adam's fall, sin, guilt, punishment, repentance, and forgiveness and salvation—finally achieved through Jesus (the second but unflawed Adam) as both model and intercessor—became a quintessential characteristic of their faith.

In spite of, or rather because of, the similarities, a painful divorce of Christianity from Judaism ensued. It did not occur in a single short, sharp break; it was a protracted and repeatedly negotiated separation, which dragged on from the middle of the first to the middle of the second century, and beyond. Christian ideologues had a delicate operation to perform. They could not, like Marcion or some Gnostics, repudiate the Jewish God and scriptures entirely. Orthodox Christians wanted all the antiquity which Judaism conferred. Judaism was, after all, they argued, much older than Greek civilization; Moses had lived one thousand years before Troy was destroyed; Jewish thinkers both preceded and informed Greek thought. Christianity was therefore not a recent upstart, founded in Judaea in the reign of Tiberius, but the true heir of the ancestral Jewish tradition. And Jesus himself was not merely a human born in the reign of Augustus; he was also the ever-existent and preexistent Word of God, who coexisted with God at the very creation of the universe.[34]

To argue all these points convincingly, Christian preachers needed all the proof texts which the Hebrew Bible provided, to show that the prophets of old really had predicted Jesus as the very Messiah. Their interpretations were rarely boringly literal, but with judicious quotations, inspired allegorization, and some well-chosen amendments to the text (after all, the Jews themselves, so Christian critics alleged, kept on changing the Greek translation of the Hebrew), it could be convincingly shown that the prophets had indeed repeatedly predicted all that now had come to pass. The Jews had willfully failed to understand the true meaning of the Bible. They had taken literally what should have been understood spiritually (carnal circumcision, for example, instead of the spiritual circumcision of the heart and ear). They had therefore forfeited their temporary possession of God's Word. The Bible now belonged to the Christians, and not to the Jews. Their literal misunderstanding of the Law had justly imposed on Jews absurd ritual obligations, which were their due punishment for their ancient sins of idolatry, magnified now by their recent slaughter of Jesus. But Abraham, himself a proto-Christian, had been duly rescued by Jesus from hell, and the ethical laws of Moses were still valid.[35]

To these ends, all the rhetorical clichés of a bitter divorce were used. History was selectively rewritten; it was all the Jews' fault: they had never understood, they concentrated on the flesh instead of the spirit, and they deserved all that had befallen them (God and the Romans had even joined forces to destroy Jerusalem). That alone proved their guilt—besides, the Jews had cunningly doctored the evidence. And finally (this was probably the main point of their Christian adversaries) the intellectual property which they had previously shared now belonged only to

Christians. It is not the Hebrew Bible, it is the Old Testament. The synagogue has become the church. It is Christians who are now the true race of Israel, the chosen people, the people of God.

Needless to say, the Christian case was only one side of the story. The Jewish side was either censored in later Christian times or originally less shrill, if only because at the time of the divorce, in spite of temporary difficulties, the Jews were by far the superior (that is, larger and legal) party. But by the mid–second century or earlier, some Jews began to curse heretics, which obviously included Christians, in their daily prayers. Both sides supplemented their formal, intellectual arguments with scurrilous stories. Jews told tales about the wicked Jesus (see Chapter Six below), Christians about the humiliating failures of ineffectual Jewish magic. Only very occasionally, in the chinks of surviving records, can we spot shy examples of mutual support and admiration. The great bulk of the record on both sides is irremediably hostile.

THE STRINGENT DEMANDS OF FAITH

Early Christians were deeply embattled, and on many fronts. Externally, they were surrounded by Jews and pagans, at best indifferent, at worst aggressively hostile. Even if murderous persecutions were in reality only intermittent, threats of casual violence and anonymous denunciations hung over Christian communities like racial hatred against ethnic minorities in modern inner cities. Christians were, or soon became, an illegal sect. Everywhere they went, they were reminded of their difference. In the Forum, baths, theaters, at gladiatorial games and at crossroads altars, in street processions, they confronted man-made idols of false gods, the demons of temptation, to say nothing of public brothels and the seductive glances of unveiled women, demons in disguise.

Christians lived in an alien world, filled with impiety, poisoned by immorality and by the oppressive forces of the Roman state, the powers of Darkness. Jesus' very incarnation was hidden from the Devil, the ruler of this world.[36] When Jesus was born, it was only by God's aid that he had escaped the clumsy plot of an evil king (Matthew 2.7,16). Roman emperors, astride their seven hills, like whores of Babylon drank from a golden cup full of abominations and the blood of martyrs (Revelation 17.4ff.). Christians internalized the hostility which they experienced around them and used it as extra insulation, in order to protect their sense of idiosyncratic distinctiveness.

Even inside their small, intense conventicles, where the devoted faithful knelt, prayed, and confessed their sins, sang hymns, fasted, and ate regularly together, enemies proliferated. Early Christians had always to be on their guard against the devilish wiles of sinners, false teachers, hypocrites, rebels, and heretics. They themselves were the beloved, the elect of God, the righteous, the brotherhood of Christ. Enemies added to that very special sense of being the chosen few. Several early Christian writings leave the distinct impression that virtues could emerge only by contrast with the vices of others, or indeed of Christians themselves. Clement's *First Letter to the Corinthians*, for example, written perhaps toward the end of the first century, begins by denouncing "the hateful and unholy schism so alien to those whom God has chosen," stirred up by a few "impetuous and headstrong younger" Christians whose madness had ruined the reputation of the church at Corinth. They used to be humble, obedient, and devout. But now they had become quarrelsome, envious, uncontrollable, rivalrous, and rebellious, and were attacking their elders. They must once again, like the prophets of old, become humble, obedient, submissive, and peaceful.[37]

But the main battleground for early Christians was inside their hearts and minds. Theirs was a lifelong struggle between desire and self-control. Christians could sin not only in their behavior but also by their looks or thoughts, even those which surface in the half-consciousness of sleep and dreams. If God is just, no true Christian can be sure of salvation. God's mercy is the only hope. There was simply no place to hide. Apostasy meant hell and eternal damnation. God and his recording angels saw straight into the human heart and listed everything, like superefficient Roman bureaucrats. Without computers, the final judgment must have been laborious, so that even God in one case, as it is confidently reported, truncated the proceedings and limited consideration to the sins of a poor man's five final years on earth.[38] For a true Christian, the only answer was unremitting virtue, self-control, humility, generosity, and sexual continence, but above all prayer, confession, and repentance.

But precepts do not equal practice. By no means all early Christians can have lived up to the ideals of their preachers. Some sinned, lapsed, or went their different ways. Indeed, our use of the idealizing term "Christian" unconsciously assumes that religious affiliation was the sole or primary identifier of a Roman's social persona. But were all nominal Christians, even then, dedicated members of a cult group? Perhaps they should have been, but were they? We simply do not know. We do not know how early Christians actually behaved. We know that some writers were proud of and boasted about Christian piety and morality, compared with the pagans around them.[39] But by and large, all that survives is statements of belief, prescripts, and exhortations. We have to read them, with and across the grain, in order to understand ideals and tensions within early Christian groups.

Ideally, early Christians were acutely conscious of their difference. They were the chosen, the elect, the beloved, the saved. But among Jews and pagans they were or became outcasts. Again ideally, Christians did not participate in pagan games, theaters, and processions, they did not put garlands over their outside doors at festivals. If they were brave, or foolhardy (Christians disagreed about this among themselves), they would make the sign of the cross over the heart or forehead at critical moments throughout the day. Perhaps that was best kept for private moments. The Christian difference was founded on a combination of brotherly love toward insiders and hostility toward outsiders. But even here Christians were different: good Christians prayed even for their enemies.[40]

They all believed in the one true God, and in Jesus Christ, his son. Complementarily, they despised the immoral and demon-inspired idols and Gods of the society around them. They hated its blatant immorality, its easy acceptance of brothels, adultery, and homosexuality. In due course, perhaps soon, all unbelievers would burn in unquenchable fire. Christians, by contrast, prided themselves on their chastity, modesty, generosity to the poor, mutual love and support. For women, conversion could mean, if preachers got their way, a dramatic down-dressing from the vainglory of jewels and cosmetics to plain simplicity. And there was something else. Christians ideally paid no regard to social differences. All were equal in the sight of God. Some Christians went further: they recognized how savagely the rich oppress the poor and how difficult it would therefore be for the rich to gain salvation. For Jesus said, "Blessed are the poor." Extra charity was the only possible answer, and that, of course, in a wicked twist, benefited the rich: they could give more ("You buy immortality with money"). The widow's mite didn't get her so far. But at least in their ideals, and to some extent also in practice, early Christians turned Roman social order and perceptions upside down: equality instead of hierarchy, charity instead of greed.[41]

In the beginning, what mattered most was inspiration. The spirit moved worshipers to a better understanding of divine glory. They all had something valuable to give: prophecies, speaking in tongues, interpretation, preaching. Their preachers were wandering beggar missionaries who relied on the faithful for simple food, stayed a day or two, and went on their way: "Every true prophet who wishes to stay with you deserves his sustenance." Together they sang psalms and hymns; they ate together in a pattern which (at least in some groups) evolved as the liturgical eucharist, with bread and wine blessed to represent Christ's body and blood. As new initiates, they were baptized "into Jesus Christ and into his death," so that like him they were, even while still alive, resurrected into a new life, after which, once their old sins had been washed away, they would sin no more.[42]

But it could not last. Even in the paradise of primitive Christianity there were vipers: heretics, false teachers, self-seekers, hypocrites, schismatics, sinners. And it was not always easy to tell who was which. Of course, one could easily tell the self-seeking prophet who fell into an ecstatic fit and asked for a large dinner, or who tried to stay on beyond the permitted two days. But those who believed that Jesus was wholly divine and merely *seemed* to suffer, or those who believed that Jesus came to preserve the Law, not to abolish it (and so Christians should obey the Jewish Law)—clearly these abominable "heretics" had significant followings. Christianity was a religion which provoked passionate commitment and passionate disagreements. But amazingly, all sides, whatever their views, seem to have colluded in the fiction/ideal that there was only one universal Church, which they represented. Christians, wherever they were, belonged, in their own minds, to the Church of God.[43]

Sinners always posed a threat to the Church's self-esteem and reputation. Of course, some were punished dramatically by God: Ananias and his wife sold their property and brought the proceeds (Qumran style) as their contribution to the earliest Christian commune; but secretly they had kept back a nest egg. St. Peter saw through their deception, and both died immediately (Acts of the Apostles 5.1ff.). The Christian God was to be worshiped and feared. But he was also a God of justice and mercy. Sins could be forgiven after due repentance and prayer. Baptism washed away all previous sins, and some Christians bought time for sin by delaying baptism until near death. Infant baptism was not common apparently until the third century.

There was no uniform response to the problem of sin. How could there be? But we can trace different strands. House cult groups were small, and presumably exerted close and inquisitive control over members' behavior. Believers were expected to confess their sins in public, show profound repentance, "groan, weep, roar, roll at the feet of priests, kneel, and abase themselves," do penance, give alms, and receive forgiveness before readmission. Occasionally, groups announced a general amnesty for postbaptismal sins, but only one, and this would be the last. Others subdivided sins into the forgivable and the unforgivable (murder, adultery, and apostasy). But under pressure of rising numbers and the harsh experience of mass persecution, even these mortal sins, except for murder, were eventually forgiven by laxist bishops. Rigorist sects and schismatic churches stuck to what they claimed were the best traditions of the church. And they imposed even tougher standards, such as no second marriage (adultery in disguise), no marriage for clergy, no sex after baptism. They were the Church of the pure (*katharoi*).[44]

Above all, sins were dealt with, at least in the surviving early exhortatory texts, by the fictional ideal that prohibitions worked. So in effect it was outsiders (whether pagans or heretics) who sin, and believers who practice virtue. Christ's death has made us free. The ethical template of early Christian virtues and vices was fairly standard, and close in many of its elements to Graeco-Roman and Jewish ideals. Basically, true Christians should have sincere faith, mercy, grace, a pure heart, and a good conscience; they should believe, love, and be free "as slaves to God"; above all they should be obedient, like children, and should not speculate. Christian women should show faith, love, piety, and modesty, be serious, temperate, and faithful, and bear children. They should submit to their husbands just as husbands submit to Christ; and husbands should be considerate to their weaker wives. Christians should love one another, be as newborn babes, honor all, be considerate, and obey all human regulations.[45]

And of course, by contrast, Christians should avoid malice, guile, insincerity, envy, slander, adultery, homosexuality, passions of the flesh, licentiousness, drunken revels, lawless idolatry, blasphemy, theft, and murder.[46] These are the sins which characterize gentiles and heretics. This separation of virtues from vices is analytically convenient, but distorting. In ancient Christian texts the matrix of virtues was interwoven with the web of vices; they took strength from each other.

What was specially different about early Christian morality was its interpenetration with the fervent belief that God would reward virtue and punish vice. This, combined with the exercise of close moral control—at first by the cult group collectively, and then by priestly leaders acting with, and later for, the group—gave Christian morality its distinctive timbre. Vices were socially punished and demonized, virtues were both sanctified and sacramentalized. I mean by this that in the intense face-to-face world of early Christian house cult groups, sins (or accusations of sin) were communal possessions. They therefore were communally exorcised. Sin was the work of the Devil, and demons were everywhere. They aimed at the weakest part of every human. Similarly with virtue (or claims to it); virtues were a blessing from God. In the Pauline tradition, virtue was a matter of conscience; it was each believer's individual and internal spiritual possession, a function of his/her faith. But other early Christian communities favored good works and hierarchy. Virtue had not only to be felt but also shown. And it was priests, acting for the community and God, who rewarded virtue and forgave sin.[47]

Yet such were the demands of conscience that no performance could be quite good enough. Lustful thoughts opened up a bottomless pit of potential guilt. A pious Christian slave once saw his beautiful mistress emerging naked after a bath. Consciously, he thought he would like a woman as beautiful as her as his wife; but in his dreams God rebuked him for his wicked desires and shameful lust. Two centuries later, a Christian monk saw a gang of nuns walking toward him. In order to avoid them and the temptation they represented, he moved aside and looked the other way, only to be rebuked by their leader, who said, "If you were a perfect monk, you would not have noticed that we were women."[48]

INSTITUTIONS OF FAITH

Early Christian faith was a vigorous combination of doctrine, ethical injunction, and passionate exhortation, part realized, part imagined so that it seemed real. In doctrine, one of early Christianity's triumphant achievements was to translate the intensity of religious piety and devotion into capsule formulas of explicit belief: for example, "one Lord, one faith, one baptism, one God" (Ephesians 4.5). Christians were taught and knew precisely what they believed, even if what they precisely believed differed from person to person and from group to group, from region to region and over time. That said, it is plausible for us to see Christianity as unified by a core of common beliefs, however diverse their expression.

Slogans—*Jesus Christ is the Messiah; Jesus Christ is the Lord; Jesus is the Son of God; He died for our sins; Repent now and your sins will be forgiven; Kneel, pray, repent, and confess*—were at the heart of early Christian confession.[49] They served as rallying cries for groups whose loyalty to the cause always needed boosting. And they functioned as emblems of belonging, as full members, to a movement which was so varied and growing so rapidly that it could not exact the detailed norms of practice and ritual on which traditional and ethnically based Judaism depended. Early Christianity was a religion of converts. The forceful simplicity of Christian slogans reflected Christianity's missionary appeal and its target audience among the underprivileged, or those who felt themselves poor or relatively deprived by Roman rule of civic power and identity. Christianity began as a religion of the underdog. But as with most revolutionary movements, those who ran it and left records were not themselves, and could not be, the truly deprived.

Early Christians in their collective memory long preserved the tradition that their religion was a religion which cared about the poor, the sick, and the weak. It was "easier for a camel to go through the eye of a needle than for a rich man to enter the kingdom of God" (Mark 10.25); though already in the late first century, the original, radical message was being diluted. Jesus' advice to the rich young man, as recorded by Luke, was: "Sell all that you possess and distribute the money to the poor," but this was qualified by Matthew (and was quoted predominantly in this form by later church fathers) into "If you would be perfect, go sell your possessions and give the money to the poor." But in the mid–second century, the *Shepherd of Hermas* declared roundly that those who gloried in their wealth had no hope of salvation, even if they repented. They were spiritually dead.[50] The ideal of poverty for long remained a Christian hallmark.

And Christianity also for long preserved its early egalitarian sense that God's messages had come as an inspiration directly to all believers, who can therefore be equal in their faith and common humility, as fellow slaves (not "servants" as in modern English translations), as slaves before the majestic glory of God. As Paul put it, "*To each* is given the manifestation of the spirit for the common good" (1 Corinthians 12.7). And again according to Paul, God's gifts, that is, wisdom, knowledge, faith, healing, the power of miracles, exorcism, prophecy, interpretation, are all shared among the faithful (1 Corinthians 12.8–11). In this powerful tradition, Christianity was a religion in which each believer has potentially a direct line to and from God.

Almost inevitably, hierarchy and sophistication at first supplemented and then gradually overcame equality and simplicity, though the tension between the two poles persisted for centuries. Already during the second century, Ignatius, bishop of Antioch, was trying to impose episcopal authority. His letters, addressed like Paul's to several churches in Asia Minor and Rome, are written with a great simplicity, all the more striking because the Greek of contemporary sophisticated litterateurs was notoriously complex. Ignatius' simplicity had a polemical point. At the same time, Ignatius repeatedly and hectoringly insisted on the supremacy of episcopal power. His very insistence assures us that his claims were heartily opposed, whether by clerics or lay believers, or both. On the other hand, his hierocratic rhetoric, its survival and high reputation tell us that his arguments represented the side which eventually triumphed.[51]

Individual ingredients of Ignatius' message can easily be traced back to Jewish and Greek antecedents. But the total impact of the whole message is radically different. Ignatius stresses his own unworthiness, his imminent martyrdom (he personally leads by his own self-sacrificing example), his joy in suffering, the ideal of unity of the Christian collective under the firm leadership of the bishop (who is ex officio the mind of God), the willing obedience of the faithful, the excommunication of false teachers/heretics, and the virtues of meekness, humility, and generosity.

Love does not allow me to be silent. Unite in submission to the authority of your bishop and his priests. I do not command you as though I were someone; for I know my limitations. But it is clear that we should look up to the bishop as to the Lord himself. Bishops are the mind of Jesus. The honorable clergy are attuned to their bishop like the strings of a harp; you ought to join the choir and sing in unison.

The end of the world is near. Don't be deluded; judgment awaits. Be humble, tremble, and fear God. Pray for mankind, that they too may repent and find God. Greet anger with meekness, pride with humility, slander with prayers, and love each other. Have faith and love for Jesus. Faith prevents sin, and love prevents hatred. Let no one mislead you. False teachers are evil hypocrites, and like mad dogs; beware their bites. They stay away from Eucharist; they are doomed because they question; they do not care for widows, orphans, prisoners; they will be consumed in everlasting fire.

I know who I am; I am condemned to death. I am in love with suffering. I lust for death with all the passion of a lover. All should know that I die for God of my own free will. I am dedicated to the cross, the cross which so offends unbelievers, but to us it brings salvation and immortality.

Jesus Christ our God was conceived by Mary; he was born and baptized. He was persecuted in the time of Pontius Pilate, and was crucified, died, and was raised from the dead. And through Jesus Christ, his Father will raise up all who believe in him. At his coming, all magic was dissolved, all superstition was destroyed; the old empire of evil was overthrown. God had appeared in human form and introduced a new order, life without end.[52]

Here hierarchy, unity, ethical prescription, hostility to heretics, faith, passion, and doctrine are persuasively woven together, and used to reinforce one another. But as long as Christianity remained a persecuted sect, unity through hierarchy remained only an ideal, an unrealized dream, an ambitious gleam in a baronial bishop's eye. Throughout the second century, Christianity was fractured by an inventive variety of heretics and schismatics: Marcionites, who rejected the Jewish God of the Old Testament and separated creation from salvation; Gnostics, who invented new and more fantastic stories about the origins of God and evil; and Montanists, who added their own leader and his assistant prophetesses to the sacred succession of inspired revealers of divine wisdom. And even to call these Christians heretics (they called themselves simply Christians) is to collude with the anachronistic fiction that the winning orthodoxy was fated to win. Orthodoxy is the winning side viewed retrospectively.

And yet, in this period, core Christianity, partly in reaction to pressures by heretics, made substantial progress toward its own institutionalization. It gradually established a sense of true doctrine, the so-called rule of faith. Its leaders asserted that they alone had legitimacy, by virtue of following in the tradition of a well-recorded (though fictitious) line of bishops, all the way from the time of the apostles. And they asserted, gingerly at first and with some persisting doubt at the edges, that there was a set canon of sacred Christian scriptures, consisting of the four gospels (John seems to have been the gospel most in dispute), together with Luke's Acts of the Apostles, the letters by the apostles (none of them, except for seven by Paul, probably by their purported authors), and the vengefully prophetic Revelation of John (for long not accepted in the east, but helped by its purported, though baseless, apostolic authorship).[53] These three developments of the late second century—the closed canon of sacred texts, the apostolic succession of bishops, and the rule of faith—were fundamental steps toward the supremacy of the Great Church.

It seems amazing now that the New Testament was not recognized as a single set of privileged Christian scriptures before the end of the second century. Long before that, to be sure, the sayings and commandments of Jesus were reverentially cited (though surprisingly seldom in surviving texts), but it was the words themselves which demanded respect, not the books in which they were written. For some time, Christian writings had to compete with spoken traditions handed down within Christian communities. Indeed, it was a cliché of early Christian rhetoric that these collective memories of, and traditions about, Jesus were themselves more authentic than any written records. When early Christians wanted to legitimate their beliefs from writings, they did it mostly by quotation from the Old Testament, and in some Jewish-Christian circles they even rejected new teachings because they conflicted with the teachings of the Old Testament. (Jewish-Christian is a technical term for those who are both.) But gradually the letters of Paul and the gospels began to be cited, though the fragility of their authority is indicated by editorial changes, interpolations, and the absence of any common word to describe them individually or collectively (they were known variously as writings, memoirs, records, commandments).[54]

No one knows how or why the New Testament was finally formed. But it seems plausible that three "heretical" innovations spurred the "orthodox" to compete. First, Marcion in the mid–second century formed his own (and the first) Christian canon, consisting of a heavily revised gospel by Luke and the ten letters of Paul which he considered authentic. Marcion's canon, like the subsequent New Testament, consisted of

gospel and epistles. Secondly, Gnostics relied on their sense of secret traditions to invent, as the orthodox saw it, new and fantastic stories about
Jesus. For example, the Secret Gospel of Mark, whose only surviving
fragment hints at an otherwise unknown homosexual episode in Jesus'
life, was preserved by the egalitarian and ascetic (or libertine) Carpocratians. Finally Tatian, again in the middle of the second century, produced
a single gospel which ironed out the inconsistencies in probably more
than four gospels; it proved popular in his native Syria for centuries.[55]
The closure of the canon in the New Testament firmly, if only gradually,
ejected these later and spurious accounts (as the orthodox saw them) to
or beyond the outer fringes of normative Christianity. Henceforth only
the approved Bible was to be the pillar of faith.

The creation of a closed canon of specifically Christian scriptures was
a stroke of genius. It united the Old Testament with the New Testament.
And it combined the Judaeo-Christian creation myth with the Christian
history of Jesus' incarnation, death, and resurrection, together with hopes
of imminent salvation. It fused the humanizing but divergent synoptic
gospels and Acts to the mystical Gospel of John, and united them all with
the inspired if obscure exegesis of Paul and the domestic exhortations of
the later apostolic letters. Doubtless, given the absence of central control, the New Testament was a compromise between competing but embedded local traditions. But it was a compromise which incorporated
diversity within an image of unity. The New Testament became a central
symbol of Christian history and doctrine, a stimulus to study and inspiration—and to further discord, through ingenious allegorical and
creative exegesis. That way, the sacred texts could be made to mean
whatever believers wanted.

The second new instrument of orthodoxy and unity, designed to defeat heresy, was the notion that only some Christian communities were
legitimated by tradition. This tradition purportedly went back in an unbroken chain of bishops as far as the apostles, who, of course, themselves
had been sent around the world by the risen Jesus. According to this new
tradition, the apostles had perfect knowledge, which they put into the
gospels. But they also transmitted tradition to a succession of priests in
churches. "In every church, those who wish to see the truth can clearly
contemplate the tradition of the apostles in the whole world. We can list
who were instituted bishops by the apostles and demonstrate their succession until now."[56]

Irenaeus, bishop of Lyon in the late second century, divided his Christian world into orthodox and heretics. And for him the orthodox were clearly stratified into bishops, clergy, and laity. He either didn't know or chose to disguise the fact that bishops as dominant church leaders were themselves a second-century innovation or ideal, and not one which was either universal or universally admired. And he reinforced his invented line of bishops by personal reminiscence: he himself when young had seen the aged martyr Polycarp, bishop of Smyrna, who had rebuked the heretic Marcion as son of Satan, and had lived before the apostle John had died. The ancient church, founded on this combination of memory and tradition, was the sole guardian of Christian truth. Heretics were malicious innovators. Tertullian (Irenaeus' rough contemporary), when he was still orthodox, argued similarly in Carthage. But when he changed his mind and became a follower of the inspired prophet Montanus, it was not tradition but truth which became for him the critical arbiter of correct doctrine and practice.[57] This battle between religious truth and tradition was to have a long history.

A third weapon used against heretics and for disciplining the faithful was the rule of faith. Assertion that a rule of faith existed was much easier than establishing its contents. As long as the church was dispersed, small, and illegal, there could be no general agreement about precise wording, because there was no mechanism for securing it. But in spite of the practical difficulties, Christian ideologues at the turn of the third century were carefully and repeatedly specifying the precise terms of their beliefs. Tertullian, for example, wrote: "The rule of faith is absolutely one, single, immovable, and unchangeable, namely belief in the one almighty God, Creator of the world, and his son, Jesus Christ, born of the Virgin Mary, crucified under Pontius Pilate, raised from the dead on the third day, received into heaven, sitting now at the right hand of the Father, destined to judge the living and the dead through the resurrection of the flesh."[58]

One irony is that Tertullian wrote this when he had already joined the Montanists. Irenaeus' statement of faith is more ambitious (the original is dozens of pages long, so I have summarized it here). It combines pure dogma with ethical exhortation, in the traditional Christian style. In both these versions, the core belief is conservative, and is similar to that of the more familiar Nicene creed from the fourth century.[59]

Irenaeus' Statement of the Christian Faith

Ours is the one true path to salvation, leading men through faith to God and to the kingdom of heaven. Turn aside from worldly desires, be pure in body and soul, abstain from all shameful and unrighteous actions. Believe in God, fear God as your Lord, love God as Father, obey the rule of faith. Faith is everlasting salvation.

This, then, is the rule of our faith. First, God the Father, invisible, Creator of all things. Second, the Reason (Logos) of God, Christ Jesus our Lord, made manifest to the prophets; through him all things were created; he was made man among humans, visible and tangible, in order to abolish death and produce a union between man and God. He is Reason made flesh, so that flesh might lose its power. Third, the Holy Spirit, through whom the prophets prophesied and the fathers learned about God, and who was poured over us humans, so that God was renewed in us.

God made humans out of earth mixed with his own Spirit, in his own image. At first they were innocent of lust, but subject to God's rule, complete with free will and self-control, and fit to rule over the earth. But a wicked angel misled them into disobedience and sin. They were cast out of paradise, and the wicked angel became the Devil. Wickedness long ruled the earth. But God flushed it clean with a great flood, and then sent many prophets through the Holy Spirit as heralds of the revelation of our Lord Jesus Christ.

Jesus, who preexisted with the Father and was begotten before all creation, was born on earth as man. Until then, all of us were bound to death by the disobedience of Adam. Jesus, the second Adam, and Mary, the second Eve, by their virtue released us from sin. The tree of disobedience was displaced by the cross of obedience. Jesus Christ our eternal king achieved our redemption, abolished death, and gave us life.

God is merciful, compassionate, tender, and good. He is just, without favor to the privileged or humble. He is God of all, Jews, gentiles, believers; he is our sustainer, nourisher, king, and judge. The disciples of Jesus Christ heard his teachings, witnessed his deeds, suffering, death, resurrection, and ascension. He called men to fellowship with God. Turn from idols, fornication, greed; be cleansed by baptism, which is rebirth and the seal of faith. Believe in and love the Lord; through faith, love, and hope, practice holiness so that you may gain eternal life. For unbelievers, there is vengeance without pardon.

All that has come to pass was long foretold by many prophets. Our faith is therefore well founded, and our tradition of preaching is true. The Word of God is law; but faith in the Son of God and love will ensure our salvation. With a pure heart, let us call on Jesus Christ.[60]

THE SOPHISTICATIONS OF THEOLOGY

There was an inescapable tension between the ideal of a stable un-changeability of belief and the rapid evolution of the church. Tertullian argued fiercely against the intrusion of pagan philosophy into Christian dogmatics. "What has Jerusalem to do with Athens?" But the tide was against him. As Christianity went socially upscale, and especially after the conversion of Constantine (312), when it entered into an alliance with the state, its improved status was marked by a gradual cultural fusion, at least in the Christianized elite, of pagan classicism and Christian theology.[61]

Fourth-century Christian ideologues showed off their new status (or pretensions) as accepted members of the cultured elite by arguing in sophisticated terms, like or almost like pagan philosophers. Even the emperor Constantine got involved. He personally attended the first reputedly universal council, held in western Turkey, at Nicaea, in 325. About three hundred bishops had been summoned, at state expense, partly to resolve the Arian controversy. According to Eusebius, bishop of Caesarea, who wrote to his see justifying his own agreement to the Nicene creed, Constantine himself had assured the meeting that the Son was to be called consubstantial with the Father, "not in the sense of any corporeal experiences, nor did he exist as a result of division or any subtraction from the Father, for the immaterial, spiritual, and incorporeal nature cannot be subject to any corporeal experience, and it was right for us to think like this about divine and ineffable matters."[62]

The Arian controversy was superficially about the nature of Christ's humanity/divinity, but it also involved power struggles within the church—between bishops and their priests, between bishops in their regions, and the nature of the emperor's involvement in church politics. In its aftermath, Christian thinkers wrestled endlessly with a whole series of problems. Was Jesus of the same, or similar, substance as the Father? Was he created, or begotten? Did God the Father suffer as well as Jesus on the cross? Did Jesus have a human soul, or did he take only the flesh of a human? To answer these questions, Christian leaders produced summary statements of belief to be decided by majority votes of bishops at regional or universal councils. For example, the Fourth Sirmian creed of 359 begins:

We believe in one true God, the Father Almighty, Creator and maker of all things; and in one only-begotten Son of God, who before all ages, before all beginning, and before all conceivable time, and before all comprehensible substance, was begotten without passion from God, through whom the ages were framed and all things came into existence; who was begotten as only-begotten, from the Father, only from only, God of God, like to the Father who begot him, according to the scriptures, whose generation no one understands except the Father who begot him.

But lack of understanding did not prevent twenty more lines of detailed specification of belief, with or without the realization that each new twist in expression opened up possibilities for further intellectual controversy. But they hoped or attempted to stop that by anathematizing those who persisted in disagreement.[63]

There was more to all this debate than intellectual exhibitionism and a narcissistic obsession with minor differences about irresolvable problems. Theology served as an arena of symbolic politics, ideally suited to a preindustrial society with scarce, redistributable resources. Councils of bishops could argue for years over the finer points of theological doctrine, without any, or only minor, practical implications. What mattered in the grand scheme of politics was that these religious elites were united in discord.[64] Theology served to veil their power. On the quiet, and away from the metropolitan centers of power, bishops in their hometowns gradually negotiated their way toward creating a secondary web of social control which was, practically speaking, with a few minor tensions, at the service of, as well as in competition with, the state.

To be sure, bishops sometimes got above themselves and claimed that the authority of God gave them precedence over secular rulers. But bishops themselves also desperately needed the prestige and armed might of the state to settle their own disputes. Emperors occasionally genuflected. For example, at the insistence of Ambrose, bishop of Milan, the pious emperor Theodosius in 391 dramatically did public penance in the cathedral at Milan for having ordered an indiscriminate massacre as a reprisal for the murder of a general at Thessalonica. But emperors also summarily exiled bishops who displeased them. Emperors could declare themselves to be firmly on top. "What I wish must be regarded as the canon," said the Arian emperor Constantius; "either obey or go into exile."[65] The dissident bishops replied from exile with vicious pamphlets, probably published only after the offending emperor was dead. But in spite of occasional tensions, the broad alliance of church and state ensured that by the end of the fourth century, for the first time, the whole population of the Roman empire was marching to the same religious music, or at least knew that the music was being played.

Theology in the later Roman empire provided a loose ideological cohesion between rulers and subjects which had previously been lacking in a state which had started as an empire of conquest, divided between conquerors and conquered. Theology created a complex and abstract discourse in which it was possible to find a significant variety of arguable positions. Some theological arguments, which overtly related to God, subtly veiled discussions about the distribution of political power. For example, was the ruler (like Jesus) divine, or human? Hence, perhaps, some of the partisan passions, not just among the elite but also occasionally in the populace. Religious politics were the politics of fluid alliances, not fixed parties. From the state's point of view, adoption of Christianity achieved an empirewide symbolic harmony at the relatively low price of religious conformism (oppression) and a tiny number of excommunicated clerics. These marginal deviants, from Arius to Athanasius, have attracted disproportionate attention, like criminals in an ordered society. What mattered much more was the total system of debate and control, which gave the empire a degree of symbolic unity which it had never previously achieved. Excommunicated priests and bishops were the system's expendable frontier guards.

From the state's point of view, the time and effort spent on theological debate was a small price to pay for symbolic unification. The donation of sizable gifts to the church from private and public funds was part, too, of that gradual unification. Besides, state generosity and popular piety helped divert attention away from the vast profits which the Roman state extracted by monetizing the huge stored treasures of pagan temples, accumulated over centuries of piety and peace.[66] The change of official religion from paganism to Christianity created enormous windfall profits for the Roman state.

Of course, from the Christian point of view it could be argued that preoccupation with dogma was at its worst a displacement activity, which distracted Christians from their true mission of seeking salvation through faith and/or good works. But at its best, theological passion was itself a motivating force which drove, shaped, and justified Christian commitment to self-sacrifice, good works, and apolitical spirituality. Right from the start, Christianity had combined fervent beliefs with ethical practice. It was belief in God and Jesus, belief in the hopes of salvation and the imminent end of the world, in the rewards of heaven and the punishments of hell, which lent urgency to ethical precepts and exhortations. Christianity was just the sort of religion which a preindustrial empire needed.

INTERLUDE: RELIGIONS AS SYSTEMS OF DISAPPOINTMENT

Department of Social Anthropology
Brunel University

Dear Keith,

I enjoyed discussing religion with you yesterday. But I wondered whether you were emphasizing underlying structures sufficiently. Perhaps a stricter, more formalist approach might reveal the bare bones of religious evolution better. So I thought I'd jot down a few basics. What follows is bog-standard sociology of religion, put in a quasiuniversalist style, although most of us realize that a single definition is unlikely to cover religions in all societies.

All, or most, sophisticated religions work on three intersecting planes.

First, religions are ethical systems; they affirm core moral values.

Second, religions are powerful social institutions, which generate, design, and promote packages of beliefs and rituals, and claim them to be of suprahuman origin. Like other powerful social institutions, religions reward members for participation and commitment, and try to belittle or punish deviants and outsiders. For example, religions offer insiders pleasure in the changing seasons, or consolation for life's tragedies; and by ritual, prayer, or sacrifice, they offer to the faithful some control over the supernatural, whether to bring benefits to ego or friends, or harm to enemies.

Finally, through myths, they offer the faithful a vision that, in the end, the God(s) or divine justice will prevail. The virtuous will be rewarded and the wicked punished, if not in this life, then in an invisible afterlife. By myths I mean here stories about the past which the faithful believe to be true, and which they use repeatedly as models for their own behavior.

By this tentative definition, religions are inherently both satisfying and disappointing. They satisfy in so far as they succeed in giving the faithful a sense of community, and by helping insiders make sense of the world and their place within it. Religions often achieve this by making the present social and natural world fit in with their particular view of what is supernaturally ordained. For example, "I'm suffering; it's part of God's will; he is testing me."

But religions also, as I see it, inevitably disappoint because they cannot deliver to their followers all or even most of what they want from God(s). Life, even in an advanced preindustrial society like Rome, was recurrently nasty, unfair, and out of an individual's control, however virtuous the worshiper had been and however much she had sacrificed or prayed. In practice, virtue is not rewarded, nor vice punished, at least not proportionally, or not in many individuals' view. But don't worry, God(s) will put things right—in the end.

Actually, as Max Weber saw ages ago, some religions, run by upper-class priests, ooze a triumphalist sense of satisfaction; a theodicy of good fortune, he called it, which means roughly speaking: we're on top and, praised be the Gods, we deserve to be. You find this theodicy of good fortune in Rome too, and you also find a lot of collusion between upper classes and the Roman populace (at least in the surviving records, written primarily, of course, by the upper classes, but how else could Rome have conquered and controlled a huge empire?). Eventually, upper-class triumphalism opens up opportunities for an antitriumphalist religious opposition. I suspect that is where Christianity fits in historically, as a religion of opposition—based initially among defeated but rebellious provincials, though of course that is not all it was.

Anyhow, in reality, disappointments flourish. So sophisticated religious systems preserve their validity and authority by a variety of tactics. For example, polytheistic religions offer their followers a sequential choice of complementary gods. The consumer moves from God to God, calendrically, by life-cycle events, and as need/fashion dictates. The disappointment engendered by any one choice merely evokes the hope that the next choice will be more satisfying. This is what happens in the modern, postindustrial secular religion of consumerism. Each choice implies a disappointment ("Damn, I think the other cake/dress might have been better"). These religious systems both satisfy and disappoint their circulating customers.

Sophisticated religious systems secure greater success (that is, have more power and influence and more adherents) if they manage to restrict access to the supernatural. Ideally, access is permitted only through accredited specialist intermediaries, such as a professional clergy. I suspect, though I cannot prove, that in complex preindustrial societies, the more complex and the more ambiguous the religious rules or creeds, and the more difficult and demanding the prescribed virtues (for example, lifelong chastity), the more powerful the intermediary clergy.

But again, any monopoly breeds opposition. Surprisingly, religions sometimes preserve their overall, long-term power by generating a series of subversive, subterranean versions of themselves. For example, discontented ecstatics, critical visionaries or prophets, and even quietist ascetics by their actions all highlight the corruption of a privileged priesthood/rulers and a sinning population. But then each subset, from establishment religion to rad-ical sects, has its own market segment, and together, in spite of their mutual opposition, they can sometimes tighten the overall hold of the religious over the social. Of course, the dominant religion attacks these "heresies," or alter-native approaches to the supernatural (such as magic or inspired prophecy), as disruptive, illegitimate, or evil. Or the dominant religion tries to incorpo-rate deviant versions into its own myth package (in the trade, we call these "secondary elaborations"). But for all their disruption, heresies are also vital to orthodoxy's enduring identity, rather like children or young siblings in a family.

A clergy's creation of an effective monopoly, or oligopoly, of access to the supernatural or sacred helps ensure a broad identity of belief and/or ritual practice across widespread and heterogeneous sets of the faithful. Restricted access to the sacred also affords the clergy higher status, symbolically and ma-terially. I do not want to sound too cynical, but from the little I've read it seems sensible for you to point out in your book that the ancient Christian clergy, for all their notable charity to the poor, used their privileged positions as closest to God to get wealthier, both individually and collectively. Cathe-drals were grand but expensive monuments to God; and of course the more glorious they were, the more it helped prove the benefits of normative reli-gion. Christian bishops may have been generous to the poor, but they used believers' donations.

Tactics for the clergy's status enhancement and self-enrichment varied widely. But two tactics deserve special mention. First, the creation of a com-plex, intellectualized theology or complex set of ritual rules helps, since a long-trained priesthood exploits an oligopolic advantage in legitimate inter-pretation of the sacred. A second useful tactic is to widen the scope of sacred rules so that they cover all that people regularly do, or prohibit especially what people intermittently would very much like to do (dance, eat too much, adulterate).

The risk of monopolizing access to one God is that the faithful have only one God, and only one set of clergy, on whom to rely for help, health, pros-perity, favour, or a state of grace, and only one set of clergy to blame. As I have said, both satisfaction and dissatisfaction are inevitable. So successful re-ligions develop mechanisms for the transfer of responsibility for disappoint-ment from the inadequacy of the divine, and from the incompetence of professional clerical interpreters, to the inadequacy of the lay believers them-selves (not enough faith, unconfessed sins, guilty thoughts, deviance).

In Roman polytheism, blaming gods for failure to provide what a wor-shiper had asked for was not, you told me, considered blasphemous, though it could be risky. Blaming a priest for the faulty (and so inadequate) perfor-mance of a religious ritual was routine. But in polytheism also, religious prac-titioners with paying customers developed techniques for shielding the god or his/her priest(s) from blame: Greek oracles, for example, as in the Oedipus myth, gave obscure messages which tempted wrong interpretation by the unfortunate punter, who at least in the literature blamed himself for his wrong reading.

The Christian tactic of demanding from its followers, not ritual purity, but committed faith and a pure mind, constituted a critical development in enlarging the arena of believers' responsibility. Christianity's success in the marketplace of competing religions was due, I think, to a combination of factors (and not least the successful conversion of a succession of emperors). But the following must surely have contributed significantly:

(*a*) The creation of a monopoly of access to a single god through a hierarchically ordered professional clergy, dependent for their livelihoods and self-esteem on customers' continued loyalty and fees. The clergy therefore had a considerable self-interest in maintaining the religious monopoly and the boundaries of orthodoxy.

(*b*) Instilling among believers a profound sense of their own unworthiness, and a conviction in them that disappointments were the result of their own sinful actions or thoughts—a system held in place, I imagine, by weekly preachings and public (or private) confessions.

(*c*) Its development of the idea as a core belief that, whatever the satisfaction or dissatisfaction of the believer with his life in this world, the wicked (or rich) would be punished eternally after death, and the good (or poor) would be rewarded with a blissful immortality. Heaven and hell are packaged differently for the different market sectors; the powerful see them as confirming current status; the radical visionary sees them as inverting the wickedness of the current world—at the end of time, the virtuous will enter the kingdom of God. The invisibility of the reward system, except by symbolic representation, was a masterstroke.

I hope this helps, though of course it's not a way of looking at religion which believers ordinarily like. It seems so cold and analytical, and it misses out all the joy and pleasure that religions bring. Let me know what you think.

Yours ever,

Josh

CHRISTIANS AND THE ROMAN STATE: MARTYRS AND PERSECUTIONS

At first sight, it may seem tempting to characterize relations between the Roman state and Christianity as a conflict between oppressive authority and faithful endurance. Romans persecuted Christians. But for the first two centuries after Jesus' death, persecutions occurred only on a small scale, spasmodically, and locally. Christians were tried, tortured, imprisoned, and executed in occasional crises, whether in response to popular outcry against their deviance and atheism, or when aggressive Christian exhibitionism provoked retaliation, or as a result of an occasional governor's religious zeal. But in the surviving record, Christians were largely protected against illicit pogroms by Roman law and punctilious legalism: Christians were to be executed only after a proper trial; and there were not many judges available.[67] The Roman state, however unintentionally, protected Christians.

The small scale of early Christian persecutions did not diminish their symbolic importance. Christ's own suffering death was central to Christian belief. Fervent Christians (like Jews before them) believed that their religion was worth dying for.[68] Suffering death was both an imitation of Jesus and a privileged gateway to salvation. Martyrs went direct to heaven, while lesser mortals had to wait for immortality until the imminent end of days. The realities of persecution, however slender in fact, were magnified by fear, fantasy, and legend. The threat of persecution, not knowing whether or when it would strike, the memory of heroic deaths and their glorification in stories all helped confirm Christian collective identity in an alien and hostile world. Being a Christian was all the more worthwhile because some Christians were ready to pay such a high price for membership. The glory of the few was an inspiration to the remainder.

From the middle of the third century, the scale of persecutions increased dramatically. In 250, 257, and 303, when Christian numbers had grown so that they were more noticeable, the Roman government launched three successive large-scale, increasingly systematic, and purposeful persecutions, which were targeted at Christian leaders and church property. But even these persecutions were not universally executed, because the Roman state lacked the steadfast will, the total control of its local administrators, and the dispersed resources to wipe Christianity out completely; besides, it always had other more pressing needs. And amazingly, in this period of relatively thorough persecutions, overall Christian numbers continued to grow. Persecutions and the bravery of Christian resistance stimulated growth, or so some Christians claimed. These persecutions effectively ended with Constantine's conversion in 312, a general Edict on Religious Toleration (313), the defeat by Constantine of his rival coemperor, Licinius (324), and the Christianity of his successors, who increasingly favored the Christian church.[69] The persecution of Christianity was then replaced by Christian persecution of heretics and pagans. And the volume of Martyr Acts, like Second World War films, increased with victory. Everyone by then knew who the true heroes and villains were.

But we need to pause for a moment. Persecutions and the heroic deaths of martyrs were only one strand in the complex of Christian relations with the Roman state. Long before the fourth-century alliance of church and state, at least in mythographic fantasy, Christian missionaries had the conversion of the social elite and client kings firmly on their agenda. The Roman elite was a potential ally and convert, as well as a worldly enemy. Some Christians repeatedly prayed for the health of the Roman emperor and for the welfare of the Roman state, and advertised the fact that they did so.[70]

So total interaction between Christians and pagans varied considerably, and along multiple axes. On the Roman side it fluctuated, if we can trust our sources, from cruel oppression to legal protection to benign neglect. And on the Christian side, interactions with Roman officials varied (with the same caveat) from contumacious provocation to public bravery, from cowardly flight to careful avoidance, from pacific retreatism to manipulative collaboration and ambitious accommodation.

Christian leaders both assaulted and wooed the Roman state. They wrote long petitions ostensibly addressed directly to successive Roman emperors, though it's doubtful that any emperor had the time or patience to read them, or indeed ever received them. The apologists argued forcefully that it was obviously unjust to persecute Christians merely for being Christian, rather than for any crimes they had committed, and that Christians lived more morally than most pagans. Tertullian was apparently the first thinker in the ancient world to offer a reasoned defense in favor of religious liberty: "There is a natural law and a man-made law that each person should be free to worship whom he wants. One man's religion does not harm another's. It is not for religion to compel religion. Gods do not desire unwilling sacrifice." Besides, pagan Gods, man-made idols of wood, metal, or stone, were really demons. And it was these demons who scattered false accusations against Christians, made men hate and kill Christians, and controlled unjust governors in the Roman empire. How could Christians sensibly pray to demons? They were powerless. But Christians did repeatedly pray to the "eternal, living God for the safety of the emperors." It was this God who alone had appointed the emperor. The Roman empire, its prosperity, wealth, and peace were all part of God's divine plan.[71]

So were persecutions. They tested Christians' virtues and punished their vices. They enabled true Christians to show their colors and win salvation. Martyrs were the new heroes of the Christian revolution. Martyrs expressed and symbolized the powers of charismatic inspiration, dedication, faith, and suffering, but in a church whose inspiration was being gradually routinized through the power of bishops. Martyrs were holy saints whose suffering deaths granted them immediate immortality. They rose into the heavenly presence and had the ear of God. They were or became iconic intermediaries between the faithful and an invisibly transcendent deity. Even confessors, who had publicly declared their faith and waited in prison for possible execution, were thought by some Christians to have the charismatic power of forgiving sins. In short, martyrs could undermine the powers of bishops. Martyrs and confessors had to be revered and celebrated—but also controlled.[72]

Martyr Acts were a new genre of Christian literature, invented in the second century. They were brief and purposive accounts of martyrs' heroism, suffering, and death, written and preserved by Christian leaders. They were read out in church meetings on the anniversaries of martyrs' deaths. The Martyr Acts describe and celebrate, sometimes with affecting beauty, the faith, endurance, and bravery of Christians imprisoned, tortured, and cruelly executed by Roman governors and emperors. The noble martyrs, men and women, in spite of all the risks, publicly declare their firm allegiance to Christ, and pay for their faith with their lives. The Martyr Acts often celebrate Christian joy in the grisly details of physical suffering. They are a sacred pornography of cruelty. But they also contain and delimit the power of martyrs within the church's own rhetoric and in its liturgy.

At first sight, these Martyr Acts may seem an incitement to further rebellion against Roman oppression. They obviously glorify the heroics of defiant resistance. But even more important, I think, they enable readers (or listeners) vicariously to act out the effrontery of opposition with impunity. In the story, the hero bravely confronts the oppressive Roman judge, is uplifted by the cheers and jeers of the hostile crowd, and after much torture, without a squeal of pain or whisper of doubt, he/she heroically dies.[73] But the reader *survives*, and can read the story again and again—unless, of course, he/she foolishly confuses fantasy with reality and rashly takes the story as a spur to imitation.

In the story, the reader can get away with murder. For most readers, in antiquity as now, reading was the displaced heroism of fantasy. Christians read about martyrs instead of being one. And the extra beauty of the story lay in its performative repetitions. Reality may rarely have conformed to its fictional depiction. But independently of reality, in fantasy, each time the story of faithful death was retold, the event recurred, at least in each believer's mind. The story was the best (and often the only) performance.

The Martyr Acts may seem realistic, like Romano-Egyptian mummy portraits, especially if we look at only one or two.[74] But en masse, they are apologetic, self-heroizing, and routinely standardized, plausible only if we think that pagan Roman governor-judges had prelearned a Christian script. They are made to look like authentic court dramas, but in fact the characters say too much that fits only in a Christian play. Most Christian Martyr Acts are completely different from the staccato compactness and mild chaos of genuine court records, which survive in their dozens from Roman Egypt in the same period.[75]

In the Christian Martyr Acts, we find a structured series of ingredients. For example:

- the hero/heroine's modest reluctance but unshakeable faith
- the lily-livered volunteer who fails and recants when put to his first stern test
- a crude, uncultured Roman underling
- the governor-judge's initial courtesy and evolving cruelty
- his curiosity about the Christian religion and his easy deception by the witty Christian martyr, whose double-entendre jokes only the Christians understand
- the martyr's incredible bravery and endurance under torture
- the crowd as chorus and swing voters, admiring, pitying, but yet pagan, and so, hostile and ever baying for blood
- a loyal minority of fervent Christians
- miracles
- death, burial, and more miracles

And finally, the unsung, unmentioned, but essential hero/heroine is the Christian reader.

This is only an illustrative list; we find some but not necessarily all elements in each Martyr Act. And once the genre was established, author and audience could play with it, by variation and inversion: a female martyr, dreams, internal conflict within the martyr's family, and so on. The genre does not stand still. There may well be an admixture of truth in the reports and fantasies. But sifting for nuggets of truth and regarding fantasy as dross is to overvalue fact and undervalue imagination. What we can do instead is to analyze how the story functions, how it reveals tensions within the Christian church and between Christians and the Roman state. We can write history not about what happened but about how Christians constructed and represented their own present and past.

We can see the blend of these ingredients best by looking at one document in detail. It is a classic Martyr Act, that is, a dramatic, apparently near-contemporary account of the arrest, trial, and death of a Christian holy man—Polycarp, bishop of Smyrna—in the mid–second century. The *Martyrdom of Polycarp* opens with a brief statement of faith: "It is a mark of true and solid love to desire salvation, not only for oneself but also for brethren. . . . Blessed and noble are all martyrdoms which take place in accord with God's will." Two points immediately: First, martyrdom was innovative in its heroization of individual salvation, but Christian leaders also wanted to preserve it as a collective good. Martyrs are our new heroes. They die not just for themselves but, like Christ, for all of us. Second, Christian leaders who wrote and read the Martyr Acts publicly in church on the anniversary of the martyrs' death wanted to keep firm control over who could be regarded as a true martyr. It is, I think, significant that the martyr here was a bishop. The church set itself up repeatedly as the arbiter of what was and what was not "in accord with God's will."

The first scene is a warm-up, a minor martyrdom before the big one. As usual the text turns on the standard conflicts between the martyr's courage and Roman official cruelty, the bystanders' admiration and their pity, and the unimportance of this world compared with the next. "Fixing their eyes on the favor of Christ, they despised the tortures of this world, buying themselves in one hour exemption from eternal fire." Ostensibly, the aim of the official torture was to persuade the Christians to turn from their faith—but in vain. The kindly governor (who is subsequently called a tyrant and the wily Devil) tries to persuade the noble Germanicus to spare his young manhood. Of course, as a young noble should (no proletarian Christian heroes yet), Germanicus courageously suffers, "whipped until the veins and arteries were laid bare," and finally drags a wild beast on top of himself, "so as to be released all the faster from this unjust and lawless life." The crowd of spectators was amazed at the courage shown by the pious Christian, and shout for more Christian victims, especially Polycarp.[76]

That was the brief opening act; now we'll get the star attraction. But no, not yet. First we have a diversion: a false martyr, an immigrant (even then!), perhaps also, so our text hints, a heretic, who has rashly volunteered for death and has foolishly incited others; but as soon as he sees the wild beasts he is scared stiff, listens to the governor's sweet talk, recants, swears by the gods, and sacrifices. "We do not approve of volunteers," our Martyr Acts state magisterially; "it is not the teaching of the gospel." The gospel, or rather this interpretation of it, legitimates proper Christian action. True martyrs, like sacrificial victims at pagan temples, needed the official stamp of approval.

Flashback. Bishop Polycarp, old man, eighty-six, knows his impending fate. It was revealed to him in a prophetic vision. But to avoid confrontation, and on the advice of many friends, he slips away to the country. By no means all Christians approved of evasion, so just in case we accuse Polycarp of cowardice, these Acts reassure us: while waiting for his death, he spends all his time, "night and day, in prayer for everyone, the respected and the insignificant, and for all the churches in the world."[77] For him, for us, the church in the mid–second century is a single grand entity, "the Catholic church throughout the world," serving both rich and poor. The Christian message is self-consciously aware of social differences and yet it is firmly egalitarian, and in this respect radically different from anything pagan.

But inevitably, Fate catches up with Polycarp. The captain of the local guard, conveniently called Herod (this is a tract against Jews as well as pagans), comes to arrest Polycarp in his local hideaway. Polycarp, like Jesus, has been betrayed, by a slave from his own household who informed against him under torture. Herod and his attendants are generously entertained (food and drink, as much as they want) while Polycarp prays continuously for two whole hours. Even in danger, Christians must be kind to and pray for those who persecute them. At first Herod is friendly, but he soon reverts to type and becomes threatening. Polycarp responds initially by refusing to speak, but then changes tack and speaks bluntly. He refuses to desert his faith. He is taken to the city, which he enters (again like Jesus) on a donkey. It is the sabbath.[78]

As Polycarp enters the amphitheater, a voice from heaven, heard only by the Christians present, says: "Be strong and manly, for I am with you." The governor tries to persuade Polycarp. "Swear by the genius of the emperor. Take account of your age. Recant. Say: 'Down with the atheists.'" It's too good an opportunity to miss. Polycarp readily agrees, looks at the mob, shakes his fist at them, looks up to heaven, and shouts: "Down with the atheists." Jewish martyr stories have similar anti-Roman double entendres. Rabbi Eliezer ben Hyrcanus once was brought to court and was asked a tricky question. He looked up to heaven and said: "I have trust in the judge." The Roman judge, stupidly misunderstanding, was flattered and let the rabbi go: "Case dismissed."[79]

But in this Christian case the governor persists and orders Polycarp to curse Christ. Polycarp understandably refuses. The two of them have a brief (but deeply implausible) conversation about Christianity, secular authority, morality, and the futility of earthly punishments. The governor gets tough, and we reach the final confrontation. Polycarp is to be executed. His face is suffused with grace; the governor is amazed; the pagans and Jews in the crowd are enraged. They demand that Polycarp be burned, and collect wood from surrounding shops and baths, quicker even than this story can be told. Polycarp's prophetic vision is to be fulfilled.

Meanwhile, Polycarp himself undresses and even tries to take off his own sandals, something he had never done before in his life. Even Christians, especially bishops, live in a world of slaves. Polycarp is not nailed but tied, to be offered up like a sacrificial ram. He prays: "O Lord, almighty God and Father of your beloved and blessed son, Christ Jesus, through whom we have received our knowledge of you, God of the angels. . . . May I be received this day before your face as a rich and acceptable sacrifice. . . . I praise, bless, and glorify you through the eternal and heavenly high priest Jesus Christ. . . . Amen." The flames are lit and blaze mightily. But then "we saw a miracle"; and the very fact of their autopsy authenticates the truth of the account. The flames surround the saint but do not burn him, and a fragrance arises as of expensive spice.[80]

When the Roman bandits (*sic*) see the flames are not working, they order a soldier to finish the blessed Polycarp off with a dagger. But when he plunges the dagger into Polycarp's body, a flood of blood gushes forth and extinguishes the flames. And at the very same time, a dove flies out, (though some editors, ancient and modern, delete this detail because it seems incredible).[81] The miraculous flow of blood alone shows the crowd the real difference between pagans and the Christian elect.

Afterward, the Devil, who is also the governor, at the instigation of the Jews, refused to give up Polycarp's body. The Jews even had the temerity to insinuate that the Christians might cease worshiping Jesus and worship Polycarp instead. Of course, that was absolute nonsense.[82] The Acts remind fellow Christians who are too enthusiastic about martyr cults that there is a huge difference between Christ and the martyrs, his imitators. In fact, many Christians did want a portion of the saint's corpse. But because of pressure from the Jews, the Romans burned the saint's body. All the Christians could do was to bury his precious bones, more valuable than jewels, and be grateful to the Lord for allowing them to celebrate the anniversary of Polycarp's martyrdom every year, both in commemoration of his death and as a preparation for future martyrs.

Polycarp was the twelfth Christian martyr at Smyrna, including those from the neighboring town. And this was by the mid–second century: not a huge score. "By his endurance he conquered the unjust governor and won the crown of immortality." This was a summary of the short version of his martyrdom, copied from an ancient manuscript. Incidentally, the date of his death was February 23 in the Roman calendar, and on that very day Irenaeus (later bishop of Lyon, but then in Rome) knew about Polycarp's martyrdom, through a heavenly voice. This is the true story of Polycarp's martyrdom.[83]

Once Martyr Acts had become established as a literary genre, others climbed on to the bandwagon, and the Christian genre itself evolved.[84] Christian Acts became more elaborate and inventive: female martyrs, young mothers even with infants at the breast, baroque dream sequences, prison diaries, talking animals, angry crowds attacking pagan leaders, mass conversions, the martyr executed but then revived by a healing angel so that he can face fresh tortures. The Christian Martyr

Acts revel in the sadism of Roman justice and in the power of their im-
agery. They rival the real savageries of gladiatorial games. But they were
also incitations to faith, dramatic reminders of what Christians believed
and of the struggles which had enabled the Church ultimately to triumph. Of course, these martyr romances did not tell it like it really was.
But through their fictions they gripped their readers'/listeners' imagination and so imposed their own simplified version of a complex history on
the collective memory. God was on the Christians' side.

Martyr Acts were not just innocent histories. They could also serve as
powerful weapons in contemporary politics, in the ongoing struggle between local and central authority. For example, one story, from Roman
Egypt, describes how in the terrible persecutions under Diocletian (303–
11), a beautiful young man was being taken in chains to court. On his
way he took mercy on a Christian who had just been executed, and raised
him from the dead; martyrs had the power to forgive sins, and even to
resurrect. When this mighty miracle had been performed, the crowd of
bystanders shouted: "The God of this holy man is the only God." But
the emperor, hearing the shouts of the crowd, was terrified, thinking that
the city had risen up against him, and asked: "What is this noise which I
hear?" They told him, and he was filled with fury, and said: "Bring him
to me."[85]

And so the stage is set for one of those classic confrontations between
emperor and saint. The saint, buoyed by faith and consciousness of
truth, stands firm, even when subjected to the most horrifying tortures.
The text is interspersed with his prayers and with the shouts of the newly
converted crowd, who themselves loudly confess their faith and are duly
put to the sword. Death is the essential punctuation of the story, and the
expectation of the reader. The archangel Michael repeatedly reappears
and makes the saint whole again, so that the tortures can start afresh.
The emperor boasts of the effectiveness of legal torture, swears by his
Gods and by the might of the Roman empire, and promises to wipe
Christians from the face of the earth.

It is a primal battle between the power of God and the secular state.
The emperor sees the martyr as a usurper "rising up against the state,"
whereas the martyr sees Jesus Christ as "the helper of the poor, of orphans, and the needy." The emperor's power rests in his soldiers, but
even they cannot be completely trusted. The saint miraculously blinds

them until they repent of their sins, so they convert to Christianity and turn against the emperor, abuse him, and throw their sword belts, their badges of office, into the emperor's face. The emperor's paganism legitimates an effrontery, a rebellion against established authority which, I think, is unparalleled in surviving writings from the Roman empire. But in an empire now Christian, when these stories were written and circulated, what remains in the mind is the possibility of rebelling against authority. To be sure, the rebellious soldiers are in their turn executed; civil authority is in the end reconfirmed.

This Martyr Act (and there are several others like it) is a drama of political confrontation. Emperor and nobles are on one side, martyrs and people on the other, with soldiers as a pivotal power bloc whose loyalty decides the outcome. But since this is a story, and not consistent political analysis, the lines are indistinctly drawn. The saint is condemned to the wild beasts. The emperor demands the most vicious animals. But what turns up is a lactating she-bear, a tiger, a lion, and a panther. Even an emperor cannot always get exactly what he wants. The crowd (the whole town is there) is filled with pity for the beauty of the youthful martyr and wishes that he would sacrifice. In vain. We haven't come all this way for a tame surrender.

The she-bear is sent in first and (surprise, surprise) licks the martyr's feet; the lion carries him on his back right up to the emperor, and in a human voice says that wild animals too acknowledge the only God as their creator. With that, the human lion leaps on the king and his surrounding entourage and lacerates them. Six hundred men, "to say nothing of children and women," were immediately converted, and eventually executed for their faith. The martyr publicly upbraids the wounded emperor for his obduracy but kindly restores him to health.[86] Even saints cannot be seen as regicides.

By no means all Christians thought it either necessary or sensible to die for their faith. Christian Gnostics, for example, thought martyrdom was self-indulgent and misconceived, the mark of an inferior understanding. For them, at least in theory, salvation was to be found in the spiritual pursuit of self-knowledge. Enthusiasm for loud public professions of faith and martyrdom reflected an exhibitionist concern for the body; true salvation was to be sought inside the spirit.[87] Other Christians thought that voluntary martyrdom was as futile as the showy suicides of

Indian fakirs; true martyrdom ("martyrdom" means literally "bearing witness") was to be sought in the pious self-control and dedication of a Christian's daily life. Each side, rigorist and laxist, argued its case with passion.[88]

Many Christians, less loftily, through understandable terror, under threat of losing their property and being imprisoned, starved to death, tortured, and executed, simply recanted. Sometimes whole Christian communities, led by their bishop, apostatized and cravenly submitted to performing the pagan rites of pouring wine and burning incense at the altars of local Gods. In 250, in Carthage, at the height of the first empirewide persecution, crowds lined up for days to participate in the sacrifice to the Gods at the Temple of Jupiter. In fact, this massive public display of loyalty to traditional cults may have itself precipitated the persecution, but it also reflected the huge pressures, both social and legal, on Christians to recant and conform. Christians were jeered at in public, threatened, reported, and attacked. In several provinces, pagans who sacrificed received official certificates (libelli), and this official registration systematically differentiated Christians from the rest.[89] Being Christian in a predominantly pagan world was an explicit act of social rebellion.

Many Christians (we have no idea how many) tried desperately to find a middle ground. Some simply withdrew; why draw attention to themselves by going in crowds to church? Some slipped away to the countryside and lived in fear and hiding, or went to towns which persecution had not reached or where persecution was less persistent. By no means all Roman governors were keen on executing Christians. One governor dismissed a case because he thought the accusation vexatious; another told a crowd of overenthusiastic would-be martyrs that if they wanted to die they should hang themselves or jump over a cliff. Besides, Jesus himself said, "When they begin to persecute you, flee from city to city" (Matthew 10.23). It was just sensible to escape in order to fight another day, rather than risk succumbing to torture. Confrontation merely increased the risk of escalation; persecutors thrived on their own success.[90]

Some Christians (again we do not know how many) bribed their way out by buying off informers or soldiers sent to arrest them. Or instead of sacrificing, they just bought official certificates to say that they had performed pagan rites, and in sufficient numbers that there was a special name for them: certificateers (libellatici). Still others, who had actually recanted and sacrificed, cut short the period of humbling penance normally required before readmission to church by simply getting unofficial certificates of reconciliation (the bishop of Carthage said "thousands were being issued every day") from Christians in prison waiting to be martyred. Since martyrs, once dead, could intercede for sinners with God, it was a simple extension to imagine that those about to die could also forgive sins.[91] Unsurprisingly, this maverick martyr power, flamboyantly paraded, upset bishops determined to maintain control over their diminishing flocks.

Persecutions tore the church apart. Tensions between zealots and compromisers, latent in times of peace, rose to the surface and festered all the more because in the turmoil of persecutions, bishops and clergy could not impose peace. Martyrs and confessors bypassed or upstaged routine authority. Rigorists insisted forcefully that it was a Christian duty boldly to profess the faith; almost everyone should offer themselves up for martyrdom. Laxists, by contrast, thought that unity and strength (and occasionally their own status) could most easily be restored in the aftermath of persecutions by forgiving and forgetting. Between the extremes, compromisers tried uneasily to tread a path which would unite the two opposing camps—often in vain. The status of martyrs was so high that even laxists and compromisers often judged it expedient to join the chorus of unstinting praise. The heat of persecutions squeezed out the reasonable middle and transformed the language of Christian morality. Suffering became a supreme good.

THE GROWTH OF EPISCOPAL POWER

Ancient Christians were both divided and united in the passions of disagreement. Even after the church's final triumph, the bitter wrangles, outed in the disorder of persecutions and their echoes continued and magnified internal discords. In some regions, divisions started in the persecutions persisted for well over a century. Those who had stood firm and believed that only the pure elect should be full members of the church fought with those who had (often allegedly) betrayed their sacred trust and sacrificed, or handed over the holy scriptures, or laxly readmitted recanters without due penance. Or rather, the symbols of past conflicts were continuously reused to fight present battles.

Rigorists claimed (with variations) that all those who joined the church knew the risks and had dedicated their lives to God in hope of gaining the promised rewards in heaven. The faithful should be ready to die, and not be afraid. Clergy had a particular obligation to stand firm and stay with their flock. Flight or bribery was a sin for anyone, because it betrayed a lack of commitment to God. For clergy, flight was simply not permissible. The Roman enemies could do their worst, but God is on the Christians' side, and he is far greater than Rome. One cannot serve both Caesar and God. In fact, persecution comes from God, via the Devil; it is the great test which sorts deserving Christians from the undeserving, who by their sins have brought persecution upon themselves. Death will come anyhow; why wait for it in bed or sickness? "Let me be fodder for wild beasts; that is how I can attain to God. I am God's wheat, and I am being ground by the teeth of wild beasts to make a pure loaf for Christ. . . . I shall be a real disciple of Christ when my body is no more." Roman cruelty is our opportunity for glory. We love and pray for our enemies and persecutors. Our church is the pure church of the elect.[92]

Idealists force the world to conform to their prescriptions. Pragmatists have to work through its troublesome complexities. Cyprian, upper-class bishop of Carthage from 248 to 258, was, or was forced to become, a pragmatist. During the first large-scale persecution, of 250–51, he ran away and stayed in hiding for a whole year. He claimed that his continued presence in Carthage would have been a provocation: it would have incited popular demands for his and other Christians' deaths. But his flight seriously weakened his control over his troubled and unruly flock, both clergy and layfolk. Some of the clergy, both in Carthage and at Rome, were critical and understandably resentful, especially when the absent Cyprian paraded his high moral standards from the safety of refuge—and left them with all the difficulties of imprisoned confessors and lapsing parishioners. And when they did not do all that he ordered, he accused them of paying no heed to their bishop above them and insufficient attention to their future judgment in the court of Christ. Some of them in turn responded by setting up their own, schismatic church, with its own laxist counterbishop. Eventually, to be sure, St. Cyprian's reputation was salvaged, by his martyrdom in 258 and by his voluminous correspondence. In effect, he wrote the minutes of his own controversies.[93]

The central problems which Cyprian faced were unity and forgiveness. To maintain his authority and his power base, he needed to keep the church together ("One Christ, One Church, One Chair"). He needed to find some way to forgive the thousands of ex-Christians who had recanted, in action or conscience, but still sought readmission to the church, preferably without the long humiliations of penance, kneeling outside the church door in sackcloth and ashes. And he wanted to buttress his own episcopal power ("God makes us bishops") against the competing influence of lesser clergy and the maverick charisma of lay confessors and martyrs, temporarily inflated by imprisonment and torture. His chosen weapons were fulsome flattery, harsh criticism (confessors were undisciplined, drunk, quarrelsome, boastful, and sexually corrupt), delay (just until times are more settled), pacificatory promises subsequently forgotten (we'll all consult together before a decision is taken), the excommunication of rivals (that is, heretics), collective decisions by whole councils of bishops, harsh talk followed by soft action, personal visions, and inflated claims of his own that he spoke and wrote (on behalf of the church) with the voice of God.[94]

Four developments, visible in Cyprian's policy, were of particular significance for later church history: the forgiveness of major sins through penance, the enhancement of episcopal power, the establishment of regional councils of bishops, and the control of martyrs by their sacralization and liturgical commemoration. Cyprian had been outraged by confessors in prison who had, as he saw it, indiscriminately handed out collective certificates of reconciliation (probably in return for money) to whole families of recanters. He wanted a proper church procedure, interregionally agreed upon once the persecution was over, but locally under his own control. There were to be individual investigations and careful distinctions. Had the guilty recanted voluntarily or willfully blasphemed? Had he/she been tortured, or just pressured? Had he sacrificed, or only burned incense, or bought an official certificate? Or finally, had he secured a certificate of reconciliation from a confessor? The variations were almost endless. And in the end the penitent apostate could be readmitted only after public acknowledgment of guilt in front of the whole congregation, (protracted public penance) and the official laying on of hands.[95]

Even that was a concession. Previously, many committed Christians considered apostasy, along with adultery and murder, as irremissible sins, which no cleric could, and only God in his infinite mercy might, forgive. Adulterers and apostates were simply ejected from the elect. Baptism provided the single and sufficient remission of sins, after which a true Christian would sin no more. Some rigorist sects even required celibacy as a precondition of baptism. And some believers postponed baptism till late in life; at risk of eternal damnation, they bought time for sin.[96]

Of course, beneath the salvos of exhortation, no one knows what actually happened. Christian propagandists prided themselves on the virtue of normal Christian practice, and it seems churlish to distrust them completely. But even in the second century some pious Christians thought the regimen too harsh. The anonymous *Shepherd of Hermas* proclaimed both the imminent end of the world and the fast-approaching possibility of a second, postbaptismal amnesty for sincere penitents. And early in the third century, the bishop of Rome had, according to indignant rigorists, even allowed penitents to be forgiven adultery: judge not, so that you be not judged. The Church, like Noah's ark, should embrace the good and the wicked.[97]

The Church, if it was to continue to grow, indeed if it was to maintain the semblance of unity, had to readmit the lapsed. Hence Cyprian's flattery of martyrs, tough talk on penitence, overt modesty, insistence on church unity and discipline and episcopal authority (in his view synonymous), and eventual soft concessions to penitent certificateers. Under renewed threat of further persecution (which then didn't materialize), it seemed more sensible to readmit them wholesale than to alienate willing, if flexible, supporters. Better to offend the rigorists than lose the weak. They had more money. It was their sins, Cyprian argued, which had brought persecution on them as just punishment. Their attachment to property had made them lose faith. But now was the time to beg, pray, weep, lament, fast, and give.[98]

Since sin could not be eradicated, it might as well be exploited. The careful stratification of different degrees of apostasy (voluntary/forced; thought about/done; sacrifice/incense only; official/martyrs' certificates) was an initial stage in the flotation of a new moral economy of sin and penance. Over time, the Church gradually elaborated an effective list of sin prices. To put it crudely, the Church marketed sin, and expanded into guilt. Sin was not just a matter of behavior; it could occur in the desires of thought and in the unconscious fantasy of dreams. Christian clerics were determined to make the faithful pay for their dreams, as though they could salve their conscience by generosity to the poor and to the church.[99]

All charities need money. The Christian church was exceptional (though not unique) in the ancient world in its reliance on believers' contributions for the support of a professional clergy. It was also exceptional in its visible care for the needy and sick outside the family. In a harsh culture in which the rich typically prided themselves on their thoroughly justified good fortune, Christians stood out in their heroization of self-sacrifice and in their private generosity to the unfortunate. Even pagans were deeply impressed, and eventually also attempted to imitate Christian charity. But it is also worth noting that as the church grew, it grew richer. From the fourth century, church buildings (like pagan temples) were increasingly decorated with silver and gold, and bishops rose up the social scale, with incomes to match. Guilt, sin, laxity, repentance, penance, and the readmission of the fallen, to say nothing of alms and legacies, used in combination, were all important forces in the church's drive for worldly success. St. Jerome, himself an avid netter of rich virgins devoted to chastity, caustically remarked that while "the scriptures were being decorated with purple and gold, and with jeweled bindings, Jesus lay abandoned outside, naked and dying."[100]

Episcopal power was another key to the church's success. Cyprian himself in the mid–third century acted like a baronial bishop, or rather as a bishop who thought that his authority ought to be obeyed without question. Just as there was only one God, one Christ, there was one church and one episcopal chair. The bishop's power was unique, unshareable, and irresistible. Rebellion against a bishop was tantamount, he claimed, to rebellion against Christ or disbelief in Christ. It was God who made bishops. Cyprian also acted like a local patrician who expected obeisance from his social inferiors. He combined Roman upper-class hauteur with the authority conveyed by the Christian God. For some of his subordinates (confessors in prison, parish priests, and presumably their supporting parishioners), not to mention his fellow bishops, this was too much. Besides, Cyprian's power base had been weakened, as we have seen, by his flight, by the divisive chaos of persecution, by inescapable doctrinal discords, and by the competing interests of other priests and bishops, accustomed to local traditions and independence.[101]

Cyprian's reactions were partly routine: heady rhetoric, expostulation, exhortation, flattery, threats of eternal damnation, appeals to personal visions sent by God, and invective. We cannot realistically gauge their total effect, mostly because Cyprian's own account is effectively the only one to survive. But his account fits neatly into the known evolution of ecclesiastical power. During the third century, the power of bishops to control church policy and doctrine, individually and collectively, increased significantly. And Cyprian's episcopacy marks a significant step in that centralization of power, at least in its ideology, if not in thoroughly effective actions. Seen retrospectively, the image of Cyprian as a powerful and authoritative bishop was of more significance than the reality.[102]

But one of Cyprian's innovations was of critical importance for later church history. In order to shore up the weakness of his personal authority and to ensure uniformity of church response within and beyond north Africa in the immediate aftermath of persecutions, Cyprian summoned successive councils of local bishops and clergy to reach collective decisions on policy. These congresses involving dozens of bishops and associated clergy (six of them in as many years) met publicly, undisturbed either by the Roman civil authorities or by popular objections. These councils decided on a uniform policy about the lapsed; excommunicated local schismatics; communicated their collective decisions to bishops overseas and sought their support. But when support was not forthcoming, Cyprian reasserted both his own independence from any supremacy of Rome and the freedom of local bishops to make their own decisions, within a canonical frame. And it is noteworthy that, such were the difficulties of communication then, bishops found guilty by one synod had no apparent difficulty in seeking redress with another congress or bishop elsewhere. The system was not yet, and never effectively became, fully integrated. But the fatal first steps had been taken. The Catholic church had decided that it was expedient to decide the nature of religious truth by a majority vote of bishops. But in fact, uniformity of belief or practice was not so easily achievable. And within the broad frame of council decisions, variety persisted, even if some versions were occasionally persecuted out of existence.[103]

Finally, confessors and martyrs. They were loose cannons in an increasingly hierarchical and institutionalized church. But confessors were only a temporary problem; their influence flourished and waned with the chaos of persecution. In the short run, Bishop Cyprian was irritated beyond measure by what he saw as the arrogance, indiscipline, and self-importance of confessors, all the more so because they breached the clerical monopoly and episcopal privilege of pardoning sins. But when the persecutions ended, so did the confessors' authority; and their glory could be retrospectively stage-managed by the collective decisions of bishops. In the end, as with heretics, confessors were useful infantry, whose passionate activism and heroism had helped protect and buttress the power and authority of the bishops behind them.

Martyrs (confessors who had died for their faith) were a different matter, both a bigger problem and an enduring glory. Martyrs were the new saints of the Christian church. They represented the inspirational element within Christianity, which always both enhanced and threatened to undermine routine institutional authority. Martyrs, like prophets and ascetics, reminded workaday priests of how much further true faith could have taken them. But there was more to it than that. Martyrs were dead humans. Their worship, as semidivine intercessors with the ear of God, violated both pagan sentiments and strict Christian monotheism. Drunken orgies at martyrs' tombs offended Christian puritans. Worship of relics, a dead saint's bone or robe, made pagans smirk and offended conservative Christians. It was a stern cleric's reproof in church of a rich lady's kissing a dead martyr's bone before the eucharist which sparked the Donatist schism. In dudgeon, she backed her steward as the break-away bishop of Carthage.[104]

What began as an oddity evolved into a norm. Sacred relics, fragments of the true cross, bones, even dust from a saint's corpse became central symbols of veneration for the ancient Christian church. The annual commemoration of martyrs' deaths had for long been a regular feature of Christian liturgy. But gradually it came to be controlled centrally by bishops. Bishops effectively decided precisely who was to be commemorated. The earliest surviving martyr list, which comes from the city of Rome in the mid–fourth century, juxtaposes the commemorative days of twenty-four martyrs with those of twelve bishops, only a few of whom had died for their faith. The next-earliest surviving martyr list, from Syria at the beginning of the fifth century, celebrates martyrs on over 160 days in the year. The prestige of individual martyrs had been fractionalized by inflation. But simultaneously, the prestige of some martyrs was enhanced by their empirewide reputation and the magnificence of their commemorative shrines. Grandiose churches were built over martyrs' tombs—whether real or alleged—on the outskirts of old cities. The churches of St. Peter in the Vatican and of St. Paul "beyond the walls" are famous cases in point. The commemoration of dead saints redrew the symbolic map of the ancient city. The new churches had begun to rival the old Forum as the city center.[105]

The end of the "Great Persecution" (effectively in 312), the Edict of Toleration in 313, Constantine's military victory over his rival coemperor, Licinius, in 324 (in whose territories the persecution had continued), and Constantine's and his successors' consistent support together marked a new era for the Christian church. Christianity advanced simultaneously on several fronts, legal, moral, self-regulatory, exhortatory, and symbolic. Laws were passed restoring church property confiscated during the persecutions, granting privileges of tax exemption to priests, and allowing bishops to act (with the agreement of the contending parties) as judges in civil cases. And eventually, by the end of the fourth century, as we have seen, laws were passed prohibiting pagan rites and membership of heretical sects. The favors showered on the church, both institutionally and personally, by the preferential promotion of Christians to high office stimulated a rapid rise in the number of Christians and in their visibility.[106] In the fourth century, Christians publicly celebrated their religious commitment. The number of Christian churches and tombs grew dramatically, though paganism sturdily persisted.

Laws to enforce Christian morality were quite slow in coming. Old pagan laws penalizing childlessness were revoked, divorce initiated by a woman was severely restricted, adultery by a slave was punished by burning, no executions were to be performed on Sundays. The increasing savagery of punishments instigated by Christian emperors during the fourth century is notorious.[107] But we have to be cautious. Laws were rhetorically persuasive public pronouncements of governmental attitude or intent, and as such, valuable indicators. But there was no effective mechanism for pervasive enforcement. Imperial laws did not determine moral performance, or even religious adherence.

But the Roman government's support for the church's own self-regulation promoted a considerable concentration of power. In effect, the Roman government allowed the creation of a new ecclesiastical estate, a self-governing church within the civil state. The first great universal church council, at Nicaea in 325, carved the Roman empire up between four superbishops, the patriarchs of Rome, Alexandria, Antioch, and Jerusalem, with provision made later for Constantinople (second only to Rome) and Carthage. It took some time to settle the exact limits of each patriarch's powers. And the powers of metropolitan bishops, that is the bishops of provincial capitals, within the six regions varied. But in principle no bishop could be appointed without the metropolitan's permission.[108] With state support, the church had moved toward a centralization of power and a homogeneity of ritual and belief.

At the Council of Nicaea, all three hundred bishops, once they had made their first collective decision that no voluntarily self-castrated man should become a priest, settled down to the more serious business of dogma, morality, and dividing the spoils: no immediate elevations to the clergy or bishoprics for recent converts to Christianity, no women to cohabit with priests unless closely related, fixed jurisdictions for competing bishops, all bishops to support one another's decisions about heretics, no mobility between bishoprics for either bishops or priests, limited forgiveness for those who had apostatized without torture during the persecutions (they should be readmitted after seven to ten years' waiting—"they should be treated with gentleness"—among those not admitted to Communion).[109]

Perhaps other, local councils reacted to their newfound powers with a greater generosity of spirit. The Council of Elvira, in Spain (early fourth century), for example, ruled that a man who sacrificed to idols after baptism could not be admitted to Communion even on his deathbed, and that a woman who flogged a slave so that he/she died within three days should serve seven years' penance if she did it intentionally, but five years' penance if she killed her slave unintentionally, unless in the meanwhile the mistress herself were on her deathbed, in which case Communion should be given. If a priest committed a grave sin, he should do penance only before the bishop; priests and bishops should abstain from sexual relations with their wives; candles should not be lit during the day on graves, because the spirits of saints should not be disturbed; no pictures were to be set up in church.[110] That was a battle, inherited from Christianity's antipagan, anti-idol past, which would soon be lost.

The Council of Gangra, in central Asia Minor in the mid–fourth century, was aimed principally at controlling and expelling a fervent sect of ascetic Christians, the Eustathians, who allegedly set themselves up as spiritually superior merely because they remained unmarried. They had introduced monastic dress for men and women (getting women to wear men's clothes); they fasted on Sundays, diverted the revenues of the church to themselves ("because they were the true saints"), despised married priests and the feasts of martyrs, and claimed that the rich would never be saved; in addition, some of them did not eat meat. In response, the council of bishops anathematized any who blamed wives for having sex with their husbands, or advocated vegetarianism among devout Christians, or attacked the celebration of the eucharist by married priests, or set up private religious meetings outside the church, or diverted the revenues of the church.[111] This rare overt attack on incipient monasticism is a sign of the continuous tensions within the church. Yet once again the church's future lay with the opposition; monasticism flourished, and preserved the records of the church's turbulent history.

The church's greatest advance during the fourth century lay in the fields of symbolic self-advertisement and the practical creation of an ideal Christian personality. Its symbolic growth was achieved not only by the construction of churches as central monuments of the new faith (accompanied by the destruction or conversion of temples) but also by the pervasive penetration of Christian symbolism into the visual and private worlds of believers. Christians saw, carried, and perhaps internalized crosses as emblems of belief in Jesus Christ, suffering, and salvation. They painted and saw Christian pictures, pictures of Christ and his apostles, and scenes from the Bible. The visual world of Christianity was startlingly different in image and meaning from the classical world of paganism.[112]

But the greatest achievement of ancient Christianity in this period was, I think, its remolding of social ethics, its purposeful construction of the virtuous believer. I am not thinking here of the radical and influential wing of Christian ascetics, who put so much stress on asexuality and withdrawal from the world as the holiest path to salvation. Their extreme ethic was perhaps admired, but certainly not imitated, by the broad mass of Christians. It put the apex of virtue out of ordinary believers' reach, even if ordinary believers could admire the holy man as a collective benefactor who might by his prayers help them too to salvation.

Rather, I am thinking here of the patient and cumulative effect of sermons and the rituals of confession and penance, on teaching and thereby creating a new nexus of charity and virtue. Of course, there is always a gap between ideals and practice, between prescription and performance. But diligent Christians in the fourth century were bombarded by repeated exhortations to obey Christian commandments, and were tempted to obedience by the double incentives of eternal punishment and blissful immortality. We have no idea, and may be skeptical, of the extent to which their normal behavior changed. But their preachers have left us a powerful legacy of continuous striving, revealing at its best a quivering self-examination as to whether the believer had lived up to his/her own unrealizable ideals or had sinned through thoughtless self-indulgence.[113]

CODA: FORCIBLE CONVERSION AND CHARITY

The end of a long chapter is not the best place to embark on a detailed description of the process of change in late antiquity from paganism to Christianity. But three very brief vignettes capture some of the problems implicit in the painful transition.

It's tempting to imagine conversion to Christianity as an intensely personal experience, whether as a blinding revelation in the style of Paul on the road to Damascus or as a gradual process of increasing certainty, in the style of Augustine (Confessions). Occasionally it must have been like that. But far more often, in Christian stories, conversion was sudden and collective. A saint performed a dramatic miracle, and on that very day thousands saw the light and were immediately convinced of the truth of the Christian message, converted, and without further ado were baptized. That seems too dramatic to be realistic, too superficial to be meaningful.[114]

By contrast, the ideal practice recommended in liturgical handbooks was that new Christians normally be admitted only once a year, at Easter, after three years of instruction and a strict examination of their morals and their scriptural knowledge and baptism. A strictly controlled process like that, complete with careful registration of individual names, could not cope with a massive increase in Christian numbers during the fourth century. So we have to choose between competing pictures: growth was so rapid that most new Christians entering the church, once Christianity had allied with the Roman state, knew very little about their faith; *or*, the growth of Christianity was nowhere near as rapid as often envisaged: pagans persisted, but simply kept quiet or were expunged from elite Christian consciousness; *or*, growth was more jagged and violent than the word "conversion" usually implies. Realism suggests a mixture; my personal inclination lies toward the first and last options.

Two stories, arbitrarily chosen, illustrate a two-edged process: group conversion through social pressure, or persuasion by threat of force. But of course, we have to be cautious; this is a story, not history. The first story is set at first in Jerusalem, then in Minorca, Spain. In December 415, a priest called Lucian received a vision: Rabbi Gamaliel, St. Paul's teacher, a tall man with a bushy beard, dressed in gilded boots and a white cloak decorated with golden crosses *(sic)*, appeared and told Lucian where St. Stephen, the very first Christian martyr, was buried. Gamaliel had buried Stephen himself, in hope of resurrection. Now, Lucian knew that Satan lays traps for the unwary by adopting disguises, so he was initially suspicious and did nothing. Gamaliel came back not once but twice, and scared Lucian into telling everything to his bishop, John of Jerusalem.

At that very moment, John was embroiled in the hotly contested trial of Pelagius, accused of heresy before a local synod of bishops. John was a supporter of Pelagius. He was overjoyed to be the discoverer (after further topographical help from Gamaliel) of the genuine bones of the first martyr. On the very first day of the disinterment, seventy-three people were cured of serious ailments. Most of the holy relics were kept in Jerusalem, where a splendid new church was erected over the site of Stephen's death. But a young Spanish priest, Orosius (famous later for his universal history) took some of the bones to Spain and north Africa.[115]

In 416, the bones of St. Stephen landed in Minorca and were deposited in the church just outside Magona (modern Mahón), one of two towns on the island, and the one with a large and powerful settlement of Jews. The arrival of the saint's bones or of a new bishop, or both, excited considerable religious enthusiasm and a distinct tension between Christians and Jews. Battles broke out in public and private. "The sinful appearance of long-standing affection was transformed into temporary hatred through love of eternal salvation." The leader of the Jews, Theodorus, ex-magistrate, ex-official, wealthy, learned, and influential, did his best to quiet things down. A truce was arranged; a day was even fixed for public debate. But then the Christians from the other town on the island, where the bishop was based, decided to join the fray. The Jews gathered stakes, stones, and spears and stored them in the synagogue.

Three dreams, two Christian, the third Jewish, had already shown the shape of the future. Theodorus the Jew, as he told us later, had a fearful dream that when he was going to synagogue, twelve men barred his way and told him that there was a lion inside. Although terrified, Theodorus peered in and saw Christian monks singing. He ran away to a relative's house, and she comforted him at her breast. The Lion was clearly Jesus, the Lion of Judah! Meanwhile, and all this was before the miraculous events to come, a Christian consecrated virgin called Theodora dreamed that a widow (obviously the synagogue!) offered the bishop all her fields to sow; and Bishop Severus had an almost identical dream.

A huge crowd from the Christian town (where no Jews live) converges on Magona. The Christians (it's the bishop's story) invite the Jews to church. The Jews refuse; it's the sabbath. The bishop suggests a debate near the synagogue; that's not breaking the Law. The Jews refuse, but come round to his lodgings, armed. The bishop says: "You thirst for our blood, we want your salvation." They all march toward the synagogue to see if there is a cache of arms, both sides singing psalms. Then, by God's will, some reckless Jewish women throw huge stones; miraculously, no one is hurt. But blood is fired, and the synagogue is burned. We kept their books to save them from misuse, but gave the silver back to the Jews so there would be no accusations of theft.

The Christians are exultant. One leading Jew converts. For the next three days, the Christians pray. Then, near the destroyed synagogue, Theodorus and the bishop debate; Theodorus is clever and learned. No victory here. The crowd prays to heaven for help and shouts: "Theodorus, believe in Christ," but the Jews all think that what they've heard is "Theodorus has believed in Christ." This miracle works. Theodorus himself is thunderstruck, but the first renegade Jew encourages him; by conversion he can remain safe, honored, and wealthy. Theodorus plays for time, but the battle is over. The broad mass of Jews convert, in groups, and then in dribs and drabs. Only a handful of obdurates remain, and a few miracles rapidly salvage them. In all, 540 new Christians, a good haul for an eight-day campaign. And the ex-Jews, of course, pay for the leveling of the synagogue and build a new church on its very site.

The second story, on the death of Homer, or the end of classical antiquity, is shorter but equally distressing. In the mid–fifth century, in a small village in southern Egypt, the pagan worshipers of a local god called Kothos were arrested and interrogated. They readily admitted, even without being tortured, that they had tempted Christian children with tidbits of food, then kidnapped them, sacrificed them, and poured their blood on the altars. They even confessed that they used the murdered children's guts as strings for the harps on which they played hymns. In spite of their confessions, they escaped punishment by bribing their way out of prison.

When the holy bishop Macarius heard of this, he went with a handful of companions to the pagan temple, which was some way out of town. As the Christian party approached, the villagers, both men and women, were extremely hostile; the women threw stones from the temple roof, the men gathered round with rakes and axes in their hands. But the blessed Macarius coolly asked to see inside their temple (though two of his priests were scared and ran away). No sooner were the persevering Christians inside than twenty men seized them, tied them up, and put them like sacrificial victims on the altar. Their last hour had come. But Macarius said: "Do not be afraid. God the Christ will help us."

And behold, the holy Besa, abbot of a nearby monastery, burst in with fourteen monks and freed them. Together, the bishop and the monks prayed for the destruction of the temple; a voice from heaven warned them to escape, and immediately a great wall of fire burned it right down to its foundations. Just then the chief priest of Kothos, an old man called Homer, came along to participate in the sacrifice. But Macarius told the monks to seize him. Homer prayed to his "Great God, Kothos, general of the air," to save him. To no avail. Homer was trussed up and, while the Christians sang hymns, burned alive in the fire made out of 306 idols from the temple and his own house. And that very day, some pagans became Christians and were baptized, while others polluted the wells and escaped to the desert; so Christians occupied the fugitives' houses.[116]

My final image of the Christian revolution is kinder, and in the end, more influential than the horrors of Christian destructive intolerance. But at the same time, it is more demanding and threatening. Basil, aristocrat and radical, was bishop of Caesarea in central Asia Minor in the late fourth century. With a combination of his own funds, church income, and contributions from believers, he built a monastery with cells nearby for solitary ascetics, a poor house from which he distributed soup during a famine, and a hospital. He himself lived as a devout ascetic, ate simply, dressed poorly. But he was learned, wrote beautifully, preached powerfully, politicked successfully, looked after the poor, and with his own hands cared for lepers.[117]

For all its idiosyncratic excesses, Christianity also promoted an image of self-sacrificing piety, of virtue, generosity to the poor, and kindliness to the sick. Of course, by no means all Christians, perhaps only a minority of them, practiced the virtues preached. But by the end of the fourth century, the whole symbolic world of the Roman empire had changed. It was now an empire of churches, not temples, an empire of prayers and sermons, not sacrifices. Everyone knew that they should now be marching to a single and Christian tune, even if by no means everyone kept in step.[118]

FOUR

Jesus and His Twin Brother

VARIETIES OF JESUS

Ancient religions did much of their business with stories. Poets, priests, and temple attendants used stories to help confirm faith among the faithful, to explain the origin and future of the world, and to describe the complex relationship between gods and humans, and the importance and identity of the particular cult which they favored. And they used stories to bridge the gap between everyday realities and metaphysical fantasy. Through stories, the unreal, the improbable, the miraculous, and the transcendental, all vital ingredients of religion, could be legitimated, captured, and brought to earth by a judicious mix with the recognizably factual. In order to be understood, the miraculous had to be partially dressed up in everyday clothes.[1]

Any new religion, when it enters the already crowded marketplace of competing religions, faces particular problems. But a new monotheistic religion in a predominantly polytheistic world confronts a double challenge. Like any new religion, it must recruit believers in order to survive; but unlike other new polytheistic cults, it cannot be content merely to claim that its god is powerful; it must also claim, against the common and entrenched opinion, that all other gods are powerless. A new and exclusive religion must claim that its stories are the only truth; all other religious stories are false.

And so, in the battle for survival and victory, old stories had to be retold with a new twist. Or even better, in order to win and keep followers, missionaries of each new religion, whether Christian or Manichaean, told new and therefore more transgressive stories, which were attractively shocking at least to some of their listeners, and inevitably just shocking to others.[2] Only in this way could the followers of Jesus, who were from the beginning just one among many of the religious sects struggling for recognition, establish a niche appeal in what had always previously been a fractured and volatile market. In the end, as we all know, their monopolistic and exclusivist strategy worked. But it would have been a rash prophet who could predict that it would succeed.[3]

Of course, stories were only one tactic in the wide-ranging battle for believers. Ritual, exhortation, exemplary piety, and ideology all played their complementary parts in what turned out to be the triumphant though troubled progress of Christianity. Over time, the relative importance of each ingredient fluctuated. And eventually, as Christianity went upscale socially and intellectually, its leaders created for themselves a relatively self-sufficient and dense network of symbolic meanings whose validity was established for insiders by reference to other symbols within the same set. Then this self-contained and self-referential theology could replace narrative as the religion's preferred instrument of self-confirmation. But humble storytelling, though often despised, particularly by the intelligentsia, was never completely replaced.

So let me tell a story, taken from the apocryphal, noncanonical Acts of John, written in Greek by an anonymous and devoted Christian in the second century. John in this account is Jesus' most favored disciple. He cannot bear to watch Jesus' crucifixion, so he takes refuge in a cave on the Mount of Olives. In the dark cave, Jesus appears to John to instruct him before he disappears from earth. And Jesus says that the ignorant multitude in the crowd around the cross, down below in Jerusalem, think that it is Jesus who is being crucified. But Jesus, as he himself tells John, is not a body but a voice, just as the cross is made not of wood but of light. To different people (and this is what the privileged elite of Christians should know), the cross appears differently: it can be the Word (Logos), Christ, the Way, the Resurrection, the Son, the Father, the Spirit, or Life itself.[4]

Jesus tells John: "I am not the man who is on the cross. I was understood to be what I am not. I am not what for the many I am. And what they will say of me is mean and unworthy."[5] What *they* will say of me is mean and unworthy. Of course, such sayings are difficult to interpret. Ambiguity and multiple meanings are necessarily built into religious texts; they usefully allow a whole host of complementary and conflicting interpretations. But as I understand it, what Jesus means here is that the orthodoxy which we find in the canonical gospels ("what they will say") is to be rejected in favor of direct personal knowledge. In its place, or rather above it, the privileged elite of true Christians can and should aim at direct knowledge of the spiritual, not the bodily, Jesus.

Later, as John went down from the cave to the city and met others who told him about Jesus' crucifixion, John laughed, presumably because he now knew, what they did not yet know, about Jesus' *un*suffering immortality. Complementary apocryphal accounts go even further. For example, the canonical synoptic gospels tell us that the Roman soldiers accompanying Jesus to his crucifixion forced a certain Simon of Cyrene to carry Jesus' cross; but another account has Jesus swap identity with Simon, so that while Simon (who now looks like Jesus) is being crucified, Jesus himself is said to be in heaven laughing at the triumphant success of his deception. Yet another account has one Jesus being crucified, while another and superior, spiritual Jesus ("the living Jesus") hovers above the cross, laughing: "And the Savior said to me: 'He whom you saw being glad and laughing above the cross is the living Jesus. But he into whose hands and feet they are driving nails, is his fleshly . . . substitute.' "[6]

These variations of a sacred tale may now seem frivolous or shocking, and may well have seemed shocking to some people then. For us, at least in the official western Christian tradition, laughter usually undermines religious piety. Humor is not what we expect to find in committed religious texts, or indeed serious academic discussion. Laughter, Clement of Alexandria wrote disapprovingly, is the prelude to fornication. During religious services in church, the Christian faithful are conventionally expected to be solemn and restrained.[7] But in these apocryphal writings, humor works in partnership with miracles to break up our normal understandings. Humor works by inversion. It turns the normal world upside down and fractures conventions with unconventional juxtapositions. Humor softens us up, and so makes us all the more prepared to accept the extraordinary elements in Christian belief, such as man made God, the virgin birth, the resurrection of the body, and life after death. Eventually, the incredible becomes, at least for believers, part of an expectable, acceptable normality.

Behind the laughter we can see a serious message. In these apocryphal stories Jesus enhances his divinity, not by his humanity but by his mysterious defiance of nature. And so Jesus is represented in various stories and in rapid sequence as both young and old, small and large, soft and

hard, father and mother and son, male and female. The binary oppositions which are so central to religious myths are offered here only to be
dissolved.[8]

In the Acts of John, for example, a woman had a vision of Jesus simultaneously appearing both like John himself and as a youth. In puzzle-
ment, the woman asks John for an explanation. John says he cannot tell
her, or indeed write down, all that he saw and heard when he was a disciple of Jesus. Typically, the revelatory text reveals only part of the truth.
Some inner secrets are held back for the elite of believers. For the moment, John replies, he can reveal only what different people are capable
of understanding. So to help us understand, he tells us a story from his
own experience. Once Jesus had summoned him and his brother James.
As they approached, James saw Jesus as a child, while John saw him as a
beautiful man. Later that day, Jesus appeared to John as bald but with a
flowing beard, whereas to James he appeared as a young man whose
beard was just starting. Both disciples were perplexed at these inexplica-
ble differences in Jesus' appearance, and for John the problem was compounded because Jesus also sometimes appeared to him as an ugly dwarf,
and at other times as a huge giant. And even stranger, when at table, John
would sometimes sit on Jesus' knee and cuddle him. And sometimes Jesus' breast was tender like a woman's, at other times hard as a rock, like a
man's.[9]

We can speculate about interpretation. Perhaps it is all about the un-
trustworthiness of external appearances, but I think that such passages
are meant to be puzzling and confusing. After all, for religious leaders, a
lack of understanding among the faithful is advantageous. These texts
help instill in the faithful a recognition of the glory of the divine and of
the enormous gap between divinity and humanity, and so induce a necessary sense of dependency. Our failure to comprehend piques our curiosity but also makes us feel humble, inadequate, and guilty because of
our inadequacy; and so we are in an ideal state for instruction by specialist religious interpreters. They instruct us kindly, but also (like modern
physicians) leave us not quite understanding what they say. As Jesus says
in the Gospel of Thomas: "Let him who seeks continue seeking until he
finds. When he finds, he will be troubled. When he becomes troubled,
he will be astonished." These texts are miracles of the word. They leave
us cowed, overawed by the magical power of a confusing divinity.[10]

Many other early Christian texts are similarly astonishing. For example, in a second- or third-century collection of Christian hymns, the Odes of Solomon, the nineteenth ode celebrates God the Father as a woman with breasts:

> The Son is the Cup,
> and he who was milked is the Father;
> and the Holy Spirit is she who milked him.
> Because his breasts were full,
> and it was undesirable that his milk should be spilled without purpose,
> the Holy Spirit opened her bosom/womb
> and mixed the milk of the two breasts of the Father.[11]

Or again, the Secret Book of John reveals a vision in which John saw Jesus change before his very eyes from young boy to old man and say: "Do not be afraid, I am with you always. I am the Father, I am the Mother, I am the Son, eternal, immaculate."[12]

In some of these images we can spot a specific theological message. For example, the scene above the crucifixion of Jesus in the Acts of John, with which we began, implies that for some Christians, as for many pagans, it was impossible to conceive of God dying. These Christians, the so-called Docetists, in their version of the central Christian myths, tried to avoid representing the physical death of the divine Jesus with as much passion as the more orthodox Christians, then and now, seek to avoid the sexuality of Jesus' conception. Where orthodox Christians proclaimed the virgin birth, the heretical Docetists claimed that Jesus was God, not man, and did not suffer on the cross.

But we have to be careful when we attribute motifs within a story to a particular theological sect, lest we privilege only one strand in a complex tale. As I see it, each nexus of religious myths offers a set of solutions to core human problems (where did we come from? who are we? what is good about our lives? how should we behave? what is going to happen to us when we die?). The myths often work by setting up a series of binary oppositions (man/God, good/evil, life/death) and then seeking to resolve the problems which the oppositions have posed, by offering mediations; for example, Christians offer a Messiah who is both human and divine, a God who hates but forgives sins, and an everlasting life which overcomes death.

The bald simplicity of my outline may seem objectionable to some believers, partly because the structural core of Christian religious belief is seductively obscured in the charter myth package. For example, the life and sayings of Jesus are accompanied by dramatic stories of miracles, confrontation between good and evil, ethical heroism, persecution, cruel death, and salvation. The variety of slightly incompatible but complementary stories (such as we find in the different canonical gospels with or without the apocrypha) allows the ambiguity which is necessary to attract a wide variety of the faithful, and also rams home the same basic message in different styles. Besides, believers never seem to be satisfied with a single, uncomplicated account of their religion. They repeatedly invent new versions of the old story. That is not surprising. What is amazing is that some sectarians within each religion claim that they alone understand the true meaning of the ambiguous message.

An analogy may help clarify my argument. Take Christmas, for example. At home, at Christmas each year, we give one another gifts. Ask young children what happens at Christmas, and they might tell you that they celebrate the birth of Jesus, but they will probably tell you of the gifts which they have received, or hope to get. Typically, these gifts are elaborately wrapped in days of expectation, and in glittering paper tied with colored string, designed both to disguise the present and to delay the impatient opener. Afterward, the reluctant child in well brought up families is expected to write letters, or nowadays to make telephone calls, effusively thanking relatives for presents which perhaps the child did not particularly like. I hope that my point is by now clearer. Of course, we could say that the central point of Christmas is the birth of Jesus, or getting presents, or both, just as we could say that the central point of myth is its implicit theology. But we can also say that reducing complexity to single, simple meanings is to miss the point, and that both the presents and the theologies are given delicious uncertainty, even by the seemingly hackneyed rituals and wrappings, stories and dramas, with which they are surrounded. Specialist interpreters may know what complex rituals mean; the faithful are probably less certain.

LAUGHTER FROM THE CROSS

Up to now I have been arguing that each nexus of religious myths contains mildly incompatible but complementary narratives, embodying ethical prescriptions, purported solutions to central metaphysical problems, and tales of physically improbable wonders. What I want to do now is to present a Christian apostle narrative, constructed in antiquity as a complement to the canonical gospels and the Acts of the Apostles. It is the Acts of Andrew, written in Greek probably in the second half of the second century, translated into Latin, Coptic, and Armenian, and widely known up to the fourth century and later.[13] The central character is the hero, apostle Andrew, who traveled around the eastern Mediterranean working miracles, exorcising demons, resuscitating the dead, curing the sick, slaying the odd dragon, having visions, making prophecies, and converting both the masses and politically important individuals.[14]

The villain is the wicked Roman provincial governor; the ingenue heroine is the governor's wife, recently cured from a serious illness by St. Andrew and converted to Christianity.[15] She is assisted by the governor's brother, also a new Christian convert. There is a small cast of extras, mostly soldiers and slaves, with the general populace acting as chorus. The dialogue between these characters gives dramatic tension and allows the overt expression of the divergent views which flourished and fought for supremacy within early Christianity.

The action begins with a miraculous cure by Andrew. A favorite slave of the governor's brother has fallen incurably sick, "smitten by a demon." All the pagan magicians have given him up for lost. But the apostle, old and poorly dressed, pushes his way through the ranks of suspicious household slaves who try to block his path and hit him. The apostle prays to the Christian God and dramatically cures the slave. The apostle's primary identity here is as a miraculous healer. He cures, of course, not by magic but by a simple appeal to the God ("who does not listen to magicians"). The contrast between Christian "religion" and the opposition's "magic" is recurrent in these tales.

The governor's brother is impressed by the slave's miraculous recovery.[16] So he too, helped by his sister and the apostle, is converted to Christianity. In fantasy at least, early Christians were already aiming at, but not yet quite reaching, the apex of political power. Their targets were the weak links in the power chain, the top man's wife or brother but not yet the top man himself. The chief power holder is still represented as an enemy. So upper-class conversions inevitably have a political dimension because they invite open conflict between the Roman civil power, which has made Christianity illegal, and committed Christians.

But back to the governor's brother. His conversion is portrayed as a pregnancy. He comes to realize inside himself that the old gods are vacuous, that his pursuit of philosophy (that is, of Roman secular culture) has been a waste of time, and that with the help of the apostle as midwife, he can bring out from inside himself the new Christian person latent within him. But as a member of the elite, he also expects the privilege of private instruction. The apostle obliges, but insists that his new birth, his rebirth as a Christian, must be heard out loud like a woman's labor pains, in public.[17] This repeated metaphoric gender glide, man as woman, reminds us that our story inhabits the mysterious world of religion, in which normal boundaries can be, should be, easily transgressed.

Enter the villain, the provincial governor, representative of Roman power, but also the snake and the son of the Devil. On the Lord's day the new Christians and Andrew gather, in response to the persistent requests of the governor's wife, spoiling for a showdown, in her bedroom.[18] Then, as the story demands, the husband returns home unexpectedly from a long trip abroad.[19] The wife is understandably worried about what his reaction will be when he finds so many people in her bedroom. So Andrew prays for a miracle to save the Christians. The husband enters the house, has crippling stomach pains, asks for a chamber pot, and is too preoccupied with his insides to notice the crowd of Christians filing past him on their way out. Rich pagan rulers clearly deserve all that is coming to them, but this is low comedy with a moral drive.[20] Christian literature is telling us here that beneath their rich robes, even rulers have their problems.

Once recovered, the governor goes to his bedroom burning with sexual passion after his long absence, but finds his wife at prayer. He is delighted to hear her say his name, and optimistically imagines that she is praying for him. But *we* know that she is actually asking God to save her from her husband's filthy intercourse. She wants to remain pure and chaste, giving service only to God. I cannot be alone, now or then, in feeling some sympathy for the husband. For twelve years she has been a good wife, forgiving his occasional peccadilloes, and just when he wants to kiss her on the mouth, she pushes him back with a priggish excuse: "After prayer, a woman's mouth should never touch a man's." As I see it, the effect here is both to exploit sexual tension as a storytelling device (we want to know what happens next) and to represent Christianity as a religion of sexual denial and social rebellion. In the Roman world of taken for granted male supremacy, the wife's rebellion, legitimated by the claims of Christianity, must have seemed shocking, even outrageous.

And yet it must have reminded every pagan woman who thought about what her secret Christianity might involve of the dangers she would encounter, or already had.

The stage is set for the inevitable conflict between Christianity and paganism, between male civilian power and the Christian wife aided by the apostle. The struggle is unequal. We know who will win, but not yet how. While the husband sleeps alone, the wife invites Andrew to visit her in another bedroom of the house. The implied relationship between saint and heroine is of repressed sexuality. St. Andrew comes. He prays to God for the wife's purity, for her protection "from this disgusting pollution" of sleeping with the vile body of her earthly husband, that insolent and hostile snake. Instead, she should wed her invisible inner husband.

To help her out of her predicament (pushy husband versus asexual desire), the wife gets one of her slaves, a pretty and extremely lascivious slut, to take her place in bed (so much for the story's alleged feminism).[21] And for eight months (note the carefully chosen period) this scheme works, while the wife spends all her time, even overnight, with Andrew and, of course, the other brethren. But the slave girl, exploiting her utility, begins to blackmail her mistress. She brags about her prowess to her fellow slaves and, when the governor is drunk, even gets them to watch her at work.

The apostle has a dream and predicts trouble. Sure enough, the wife's other slaves betray her to her husband. He is outraged, cuts out the sexy slave's tongue, cuts off her hands and feet, and throws her to be food for the dogs. The three slaves who have betrayed their mistress to him are crucified. Rough justice this, but it all goes to show, doesn't it, that sexuality, hypocrisy, and being a slave don't pay. Admittedly, the Roman governor, the villain, is made out to be unspeakably cruel, but the story's implied morality is that the suffering of a slave or two is as nothing in the pursuit of the asexual virtue of an upper-class Christian mistress.

After such a bloody human sacrifice, the wife persists in her holy task. The husband first grieves, fasts, and reviles his gods; then, rather touchingly, he begs his wife to let things go back to how they used to be. He is prepared to forgive her, even if she loves another; he still loves her deeply, and wants to sleep with her, have intercourse with her, have children by her. Indeed, so he says, he has always treated her like a goddess. This is a nice touch, since in this Christian novel, it is exactly the approach (as so often at this stage of a relationship) which is least likely to pay off. She is adamant: she is in love—she repeats, in love—with another world.

The denouement of the struggle between Roman civil power and Christian spiritual authority is at hand. Civil power is forced (as often too in modern times) by saintly intransigence into unjust repression, which in turn undermines the government's own legitimacy. Andrew is arrested, imprisoned, and threatened with cruel punishment. The governor's last desperate play is worthy of an opera by Puccini: return to sex and I'll free your lover. But the offer is firmly rejected; sex and Christian virtue are incompatible.[22] With divine aid the governor's wife becomes invisible, and so magically evades the guards put around her bedroom at home. With the help of an angel she visits Andrew in his prison cell, kisses him (he is, after all, "the Lord disguised as Andrew"), and says adieu.[23] He advises her warmly against sex, and next day walks willingly to his place of crucifixion. Death, especially a martyr's death, in this type of literature, is to be welcomed calmly. Death is the gateway to a better life.

When Andrew is being crucified in a particularly cruel way—tied, not nailed, and with his knees unbroken—he too smiles and laughs, and addresses the crowd in a striking speech, delivered from the cross itself: "Men, women, children, old, slaves, free, and any others who hear me. . . . I exhort you all to rid yourselves of this life, which is painful, vain, senseless, boastful, empty, perishable, transitory, the friend of pleasures, the slave of time."[24] So enthralled was the crowd by the fervor and brilliance of St. Andrew's teaching that they all listened to him, all two thousand of them, and not a single one of them left, even though Andrew went on preaching "for three whole days and nights." But on the fourth day, the crowd, filled with admiration for the saint's abundance of words, clear reasoning, and noble spirit, rushed off angrily to the governor and protested at his sacrilegious judgment. They asked for the holy man to be pardoned, spared, and let down. At first the governor was inclined to ignore the crowd. But then he worried that they might get out of hand and riot. Governors were above all expected to raise taxes and keep peace. If the crowd caused trouble, his own reputation and head might be at risk. So he promised to set Andrew free. The crowd was jubilant.

And so this scene ends with the implausible image of a triumphant crowd and of the Roman provincial governor personally stooping to untie the bonds of a convicted Christian martyr. But the martyr himself angrily rejects the governor's clumsy and belated attempts to deliver human justice. And he is disappointed with the joyful crowd, because they have simply failed to understand his spiritual message, namely that he must die, and that he longs to die, and that life on earth is not worth living.

Behind the apparent simplicity of the story there lurks a whole series of serious messages. Implicitly, the canonical history of Jesus' own crucifixion is being rewritten. Jesus himself, like Andrew, could have been spared. If only Jesus had wanted it, the Roman governor could have been made to change his mind. But perhaps Jesus, like Andrew, actually wanted to die. In the canonical gospels, the governor Pilate is weak minded; in the apocryphal Acts of Pilate, he is on Jesus' side, is extremely reluctant to kill Jesus, is forced to by the Jewish leaders, and later repents.[25] Here the governor crawls at Andrew's feet. At least in fantasy, Christianity has already conquered Rome and made her its subject. In the canonical gospels, the Jewish crowd is anti-Jesus; but here the crowd is pro-Andrew, on the Christian side; they are the powerful and outraged defenders of justice, humiliating the Roman governor and getting him to undo his unjust decision. But complementarily, the masses, as in the Acts of John, do not understand spiritual truths and necessities—they are crudely and unthinkingly prolife. Their hearts are in the right place, but true understanding is reserved for an inner elite of knowing Christians.

One seemingly incidental, unrealistic, and amusing episode reinforces my suggestion that the Acts of Andrew are implicitly rewriting the canonical gospels' account of Jesus' crucifixion. Andrew's sermon to the crowd lasts for three whole days and nights. By implication, as I see it, Andrew now does what Jesus should have done. Andrew spent the three days after his crucifixion in teaching the living, not in saving the dead, in rescuing the great Jewish leaders from hell. By implication, understanding and knowledge for the living counts for much more than the resurrection of fleshy and corrupt bodies. And of course, Andrew, like Jesus in the Acts of John, does not suffer on the cross; instead he smiles and laughs. And in explanation, Andrew tells the governor that Jesus (but here Andrew is clearly speaking of himself) "is not a man who can be punished" (AA 149). Andrew is like Jesus. He is a Jesus look-alike.

Theologically, the message of these Acts is complex, and interestingly inventive in its particular blend of well-known ingredients. Each of us has within us a seed of immortality, an element of the divine. After all, man is made in God's image, or as the Gospel of Philip aggressively puts it, humans make God; it is therefore God who should worship humans.[26] At the very least, in this view, humans and gods are reciprocals. Each of us, with effort, can and should use all his or her spiritual energy to foster the God within us. Each of us, to express the idea with stark clarity, should create our own Jesus. Unfortunately, this optimistic theology has its pessimistic complement. Each of us also has within his or her body that shell of corrupting desires, the seeds of destruction. Life is a continuous struggle between the good and the bad inside us. And the artful Devil is always trying to trap us. Only death brings freedom from this continuous tension. And only the fortunate few can win redemptive salvation.

In the apocryphal Acts of Andrew, the key to this precious redemptive salvation is Andrew himself. Andrew is in essence a Jesus look-alike, a second redeemer, "the Lord in Andrew's form" (AA 146). It is as though Christians, at this stage of the religion's development, saw no reason to rely on a single foundation myth, codified in a canonical New Testament. For later Christians there came to be only one authoritative Jesus, the "historical" Jesus enshrined as a single composite figure drawn from the New Testament gospels. So too there came to be for many Christians only one privileged set of sacred accounts of Jesus' life, sayings, and miracles, though the institutionalized monopoly of the canonical was not firmly established until the third or fourth century. But in the earlier stages of Christianity (and indeed until much later), Jesus was a figure who could be piously reduplicated. His appearance on earth was not constrained to one particular location or to one particular set of loyal and privileged disciples. The message of an interventionist God had to be sold to the faithful and to would-be converts by multiple reappearances. So Andrew/Jesus is merely one manifestation of God's spiritual emanation, appearing to humans in bodily form.

Of course, there was a significant theological difference between the original Jesus and this refurbished Andrew/Jesus. For conventional Christians, Jesus became the one and only salvific redeemer, whose suffering sacrifice gave all humanity the chance of salvation. Our Andrew/Jesus seems rather different. He is, I think, not himself the redeemer, but rather the agent through whom his followers and imitators can achieve understanding of the divine. It is as though they discover, through Andrew, how to carry God inside themselves. And to the extent that the followers succeed, they themselves become godlike, though of course in an inferior and imitative way. And so a radical and subversive theology of creating God for yourself, without the intervention of priests, is sold in a seductive way, by means of an apparently simple story.

The naivety of these stories should not lead us to underestimate the importance of their functions. The stories are not merely records of miraculous divine performances acted out by Jesus or his apostles. The stories are themselves performative. By performative I mean—and I do think that this is both a simple and a striking point—that the mere reading of the story by itself constitutes a repeat performance of the miracle which it records. For believers, that is the chief significance of the story. Christian believers benefited from a staggering human invention, made I do not know when or by whom, namely, that it was very much easier to tell stories about miracles than to perform them. One way in which we can hope to reexperience the experiences of ancient believers is to rehear their stories, albeit with twentieth-century ears. At least, that is a beginning.

ON METHOD, OBJECTIONS, AND A RESPONSE

I was not at all confident about what I had written so far, so I sent the typescript out to several friends, including a church historian in Germany whom I greatly admire. He wrote to me as follows.

> Theologische Fakultät
> Heidelberg
>
> My dear Keith,
>
> Thank you for sending me your brief manuscript. I assume that it is part of a larger project, since as it stands it violates most of the sensible rules of ordinary history. But just in case you are satisfied with it, and do not plan to frame it in the conventional way, I thought it might be helpful, since I have had a few thoughts about it, to set out my objections as clearly as I can. I hope

you don't mind my concentrating on your faults (as I see them). I'm sure you're well enough aware of your strengths without my help. I group my objections under four heads, in no particular order of priority:

1. the cream bun syndrome
2. opacity and reproducibility
3. contextualization
4. your duty as a historian

You clearly like telling stories, and you tell them quite well, for an amateur. But history and storytelling are quite different. I need hardly tell you that they diverged centuries ago. Of course, the historian can, and occasionally perhaps even should, tell a story to lighten his text (you see I am not as stuffy as you make me out to be; I too like a joke). But history, as I should not have to tell you, is concerned with fact, and if possible with truth.[27] OK, I fully realize that a purely objective history is impossible, but there are some advantages in the dominant convention that we put our conclusions as objectively and as impersonally as possible. The opposition—stories are fiction, designed for entertainment; history, by contrast, is serious business, designed for edification—is much too crude. But you know what I mean, and which side of the fence I think is preferable. And finally, I really don't feel comfortable with your superficial impressionism. A quick clever essay on a huge topic, instead of a sturdy monograph. There are advantages in German thoroughness, even over English whimsy.

My colleagues here in Heidelberg would not have to be told all this. They take it for granted, whereas I at least am willing to see that there could be an argument. And I do realize that we pay the penalty of our own commitment to truth, thoroughness, and accuracy. Not many people read our books. But, and this is my main point, your divergent tack is equally problematic. Hence, what I lightly call the cream bun syndrome. One story may be amusing; two stories may be tolerable; the third story sticks in the gullet or (to change metaphors) begins to bore; and any subsequent story makes your satiated audience feel more than slightly sick.

Stories tyrannize and infantilize their audience. When the truly professional historian describes, analyzes, and proposes explanations, we can contrapose opposing or complementary explanations, and exceptions to his generalizations. But when you tell stories, how can I respond, except with a polite smile, or a yawn, a laugh, or another story? If we all did what you are doing (heaven forbid) we would finish up only with reciprocal boredom: I tell you a story, and then I listen to one of yours. In fact, although you make a bold attempt to be more interesting than conventional historians, you finish up by being a bigger bore. I am sorry to be so frank.

That was my first objection. My second objection relates to opacity and reproducibility, and I can be briefer now. Your stories do not make sense by themselves. I think the problem is that you pose as a passive relayer of the original narrative. Peter Brown also tells stories, but no one is in any doubt that the stories which he tells are his own.[28] But you tell stories as though they were the originals, with minor and (let me stress) sometimes indistinct editorializing. Your mixture of narrative and exegesis is quite confusing. What you are really doing is simplifying and reducing quite complex originals to their bare bones. And this is not justifiable, at least not unless you tell your readers that this is what you are doing, and how you are doing it.

In any case, most scholars will have read the original sources, so I'm not quite sure what sort of audience you are aiming at. For nonscholars, the stories do not make immediate sense, or rather it is not obvious what sense the nonspecialized reader should make of them. Nor do you make clear why we should trust your particular version of an ancient story. So the mere reportage or simplification of the stories leaves your readers both uninformed and puzzled. Anyhow, you are attributing much too much importance to really rather minor and peripheral sources, which theologians and church historians have justly treated as marginal. They were not very important in antiquity and are still not important, compared with the great church fathers.

And that is not all. You are being far too idealist. History, whether we like it or not, is part of scientific knowledge *(akademische Wissenschaft)*. We have responsibilities to our students. Conventional historical knowledge, real knowledge of the sources, is testable, summarizable, objective, and reproducible. How on earth do you expect our students to reproduce your stories and subjective commentary in their exams? You can't expect it; it is just too frivolous for words. They have to pass exams.

So far you will think that I have been too destructively critical. But I really do want to help. Surely your stories (and this is my third point) would make better sense if you set them in a traditional context, and told us quite simply who wrote the apocryphal acts and who read them. You could do worse than quote or summarize the classic old commentaries in Schneemelcher, supplemented by the recent work of Junod and Kaestli on the Acts of John and Prieur on the Acts of Andrew, for example.[29] Both are exemplary editions, which show the strength of what I could call the continental European traditions of scholarship. Here we do things rather thoroughly, leaving superficial essays to the English!

I have made my three points. My fourth is a simple admonition. You are trading on your reputation as a serious historian in order to foist irresponsible work on our profession. They will quite understandably and properly reject or ignore the insights which you have, unless you show that your work is serious and scholarly.

Best wishes, and love to Jennifer,
Hartmut

In due course, after a lot of thought, I answered Hartmut's letter as follows.[30]

King's College,
Cambridge CB2 2IST

My dear Hartmut,

I am glad I don't have too many forthright friends like you. But thank you very much for being so frank. It really was very helpful. Would you mind awfully if I answer your comments in a different order? I'd like to take up your point on contextualization first. Here my response is simple surrender. Of course, you are right. I imagine and hope that the following paragraphs are something like what you had in mind.

When the apocryphal Acts were written, Christians were proscribed and occasionally persecuted. They had no effective mechanisms for ensuring uniformity of belief or practice. And so, a bewildering variety of believers called themselves, and probably sincerely thought of themselves as, Christians, even though they espoused beliefs which more orthodox Christians subsequently rejected or abhorred. By orthodox, I mean here beliefs which later Christian power holders legitimized as orthodox.

Even during this period, say 150–250 CE, church leaders were reacting to the plurality of Christian views by evolving the primacy of what we now know as the New Testament. By the late second century, there probably was a core of conventional Christian belief. But we should be cautious; most surviving second-century Christian writings outside the New Testament and before Irenaeus and Tertullian (admittedly there are not many of them) barely mention the New Testament writings. They get their legitimating texts instead from the Old Testament. In other words, the New Testament was by no means yet the central pivot of Christian self-identity which it later became.

The apocryphal Acts were written initially in the second and third centuries CE as pious Christian tracts by unknown individuals, who worked over and recombined elements of the Christian tradition with motifs and storytelling tactics drawn from the pagan world.[31] They claimed authorship by or close association with Jesus' leading apostles, and drew legitimacy from these claims. Just as bishops from the second century onward were claiming direct and continuous succession from the apostles as the basis of their monopolistic authority to celebrate liturgy and to appoint priests, so these apocryphal Acts, by contrast, implicitly made the teaching of the apostles the property of all who read them and believed in them with faith. Bishops, such as Ignatius, stressed their own episcopal authority. The apocryphal Acts do not mention bishops, and very rarely mention priests. They are thus covertly antiauthoritarian. But they are committedly Christian, offering texts which are complementary to, rather than contradictory of, the canonical gospels and Acts of the Apostles.

For centuries, reputable fathers of the church continued to cite some of the apocrypha with approval, though others were dubious or hostile.[32] But eventually, especially after heretics such as Manichaeans and Iconoclasts in the eighth century admired and used the apocryphal writings as proof texts, the apocrypha came to be disregarded and officially despised. That said, whatever the official judgment, the apocryphal texts were copied, emended, and translated into Greek, Syriac, Coptic, Latin, Ethiopic, Armenian, and Georgian. This variety and their survival in different versions bears witness to their continuous popularity among Christians.

I hope, Hartmut, that this is the sort of contextualization that you had in mind. Let me now try to deal with your other trenchant comments. Roughly speaking (I paraphrase), you thought that my versions of these Christian stories were boring, reductionist, unfocused, nonreproducible, unprofessional, and irresponsible.

Of course, I could counterattack and say that conventional scholarship on the apocryphal Acts often concentrates on systematizing and labeling the theological statements which are scattered throughout the texts, and on finding parallels with them in other literature. So the virtue of self-control comes from Stoicism, spiritual rebirth from Platonism, personal unity with God from Neopythagoreanism; the battle between good and evil is dualistic, or Manichaean; the opposition between flesh and spirit is Gnostic; the nonsuffering Jesus is Docetist. That is all good intellectual fun; and in a way it is both helpful and misleading. It helps us to see what a mixture of received wisdom the apocryphal texts draw on, but it is misleading because it tempts us to devalue the benefits of confused wisdom. At first sight, all these labels constitute enviable objective knowledge. But they tempt us to imagine that ancient readers read (or heard) these stories with these theological categories in mind. And besides, these heretical labels are also part of a conventional Christian tactic of categorizing the apocryphal Acts as marginal, populist, local, and heretical, and therefore of no particular concern to sophisticated Christian orthodoxy.

These apocryphal Acts are stories, not theological treatises, and in my view all the better for that. The art of the story is that it tries to find a way of binding together incompatible views in the same package, using suppressed sexuality, ethereal spirituality, dramatic tension, and anti-Roman sentiment as a volatile glue. For example, in the Acts of Andrew, the hero (rather like Odysseus returning from Troy) is the old and poorly dressed apostle who struggles for admission to the governor's courtyard. He is rebuffed by arrogant slaves but enters by sheer charismatic authority. Only we, the readers, and the governor's wife (like an ascetic Penelope) recognize his true virtue. The privileged governor's wife is the heroine who recognizes the errors of her former fleshly ways, but at the same time symbolizes an ecstatic, emotional, impassioned approach to God.

The subhero, the governor's brother, another rich guy, is, in effect, the apostle's exemplary disciple. His approach to God, in contrast to the heroine's, is intellectualist and mystical. But he never quite understands the master's message—a storyteller's tactic, this, like Dr. Watson to Sherlock

Holmes, which allows us to be told and retold what the message is. His spiritual trajectory is complementary to the heroine's. He begins as an offstage soldier, then renounces violence with the aim of dedicating himself to secular philosophy. But then he gives secular philosophy up too for Christianity, a process which turns him from independent man to dependent woman, who bears his/her own soul in a spiritual rebirth. The villain governor is vital to the action, since he symbolizes the enemy, whether Romans or the Devil or pagan flesh eaters, and he helps to give the heroes identity. It is only in competition with the Devil that God can show his virtue; their mutual "enmity becomes a kind of friendship" (AA 17).

The story's soft revelatory tactic of leaving most of its arguments unclearly stated and unresolved is not one which we are used to, or rather it is not one which we are taught to admire in university departments, which stress instead the virtues of formal and sequential scientific reasoning. The dogmatic theologian seeks consistency, but at the cost of recreating this messy world in his own image. The Christian novelists, by contrast, are purposefully not dogmatists but compromisers, allowing different protagonists in the dialogues to sketch their complementary views. By implication, readers also can choose to invest the text with as much meaning as they want and, if they see religion as a matter of competing beliefs, can choose whichever sect they like best.

What I am suggesting here is that the Christian romance was to theology what soft microhistory (as in the works of Simon Schama, Robert Darnton, Carlo Ginzburg) is to formal history.[33] Each creates the need for the other; they are complementary, and not necessarily enemies. The Christian apocryphal romance was one reaction, one supplement, to the intellectual transcendentalization of the Christian God in ancient theology. Similarly, novelistic, soft history is one response to the overproduction of narrow historical monographs.

A final gloss. I think you are right once again. I have reduced some of the stories to their bare bones, and stories do infantilize. I have three justifications.

First, the originals are quite long-winded, so pruning them is a mercy.

Second, I suspect, though I cannot prove, that preachers and Christian propagandists would have used some such simplified versions orally in persuading the faithful to stay faithful. Incidentally, since the originals were written in quite a sophisticated style and language, which shows a close acquaintance with classical literature, such as only a tiny proportion of the ancient population (well less than 5 percent) could master, it seems likely that these Christian novels were written in, and appealed to, exactly the same subelite social circles which consumed Christian theology.

Finally, infantilization. Religious stories are designed not merely to mix the miraculous and the real, but also to persuade, by getting us to suspend critical disbelief. Infantilization is a useful, perhaps even necessary component of religious practice. I wouldn't want to teach economic history this way, but to omit it from religious history would be misleading.

History is a broad church, Hartmut. There is room for variety. I appreciated your jibe about English superficiality: I too admire the work of Junod,
Kaestli, and Prieur. I agree their editions are exemplary. But each runs to
more than eight hundred pages. There surely should be room in the academic marketplace for briefer discussions also. My aim in retelling stories
with editorial asides is to give the reader or listener the vicarious experience
of living in antiquity, albeit for a short time, without ever leaving the modern
world. I exchange objective rationalism for empathetic imagination. Of
course, I recognize that we can never really go back so far in time, into another culture; inevitably, we always look at antiquity through modern glasses.
But at least we can try to imagine what it was like to be there; and these ancient stories, even if retold, allow us to glimpse how some ancients constructed their worlds. I may sacrifice reproducible clarity, but just imagine the
glory of being a martyr.

Love to Heidi,

Yours ever,

Keith

JESUS' TWIN BROTHER

In spite of Hartmut's criticisms, I still want to tell another story. Not
just out of obstinacy, though there may be some of that, but more because the underlying structure of these apocryphal narratives becomes
visible only when we superimpose one tale upon another. Besides, given
my chapter title, how can I quit without mentioning Jesus' twin brother?

Judas Thomas ("Thomas" is Syriac for "twin") is the twin brother of
Jesus and the hero of the Acts of Thomas, originally written in Syriac,
probably at the beginning of the third century.[34] But the work was soon
translated into Greek, and later into Latin, Coptic, Armenian, Arabic,
and Ethiopic. Like the other apocryphal Acts of apostles, the Acts of
Thomas were also used and adapted by Manichaeans (see Chapter
Seven). But they were originally written as pious Christian literature and
were long regarded as pious by loyal Christians. Witness the multiple
translations and different versions. For example, the longest Greek versions preserve more of the original, whereas the surviving Syriac versions have been altered to fit in with a later Catholic orthodoxy.

The Acts of Thomas comprise a long and complex cycle of stories,
written with some artistry and care. As I see it, the text moves on three
intersecting planes or levels. On the first level, the Acts ostensibly con-
sist of a series of miracle tales, complete with the elements we have come

to expect in these apocryphal Acts: suppressed eroticism combined with a vivid, even violent antipathy to sexuality; repentant sinners who confess their faults (and are wonderfully cured); appearances by the Devil in multiple guises—boastful, defeated, slain but renascent—like a master criminal in a TV series; exorcisms; resuscitations from the dead; spectacular conversions and miracles; even talking animals. The second level comprises some strikingly powerful prayers and exhortations, and two beautifully poetic hymns. The Song of the Pearl, a highly ambiguous tale of moral education or self-discovery, is justifiably famous. The third level is an ethical pilgrim's progress. Thomas himself and implicitly we, the readers, with him gradually get to see the errors of our ways and ascend the path to salvation through spiritual knowledge.

But first a few words about Jesus' twin brother. In a sense, we have already met him, because each of the stories I have already told contained a Jesus look-alike of their own making. Why? Because theologically, as I understand it, one of the main messages of these apocryphal Acts is that the Jesus who matters most is the Jesus whom each of us can create for ourselves, inside ourselves. Just as Jesus encased his divinity inside a human body, so reciprocally we humans can through our necessarily imperfect perception and belief in Jesus become partly divine.[35] We live *by* Jesus, *in* Jesus, as some believers still say nowadays. Even so, for some conventional Christians, ancient or modern, this implicit human identification with Jesus may seem a blasphemously self-aggrandizing self-deification. For others it may be liberating.

But how does Jesus' twin fit in? Jesus' twin is on one level, I think, a metaphor for Jesus' own and believers' alternative identities. For Jesus, the twin is a lesser reflection. For believers, Jesus' twin is an enhanced image, but not as elevated as Jesus himself, and so, perhaps, rather like a later saint or martyr, more imitable and within reach. Perhaps it is best to see Jesus' twin brother as a supersaint, or as a metaphorical bridge between divinity and humanity. And yet, the Judas Thomas of these Acts is also obstinately human and mistaken. He takes time to see and grasp the divine. On the other hand, he can reveal himself to be almost divine or at least in touch with divinity. So within these Acts, Thomas occasionally, when performing a miracle, himself becomes Jesus, and (humorously) gets mistaken for Jesus—the traditional twin-confusion joke. And just as we and other onlookers confuse the two twins, so does the Devil. The

Devil, who is the pervasive archenemy of the early Christians, is (amazingly) deceived by this simple disguise of divinity in a human shell. Or at least, that is what the Acts of Thomas tell us, just as in the *Second Treatise of the Great Seth*, the Devil (and the Jews and Romans) were once deceived when Jesus swapped identity with Simon before the crucifixion. By this simple deception, the divine Jesus, and by proxy the divine within us, can manage to evade the evil demons who obstruct the elevation of human souls to heaven.

On a more mundane level, Jesus' twin brother is Judas Thomas, one of the apostles. He is also the purported author of the Gospel of Thomas, which contains over a hundred sayings of Jesus, many unrecorded in the canonical gospels.[36] The elevation of St. Thomas to be the twin brother of Jesus was probably in part a tactic aimed at increasing the authority and legitimacy of all the writings attributed to Thomas. It was also probably an attempt at claiming primacy for Thomas, and for the Christian communities which celebrated him as their founder, over rival communities with differing practices and beliefs. In other apocryphal stories, each of Jesus' apostles is allocated a particular region to convert. The Syrian church at Edessa, where the Acts of Thomas were probably written, went one better. They retrospectively adopted the Gospel of Thomas as their own, and also had their patron founder convert India, no less, to Christianity before having his body returned to be buried in Edessa, after his inevitable martyrdom.[37]

The image of Jesus having a twin brother who somehow shared in Jesus' own charisma, and could share it with an elite of believers was too attractive to forgo. I assume also that the idea of Jesus having a twin brother developed in competition with the idea of divine conception and virgin birth. In the second century, some Christians were already promoting the idea not only that Mary, the mother of Jesus, was a virgin at the time of her conception but also that she miraculously remained a virgin after giving birth. These writers dealt with Jesus' brothers and sisters, mentioned in the canonical gospels (Mark 6.3; Matthew 13.55–56), by envisaging them as the children of Joseph by a previous marriage. So, according to this story, James, the brother of Jesus and later leader of the primitive Christian community at Jerusalem until his martyrdom in 62 CE (Galatians 1.19), becomes Jesus' stepbrother. And he is the purported author of the First Gospel of James, which celebrates Mary's perpetual virginity. When she gave birth to Jesus in a cave, she was only Joseph's fiancée, and Joseph was already an old man; after the birth, the midwife came running out of the cave and shouted to Salome, one of Jesus' stepsisters, that Mary was still a virgin. Salome did not believe her: "Unless I insert my finger and test her condition, I will not believe that a virgin has given birth." She did, and her fingers burned with fire. She immediately regretted her lack of faith and prayed. The Lord God heard her prayer and sent an angel to tell her to touch the infant Jesus, and she was cured.[38]

Yet other early Christians either rejected the idea of the virgin birth altogether or were not particularly concerned about it. For example, some second-century Syrian Christians, roughly contemporary with the Acts of Thomas, denied that Jesus was born from the Virgin Mary; they believed that he came to earth in a spiritual, not in a carnal body.[39] Still other early Christians went along with the canonical gospels and acknowledged that Jesus really did have brothers and sisters, and so implicitly accepted that these siblings were the later children of Joseph and Mary.[40] Acceptance of this fact did not prevent the faithful from also believing in the miracle of the virgin birth and in the singularity of Jesus—any more than Matthew's long genealogy of Jesus, proving him to be a descendant of David, undermined claims that he was the Son of God.[41] One of the main functions of belief is to allow humans to hold incompatible views simultaneously. All that said, for some ancient Christians, as I see it, Jesus' twin was not so much a fact or a theological statement; Jesus' twin was more a metaphor for the possibility that each of us can, with effort, become like Jesus.

IN THE BRIDAL CHAMBER

The Acts of Thomas begin soon after Jesus' death.[42] Each of the apostles is to be given a territory to convert. They cast lots, and India falls to the lot of Judas Thomas. He is extremely reluctant to go. "I am not strong enough for this. And I am a Jew. How can I teach the Indians?" Jesus appears to him in a dream to reassure him, but still Thomas is obstinate and refuses. Like a normal mortal, he does not obey the Lord's commandment. But then Jesus comes back to earth, tricks Thomas, who cannot deny that Jesus is his master, by selling him as a slave (just as the other Judas Iscariot had sold Jesus) for twenty pieces of silver.[43] So Thomas, who like his grandfather Joseph is a carpenter, goes willy-nilly on his way to construct a new world.

The two men, Thomas and his earthly master, arrive en route at a port variously called Sandaruk or Andrapolis (the names mean "City of Sandalwood" and "City of Man"; we can choose between Oriental mystery or simple symbolism). As they disembark, they hear the sounds of music and much singing. The local king is having a wedding feast for the princess, his only daughter. The heralds proclaim that everyone must come to the feast, whether poor or rich, slave or free, citizen or alien. Refusal will be punished. The Oriental king, like the Roman emperor, expects everyone to participate in public (that is, pagan) festivals. But at the wedding feast, Thomas neither eats nor drinks. When a guest asks Thomas, "Why aren't you eating?" he replies, "I am come hither for something better than eating or drinking," and indicates that he is here under compulsion, on the orders of the (earthly) king. And he makes the sign of the cross on his forehead and over his heart. So too pious Christians were expected by their leaders to stand out from the pagan crowd, even at the risk of giving offense.[44]

A flute girl is doing her rounds. She comes up to the saint and plays right near him. But the saint firmly ignores her. One of the attendants, annoyed at Thomas' churlish behavior in refusing to participate in the festivities, slaps his face. Thomas does not, as we might have expected, turn the other cheek. Instead, he makes a dreadful prediction: "A dog will drag the hand which smote me" (AT 6). Of course, since he speaks in Aramaic, no one except the Jewish flute girl understands what he said. The story moves with a certain economy of character; the flute girl is both temptress and interpreter. It is at once a simple tale of sexual attraction and rejection and a holy tale of spiritual awakening and divine power.

After his prediction, Thomas sings a song about beauty, but not about the beauty of women or of the flute girl, who is so obviously about to fall in love with him. In this pious tale, the thrust of sexuality is suppressed. Sexual desire is etherealized as a metaphor for the love of salvation. The song which Thomas sings is a spiritual wedding song about the higher match which a man can make with the beautiful Daughter of Light, and about the superiority of spiritual over temporal power. The Daughter of Light was made by the first Creator, her chamber is full of perfume and light, truth floats above her head, joy dances at her feet, the planets attend her wedding, God is the bridegroom. The food is ambrosia, and the heavenly wine brings neither thirst nor desire. "And they glorified and praised the Father of Truth and the Mother of Wisdom" (AT 7)—which is itself a coded allusion to the first Creator, who created the Jewish God. But no one except the flute girl understands him, though they all look at him as he sings and notice his radiant, ecstatic transformation, brought on by his contemplation of the divine.

Meanwhile, the offending attendant has gone out to get some water from the public fountain. A roaming lion which happens to be there tears him limb from limb, and a black dog, which also happens to be there, carries one of his hands, in fulfillment of Thomas' prophecy, back to the inn where Thomas is. "And when they all saw it, they were amazed." The Jewish flute girl, in immediate renunciation of her previous lifestyle, breaks her flutes, falls at the apostle's feet, and so acknowledges Thomas' real identity: "This man is either God or the apostle of God"; and she tells everybody that she heard him prophesy what has come to pass (AT 9). Some of those around, our narrator tells us with arresting candor, believe her, and others don't. The disbelief of some throws into relief the virtue of those who have the courage to believe.

The story of the miraculous prophecy spreads, and the king hears about it. He invites Thomas to bless the bridal pair. Thomas comes to the palace and with bad grace blesses this merely human marriage, and ostentatiously departs. His blessing, "I beseech you, Lord Jesus, that you may do to them what helps, benefits, and is profitable for them," is strikingly unenthusiastic.[45]

The king has the room emptied of guests. The door of the bridal chamber is closed. The young prince lifts the curtain so that he can get into bed with his new bride. Imagine his astonishment: as well as the bride, he thinks he sees Thomas standing talking with her. He says, "But you just went out before everyone else. How is it that you are here now like this?" Jesus answers, "I am not Judas Thomas, but I am his brother" (AT 11), and the Lord sits down on the marriage bed and speaks to them in this wise:

> Abandon filthy intercourse and you will become pure and free from afflictions, and from the heavy burden of children. If you have children, then for their sakes you will become avaricious oppressors; and in turn you will be

made to suffer for their misdeeds. Besides, most children are unrewarding; they are either possessed by demons, lunatic, or consumptive. Even if they are healthy, they are still unrewarding . . . they are caught in adultery, murder, theft, or fornication, and by these too you will be afflicted.

But if you are persuaded and keep your souls pure, your lives will be undisturbed by grief or anxiety . . . and you will live in expectation of an eternal, incorruptible marriage of the bridal chamber of immortality and light. (AT 12–13; ending slightly abbreviated)

The young couple are convinced by what the Lord Jesus said, and abstain from filthy lust. They spend the whole night in wakefulness and self-control. But although they are pleased with their newfound way of life, the king and queen are astonished and outraged. The queen asks the bride why she is sitting unveiled in front of her husband, as though they had been married a long time. And the bride answers that "the mirror of shame has been taken from me" (AT 14), as though her rejection of sexuality with a "temporary husband" and her reunion with a true, immortal husband has allowed her to return to that state of paradise in which Adam and Eve once lived, before they discovered sex, shame, and death. Implicitly, the story quietly goes in reverse, back through the creation myth. The newly converted couple rejoice in a salvation which has brought them already back into the innocent delights of primal existence, before time. But the bride's conservative and pagan parents fail to understand, and in their fury pursue Thomas as a magician. But of course, it is too late. By then he has gone, farther on his long journey to India. The flute girl is brokenhearted.

To modern sensibilities, the starkly repressive asexuality of this radical brand of ancient Christianity seems shocking. We live in a culture which idealizes sexuality as a fundamental democratic freedom and pleasure. In the Roman world also, sexual pleasure for both men and women was openly celebrated, at least in some circles, as can be seen, for example, in the ruins and museums of Pompeii. Christian propagandists who attacked sexuality as intrinsically evil (and this is the repeated message of the Acts of Thomas and the Acts of Andrew) must have realized how much their asceticism differentiated them from secular Roman culture, and probably also from most of their own fellow Christians. Perhaps that was why Jesus himself, rather than Thomas, was the chosen spokesman. But even here, the bitter pill of abstinence is given a slight sugarcoating;

our author frames his stern prescription with the semicomic mistake of taking Jesus for his twin, Thomas.

The arena for this drama, as in an episode of the Acts of Andrew, is, surprisingly for an ancient story, the bedroom. Romantically, we are pulled along by our normal expectations of a marriage, though here those expectations are frustrated by pious celibacy. Even deeply committed normal Christians must have gasped at the timing and location of this conversion. For fervent ascetics, weddings were too good an opportunity to be missed: souls had to be saved, especially on the brink. Indeed, the conflict between carnal lust and pure asceticism among newlyweds became a trope of ancient Christian literature. According to Christian ascetic ideals, Christians denounced, while pagans celebrated, fertile marriages (plate 6).[46]

Theologically, the story leads us from the bridal chamber of carnality, where sexual acts used to happen but are now rejected, to a higher moral and religious plane, the bridal chamber of the spirit. Here, as we know from other early Christian writings, the bridal chamber is a metaphor for the reunion of human with God, and of male with female. This bridal chamber offers a spiritual rebirth, through which man and woman reunite to form the androgyne from which humanity originally sprang; through this ritual and story (which mirror each other) believers imitate and so become united with their androgynous Creator God.[47] In the beginning, so this revisionist ancient Christian story goes, before sin began, men and women were united. In the bridal chamber of the spirit they can be reunited. For some Christian sects, the holy bridal chamber represented a central focus of their common worship, though conservative Christian critics sneered at the actual immorality of their behavior, in defiance of all their leaders' ascetic ideals.

The lure of these apocryphal Acts is sex, though more sex repressed than sex attempted. First, we have the frustrated love of the flute girl for the uninterested saint, and then the unconsummated wedding of the young royal couple, diverted from short-term carnal pleasures by the persuasive words of Thomas and Jesus. They desert sexuality and celebrate instead the immortal blessings of the spiritual bridal chamber. They rebel against the conventional standards of their parents, and turn from worldly carnality to asexual piety. Later in the Acts of Thomas, in the two longest stories, Thomas converts the wife of the chief adviser to the king of India (AT 82–170). She immediately denies her husband his sexual rights and becomes besotted with Thomas.

The husband is by turns bewildered, outraged, vengeful, wheedling, and seductive. Some of their speeches ("Do you remember the time we first met? I remember how beautiful you looked"—countered by "But that was then, and this is now") are impressively moving. The drama follows the twists and turns in the husband's anger, his self-pity, his denunciation, and his pleading. Inevitably, his wife rejects him, and so shows up her own antisocial (subversive, even) preference for, and commitment to, the new religion. In the end, of course, the wife, freshly converted to asexuality, stands firm for her new faith. In a further twist of the same theme, the king's own wife, sent to restore the chief adviser's wife to her senses and to her husband, also converts to Christianity and also refuses her husband sex. In the ensuing confrontation, the people support the Christians, but the men of power take their revenge. The martyr is imprisoned, he repeatedly escapes to convert yet more people to Christianity, but in the end, Thomas is somewhat unceremoniously killed.

A central theme of these stories is the conflict between two men, the Christian hero-saint and the secular political ruler (governor, king's adviser, king). But once again, the pivot of the Thomas story is the woman, who switches her affections from earthly husband to heavenly Lord and through conversion to Christianity moves from the pollution of short-lived sexual pleasure to immortal salvation and ethereal spirituality. She gains power through sexual denial. The alienation of marital affections leads, inevitably, to conflict between the two men, since the king understandably blames the saint for his wife's unreasonable behavior.[48] And as the story demands, the king eventually has the sinless saint killed. The scenario in the Acts of Andrew, as we have already seen, is very similar.

The triangular theme, two men and one woman, is common enough in western myth and literature, though often the woman is only a cipher through whom the two men explore their mutual relations.[49] And indeed, in these stories too it is easy enough to see that the main drama here depends mostly on the conflict between the men, who represent the competing poles of political and religious power, of the secular and the sacred.[50]

But behind the fiction is there any glimmer of reality? The question is misconceived. As I see it, the fiction is part of the reality. A new religion could get established only by social rebellion. These texts are partly fictional, but they also reflect the pattern of rebellion by which wives and daughters, at first covertly and then openly, rebelled against male authority and used religion as the legitimator of their actions. In the foundation myths of modern Tibetan nunneries, a similar theme recurs; holy women founded nunneries after rebelling against the marriage wishes of their fathers.[51] The story then becomes the spur and legitimator of imitation. Women feel they have the right to rebel and follow their own religious enthusiasm in spite of male opposition. But this can only be part of the story; after all, males too entered and propagated the new religion of Christianity in opposition to convention. The female pivot, the wife who deserts her husband for a new faith, is a cultural construct. She is not herself the instigator of change; the prime movers are male (the saint, the king). Rather, as with Eve in Genesis or Mary in the New Testament, the woman is used as a register of change. In these Christian stories the woman is set up as the fall guy. She takes the blame for upsetting normal family life and for putting religion first. But she also makes it possible for a virulently antisexual message to be sold in a sexy package.

THE DEVIL DEFEATED

Sex is a central theme of the Acts of Thomas. But it is not the only theme. The stories, with a kaleidoscopic profusion of colors, also deal with the virtues of charity, with resurrection, with punishment in hell, and with the pervasive powers of the Devil.

When Thomas, the saintly slave-carpenter, and his master finally arrive in India proper, King Gundnaphar (this is the name of a real king in northern India, according to coins found in the Punjab and Afghanistan, a factoid which has excited some historians unduly, given that he probably died sometime before Jesus' birth) welcomes them and instructs Thomas to build him a palace. Thomas sketches the design; the king is impressed, gives him gold and silver for its construction, and leaves them to it. Thomas sends back reassuring progress reports but spends the money instead on alms for the poor and needy. The tension of the plot lies in Thomas' extraordinarily cheeky defiance of earthly power and our conviction that the king must eventually find out and punish him, in spite of or because of his virtue. The denouement is delayed by a twist or two, and Thomas continues to live simply, teaching about the new Christian God, healing the sick, driving out demons, and spending the king's money on the poor. The message of the story (but then, it is only a story) is both subversive and revolutionary. Taxes should be spent on the poor, just as Christians, more than any other religious group in antiquity, spent alms on poor relief.

Reality temporarily intrudes. The king finally comes in person on a tour of inspection, and of course, he finds nothing built. He is as angry as we might expect, and has Thomas and his owner thrown into jail. Thomas' master (a mere foil) is frightened and no doubt regrets his choice of slave, but Thomas himself rejoices: "Fear not, but only believe, and you will receive everlasting life in the world to come" (AT 21). He knows, we know, that secular power is powerless against the spirit. Meanwhile the king dreams about how to kill Thomas painfully.

Just at this moment, the king's brother Gad dies. He goes to heaven, where angels (like friendly and respectful realtors) show him the various mansions in which he could dwell. He chooses one more beautiful than the rest, but the angels refuse. This palace is reserved. It is, of course, the real, heavenly palace which Thomas has been constructing for the king of India. Virtue on earth has its reward in heaven. As in the Acts of Andrew, the demands of the story have precedence over strict morality, since neither the king nor his brother has yet intentionally or consciously done anything worthy of heaven; but then, I suppose, some of us secretly hope that our rewards in heaven will be undeserved.

In spite of all that, the king's brother, who is clearly used to getting his way, asks the angels if he can go back to earth so that he can ask his brother, the king, if he can buy the heavenly palace, whose true worth the king presumably does not yet know. Amazingly, the angels agree, and much to everyone's surprise, the king's brother is reincarnated and finds himself in his own body, in his bed, alive. Modern views on the unbridgeable divide separating the living and the dead are much too rigid and stuffy. And in some ways, the king's brother is like Jesus' brother Thomas. The story gets its magic by having several intermediaries between earth and heaven.

The king of India is wise enough to smell a rat. He refuses to sell his new, heavenly palace and releases Thomas from prison. The king gets down on his knees, apologizes to Thomas for any mistreatment, and begs to become a Christian. His brother Gad joins in too; it seems that he gets long-term resuscitation out of the deal. Thomas prays for their forgiveness and for their immediate admission to baptism and Communion, and fervently advises the crowd against the three major sins: fornication, greed, and gluttony. In fantasy at least, Christians were now dreaming of converting the king. It took them only a century to realize their dreams and convert the Roman emperor Constantine. Meanwhile this imaginary Christian king of India feeds all those in need (which is rather more than any real Christian king ever managed to do).

The apostle, the kingly pair, the existing faithful, and many new converts riding on the royal coattails celebrate the conversion with hymns, baptism (powerfully if unconventionally arranged), and the eucharist: "Come, holy name of the Messiah; come, power of grace which art from on high; come, perfect mercy; come, exalted gift; come, sharer of the blessing; come, revealer of the hidden mysteries; come, Mother of the seven Houses . . . come, messenger of reconciliation, and communicate with the minds of these youths." And he baptized them in the name of the Father and of the Son and of the Holy Spirit (AT 27). And this solemn rite of baptism was sealed by the blazing apparition of the Lord, whose voice they all heard but which only the apostle Thomas could see. Here the account of the ritual reminds the faithful of experiences; and symbols which they have all shared. Such accounts are complementary to experience; stories can go well beyond what ordinary Christians actually sense, and (as with marijuana smokers) help neophytes to realize what the full experience ought to be like. The prayer reminds us, as some of us need to be reminded, that Christianity in this period was varied, strange, and sometimes magical but not yet, or not here, fixed in its liturgical form.

After the eucharist, Thomas preached to the assembled crowd his standard ascetic message, softened by hopes of salvation:

> Men and women, boys and girls, young men and maidens, mature and old, slave or free, abstain from fornication, avarice, and servitude to the belly [Syriac: demons]. For these are the three chief causes of wickedness. Fornication blinds the intellect and darkens the eyes of the soul; it confuses the steps of the body. . . . Covetousness brings the soul into fear and shame. . . . And servitude to the belly makes the soul preoccupied with care and sorrow, fearful of being in need, and greedy for things out of reach.
>
> Wait for the coming of Jesus, and hope in him, and believe in his name, because he is the judge of the dead and the living, and he shall recompense everyone according to his deeds at the last coming. And then it will be no ex-

cuse for anyone to say: "We did not know." . . . Repent and believe in the new message . . . receive grace for yourselves and plant the sign of the cross in your souls. (AT 28)

Vivid description of other people's conversion and baptism helped reassure existing Christians that they had made the right choice. Vicarious experience gave believers another opportunity to remember their first commitment to Christianity, just as modern car advertisements reassure recent buyers that their brand is best. Believing readers are confirmed in their faith by remembering their own conversion, just as nowadays older guests at a wedding are touched by a young bride's happy beauty and by the new couple's romantic idealism. Once upon a time, we too were there. At the very moment of tender memories, the apostle preacher tells us his stern demands: no lust, no greed, no demons; repent; you will be judged, and may be saved. It is a discomfiting and seductive religion, powerful in its recognition of universal weaknesses, appealing to some in its call for abnegation, and from my point of view, hopelessly misleading in its promises.

On Christ's instructions, Thomas goes out of town and, just off the road, by the second milestone, discovers the corpse of a fine-looking youth. He prays, and hazards the inspired guess that the youth's death is the work of the Devil. No sooner has he spoken than a large black snake emerges from a fissure in the rock, darting its head and thrashing its tail. And this is the tale which the black snake tells: I fell in love with a beautiful woman living in the neighboring village, and pursued her. But then I saw a young fellow kissing her, making love to her, on a Sunday, and doing other disgraceful things, which it would be quite easy to talk about, but not to the twin brother of Jesus. "So I watched out for him, and in the evening, when he passed by me, I struck and killed him" (AT 31). Perhaps it is even more discomfiting for us to think that the Devil too can be the jealous guardian of our morals.

And even the Devil can be induced to confess his sins. He says he is the wicked son of the wicked Devil, who sits upon the throne and has power over creation; it was he who stole through the fence of paradise and persuaded Eve and Adam to sin; who tempted angels with lust for human women; who bribed Judas to betray Jesus. "I am the kinsman of him who will come from the east; to me is given the power to do what I want on earth" (AT 32). For me, brought up in and deeply affected by a monotheistic culture, there is always a childishly subversive thrill about dualism, about the eternal battle between almost equally matched good and evil. But as a list of imaginable crimes, this is feeble stuff—barely enough perhaps to convince the ancient Christian that the apostle was justified in the Devil's murder.

Thomas prays for inspiration and tells the crowd, now gathered, about his belief in one God. They beg him to kill the snake/Devil. And Thomas speaks again to the snake. (Perhaps we could arrange for a similar confrontation on TV.) The apostle reproaches the serpent for boasting about his father's deeds. The time for his end is come. "In the name of our Lord Jesus, who contends with you even now for the people who are his own, I command you to suck out the poison which you put into this man" (AT 33). The serpent objects that this will mean his own death, but the apostle is adamant. The serpent sucks. The young man, who was purple, becomes whiter, and increasingly alive; he is suitably grateful and immediately converts. But the serpent swells up and bursts. The king and his brother are instructed to build a hostel for migrants over the snake's grave. Well, you cannot expect immigrants to get the best sites.

The young man gives a touching, though densely heretical, speech. Like a Gnostic and like a later Manichee, he has become united once again with his original nature of Light; he has become one with God. He has seen the Light, is freed from the Devil, who compelled him to sin shamefully and shamelessly. Light and Dark are competing, dualistic forces. There is no talk here of free will. The apostle warns him that he must cling to the Light which he has glimpsed, or else he will once more be banished to the world of the Devil. And to the crowd who strain to see him and the young man raised from the dead, the saint says:

> If you cannot see me, who am like you, unless you lift yourselves up a little from the ground, how can you see him who is on high and found in the depths, unless you raise yourselves out of your former lifestyle, the acts which do you no good, the pleasures which do not last, the wealth which you leave behind . . . the beauty which grows old and vanishes? . . . Believe rather in the Lord Jesus Christ. And the crowd wept, and asked forgiveness. And the apostle tells them that the Lord God forgives those sins committed in ignorance by pagans. (AT 37–38)

As a new Christian, you can start with a clean sheet. To some, that may have seemed a considerable attraction.

In the next, rather feeble episode, a talking donkey acknowledges Thomas as the twin brother of Jesus, come to give freedom and life to India (AT 39). And then, more excitingly, the apostle once more confronts the black serpent/Devil, who has migrated to another town and possessed a woman. He has engaged with her in "filthy intercourse" by night for five years. She begs the saint for deliverance. Obviously, contrary to appearances, the Devil has not been killed forever. Just as well. The Christian God needs the Devil just as modern bourgeois property owners need thieves and just as a Republican Congress needs violent crime. The virtuous get their identity from the vicious, whom they ostensibly want to exterminate but actually need to preserve. We cannot imagine the Christian church without sinners; indeed, several ancient critics accused the early Christians of manufacturing sin (see Chapter Six).

And so, once again we get a ritual confrontation between good and evil, apostle and Devil. The Devil understandably complains that Thomas should not use violence against him while advocating its renunciation among his own believers. And he suggests a rough division of adherents: "Why do you covet what is not yours?" (AT 45). To no avail; the Christian apostle, like kings, does not have to abide by his own rules. So the demon is forced to renounce the beautiful woman, which he does with a certain elegant regret. Like a wandering preacher, he will again go somewhere else. This promise sets up yet another confrontation, but for a future episode. It also reveals a certain parochialism in our author's perception of the divine economy; so long as my city is free, all is well with the world. The Devil disappears (though we know full well that he has not disappeared forever) in a trail of fire and smoke.

The apostle signs off with an affecting list of Jesus' virtues, populist, divine, bureaucratic, optimistic:

> Jesus poor and catching fish for dinner and supper; Jesus satisfying many thousands with a little bread, Jesus resting from the weariness of a journey like a man, but walking on the waves of the sea, like a God; Jesus, exalted voice arising from perfect mercy, savior of all, liberator and administrator of the world . . . Jesus, who does not neglect us in anything which we ask of you. (AT 47–48)

And then Thomas baptizes the woman freed from the demon, and many with her, and celebrates the eucharist, giving bread first to the woman and those baptized with her, then to everyone else. At least in this vision of the apostle's community, there was no precedence of priests, no routinized subordination of women in liturgy.

Beneath the varied surface of these stories there is a common underlying structure, and a whole series of ingredients. Basically, the overall purpose is to recreate a potent mixture, combining the apostle's divinity and human sin. Here is the recipe.[52]

a. We begin with: a human sinning.

b. He/she gets caught or suffers (*a* and *b* can be reversed for variation).

c. The half-divine apostle, mirroring Jesus' own mixture of divinity and humanity, perceives the sin, and his intercession is begged for.

d. The apostle prays to almighty God and draws the readers' attention to God's manifold virtues.

e. The apostle performs a miracle: raises the dead, gets an animal to talk, defeats the Devil, gives us a glimpse of heaven or hell, to stimulate or terrify.

f. The miracle impresses the sinner, the crowd, and us, the readers.

g. And so, we feel humble, and the sinner repents, has faith in the new religion, and requests admission to the ranks.

h. The request is granted.

i. The new Christian is baptized and given Holy Communion; the ritual is described so that we can reexperience our own conversion, and if necessary be told what we ought to experience next time we participate.

j. Seduced and softened up by this heady mixture—divine power; victory over the forces of evil; magic; miracles; repentance; rituals— we are in an appropriate condition for the hard sell. The narrator, through the saint, tells us what we need to do to be really, truly Christian. The demands are tough—small matter now that the task is beyond us. Ideals are there to test us, and to give us standards by which to judge others and find them wanting.

k. Meanwhile, the text, under the convincing guise of simple story telling, continuously negotiates and sells delicate, quite complex, paradoxical, and polemical theological and ethical positions. Only to the naive is it just a popular tale or religious romance. But behind the finesses, the pious main thrust is clear. Through virtue and faith, in spite of sin, we too can be saved by the redeeming messenger, Thomas/Jesus. Evil, the Devil, and corrupting sex can be, will be, defeated. Earthly eroticism may help the story along, but asceticism is the religious eroticism of the true Christian.

A VERY BRIEF TRIP TO HELL

Many elements of this complex structure are visible in the next tale. One of the people taking communion is a young man. When he is about to put the blessed bread in his mouth, both his hands wither. The apostle tells him not to be ashamed but to confess his sins; such things do not happen without cause. The young man realizes he is in a fix, falls on his knees, and begs the apostle to intercede. He has fallen in love with a prostitute working from an inn. He knows that Christianity is against "filthy intercourse, especially in adultery," but he loves the girl and wants to be baptized. So, "I begged her and tried to persuade her to live with me a life clean and pure and tranquil and chaste and modest" (AT 51). There seems little doubt that he meant that they should live as ascetics, without sexual intercourse. But she refused. So he had intercourse with her and killed her.

When the apostle hears all this, he gives a brief lecture on the corrupting evils of sex, uses some holy water to cure the young man's hands, asks him to trust in faith, goes to the inn with the usual large crowd, finds the dead body of the prostitute, says a prayer, and gets the young man to raise her from the dead. It is clearly not the apostle himself who performs the miracle, but God who empowers even the reformed sinner. The dead girl stands upright, rushes over to the apostle, and falls at his feet. He asks her to tell the crowd where she has been. The answer is, to hell and back. And so we get a brief preview of the horrors of hell. The fixation is predominantly on the punishment of sexual sins. Indeed, Thomas tells the crowd that adultery is "more hateful to God than all evil deeds" (AT 58).

Her guide in hell was a black man dressed in rags (no political correctness here). She has seen blazing pits of fire for adulterers and homosexuals. There is a pit filled with excrement and worms for youths who indulge themselves with harlots or, not content with that, lie in wait for virgins. A similar punishment awaits the girls who because of wanton lust have lost their virginity and have brought shame on their parents. Else-where, slanderous souls hang eternally by their tongues; immodest women who went about bareheaded (the young bride's joyous liberation from the veil is conveniently forgotten here) hang by their hair; thieves and those who did not give to the needy hang by their hands—while those who did not visit the sick or attend funerals, or who tripped lightly along the paths of evil, hang by their feet. Every soul, we are comfort-ingly reassured, receives its condign punishment.

And Thomas said to the crowd:

> You have heard, my children, what this woman has said; and these are not the only tortures; there are also others, much worse than these. You too, there-fore, unless you are converted to this truth which I preach, and restrain your-selves from evil deeds . . . you too will finish up in these torments. Therefore, believe in Jesus Christ, and he will forgive the sins which you have already committed, and will cleanse you from all your bodily and earthly desires. . . .
>
> Put off, therefore, each of you, the old man, and put on the new; put off your old habits and your weakness of the flesh. Let those of you who steal, steal no more, but live by toil and hard labor; let those of you who com-mit adultery be lecherous no more, so that you may not condemn yourselves to eternal punishment. For to God, adultery is exceedingly wicked, worse than all other evils. . . . Instead, walk in faith, meekness, holiness, and hope, in which God delights, so that you may become members of God's house-hold, and may receive from him the blessings which only very few receive. (AT 58)

Christianity here is presented as a simple system of faith, reward, and punishment, with a strange fixation on adultery, a surprising stress on hard work, and a sense of its own selectivity. Only the elect will be saved. "And these multitudes believed, and surrendered themselves to the liv-ing God and to Jesus Christ . . . and each of them brought much money for the relief of widows" (AT 59). Christians were exceptional in the an-cient world in their devotion to charity. It is also realistic to note that over time, and certainly by the time the Acts of Thomas were first writ-ten, some Christian clergy lived quite well, if not out of the money given for charity, certainly from money not spent on the poor.

The scene closes with Thomas' prayer:

Perfect us with your grace and mercy. Behold, Lord, it is you alone we love. We have left our homes and the homes of our families, and for your sake have willingly and gladly become wanderers, so that we may possess you, the possession which cannot be taken away. . . . Behold, Lord, we have left our fleshly wives and earthly nourishment, so that we may be united with you in true union and share in the heavenly harvest which no man can take away. (AT 61)

The truth is revealed. The multitude is converted and is set ethical tasks it cannot, and understandably does not want, wholeheartedly to fulfill. It is made to feel guilty for its shortcomings, and finally out of genuine repentance and goodwill brings money for charitable works. But the elect, the chosen few who are the true devotees, have left the social world and have dedicated themselves in spiritual union with God. This Christianity is a stratified religion: on top, by their own estimation, wandering priests; beneath, a multitude of faithful to support them; and in turn, below them, a mass of unbelievers.

The bare outline of these stories hardly does them justice. But the truth is, unless you have a yen for longish prayers, dramatic resuscitations and conversions, and ethical prescriptions, the text as it stands is rather long and rambling. In my view, there probably was a crisper set of oral versions, used in pious circles, of which the surviving written texts are literary elaborations and reflections. But I cannot prove that. Ethically, the Acts of Thomas repeatedly emphasize that sexual intercourse is filthy, contemptible, the starting point of every evil.[53] But they also prescribe meekness, generosity to the needy, especially to those who are Christian, and kindness.

Theologically, the Acts of Thomas are complex, with many interwoven elements.[54] Like the Acts of Andrew, they are a set of stories which disguise strict theological purpose in a medley of drama and words. Even so, some bits are obviously Gnostic in inspiration, while others are more or less orthodox, in the dominant tradition of the Christian church. Jesus is the savior, human and divine, who died to redeem humanity; the believer should walk in faith, meekness, and holiness, and can hope for forgiveness of sins and immortal life after death. That said, it is quite easy to collect a whole bundle of allusions which show that the author of the Acts of Thomas had read and internalized the Gospel of Thomas, and shares the encratite (extreme ascetic) hostility to sexuality shown in the Book of Thomas the Athlete. In all these works, Thomas is the very special alter ego of Jesus; Jesus tells Thomas secrets which are too holy to share with the other apostles (Gospel of Thomas, Saying 13). But Thomas will reveal these secrets now to worthy followers. Knowledge and abstinence bring a freedom from the Devil and from death.[55] And as in the Acts of Andrew, following the teaching of the apostle will make the faithful believer like the apostle, and so like Jesus himself.

For all its encratite enthusiasm, the style of the Acts of Thomas is not explicitly polemical against contrary positions. So it seems sensible to deduce that the author considered what he wrote to be broadly acceptable to fellow Christians. It was written to be within the Great Church tradition, even if it catered especially to devoted ascetic sectarians. We simply do not know how many ancient Christians read it. For modern Christians, perhaps uncomfortable prominence is given to the Devil and to painful reminders that sins will be cruelly punished for all eternity in hell.

As with the other apocryphal Acts of the apostles, the Acts of Thomas were written cleverly, in order to be popular. Can we speculate about the context of their composition? It seems reasonable to assume that only about 10 percent of the adult male population in the Roman empire could write and read (and that is a generous estimate), and scholars commonly agree that the Acts of Thomas were written in the Syrian town of Edessa. The population of Edessa is unlikely to have been above twenty thousand people. Of these, roughly one-third were adult males.[56] So there were some seven hundred adult males in Edessa with writing and reading skills, and most of these would have had only basic instrumental literacy; they could add up, sign their names, read a tax receipt. Only a very small group, well less than a hundred men, I imagine, had any facility in writing sophisticated prose and verse.

What we have, then, in the Acts of Thomas is subelite writing. The author was probably a member of Edessene high society. And that makes sense of the stories' fixation on the king. The small region of Edessa at the end of the second century was ruled by a king under Roman patronage. Our author clearly imagines a setting in which he, alias the saint, has easy access to the king and his advisers. Perhaps, too, the local context helps account for the Christian fixation on chastity. In the neighboring city of Mabbug (Greek: Hierapolis), the dominant cult of the Mother Goddess, Atargatis, required of its devotees that they show commitment by self-castration (see Chapter Five).[57] People in this region had long been used to spectacular acts of religious devotion. Christians, to win, had to compete in that tradition.

One final point about the Acts of Thomas. They project a Christian community led and inspired by a lonely, wandering prophet who preaches, prays, cures, exorcises, and raises the dead. By the beauty of his message, by the simplicity of his example, and by his charismatic powers he continually converts new Christians. As in the Acts of Andrew, we hear nothing of bishops and next to nothing of priests. The Christian community envisaged is small, volatile, unorganized, and fast expanding. It has a liturgy of baptism and eucharist, but its liturgy has no settled form either of actions or words. All this is surprising for the Christian church in about 200 CE, when bishops at Rome were trying to make rules for the whole church and when preachers such as Clement of Alexandria and Origen were already attacking the self-interest and self-indulgence of ecclesiastical fat cats. Of course, we might be dealing here with the idiosyncratic visions of a marginal sect, or even, one might argue implausibly, with an author who is trying to recreate the primitive conditions of the apostolic age. Rather, I imagine, we are dealing with a nostalgic idealization of how the church still should be; a passionate and self-denying engagement by committed believers with a leader who by his own closeness to God brings the faithful, men and women, to be close to God, and saved. Christianity, in the Acts of Thomas, is a religion of a knowledgeable and self-sacrificing elect. And it was these ideals of wandering ascetic beggar priests which Mani took over in the middle of the third century, together with the ideas and actions of the apocryphal Acts (see Chapter Seven).[58]

I want to finish near where we began, with the Acts of John. Before Jesus was arrested by the lawless Jews, whose God is the Devil, he assembled the disciples and got them to form a circle holding hands. Jesus himself stood in the middle, and all sang a song antiphonally while dancing around him. The words of the hymn (AJ 94) are mystical, paradoxical, complex, and yet impressive:

> Glory be to you, Father.
> And we, circling him, said, "Amen."
> Glory be to you, Word; glory be to you, Grace. "Amen. . . ."

Now we give thanks. I say: I will be saved and I will save. "Amen. . . ."
I will be pierced, and I will pierce. "Amen."
I will be born, and I will bear. "Amen."
I will eat, and I will be eaten. "Amen. . . ."
The whole universe takes part in the dancing. "Amen."
He who does not dance does not know what is being done. "Amen."

And so it goes on. The point of the hymn and the dance lies mostly in their performance, in the singing and in the dancing, and in the participants' experience, which is akin to an initiation. To understand it all, you have to perform it with believer friends.[59] Even without a performance, it is still clear that the hymn and dance constitute a challenge to, or at the very least a deviation from, what later became the conventional eucharist. For most sober Christians, a liturgical dance seems too orgiastic to be a proper way of approaching God. Besides, in this dance each participant has a direct relationship to Jesus, unmediated by an ecclesiastical officiant.[60] By dancing and singing, each follower is brought closer to wisdom and to personal identification with God. The Acts of John offer a personal and ecstatic approach to Christian religion.

Throughout this chapter, one point has been implicit. I have wanted to intimate that the structure, purpose, and intellectual style of these apocryphal Acts of Apostles are remarkably similar to the structure, purpose, and intellectual style of the canonical gospels and canonical Acts of the Apostles in the New Testament. All of them were proposing ethical and metaphysical solutions to core human problems. None of them was purposively telling what we would now call true histories. But that is a big subject, and one to which we shall return in the final chapter.

For the moment, it is sufficient to bear in mind that Christian sacred writings, canonical and apocryphal, offered a magical mixture of transcendentalism, hope, and history. It proved a winner. But it took some time for the history of Jesus' life, sayings, and miracles enshrined in the New Testament to gain preeminence as holy scripture. And in retrospect, we may take that eventual success too readily for granted. In the early stages of Christianity's development, as I see it, both the immanent, transcendental, invisible God and the historical Jesus needed supplementing. Additional intermediary figures, such as Andrew or Thomas, helped bridge the gap. Judaism, similarly, had supplemented the original foundation charter of the Pentateuch with prophets, laws, and apocalyptical visions. Just as Jews apparently needed prophets, angels, and rabbis, so early Christians also needed extra intermediaries from heaven, such as miracle workers and healers, and they needed stories about miracles and miracle workers, martyrs and saints, to say nothing of angels and demons.[61] In effect, the cynic might say, all these godly figures, repeatedly breaching the grand divide between life and death, mortality and eternity, made Christianity, for all its protestations, much more acceptable in a polytheistic world.

FIVE

Magic, Temple Tales, and Oppressive Power

Our time travelers are now in Egypt, under Roman rule, during the second century. Their first stop is Tebtunis, a substantial village in the Fayoum, an artificially irrigated district on the edge of the Sahara desert, about 150 kilometers southwest of modern Cairo. Tebtunis is completely undistinguished, except for its famous temple dedicated to Souchos, the crocodile God, and the hundreds of papyri discovered a century ago, stuffed and buried inside mummified crocodiles. Even so, this village temple is off the beaten track, and nowhere near as magnificent as the great Nile River temples such as Dendera or Kom Ombo (which was also dedicated to Souchos). James and Martha's remit here is to experience and report the living variety of pagan religious practices, from formal ceremony to private magic.

THE TEMPLE OF THE CROCODILE GOD (JAMES)

Martha was being impossible, hysterical. You know what angry women can be like: shouting, tears, complaining, rejecting. God knows what the rest of the travelers in the temple rest house thought of it all, through the mud-brick walls. All my efforts to comfort her were shrugged off. She said I'd never loved her, not really, not with sympathetic understanding. I'd just wanted to sleep with her—which was true, but not the whole truth. Anyhow, all that was over now. She just turned her back on me. Had done ever since that wedding in Pompeii.

Well, I thought, I might as well take advantage of the local facilities. Not the brothels, just across the broad avenue leading to the great Temple of Sobek, the crocodile God, but a priest.[1] I thought one of those bald-headed, linen-robed codgers whom we'd seen praying yesterday might have ideas about how to win a woman back, might try his luck, and mine, with a spot of ancient magic. Little did I realize what I was getting into, though the whole place was very strange, with its crocodile-headed Gods and a whole cemetery outside the temple devoted to mummified crocodiles. We saw a solemn procession carrying a large dead crocodile ceremoniously to its grave (plate 20). Here, two thousand kilometers from Rome, animal-headed Gods loom larger than rulers, and religion reflects Egypt's long history of idiosyncratic difference.[2] We seem light-years away from Pompeii.

We'd been to the temple the day we arrived. Well, we could hardly miss it, and there was nothing much else to see or do. Frankly, Tebtunis was a hellhole, oppressively hot even in winter, and sand just everywhere, in my hair, clothes, ears, eyes, food. Eating bread was like eating grit.[3] No wonder Martha was in a rage. But at least we had enough to eat, un-like the thin and hungry barefoot boys who stood and watched every mouthful we swallowed, until they were angrily chased away by the innkeeper. Poverty, rags, dirt, flies, malnutrition all around us, and heav-ily barred windows protecting the little some had scraped together. But even in this squalid village we caught an occasional glimpse of luxury and education. There was a bathhouse, a covered market, and of course, the temple.

The temple dominates the village. It's the largest building for miles. But it's not just size; it's color and the mystery of hieroglyphs massed along the walls. High on one wall I saw Sobek, carved and painted in striking colors of black, white, blue, and red. His body is human but his fearsome crocodile head stands out in profile, with jagged mouth and protruding teeth. And his head is topped with the curled tongue of a co-bra and the traditional red crown of the kings of northern Egypt. Reli-gious and political power are intertwined. Next to him stands the bare-breasted Goddess Isis, and the great God Amun painted red—a pa-gan trinity, all wearing the traditional black and blue wigs, against a white background.

The temple is the climax, but the approach is impressive too: a long, grand avenue guarded by huge stone lions; then two hundred meters of expensively paved limestone slabs, all lined with memento stalls and monuments (altars, statues, stone lions) dedicated by visiting grandees.

Religion here is obviously flourishing, and all supported by the contributions of surrounding villages and visitors.[4] We had hired a guide, partly to fend off pestering children—there always seemed to be so many of them everywhere—and partly to point out what we might otherwise miss. He showed us a massive stone altar set up soon after the Roman conquest, more than a century before, by the local district magistrate. It had a short inscription in suitably large letters to "the great God Sokneptunis" (one of the crocodile God's various names). Perhaps it was important for the new Roman rulers to make their mark and to be on good terms with native Gods.[5]

They're used to visitors here, and cater to them too: banqueting rooms, guides to show visitors the sacred crocodiles feeding tamely off tidbits in the grandiose semicircular stone basin where they were kept, sacrificial animals on sale for the guilty, oracles available for the anxious, and a library filled with traditional wisdom.[6] Religion here is meant to be impressive, evocative, and fun. Last night when I was strolling around in the temple precincts, I saw and heard a group of men feasting; they sounded very drunk and cheerful. I asked a slave waiting for his master who they were: the guild of salt sellers, he told me, fixing prices.[7] "And there's a wedding party in the next room," he added; "the children of Pantbeus, getting married to each other, and they'll probably go on all night."

I shuddered at the idea of another wedding. But then I thought about what the man had said, and checked: "The children of Pantbeus, getting married, to each other?" I asked hesitantly. "Yes, brother and sister," he said and seemed to think nothing further of it, though surely he must have known it was odd. And I remembered I'd seen a party of gaudily dressed people the day before, men in white robes striped with black and purple, women wearing shocking pink striped with black or brown, or reddish brown striped with black or white. They stuck out against the normal drab, black and gray.[8] Roman Egypt looked startlingly different from Pompeii.

I asked at the temple later, and my friend Marsisouchos the priest confirmed it: brothers regularly marry sisters all over Egypt, have done for centuries, and in all strata of society. Strange people, I thought, and they must seem even stranger to regular Romans. Then I remembered that in Egyptian religion Isis married her brother Osiris. The Egyptians were only imitating their Gods—or was it vice versa?[9]

Now I was going back to the Temple of Sobek to find Marsisouchos (his name is Egyptian for Son of Souchos, meaning son of the crocodile God), to see if he could work some magic and win Martha back for me. Of course, I'm a rationalist, I don't believe in magic, but well, I was here. And in spite of all that Martha said, I really did love her—had never managed to tell her, persuasively. Afraid of commitment, I suppose, disguised as commitment to my children. OK, you're not interested in my private problems, though it's private problems, as Marsisouchos wryly admitted, which bring customers to priests.[10]

Marsisouchos had impressed both of us considerably. An oldish man, the only one of the priests who had treated all our questions seriously and courteously and had answered with intelligent irony. It was Marsisouchos who had told us in a quiet voice how the Roman rulers had crippled the temples, taking away their lands, reducing their traditional wealth, controlling entrance to the priesthood, putting the top temple positions up for auction, taxing everything that moved.[11] In the olden days, he said, when the pharaohs ruled, and even under the Greek kings, temple priests had been the effective leaders of the Egyptian people, accustomed to meet one another in annual conventions to discuss sacred matters. But the Romans had stopped all that. "They don't want us to get together," Marsisouchos said. "Now the chief priest of all Egypt"—he spat out the words—"is a Roman bureaucrat.[12]

"But one day," Marsisouchos whispered, "all 'the foreigners in Egypt'" (he seemed to have forgotten that I was a Greek, but then, so many Egyptians speak fluent Greek, and at the top end of Egyptian society the two cultures are intertwined) "'will disappear like leaves from a tree in autumn, and the Egyptian statues which they took will be restored to Egypt.' That was a sacred oracle," he said, "and it will come to pass. Hundreds of us," he went on, "think the Romans are tyrants and robbers; and they still favor the Jews. But one day we'll get our revenge. Meanwhile, what can we do? If you rebel like the Jews, you get crushed. And the Romans do provide peace"—here he smiled, as one of his plumper fellow priests swished by with some rich-looking Roman tourists in tow—"and prosperity for some."[13]

Marsisouchos was clearly intelligent, a rebel manqué. But some of the other priests we talked to had been hopelessly self-idealizing. One of them told us that priests lived apart from other people and stayed near or inside the temple in contemplation of the divine. "We don't do manual work, we are not interested in money or sex. Our objective is to live simply, frugally, chastely, avoiding social contact as much as is reasonable. Of course, at festivals we see ordinary people, but normally we mix only with those who participate in the same rites. And we all have to purify ourselves before we come inside the temple precinct—you know, eat the right things, and not too much, and no sexual intercourse before coming to the temple to behold the God. And when we fast, we stay away from our families, and communicate only with those who are also staying in the temple for a period of contemplation."

It's difficult to concentrate when priests drone on like this. I said that I'd read somewhere that an Egyptian priest had been hired as the emperor Nero's tutor. But my irreverent diversion didn't stop his flow. "We teach our young priests to walk calmly, to keep their hands folded inside their tunic, to avoid touching what is impure, to smile if necessary but not to laugh, to drink only a little wine, preferably none, because wine befuddles the mind, prevents study, and stimulates sexual desires. We eat bread and vegetables, a little or no oil, no luxuries, no foreign foods, no fish, no meat from animals with uncloven hoofs, no birds, especially doves. In fact, the rules specifying what we can eat, or rather what different ranks of priests can eat, are quite complicated. There are learned treatises about all that. And when we are going to celebrate a particularly holy rite, then we dedicate time to preparation, never less than a week, sometimes six weeks. During this period we do not eat bread, or eggs even, or vegetables, and of course we abstain from sexual intercourse, and wash often to keep ourselves pure for the God."[14]

In a way, it all sounded like Christian monkish ideals with a different theology; though of course, I have no idea whether these Egyptian priests actually lived up to their ideals. But they did look like monks with their long robes and tonsured heads. In one of the temple outbuildings we glimpsed inside a priest's bedroom; it did seem quite sparse. The bed was a cot of palm branches, comfortable enough, but the pillow was a block of wood.[15] And the Egyptians, like the Jews, and the Christians later, but unlike most of the Roman world, had a professional priesthood. In Tebtunis there were fifty of them, who took it in turn to serve in the temple but lived otherwise with their families. Notionally, the priesthood was hereditary, but every stage of a priest's career was closely controlled by the Roman administration. They had to get permission to circumcise their sons, give notice that they had learned to read the holy scriptures, to say nothing of paying fees for each step up in the hierarchy. The top priest had paid a fortune for his post, Marsisouchos told us; but then, he kept a fifth of the temple's total revenues.[16] So Marsisouchos' angry complaints about the Romans and the priests' lost glory disguised their substantial remaining privileges.

But enough of all that. I was preoccupied by my own affairs. Martha's moodiness was niggling me. I had to do something. I wondered if and what Marsisouchos would suggest. I went across the temple courtyard, past a group of boys struggling with math exercises—some of them were working out square roots; I felt glad to be out of all that. I found him in the library, supervising the work of a young priest copying a tattered manuscript in the ancient hieratic script onto new papyrus. The boy clearly had talent and didn't mind his handiwork (a long prayer, carefully scripted in red and black) being admired.[17] Marsisouchos asked me if I wanted to see the treasures of the temple library (and I did look at them later), but for the moment I said I wanted to ask his advice, urgently.

So we sat together in the shade of a wall and I told him my woes. He listened intently and asked me what I needed. I asked him what he suggested. You know the leisurely pace of Middle Eastern conversations. The easiest way, he said, was to consult the oracle. But I'd seen people doing that yesterday. They hand in two questions on slips of papyrus and get one back.[18] Better odds than horse racing, but you'd need a lot of faith to be sure you are getting the right answer. So I looked unenthusiastic.

THE MAGIC FIX (JAMES)

The most difficult way, he said, was for me to sleep in the temple, and perhaps the God would come to me or I'd have a vision. I must have looked skeptical, because he bridled and said that he personally knew of several people who had been cured of serious sicknesses by dreams they'd had in this very temple. In fact, even if I didn't believe him, he had a scroll right here in the library which gave a vivid account, in black-and-white, of the God's astounding appearance to a sufferer, to such good effect that his mother was cured of a long and painful illness, and the son finished a book over which he had long dithered.[19] That was a direct hit.

But how had the priest guessed? It was just the dream I needed back home—though it wouldn't help me with Martha now. Marsisouchos must have noticed my change of heart, and pressed his advantage. But when he said that sleeping over in the temple required long preparation, and sacrifices afterward, he soon realized that it wasn't for me; I hadn't lost my modern taste for a quick fix.

Well, Marsisouchos said—and here he began to press me about myself and my relations with Martha: Did I still love her? Want her back? Did she nag? Did we squabble? Had I eaten meat recently? How long was it since we'd had sex? (The true answer was, almost a century: we'd left Pompeii in 77 and arrived in Egypt in the thirteenth year of the reign of Marcus Aurelius, 172 CE.) I just said it had been quite a long time. He seemed satisfied, and intimated that basically I was in a state of purity, or would be once I'd been to the baths, washed thoroughly, and dressed in fresh linen. If I really wanted Martha back, he said, he could rekindle her affections, and enable me to keep her, with a powerful spell and the aid of his own familiar spirit.[20]

"All you have to do," he said, "is bring some of Eirene's [that's the name Martha was traveling under] hair and clothes, and come to my house before dusk. I'll send a boy to fetch you from the baths." I asked if I could make a contribution to the expenses of the library, and he said that the cost of fine papyrus was unbelievably high.[21] We settled quite amiably on four gold coins, which would, I reckoned, buy a whole armful of rolls and feed his family for several months.

He seemed pleased, so I thought it was now my turn to press my advantage. I asked him where he'd learned magic and what the priests did inside the temple—not all at once (that would have got me nowhere fast), but gradually as we talked over the next couple of hours. He'd learned magic in Memphis, had studied it for years, had even walked to India to consult with the Brahmins.[22] He took it all very seriously. Some ignorant people call it wizardry, he said, but for experts, magic is simply *the* way of communing with and being transformed by the divine.

Once, he said, helped by inspired tuition from a priest, and by careful spells, he had himself succeeded in seeing God in all his incredible beauty. "'*I* always knew that I would converse with the Gods, and I continually stretched out my hands to heaven, and entreated the Gods to bless me by giving me a vision in a dream or a divine spirit,' so that I might gaze on the immortal soul. I nagged my teacher to help, and one day I fell on my knees and entreated him with tears, until he finally gave in and told me to prepare myself by fasting for three days. They seemed like years.

"And then just before dawn on the third day, I went to my teacher's house. He asked me 'whether I wanted to talk with a spirit of the dead or with the God himself. I said I wanted to talk with the God, and alone, face-to-face.' My teacher seemed shocked by my request, but agreed, took me to a room, told me to sit on a chair opposite the one on which the God might sit, left, and locked the door.

"When the God came I was astounded. 'Human words cannot describe the features of his face or the beauty of his adornment. I was thunderstruck, my mind was overawed, so that I could hardly speak, but he told me to ask what I wanted, and he would gladly tell me everything.' And that, my friend," Marsisouchos said, "is the secret of my wisdom. Since then, 'I have seen the Devil, and learned how the rulers of darkness work inside men's souls, and what they can achieve through trickery and fear.' I have cast spells which lift me up to the heights of heaven, so that I seem to be in midair, not to see earth below, but the divine order of the heavens above, and the ruler Gods."[23] Even as he spoke, Marsisouchos looked quite uplifted, and I was impressed in spite of my skepticism.

But he still refused to tell me directly what happened inside Egyptian temples. Egyptian priests seem much more secretive about all this than they were in the other Roman towns we visited. I suppose it's because in Egypt they're a group of professional priests, and they maintain their privileges and their firm grip on the people by mystery and by keeping everyone out. Here the priests worship the God(s) *for* the people. Actually, it's quite a sensible division of labor. Only priests can go right inside the temple, though privileged people are allowed into the inner courtyard. The general populace have to be satisfied with the outer courtyard. That's where they bring their offerings, principally of bread, fruit, and beer, and that's where sacrifices are burned during festivals.[24]

Martha and I had stood with a few other faithful locals and visitors in the outer courtyard yesterday before sunrise. The priestly procession comes up from inside the temple on to the roof, so that the sun's first rays strike the statue of the God which the priests are carrying. It's the same portable statue that they bring out during festivals. And of course the people all have an inkling of what happens inside the temple from these brief glimpses, as well as from gossip and stories. And because most of these stories are known only locally, there's always someone willing, for a tip or a drink, or just a respectful ear, to tell a stranger their version of the truth. Variations and the constant reworking of variations help keep the religion alive.

From what Marsisouchos told me, and snippets which I picked up from other informants, especially the scrolls which Marsisouchos let me read in the library, I gathered that the priests take it in turns to serve and worship three times a day, morning, midday, and evening. In the morning, before dawn, they open the temple doors, let light into its dim interiors. And then they wash, perfume, clothe, and feed the statue of Soknebtunis, and the other, lesser Gods who also have statues in the temple. The high point of the morning ritual is opening the God's mouth. But this is also a metaphor for making the statues alive. And meanwhile there's a lot of praying, processing, and hymn singing. One of the library manuscripts had a stunning colored picture of a priest officiating. He was wearing a red robe and a leopard skin carefully arranged so that the head and front claws were on his chest, and the rear claws and tail behind his calves. In some sense the priest had become the leopard. Pity that no one except priests ever saw it. Modern tourists who throng the temples in bright sunlight must have difficulty in imagining this long-forgotten priestly piety, the swinging lamps in the gloom of the temple, the swish of priestly robes, and the slow, repetitious chant of their lengthy prayers, recited exactly as prescribed on each room's walls.[25]

At great festivals the God, together with his fellow Gods, comes out to meet the people, so that they can see the God and the God can see them; and as a liturgy puts it, they all rejoice. The priests parade in an impressive procession. Some are masked like Gods, others carry the God's clothing and jewels, and others by way of encouragement show off the villagers' offerings. Finally, two senior priests, dressed as king and queen, with incense and rattle, precede the God himself, and look back at him in admiration: no better ritual dramatization that even rulers admire Gods. Outside the temple the God is represented by a small portable statue, so that he can tour the villages of his domain or preside over dramas staged to celebrate important episodes in his mythic history.[26]

Occasionally the God and his priests even go along the Nile to meet his fellow Gods from neighboring towns. Although each animal-headed God (ram, bull, crocodile) is sovereign locally, everybody knows that the local God is only one of a panoply of Gods, and part of a heavenly set which includes the great Gods, Ra the sun God, Isis and Osiris, and their son, Horus. This recognition of divine unity, whether conscious or subliminal, is made explicit in prayers. Sobek is the Creator God, male and female:

> He is more powerful than all Gods, Sobek Ra . . . who has created the earth to produce bread, makes the trees grow, receives offerings, and gives nourishment to those he has created, who has made the bulls mount the cows, and has let the calves be born, who creates like a God, and who is pregnant like a woman, who begets like a man. [She] renews her temple, she carves the statues of the Gods, in her name.
>
> Peace be unto him. Holy God, who came into existence at the beginning of time in the primordial water. Eternity is in front of you, as yesterday which passed. Most powerful of Gods, your name is Truth, Truth. O Lord, whose head is a falcon. Crocodile, your eye is made of fire, your fingers are serpents and tortoises. Millions of cubits of fire are your roads. King of heaven, prince of earth. He is happy when there are cries of joy. Praise Sobek.[27]

Among the faithful, this worship apparently aroused considerable passion and devotion, rather more than I would have expected from what most textbooks say about ancient religions: you know, all form but no feeling. Marsisouchos told me that in the olden days, devotees of the God used to dedicate themselves to his service with a solemn oath. He showed me one in the temple library:

> Before my master Soknebtunis, the great God, I am your servant together with my children and my children's children. I shall not be able to go free from your precincts for ever and ever. You will protect me from every spirit male and female, every sleeping man, every epileptic, every drowned man, every bird, every incubus, every dead man, every man of the river, every madman, every fiend, every red thing, every wry-neck, every pestilence whatsoever.

In return for the protection which the great God gave from pervasive evil spirits, the humble worshiper promised to pay the God (and of course, his priests) a monthly fee in silver and bronze.[28]

Marsisouchos showed me several other impressive manuscripts in the temple library: medical prescriptions with illustrations, but more learning than practicality; prayers, hymns, folktales, religious stories; books filled with sound ethical advice, even an interlinear dictionary of hieratic

Egyptian and Greek, which Egyptologists in the nineteenth century, before they could decipher hieroglyphs, would have given their eyeteeth for. I was particularly struck by a set of astronomical calculations, fitting a twenty-five-year lunar cycle to the solar year and to the zodiacal sequence; ideal for horoscopes. And there was another papyrus, which aligned the Roman and Egyptian calendars, apparently so that Tebtunis villagers could celebrate emperors' birthdays and other festivals, with spectacles and recitations, on the correct day. Even insignificant villages like this were tied into the central Roman symbolic system.[29] These temple priests not only were religious leaders, guardians of tradition, and community advisers, but they also had a tidy side business in casting horoscopes, predicting the future, suggesting cures, and as I had seen, if you paid them enough on the quiet, putting powerful magic on enemies, business rivals, or reluctant lovers.

It was time to see how it worked. I went back to the temple rest house, was civil to Martha without reciprocity, went to the baths, and waited for Marsisouchos' slave boy. Eventually, he came, a lovely boy with merry eyes. Did that bode well? Along dusty and dirty streets filled with curious children speaking incomprehensible Egyptian, we soon arrived at Marsisouchos' house. Nothing romantic about that, a mud-brick house with a few blocks of stone and palm-wood beams to indicate his status, but with your regulation chickens and two black cows in the courtyard.

Inside, all was swept clean. Marsisouchos smiled a hospitable welcome, gestured me to a chair, and offered me a glass of beer. I had time to look around. The furniture was crude; the walls were plastered and painted a bluish green, with the occasional sketch of figures and plants. A couple of windows, high up, were firmly shuttered on the inside. The style reminded me of Pompeii, but here everything was very crudely done. We were several large steps down the social hierarchy from the House of the Gilded Cupids. But it was still visibly a house with cultural ambitions: wooden and bronze figurines in the niches along the walls—one, I noticed, was of the crocodile God. And there was a strikingly garish picture hanging on one wall, its wooden frame painted dark red, of two seated Gods, each with halo, both ceremoniously dressed, one (the male) clutching a crocodile to his breast. He must be Soknebtunis, the crocodile God, I thought, though a museum label would have been useful; the woman was certainly Isis. "That's Soknebtunis and Isis with their son,

Harpocrates/Horus," Marsisouchos said from behind my shoulder, pointing to the baby ram at the Gods' feet. Strange culture, I thought, not for the first time; but at least religion pervades home as well as temple.[30]

After a bit, Marsisouchos invited me to a room upstairs. We sat at a wooden table and as night fell heard the distant sounds of people shouting, dogs barking. The bright-eyed slave boy brought lamps, and Marsisouchos told me that he was going to work a spell of great power, which would surely bind Eirene (Martha) to me for life. He had prepared potions and ointment of magical force, one from recipes handed down by generations of priests, the other a special remedy revealed to him alone by the God. I wondered again what I had let myself in for. It was to be a ritual with five acts.

From a side table Marsisouchos brought over a libation jug of wine and honey, a small wooden statue of the God, a mixing bowl into which he carefully poured fresh white milk from the black cow and wine. Then on a small tablet of soap he scratched the great name of God with seven vowels, and drew a falcon-headed crocodile. On the other side he wrote an invocation: "I call on you, creator of all, self-begotten, who see all but are not seen, who gave the Sun its glory and all its power." Then he turned to me and said, "If you wish to win Eirene back, lick this soap, and the power of the spell will be yours." Well, I thought, unpleasant but not life threatening. So I obediently licked one side, and inevitably foamed a bit at the mouth. Marsisouchos looked happy at my compliance. Luckily one side was enough. He took the half-licked tablet from me, dropped it into the bowl of milk and wine, drank half of it, and gave me the rest. I was drinking the power of the spell.[31]

Next Marsisouchos showed me the fruits of his afternoon's labors: a crude wax figurine of a naked woman, kneeling, her arms tied tight behind her back. All over her body, with a fine brush, he had written in tiny letters the names of outlandish Gods: MELCHAMELCHOU AEL on the breast, ELOAIAOE on the sole of her left foot. This was his image of my Martha. I felt ashamed, embarrassed, shocked at what I was allowing him to do, but I really didn't see how I could stop him. I was locked in. Next he took a small flat piece of lead, on which again in tiny letters he had written out an elaborate spell. With needle and thread he pierced her body and tied the lead tablet to the waxen doll. "At first light of the new moon," he said, "we'll bury all this in the tomb of a child who has died before his time, so that his uneasy soul may carry your message to the powerful spirits of the dead."[32]

Then we went onto the roof of his house. The slave boy fanned some charcoal burning on a low altar, and Marsisouchos threw some grains of wheat and incense, poured some wine as a libation, and muttered an inaudible prayer; then looking toward the moon, in a low voice he began to croon his complex spell, using, of course, the names we were still traveling under. And I had to repeat it all, word for word.

> I call on you, Mistress of the entire world, Ruler of the cosmos, Lady of the night, who travel through the air, order your angel to go after Eirene, daughter of Chrysanthe, pull her by the hair, by the feet, so that she is in continuous fear of phantoms, hungry, thirsty, sleepless because of her passion for me, Gaius son of Aelia, comes to me in my bedroom, a burning heat in her soul, a frenzied passion in her mind.
>
> I call on you, Gods of the underworld, Pluto and Kore Persephone, Ereschigal and Adonis, do not allow her to eat, drink, go out, or sleep apart from me, Gaius whose mother was Aelia. And I adjure you, corpse spirit Antinous, by Abrasax and Barbaratham cheloumbra barouch, bind Eirene daughter of Chrysanthe so that she is not fucked, buggered, cunt kissed, or given pleasure by any other except me, Gaius son of Aelia. Drag Eirene by her hair and by her entrails to me, Gaius, and make her inseparable from me until death, head to head, lip to lip, belly to belly, thigh to thigh, sex to sex. Now, now. Quickly, quickly.[33]

And in the middle of his chant, he took up his Martha/Eirene wax doll and plunged bronze needles into each of her vital parts: brain, ears, eyes, mouth. I found it quite disturbing, disgusting even, and tolerated it, I think, only because I was there employing an ancient Egyptian magician in an alien civilization, on a roof in the dark (plate 21). And it was only a doll. But what a strange, repulsive, violent way to express love. Then belly, hands, genitals, feet, thirteen needles in all, and as he pierced each one, he chanted: "I am piercing Eirene's hands so that she thinks of no one but you, Gaius." Or was it, I wondered, because we in our culture do not like to acknowledge the violence of our feelings?

I left as fast as decency allowed, but not before Marsisouchos had promised to bury the doll and tablet in a grave before dawn. Of course, he wanted me to do it myself, but I was the paying customer, so he, polite as ever, gave way. As a parting present he handed me a dark blue glass

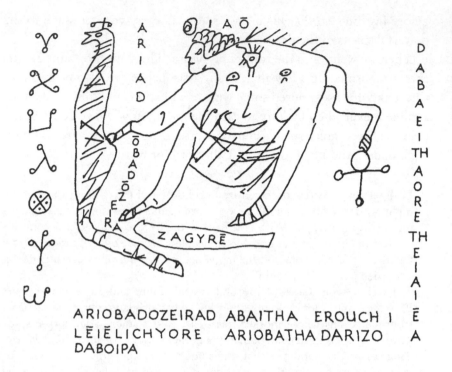

ARIOBADOZEIRAD ABAITHA EROUCH I
LĒIĒLICHYORE ARIOBATHA DARIZO
DABOIPA

phial containing, he said, a precious liquid, made according to the secret recipe given him by the God. "Smear it on the tip of your penis and you will be able to match thrust for thrust the desire Eirene feels even now."[34]

When I got back to the temple rest house, Martha was awake. She said she was cold and had been having terrible nightmares. She put out a hand and pulled me into bed. I deny completely that it was the spell working. But then, belief always defies reality.

THE TEMPLE OF THE GODDESS IN THE HOLY CITY (JAMES)

After the heat of Egypt, springtime in Hierapolis (Holy City) was a relief. It's quite a big town, on a hill, in lovely, gently undulating Syrian countryside, filled with fruit trees in blossom, just on the edge of Roman civilization, twenty kilometers from the river Euphrates and not far from modern Iraq. Not that there was a lot to keep us amused. Well, some of the local lads were trying, in their own peculiar way, to entertain themselves and everyone else by camping for a whole week roped to the tip of two giant phalli. No joke. Not for the phallus climbers either. If they nod off, they fall and kill themselves.[35] I'll explain in a minute.

Thanks to a neat piece of jiggling by Martha with the time-space calibrator, we arrived just as the annual festival was finishing. Miracle we got anywhere near it, I suppose, so I shouldn't be churlish. As a result, the burg was chock-full of pilgrims. Obviously, most were locals from Syria, but a minority had come from all over and added greatly to the prestige of the festival. Of course, we visited the great temple, which was a huge and striking combination of local limestone, white marble, and black basalt, glowing with its gilded roof at the top of the hill in the center of the town. In return for an offering we were shown the temple's haul of treasures. It was a prototype theme park, part swimming pool, zoo, art gallery, abattoir by the great bronze altar in front of the temple, part church for the faithful, and fair.[36]

Within the precinct there was a lake, a park with sacred bulls, horses, even bears, and we were told there were even tame lions, but we didn't see any, and we didn't look too hard (no Jeep, no binoculars; this was danger tourism). Inside the temple courtyard there was an impressive array of stone and bronze statues, set up to heroes and kings, and by them too, to judge by the expense. Of course, the most precious treasures were inside the temple, with its gilded walls and ceilings, filled with the scent of exotic perfumes.

And in the sanctuary, elevated so that all can see (but only priests can enter) are golden statues of the great Gods, bedecked with precious jewels—Zeus (or Hadad, as he is known locally) and, on a grander scale, the great Goddess (Hera; she's called Atargatis here), he on a throne of bulls, she on lions; between them a model temple, made of gold, filled with mysterious objects, and topped by a golden dove. I've no idea why. But what startled us most was the baldachin, or canopy, over the Gods, with marble columns and gilded roof, just like the one at St. Peter's or St. John Lateran, in Rome. Well, almost.[37]

And then, along the inside walls of the temple, there is a whole array of other Gods, Athene, Aphrodite, Artemis, none of them particularly striking, but all there to lend support and grandeur to the chief Gods, Hadad and Atargatis. Our guide wanted us particularly to notice the statue of Apollo, bearded and in armor, which is apparently rare, holding a spear in one hand and a flower in the other. There's bound to be a story about it, but I'm relieved to say we didn't hear it.

What mattered most for the locals was that this Apollo predicts the future. One of the priests told us (there are three hundred of them apparently—temple tourism here is big business) that Apollo (they mean his statue) gives oracles by moving in different directions of his own accord, sometimes even leaping up into the air, though it needs a priest or two to interpret what he means. And to prove how effective the Gods are, we were shown the precious gifts of gold, silver, and clothing brought by distant pilgrims, over centuries. Hint, hint. The store of wealth was impressive, especially given the pervasive poverty around.

We asked about the origins of the temple, but it was difficult to get reliable information. Always is, I suppose. Everyone we asked told us something different. At first I found this extremely irritating. Like getting different bus times in modern Egypt. I confronted one priest quite forcefully with some of his contradictions. He just smiled benignly and shrugged his shoulders. After all, I wanted the Gods' favor, or so I had told him, and he had the key, physically and metaphorically, to the Goddess. And in the end I realized that having a variety of accounts, instead of a single "true" account, made some sense. I suppose in a minor way that was a conversion.

As I see it, it isn't a matter principally of different levels of sophistication—you know, complex analyses for the educated, simple stories for the masses—though there is a bit of that. And obviously, when punters come out of the temple, if you ask them what happened inside, you'd find that their understandings and memories differ radically. But I think it's more important that a variety of holy stories reflects the mysterious unknowability of the divine. And curiously, this variety empowers both the storyteller and his listeners. It's mutually convenient.

The storyteller can ad-lib and embroider tradition to suit circumstances or as a reflection of his piety (you can hear the process with modern tourist guides, who often tell the most absurd and inaccurate stories). And the listener is free to forget, remember, be skeptical or impressed. But the priest has two built-in power plays: like a real estate salesman, he's been there before, and often; the punter, by comparison, is always a novice. And if the customer wants something specific, like health, wealth, a nicer partner, or relief from pain, then the priest, like my priest now, holds the key to access. And for access, the punter has to pay the Goddess, of course.

The festival at Holy City seemed quite extraordinary, especially once I put together what we saw and what we heard in to one giant stew. Mixing autopsy with narrative is not conventional, but I personally think it's fair. After all, it's what pilgrims do themselves. They supplement their actual experiences with stories, in anticipation beforehand and in memory afterward. And sophisticates, who can't bear to read or hear simple stories, do fancy allegorical stuff (or split theological hairs) to reassure themselves that they're (or their God is) special. So here goes.

First of all, your real male pilgrim (not superficial tourists like us) shaves himself completely bald (like an Egyptian priest), not just the hair on his head, but eyebrows too.[38] If he's a young lad on his first pilgrimage, he takes some hairs from his beard and puts them into as expensive a box as he can afford (gold or silver for the seriously rich), and then when he arrives, dedicates it at the temple, together with a name tag to commemorate his devotion. Young girls too dedicate a lock of hair. Looking at name tags, remembering your own, and comparing it with others' devotion is a great side attraction of the festival.

Next our pilgrim (he's still at home) sacrifices a sheep, eats the meat, but uses the sheepskin as a prayer mat, while putting his own newly bald head (can you believe this?) inside the sacrificed sheep's head. At Rome there is a famous statue of the emperor Commodus with his head inside a lion's head. I imagined that the lion was long dead, and just there as a heroic metaphor: emperor, lion slayer, just like Hercules (plate 8). But perhaps given Commodus' reputation as a first-rate hunter, it too once had blood dripping from it. The Romans are gorier than we can possibly imagine. Anyhow, these pilgrims' heads go inside the bloody, newly slaughtered sheep. After that the pilgrims cover their heads with garlands, are forbidden to wash in, or drink, anything except cold water or to sleep on a bed until they get back home from Hierapolis. I guess it's all designed to make sure that by the time they arrive, they're dirty, tired, and depressed. But it sure signifies that they take religion seriously.

As to the origins of the temple, we both just got hopelessly contradictory and incoherent accounts. Each story seemed designed to explain a particular local religious practice. First I was told a feeble version of the Noah flood story. The first humans were wicked, so they were all punished with a huge flood, except for one good guy called Deucalion, who led his family and animals to safety in a large boat. The flood drained away down a hole in the ground, and the temple is built over the hole (which, like obedient tourists, we saw yesterday). And that is why one of the great festivals here marks a pilgrimage to get seawater—and the sea is well over a hundred kilometers away.

Then another guide, I mean priest, lying in wait for gullible visitors, told Martha a quite different story about how the temple was founded. This one explains why the locals don't eat fish and do respect doves, which is, of course, what I've always wanted to know. Martha remembered, by the way, that Egyptian priests didn't eat doves either.[39] It was some incredible yarn about a Goddess mother, half woman, half fish, like a mermaid, and her daughter who became a dove. I couldn't make head or tail of it.

Martha heard a third story—we'd separated for a bit; it seemed quite safe, and we needed a bit of a break from each other. This one, at least in her version, was completely insipid, but at least it was trying to explain a central rite of the place. Hierapolis is the castration capital of the Roman empire. Young men castrate themselves in the holy service of the Mother Goddess Cybele. Actually, you find small bands of eunuch priests not just here but wandering all over the place. I forgot to tell you, we'd seen one back in Pompeii, and the mere sight of it had sent our young but simple slave Myrmex into a paroxysm of shudders. He had tried to hide behind the dwarf, Aesop, which was quite amusing, but for the fact that Myrmex was obviously terrified. Aesop eventually wormed the reason out of him and told us.

Myrmex, who in spite of his simplicity was quite a good-looking hulk, had once been slave to a group of wandering eunuch beggar priests serving Cybele and Attis. According to his story, "bugger priests" would have been more appropriate. Anyhow, these priests dressed like women, Myrmex said, in gaudy clothes, wore heavy makeup with lots of rouge on their cheeks and mascara, and lived off the donations of believers. When they came to a new town, to whip up custom they used to parade through the streets the statue of the Goddess strapped to their donkey's back, the priests shaking cymbals and castanets, and with Myrmex (the only whole male of the group) playing the horn. OK, it's a bad joke, but that's what Aesop told me. In the Roman world, you don't have to be pious about priests.[40]

As soon as they got a reasonable crowd, these eunuch priests danced like maniacs and cut their bare arms with sharp knives, so that the blood flowed; and one of them (they took it in turns, Myrmex said) worked himself into a frenzy, confessed his guilt, and cried out that he had sinned against the sacred laws of the Goddess. Then he flogged himself with a particularly painful whip, threaded with bones, until the ground around him was slippery with blood. If they were lucky, the crowd would be so impressed they would shower the priests with copper and even silver coins, food, barley, wheat, wine, cheese, real luxuries. So they lived quite well, and added to their income by telling fortunes. Myrmex said that they were complete rogues and gave the same incomprehensible oracle to everyone. But his life was hell, the priests were so cruel, demanding, and randy—he never knew how long he would stay intact. Anyhow, in the end the priests were caught red handed stealing a gold cup from a temple, and Myrmex was sold, but only after a horrendous flogging from the public executioner.[41]

But back to the story which Martha heard. Basically, it just repeated the common tale of Cybele and Attis. The Goddess Rhea (or Cybele/Atargatis—she's called different names in different places) got her lover, a handsome young man called Attis, to castrate himself so that he couldn't have sex with anyone else. At that time Hierapolis was the farthest outpost in Greek civilization to which Attis came, whipping up enthusiasm for his cult. And that's why her temple is here. Beyond Hierapolis lay the desert, the Euphrates, and the Persian empire. It's a very lame story, except it's true that Hierapolis is on the frontier of civilization; as I've said, it's only a dozen miles from the Euphrates.

CASTRATION AGAIN (JAMES)

Both of us heard the fourth story as we were strolling around the temple courtyard, looking at the various statues of local heroes. Most of these heroes figured in the story, which made it a bit more interesting, though it was a lot longer than the other versions. But just like them, it's a far-fetched, cock-and-bull yarn. (That's what we probably think about all myths adorning a religion which isn't ours.) This tale also tries to explain why young men castrate themselves in the service of the Mother Goddess. Apparently they do it right here in the street during the spring festival. We'd just missed it. Exactly as Myrmex had told us, the priests and their castrated followers whip one another and cut their arms, so that there is blood everywhere, all to the tune of flutes and drums. Others sing hymns or get carried away by inspiration. And even some of the spectators join in the hysteria, or that's what we were told. And it could be true; quite a lot of holy guys castrate themselves and dress up as women, even now in India, and in the service of the Mother Goddess. They help out at weddings, to bring fertility![42]

In ancient Hierapolis, the Syrian youth who wants to do it throws off his clothes and rushes stark naked to the open space in the center of the crowd, takes the ritual sword, and castrates himself there and then, in public. Believe it or not, they parade later, with him holding up what he has cut off. Some people say that the *galli* (which is Latin for "cocks") castrate themselves with specially sharpened shards (at least that way you avoid rust), but, my God, those shards would have to be sharp. To add insult to injury, the castrates wear women's clothing, as though to say that women are men with their penises chopped off! These Romans are disgustingly primitive.

Anyhow, this tale about how the temple was founded goes like this.[43] It's constructed like a Russian doll, with one story hiding another. This is how it begins. A king's son falls desperately in love with his father's new wife. Since he can't express his love, he becomes sick and then dangerously ill. His father summons a skillful doctor, who realizes in general what's wrong. Artfully, the doctor calls the whole household together, and meanwhile holds his hand on the youth's heart. The youth lies quite passively, until his stepmother comes into the room. Then his body trembles and his heart pounds. The doctor cleverly tricks the king into saying that the life of his son is more important than the love of a woman, and then reveals that the son is in fact in love with the king's wife. The king, true to his word, as a king should be, leaves his wife and his kingdom to his son. Do all religious stories have deeply improbable beginnings?

Now for the second act. Previously, when the queen had been living with her first husband, she had a dream in which the Goddess ordered her to build a temple in Hierapolis, the holy city. Typically, the queen paid no attention to the dream, but subsequently she falls seriously ill. Only then does she realize what is wrong, and persuades her new husband to let her go to Hierapolis with huge funds to supervise the building of a temple.[44] And he chooses one of his best friends, called Combabus, to escort the queen and be in charge of the enterprise.

Combabus is horrified. He is young; the queen is beautiful; he knows he can't come out of this affair unscathed; he begs out. But the king insists, so Combabus plays for time and requests a single week's postponement. He has to do something desperate. He castrates himself and embalms his genitals in a small pot, which he carefully seals and publicly entrusts to the king in open court: "It's more precious than gold," he says.

For three years the queen and Combabus work together at building the temple. And what Combabus feared happens. The queen falls madly in love with him. Perhaps the Goddess was still angry with her for delaying the temple building. At first she just weeps and keeps her love secret, then she determines to have her way. One evening after dinner, fortified by drink, she blurts out her passion. Combabus angrily rejects her and reveals his whole story to her. She calms down a bit, but she still loves him. And even to this day, people told us, some women fall in love with the castrated priests; things happen like that in the holy city of Hierapolis.

Naturally, others notice how much time the queen is spending with Combabus, and eventually rumors reach the king. Some people tell the story differently. They say the queen took her revenge for her rejection and herself accused Combabus of trying to seduce her. Anyhow, Combabus is summoned back home, imprisoned, and accused of adultery, abuse of trust, and impiety to the Goddess. There are many hostile witnesses, and all the courtiers were against Combabus. He is sentenced to death.

All this time Combabus remains silent (Jesus was not the only holy man to be tried by a ruler and remain silent when falsely accused). But when he is being taken off to execution, Combabus asks for the precious jar which he had so providently deposited in the king's care. The jar is duly brought and opened, to reveal both what Combabus had suffered and his innocence. The king is filled with remorse, the false accusers are themselves executed, Combabus is given rich gifts of gold and horses, and high status, and is allowed to finish building the temple, where he remains for the rest of his life. So high is his prestige that some of his closest friends decide to castrate themselves to keep him company. And they erect a bronze statue to him, which was one of those we'd seen when we were touring the temple.

I've gone on too long, but I haven't explained yet about the phallus climbers. Just outside the temple, on either side of the steps, there are a couple of impressive statues, one of the Goddess welcoming you to the temple, the other of the local cruel God Bes, with an enormous phallus. That must have given some locals the idea of decorating two giant stone pillars in front of the temple to look like penises. During the spring festival, athletic young men climb up these columns and when they get to the top they haul up clothes and what they need to make a nest. But they are not allowed to sleep while they're up there, and they have to stay for a week, which is quite an ordeal, and dangerous. Meanwhile, every day, down on the ground, ordinary people come and put money in a jar, and one of the climber's assistants shouts out each donor's name. And the phallus climber, as though he is halfway to heaven, says a prayer for the petitioner. I suppose in some way these are the slightly odd pagan predecessors of the Syrian pillar saints, though St. Symeon spent over thirty years on top of his pillar.

Anyhow, we were strolling along in the temple, looking at the various pictures and tablets which people had put up to commemorate the Goddess's miraculous healing powers. We asked an old priest about them. Unfortunately, he turned out to be an unstoppable gabber and explained the first picture in immense detail, full of moral warnings and exhortations. All I remember really is that Fortune is blind and mad; but humans beg for Good Fortune and then, when they get a bit of it, give themselves all the credit for achievement and virtue! Even so, Good Fortune never lasts, and undermines itself by vicious tricks and temptations, such as Luxury, Profligacy, Flattery—all represented in this Roman man's world, inevitably, as women. Then Repentance (another woman) may save the now poor man, but only by her own choice. According to this morality, life is decided by external forces, or by Gods dressed as virtues and vices, though humans can help or hinder by better or worse choices.[45]

It all sounded quite moderate to me, no hair shirts, no celibacy, no castration; an ideal religious ethic for a prosperous elite who had not yet suffered ill fortune. Perhaps the priest was smarter than I had given him credit for, and had seen through my disguise. No, on second thought, this was the stuff he delivered to all out-of-town pilgrims. They were bound to be comfortably off; his gentle chiding made them more generous.

Our garrulous old priest did tell us one or two more interesting stories. As a young man he had traveled quite widely, visiting temples in nearby Asia Minor and Greece. One temple he remembered particularly was in a country district near Ancyra. The people there were particularly pious and sinful. "Yes," he said, "you can be both." But when these country folk committed sins, they did not always admit them immediately, just like the queen in the previous story, who didn't pay attention to her divine dream. But the local God Men caught up with the sinners and punished them with a painful sickness, or blindness or madness. That made them realize that it was impossible to hide sins from the God, so they confessed to the temple priest, who usually imposed a mild penalty, such as a compensatory gift to the God. That, and the very act of confession, made the sickness go away, and in gratitude the repentant sinners set up simple memorials telling their stories, their sins, and their cures. It was a great warning to other people around not to ignore the power of the God.[46] Clearly, Jews and Christians did not have a monopoly of sin, guilt, confession. I was quite surprised.

"You have to be careful how you pray," the priest said. "I saw two tablets side by side in one temple of Asclepius.[47] One was quite modest; it commemorated the God's mercy in releasing a woman from a pregnancy which had lasted five years. The one right next to it told how a woman prayed to the God to make her pregnant, that's all. She became pregnant, but the pregnancy went on and on. After three years she came back to the temple and upbraided the God, but he said, quite properly, that he had given her all that she had asked for. So this time she prayed for birth, and he was merciful. No sooner had she left the temple precinct than her prayer was answered, and she gave birth successfully. If you folk need help with wording your prayers precisely, I'll be pleased to help," said the priest. After Martha nudged me, I took the hint, and we got rid of him with only two silver coins. He seemed pleased, and was bound to practice the same routine on his next visitors. It was time to leave Syria and try our luck in the great city of Ephesus.

ARREST AND TRIAL IN EPHESUS (*MARTHA*)

Ephesus was magnificent. The site helps. The city is built overlooking the sea but rises up along a steep-sided valley. The main street leading from the harbor is five hundred meters long and eleven meters wide, with grand shady colonnades either side. Off to the left, there is the giant harbor bath-and-gymnasium complex, the largest outside Italy, we were told, and only just finished. We wandered in on our first day, and gasped at the ostentatious luxury of the surroundings, ornate ceilings, with marble cladding everywhere. James said that in the men-only gymnasium young athletes, the local elite glistening with oil, wrestled naked in the sand, and showed off their muscles and status by conspicuous consumption of energy and leisure. Then we went along past the huge public market and the theater, nestling in the hillside, capable of seating twenty-four thousand spectators. We walked out of town toward the great Temple of Artemis, Ephesus' pride and joy, with its famous, amazing, and beautiful many-breasted statue of the Goddess (plate 7). Some scholars nowadays say that the Goddess' breasts are really bulls' testicles, and I've heard a modern tourist say confidently that they're figs. But that's the whole point of symbolism, it makes you wonder what it means. To me the whole design implies breasts, womanness, succor, and fertility all over. But I've no idea what the original sculptor or ancient worshipers thought. I do know that some of the faithful buried the Goddess carefully when triumphant Christians began replacing statues of Artemis with crosses.[48]

Back in the city, of course, we were impressed by the streets paved with marble, artificial waterfalls, the grand ceremonial arches topped with statues of Gods and emperors, by rich grandees' terraced houses on the steep hillside overlooking the main street, and by the Library of Celsus, recently built, and looking even grander than it does now. We were astonished by the sheer mass of statues and altars set up by dignitaries and visitors to honor the city and themselves. We could have spent days rediscovering the city's history by reading inscription after inscription honoring priests, donors, magistrates, and Gods, and amassed higgledy-piggledy, or so it seemed, on every available surface of wall and column. In some sense this was your typical Roman city, such as we can still see glimpses of all over the Mediterranean basin, in Italy, southern France and Spain, north Africa, Jordan, and Turkey. But of course, it was on a grander scale because Ephesus was the chief city of the province of Asia. So there were temples and a theater, baths and basilicas, the hallmarks of Roman culture and civilization.

But it was more complicated than that. To be sure, Rome had stamped its mark on the city. Four central temples dedicated to Roman emperors, buildings dedicated to Augustus and Tiberius, over-life-size statues of Titus and Trajan, statues of Hadrian and his wife, and all this by the time of our visit (c. 138 CE), ensured that no one in Ephesus could easily forget Rome's overlordship. Temples to Roman Gods had changed the whole symbolic landscape of the city.[49] And halfway up the hill, well above the theater, the official residence of the Roman governor, with its fresh breezes and panoramic views, symbolized the supremacy of Roman power.

And yet, beneath the Roman heel, a proud if transmuted tradition of Greek cultural separateness and antiquity survived. It is probably most apparent for us in Greek speeches and writings of the period, and in the obligation which Roman leaders felt to speak and write Greek fluently. But the tension between ancient Greek culture and Roman power was visible in the city. For example, the Temple to Domitian and his family was decorated with imperial statues set up by donations of the "free and autonomous" cities of the region. A cynic might sneer at these pretensions of freedom as incompatible with the gifts of subservience to Roman power. But the claims of autonomy and freedom probably mattered to the Greek town leaders. And the harbor baths, built out of respect for Roman customs, were dwarfed by the adjacent gymnasia and palaestra (wrestling school) built firmly in the Greek tradition.

Finally, a generous donation by a Roman knight in the early second century funded a yearly procession to honor the birthday of Artemis. At the head of the procession, thirty gilded and silver statues celebrated Roman imperial and Greek traditions. The imperial family, the Senate, the Roman people all featured. But both in image and ritual, the center stage was filled by the invented antiquity of local traditions and the traditional cult of Artemis. Rome mattered, but in this ritual celebration it mattered less than competitively refurbished local Greek pride.[50]

And yet again, the shadows of Roman power were not so easily swept aside. Even time in Ephesus was dominated by Rome. One of the inscriptions we saw, carved impressively on marble, recorded that in 9 BCE, twenty years or so into the reign of the first Roman emperor, Augustus, the provincial governor of Asia proposed that out of gratitude for the benefits of universal peace the calendar should be recalibrated. He suggested that Augustus' birthday (September 23) should now mark the start of the calendrical year, because it was "equivalent to the beginning of everything . . . the beginning of life and living, which has set a limit to regret for being born." The council of Asian towns responded enthusiastically: "The birthday of the God [they meant Augustus] marked the beginning for the whole world of the good tidings which he brought."[51] So, a few years before Jesus' birth, God Augustus' birthday was used to mark the start of a new era, at least in western Turkey. And the term "good tidings" in the council's decision is the same as the later Christian word for "gospel." The equation man-made-God and God-made-man was being worked out almost simultaneously but differently in neighboring provinces.

One other inscription particularly caught our attention. It was set up outside a small house temple dedicated to Zeus and Hestia (the Latin Vesta, the hearth Goddess). Worshipers entering the temple, whether male, female, slave, or free, were to obey the following rules: they were not to administer abortifacient or contraceptive charms or drugs, rob or murder, or assist anyone else, or stand silently by. Men were to have sex only with their wives, and not have sex with slaves, male or female. Women too should have sex only with their husbands. Any infraction bars a worshiper from entry. The Gods of the temple observe behavior carefully and will punish transgressions terribly. "To those who obey, the Gods will be gracious as they customarily are to those whom they love." Men, women, slave, and free should believe within themselves and obey these commandments, so that they can take part in the monthly sacrifices. The inscription seemed quite old and worn, and we had no opportunity to check out who or how many people belonged. But the morality and commitment sounded quite committedly Christian.[52]

It all happened so suddenly. We'd had quite a good time. For a change, James was being quite reasonable. Anyhow, there we were, strolling up the grand marble street from the Library of Celsus, past the oversized statue of the emperor Trajan, when someone shouted for us to stop. Then this arrogant, foppish-looking guy, carefully coiffed, with a small retinue of tough but well-dressed slaves, sauntered up to James and said: "Can I have back now what you've been owing me for too long?" For me, just one look at him was enough; he spelled big trouble. This definitely was not the time or place to be British. But James, never one to kowtow, was having none of it and retorted truculently: "I don't understand. You're mad."

Caius (we later found out he was a local grandee, Caius Terentius Flavianus, from a family with all the right connections): "I lent you money and you call me mad; don't you recognize me? Are you trying to cheat me?"

James: "Back off, and find the real guy you lent money to. It wasn't me."

Caius: "I can't believe what you're saying to me. You're insulting me. I'll get my own back and in good measure, you scum. You don't know what's good for you."

And at a nod, his slaves, who looked used to this kind of business, grabbed James, who rather feebly said: "Take your hands off me."

Caius: "Hold your tongue." (And to his slaves) "If he causes trouble, knock his teeth out." (To James) "You're a rogue or an impostor. I want to know whether you're slave or freed. Your master shall hear of this, and he'll either have you crucified or you'll rot in prison until you're old."[53]

And that's where James went, with me weakly following.

Once in prison, things went from bad to worse. James was asked who he was and who would go surety for him. Of course, we knew absolutely no one. In the circumstances, we could hardly claim that we came from Ephesus, as we had in Pompeii. James extemporized cleverly enough. But in the Roman world, if you don't have a patron to speak up for you, you're in trouble. The prison clerk was already hostile. James' accuser was a citizen of note, one of the priests of Artemis.[54] James was roughly searched, his money bags discovered, counted. By the poor jailer's standards, he was carrying a small fortune in cash. It was our insurance against disaster. It didn't turn out that way. Exactly the opposite. The jailer looked curiously at some bronze coins we had with the Goddess Isis on one side and an emperor's head on the other. He called a buddy, and then a superior, then a money changer. The coins, they claimed, were counterfeit. Now James faced not just a civil suit for nonpayment of a debt but the serious criminal charge of dealing in false coins.[55]

Only when we had got back to England did we work out what had gone wrong. By mistake, the Netherlands Coin Cabinet had given us some Isis coins minted in the fourth century under Christian emperors.

So now we were being tried for producing coins two centuries early, rather like the Seven Sleepers of Ephesus, those ancient time travelers who by a miracle died in the third century during the Decian persecutions and woke up in the middle of the fifth century. They too were arrested, but for producing coins two centuries late. But at least they had proved to the satisfaction of the local bishop that physical resurrection of the body was possible.[56] We'd proved nothing.

But for now prison was the new reality: dark, dank, dirty, airless, though with a small bribe I was allowed to visit and bring the manacled James food. Just as well I did, because as far as I could tell, none was provided. Luckily the assizes were due in a couple of days, though no one knew for sure when they would begin. And waiting was hell. But then, very early one morning, I was tipped off (for another bribe; just as well James and I had kept our money separately) that James was being moved to the long navelike basilica by the upper market. We were kept in a throng of prisoners and soldiers some way down the hall; the governor, Julius Alexander Berenicianus, ex-consul, entered, preceded by his rod-bearing lictors and followed by his younger assessors. A herald told everyone to stand, while the judges sat on thronelike chairs on a raised dais at one end of the hall.[57] At the other end, Augustus and his wife, Livia, sat serenely as statues, overseeing the administration of justice. James' wasn't the first case to be heard. Thank God.

The first accused was on a charge of highway robbery. We couldn't hear much or see much because of the hubbub around us. But we heard his screams as soon as he was strung up and flogged. He obviously persisted in pleading not guilty, and so his torture didn't stop. In the end, he was sentenced to death.[58] Poor fellow, and it hadn't taken long either. Roman justice at this level was rough. Perhaps it was designed to make a deep impression. It did on us.

The second case was more complicated, with lawyers acting for both sides. No long-winded Cicero-style declamations, but brief depositions, legal documents read aloud or passed around, mutual interrogations with frequent interruptions by judge, advocates, and litigants, and loud partisan reactions from claques of bystanders. This trial mixed justice with theater. The claimant was trying to recover an outrageously over-due debt from the son of the alleged debtor, his social superior. We listened all ears; it might give us some clues. The creditor had taken the law into his own hands by locking up the debtor and his family. At least the foppish Caius Terentius had sent James to the public prison. The governor eventually gave judgment, after briefly consulting with his assessors: "You deserve to be whipped," he said to the creditor, "for detaining a respectable man and his womenfolk on your own initiative. But in deference to the crowd, I shall be generous to you. You have waited forty years to bring this charge. I'll grant you half that time. Apply to me again in twenty years."[59] Our judge was clearly a wit and liked playing to the crowd, or exercising his power arbitrarily.

We were shuffled closer up front. James' case was to be the next but one. It wasn't comforting. Brigandage again, apparently a retrial. The ragged accused was stripped, hung up, and flogged. "Now, tell the truth," said the judge. "Were you with the brigands?" The accused said: "We confessed because of the tortures." The judge looked at his papers: "But who was with you from the village?" The man screamed, and mumbled something we couldn't hear. Judge: "And who else?" By this time, the poor fellow was half dead, and pretty clearly not much more could be got out of him.[60] *Case dismissed*, said the judge. I wondered if he would ever recover. This was the savage side of Roman justice. It wasn't only Christian martyrs who suffered. But now we had ourselves to think of.

Caius Terentius Flavianus, James' initial accuser, was nowhere to be found. He'd put us into prison and then simply didn't show up. Surely, no accuser, no case. But then the jailer came greasily forward and handed the judge our suspect coins. "What is your name, and where are you from?" asked the judge. James answered as we had agreed. The judge said: "String him up, and flog him." Now, I was quite willing to experiment a little with the Roman justice system, and James could be a real piece of work at times, but I saw no reason to have him tortured for the sake of ancient history. So I pressed the panic button strapped to my thigh, and in a microsecond we both dematerialized, I imagine to general astonishment. "I bet that foxed them," I said to James. "Oh, I dunno," he said; "if they've read the New Testament or the life of Apollonius of Tyana, they should be used to miracles."[61]

SIX

Pagans vs. Christians vs. Jews

PRELUDE

King's College,
Cambridge CB2 IST

My dear Hartmut,

What a stroke of luck. I've unearthed two previously unpublished third-century letters written by and to an earnest new Christian, called Macarius, about a dinner party he's just attended. He innocently accepted an invitation to dinner with some old pagan friends and got roundly attacked for his new "superstitions." He's more shaken than wounded, and a bit unsure of himself. Actually what hurt him most is that his friends confused his Christianity with Judaism. Not something that either he or the Jew sitting next to him at dinner appreciated.

What apparently worries him is, did he say the right things? Of course, we can't tell, because only his account, written to his spiritual guru, survives. But his account has a naive plausibility, though Macarius comes over as slightly self-indulgent, indecisive, and well-meaning. But then, is his naivete, the fact that he doesn't get his arguments quite right the first time, in itself a rhetorical ploy to be persuasive? And he can always tell us what he should have said. He does, in a second bite at the cherry of truth. And then his adviser, Clement, who obviously fancies himself as a thinker, puts him right.

I know you had serious misgivings and some criticisms of what I sent you last time, about the New Testament apocrypha [Chapter Four above]. But I thought it worth persisting, and you know how much I value your comments for their learning, acumen, and honesty. I still want to experiment with a different style of history writing. Here I've tried to catch the atmosphere of educated Romans socializing, and discussing religion seriously. Could you possibly look through and comment?

It begins with a mosaic of second-century Christian apologists, similar to those found in other writings, with some linking stage directions. The characterizations seem genuinely classical, and all the criticisms made against Christians and all the defences of Christianity are found in Christian sources.[1] It's surprising, isn't it, that Christian writers were so thorough as to include the vulgar accusation that Christians murdered and ate babies, worshiped an ass head, and even that they venerated Jesus' erect penis. You probably think that such vulgarities are not worth recycling. But I can't help thinking that whatever the justification (or lack of it) for such wild accusations, these were the rough ideas which underwrote popular anger against Christians and their repeated persecution. Anyhow, what matters most for my present purposes is that these were the arguments which clever and educated Christians chose to defend themselves against. For the most part, we know about attacks against Christianity only because Christian writers have preserved them. Please let me know what you think.

The second section reflects Jewish impatience with Christians, not the usual discussion of ritual curses made at least by some Jews in their daily prayers in synagogues, but instead some crude stories told by Jews about Jesus.[2] The surviving manuscripts of these stories are quite late (sixth century onward), but then, the earliest surviving manuscripts of Ovid come from the ninth century. I can't believe it took hostile Jews six hundred years to invent invective against Jesus, so I'm quite happy with the notion that Jews for centuries told some such stories among themselves to discredit Christians.

Macarius' letter finishes with a ghost story. At first sight it may seem a bit out of place. But it illustrates perfectly how pervasive demons were in the thought world of Jews, pagans, and Christians alike. Nowadays we despise demons as vulgar superstition and exclude them from our everyday understanding—though even now they occasionally get their revenge, especially (?) on children at night—about how our idealized ancients thought. Apparently, most people in the Roman world, whether Greek, Roman, Syrian, or Egyptian, educated or uneducated, pagan, Christian, or Jew, believed in demons fervently, in many cases as fervently (perhaps on a different register) as they believed in gods. Do you agree? Anyhow, I think it's a really good ghost story. When I first read it I had nightmares.

The chapter simulates the atmosphere of a real dinner party—normal conversations go in dozens of different directions. Sure, the author necessarily imposes some sort of order in his reportage. Actually, I think even in academic history it's important occasionally to reproduce the chaos of the lived experience. Historians regularly write objective history as though they were birds of prey, viewing historical actors from an objective height. This is atmospheric observation, written from the ground level, semichaotic history—I think that's what I'd like to call it.

Anyhow, I'd be terribly grateful if you would let me know what you think about my find, again as frankly as you wish.

Yours ever,

Keith

DINNER PARTY CONVERSATIONS

Cast, in Order of Appearance

Macarius, *a slightly earnest but insecure Christian, the author of this letter*

Clement, *his learned and supercilious mentor*

Celsus, *sharp eyed, silvery hair, a liberal pagan*

Crispus, *their wealthy and courteous host*

Avenna *and* Lucius, *two leading town officials and pagan priests; Lucius is also a well-known writer and storyteller*

Epiphanius, *an aggressive and ugly pagan*

Isidorus, *aka Simon, son of Judas, a hellenizing Jew, also a town official*

There are women in the background, sitting at a separate table. Macarius records nothing of what they said—typical.

Macarius to Clement, Brother:

It was very cold, just the weather for hot food and good company. Celsus, a freethinking philosopher, had asked me to go along to a dinner with friends at the house of Crispus. I've known some of them since we went to school together, and we have always got on well. So I thought I ought to go, although I don't often go out to dinner with unbelievers. As you know, one problem which always crops up is that we can't eat meat which has been offered up as a sacrifice to one of their gods. And once you are in company, it can be quite embarrassing to avoid eating what you are served. Of course, some people just pick at the vegetables, but even that attracts people's attention.[3]

But here was a chance for serious conversation, an opportunity for me to discuss the nature of beliefs with educated and sophisticated men. I'd known some of them besides Celsus since we were students together in Athens. Secretly, I thought I might persuade them all to believe in the true God—or at least to take our sacred writings more seriously. Of course, I knew I would have to put up with some criticism, but then tough arguments in a good cause are easier to bear than the pains of martyrdom. But I didn't realize quite how trenchant their criticisms would turn out to be. Obviously, Celsus had been rehearsing, so that I got home quite shaken up. To tell you the truth, after that bombardment I was not really so sure after all about my own faith. I thought you might be able to help me, tell me what I ought to have replied.

Some of it was rather shocking and irreverent. But I expect in your position you've heard it all before, so I'll pluck up my courage and tell you the gist of what he and the others said. Needless to say, one of them started off by accusing us Christians of being a recklessly revolutionary secret society, drawing our members "from the illiterate dregs of the populace, and credulous women with the instability natural to their sex." Avenna, who is one of this year's chief magistrates here and a priest of the imperial cult, piled it on (he's rich and rather obnoxious, with a thin, grating voice, the sort of person who rolls his eyes, cocks his head, and keeps on looking round for approval): "You Christians are just a rabble of profane conspirators, bound together by nighttime meetings, ritual fasts, and disgusting feasts. You spit on our Gods, laugh at our sacred rites, despise our civic titles and robes of honor, while you yourselves go around half naked."[4] I had absolutely no idea what he had in mind, and was just about to object when Lucius, his senior colleague and a lawyer, butted in.

"You are quite right," he said. "I asked one of my slaves about these Christians, and he told me that they recognize one another by secret signs and tattoos. They work themselves into a kind of religious lust, fall in love almost before they know each other. They are a promiscuous brotherhood and sisterhood, in which fornication is turned into incest under guise of holiness. Did you know? Some of them consecrate the head of an ass, and actually worship the genitals of their founder and priest, and adore his organs as the Creator of their being [plates 22–23]. And he was nothing but a crucified criminal.[5]

"As for their initiation rituals, they are absolutely shocking. It's quite beyond belief, but this is exactly what my carriage driver told me. They actually get a live baby, case it in dough, and put it beside the initiate. The neophyte is ordered to hit the dough as hard as he can, and so unintentionally kills the infant. Then the Christians drink its blood, tear its limbs to pieces, swear an oath of covenant over its body, and so pledge themselves to silence by complicity in guilt. After that, as if this were not enough, and only the Gods know why they do it, they tie a dog to a lamp, and when everyone of all ages and sexes is thoroughly drunk, they throw a morsel to the dog slightly out of its reach. Of course, the dog pulls the lamp over and then in the ensuing darkness, they have indiscriminate intercourse with drunken lust" (plate 24).[6]

Now, I thought that all this nonsensical stuff about Christians having nighttime orgies was old hat and no one believed it any longer, though I have heard fellow Christians make the same accusations about heretics—you know some Gnostics behave very strangely.[7] But here were grown-up, sophisticated, and educated men talking about it as though it were true. I could hardly believe my ears. And I said so, in no uncertain terms. I said they were reducing a serious religion to the level of one of these newfangled erotic novels which are filled with dramas involving canni-balism and fake deaths. Novels and real life have little to do with each other.[8] Of course, Christians didn't have nighttime orgies; they are, as you know, brother, kindly, hardworking, charitable, and God-fearing.

"That may be true," said Celsus good-humoredly. "I personally am quite willing to believe you. But even you, Macarius, must agree that on the political level Christians have serious charges to answer. To put it bluntly, Christians are an antisocial, illegal, secret, and seditious sect. Christians exist within the Roman state, take the benefits of Roman rule, but refuse to cooperate with the government. They have been univer-sally unpopular at all levels of society, from emperors to provincial gov-ernors and town councilors, right down to the common people." Celsus said that our leaders just throw themselves at the authorities, almost beg-ging to be tortured and crucified for their faith, and to no purpose.[9]

"Why can't you compromise?" he said. "After all, different peoples all over the world call their Gods by different names. All except you and the Jews agree to worship the highest Gods in public for the common good. And the Jews have the age-old justification of long tradition. Besides, they used to worship their God in a temple like ours, with altars, victims, and rites, though their God didn't help them as much as they hoped, given that their temple is now destroyed and they are ruled by us Ro-mans. But they at least came sufficiently to their senses, and agreed long ago to sacrifice *for* the emperor, even though not *to* him. It surely wouldn't be too dreadful if someone told you Christians to take an oath 'by an emperor,' or pour a simple libation 'to the emperor's health.' Couldn't you just participate in our public festivals, for the sake of form, and take the occasional public office, and perform public duties for the common good? Actually, I personally know of some quite respectable Christians who do just that, however much it goes against their highest ideals. After all, what would happen if everyone refused to serve in the army on religious grounds?"[10]

Celsus paused, his keen black eyes sparkling. He has a shock of silver hair, is very handsome, knows it, and uses his good looks and charm to get his way. Under his influence, I began to have an inkling as to why some people do think of us as obdurate radicals, and why the general populace blames us in a crisis for famine, plague, or earthquakes.[11] To them, we seem impious. Of course, I tried to explain as best I could that we cannot serve two masters. We cannot serve both God and Mammon. And if they conflict, we have to prefer God. We do pray for righteousness, and our prayers destroy the wicked demons who cause evil in the world. With our prayers, frugality, and charity, we are fighting for the emperor more effectively than his soldiers do. Our piety does more good than their violence. We cannot compromise our faith if compromise involves us in the licentiousness of public festivals, the savagery of war, or the blasphemy of equating the emperor with the true God.[12]

"As to swearing by the Genius of the emperor, or by his Fortune, I'm afraid that is just a specious disguise for deifying an entity which is not divine. And I personally feel I would rather die than swear by a nonexistent or wicked demon."[13] That's what I said, with some vigor, because I had heard our preachers say similar things in our church meetings. But this time, I'm afraid, they all seemed either puzzled or unimpressed. I even heard one of them mutter, "That would be difficult to prove," but I don't know what in particular he was referring to. I just wish I'd had some of the brethren there to help me out.

"That's just the problem," said Celsus. "You Christians don't like being closely questioned. You want people simply to believe without question and to have faith. You don't want educated and intelligent men, like us, at your meetings; they scare you. You don't come and preach to us. Your whole religion is aimed at the gullible, the uneducated, and the poor. Your converts are slaves, women, and children. You meet in secret, in private houses, with low-class workers, weavers, cobblers, laundrymen, yokels, all illiterates, who would never dare to speak up in the presence of their betters, who are more educated and intelligent. But you Christians get hold of children in private and some weak-minded women, and try to subvert them.[14]

"And it's quite shocking what you tell them, to obey Jesus Christ and not their schoolteachers or fathers. Fathers and schoolteachers, you say, talk complete nonsense, and don't really understand. Only Jesus Christ knows the right way to live. But then if by chance a schoolteacher or father comes into the room, the cautious Christian preacher takes to his heels. He urges women, children, slaves, workers to rebel, surreptitiously. He whispers that he can't say anything more now; the teacher is wicked, evil, and bent on punishing the children. Why not come along sometime with their friends to so and so's little shop, their mothers will be there, and we'll teach you perfection. That's the road to their corruption."[15]

You can imagine how angry I was inside, but I trust I kept my indignation concealed. "It's not true," I said, "that we attract only the poor and the stupid. We try to teach the universal doctrine of Jesus Christ in towns, villages, and the countryside. Lots of people, even rich and honorable men, some scholars too, and ladies of refinement and good birth have joined us. We teach them to believe in the one true God, and in Jesus Christ, his Son, the Holy Spirit, who made the world. We are proud of the fact that we worship a spiritual God, not idols made by common workmen. We teach our followers to despise idols; whether made by great artists or common craftsmen, idols are man-made.[16]

"Above all, we teach our followers virtue, how to be pure in heart and mind, meek, and peace-loving; they respect their neighbors' and their relatives' rights; they are willing, glad even, to suffer for the sake of the faith. We deliver women from licentiousness, perversion, and a mania for theaters, dancing, and wild superstitions. We make young lads self-controlled. You know how most grown-up men hang around the brothels. Instead we teach them to suppress those sexual desires which otherwise dominate adolescent minds. We teach them what penalties they will suffer and how they will be punished for their sins in the afterworld. In this way they make progress toward self-control and righteousness. And even slaves can be taught how to exercise their minds like free men. It is true that there are different levels of understanding, but that is only to be expected. And we do teach our new members thoroughly, and examine them individually to see how carefully they have embraced our values. If they have sinned, they are driven out and readmitted only after penance."[17]

"Actually, I think you encourage sinners," said Celsus. "All they have to do is repent. Whereas our pagan cults explicitly exclude sinners from the precincts of the temple." I replied, rather too hotly perhaps, that people are sinful by nature, that pure virtue is impossible, and that evil just exists in man, though by determination humans can improve themselves. Celsus said dryly that he still thought we Christians concentrated on sin, inventing terrors and using the threat of eternal punishment as bait to attract popular attention. "You are all right, Macarius," he said; "you are very intelligent and educated. But lots of Christian preachers, you must admit, are wandering beggars, charlatans who get into ecstasies, incant the names of demons, pretend to drive out spirits and do other miraculous cures. They prophesy the future, the imminent end of the world in which everyone will be thoroughly roasted alive, except, of course, for the Christians, who will be saved—and not just those who happen to be alive at the time, but all dead Christians too will rise up and repossess the very same bodies as before."[18]

At this, everyone burst into laughter, and several people said: "Macarius, you can't really believe all this nonsense, can you?" and I said, quite boldly I thought, that I used to laugh at these things, just like them. "I too was once one of you," I said, and they knew it was true, and it quieted them for a bit.[19] I was about to go on and explain about the mystery of bodily resurrection, and the difference between literal and allegorical interpretations of the sacred texts, when Celsus got in before me. Of course, I wanted to interrupt, but I really thought it would be best to let him run on; he seemed to have quite a strong wind behind him, and most of the people there seemed to be on his side. I couldn't quite see how to deal with him.

"There are lots of them," he said; "they hang around temples and military camps, begging and offering prophecies. They pretend to be spiritually inspired, and every one of them commonly says: 'I am God, or I am the Son of God, or a divine spirit. And lo, I have come. Already the world is on the point of destruction. And you, O men, because of your iniquities, are doomed to perish. But I want to save you. And you shall see me in due course returning with heavenly power. Blessed is he who worships me now. But on the others, I shall cast everlasting fire, whether they live in cities or in villages. And those who fail to realize the dire punishments in store for them will repent and groan. But I shall save forever those who repent and groan.' And then these fellows go on to shout incomprehensible, incoherent, and utterly obscure phrases, the precise meaning of which no intelligent person could discover, simply because they are meaningless and nonsensical. In fact, the incomprehensibility has a point; it gives any fool the opportunity to interpret what has been said in any way he likes. And in fact," said Celsus, "I've heard similar predictions with my own ears, and have personally questioned these fake prophets about where they got their ideas from. And they told me quite clearly that they had invented it all themselves."[20]

At that very moment the majordomo came in and announced that dinner was ready, so we had to stop talking and think about eating. I was quite flustered; it's not very nice to have what you hold dear so bitterly attacked. I shouldn't have worried so much beforehand about eating sacrificial meats. Celsus' attacks had quite taken my appetite away. Of course, I knew absolutely what I wanted to say in reply, that such charlatans aren't real Christians, that we can't be held responsible for all the excesses of people who call themselves Christians but who aren't members of the churches of God. Have you heard by the way that the Ophites, whom some people confuse with us, actually require their new members to curse the name of Jesus?[21] It just shows how stern we'll have to be in deciding who exactly does and who does not belong to the true Church.

Anyhow, I was thinking about all this, running over the arguments in my head, naturally disappointed that I hadn't had the chance to speak my mind, a bit in a dream, I suppose, while the others were chatting and laughing as we went to our places in the dining room. The others were clearly more at home together, or more adroit, so that they all took their places, with the womenfolk together at a separate table; and as luck would have it, I was seated next to Isidorus, who is a town councilor and the market officer here, though actually everyone knows he is really Simon, the son of Judas.[22] He's jovial enough usually, with a long beard flecked with gray, really quite clever, and I like him on the personal level—I've known him for years—but he's quite extraordinarily touchy on religious matters. And here we were, being lumped together, whether consciously or unconsciously by my host, as birds of a feather. It was all a bit much.

In fact, dinner went quite well. The food was rather grand, with sesame cakes and honey, fried fish, goose, and wild boar. (Simon said he wasn't going to eat any of that! There were limits. I said mildly that I didn't think most Jews nowadays—of his class, I meant—bothered with food rules.) The wine flowed, but most of the guests drank moderately, except for Epiphanius, the rhetorician. He is a short, irascible man, going bald, with a thick neck; he has rotten teeth and poisonous stares, though that doesn't stop him pursuing young boys. In fact, I saw him make up to the slave boy pouring his wine, squeezing his fingers suggestively—you know the disgusting habits of some of these unbelievers.[23] But our host, Crispus, also noticed what was going on and had the wine boy moved to another table.

It was this Epiphanius who started on religion again, although I suspect he had been talking things over with Celsus, because I was surprised at how well informed he was, or rather how detailed his misinformation was. He's a vulgar man, so I'm a bit ashamed really, even to tell you what he said.

"This Jesus," he said, "I don't see how you can think of him as the Son of God. Of course, there were several people at the time who made similar claims: Theudas, Simon, Judas of Galilee, and Dositheus the Samaritan. In fact, Dositheus claimed that he was the prophesied Messiah, and there are still people to this day who believe in him, have read his books, and claim he never died but is still alive. How on earth do you decide between the rival claimants? After all, Jesus was a convicted criminal, betrayed by the very people he called disciples. If he was God, how could he have allowed himself to be arrested? If he was the savior, the son of the greatest God, and an angel, how could he allow himself to be deserted and betrayed by his closest followers, who had privately shared everything with him and who had been favored pupils, with Jesus as their teacher? If Jesus was God, surely he should have done good to those around him. And when he was on trial, at least he could either have instructed his judge or, like Apollonius when he was tried by the tyrant Domitian, have magically disappeared from the courtroom. But all he did was to endure in silence.[24]

"As to the story of his birth from a virgin, conceived by the Holy Spirit, it is obviously a nonsensical fabrication. I have heard the true story. Jesus' mother was a poor spinner in a Jewish village who committed adultery, probably with a soldier, and was driven out for her sin by her husband, the carpenter. She wandered about in disgrace, and secretly gave birth to Jesus. Because he was poor, he hired himself out as a workman in Egypt, and that is where he learned magic (you know what the place is like), began to have delusions, and called himself God. In fact, Jesus was a mere man, and probably a charlatan pretending to effect magical cures and mass illusions in return for a few obols. It is inconceivable that God, who is perfect, would have become an imperfect man (and incidentally, even some Christians admit that Jesus was ugly), or that God would have tried to deceive humans into thinking that he had done so. It is simply impossible for me, for us, to credit that God, or a son of God, has or ever would come down to earth.[25]

"Above it all, these Christians believe—it's quite absurd—in an invisible God. And at the same time, they make him out to be an interfering troublemaker, busy with the whole universe and every little thing that happens in it. Then they threaten the whole world with destruction by fire, and delude themselves that they themselves will be born again after death, and actually seem to have confidence in one another's lies. They believe in bodily resurrection, but quite irrationally avoid cremation as though the body can be reconstituted not from ashes but after years of corruption or the final world destruction.

"They should just look around. The great mass of the world is suffering from want, cold, hunger. Meanwhile the Christians, racked with fever and disease, dream of posthumous immortality. Who is this God who can help you in the next world but not in this? We don't need your God, thank you. Besides, you Christians deny yourselves all the satisfying pleasures: you have no shows, no processions, no public banquets, no meat from victims, no drink, no perfumes for the body. We don't need your false certainties. No one knows the secret of the universe. 'Ignorance,' as Socrates said, 'is wisdom.' What is doubtful is best left in doubt."[26]

"You just don't understand," I protested, "although I admit it's difficult to describe the nature of God in words. Jesus was the Son of God, both human and divine. Just as we can all be united to God in spirit, so the Spirit of God was united into the soul and body of Jesus. The divine Spirit spoke through Jesus, although his body and soul were both human. Jesus' divinity is not in question. If he had been a mere man, how could he have spread his teaching and religion all over the world, in spite of the opposition of emperors, the Roman senate, governors everywhere, and the common people? Christ has accomplished the conversion of multitudes, because he is the power of God and the wisdom of the Father [1 Corinthians 1.24]. His coming was predicted long ago by several prophets of the Jews in the sacred writings. While he lived, Jesus healed the lame and the blind, and even raised some from the dead, as is made absolutely clear in the gospels, which were written by eyewitnesses. Jesus won some people over by his well-reasoned arguments because he always expressed himself in a language appropriate to his hearers, and convinced the less well educated by his miracles.[27]

"And since Jesus died, his apostles have achieved even more than Jesus did by his physical miracles. Through their teaching, the eyes of the people who are blind in their souls are continually being opened, and the ears of those who were deaf to virtue now eagerly hear the message of Jesus: that he died willingly, in obedience to God the Father, in order to benefit the whole of mankind. A single righteous man, both human and divine, died voluntarily for the sake of the whole community, in order to overcome the ruler of the demons, who previously held all human souls in subjection. Through Jesus, through his life on earth, through his teaching, and through his suffering death for our sake, we now all have available better and more divine laws. Through them we can be delivered from the evils of the present world, and from its rulers, who have ceased to be of consequence. Jesus, the Son of God, has proved himself to be purer and more powerful than all other rulers."[28]

There was a stunned silence at this, and I confess I felt rather proud of myself that I had managed to put so many complex arguments simply and well. Looking back now, I suppose it was a bit risky to speak so openly in front of influential people and say that God is greater than the emperor. Walls have ears, and you just don't know who is acting as an official spy.[29] But I decided to take advantage of the silence and go on. "After Jesus died on earth (he was murdered by the Jews), he descended into hell and there converted many souls. He rose again from the dead, as the old Jewish prophets had predicted, and he rejoined his Father in heaven. He appeared again in the flesh to his disciples, as is revealed in our sacred books."[30]

"All that is complete nonsense," Epiphanius interrupted me rudely. "The gospels are obviously fictitious. And Christians when they are criticized simply alter the original text of the gospel (which they have already done three, four, or even more times), just in order to get out of difficulties." Of course, I said that the gospels were written by simple honest men, unaffected, if Epiphanius didn't mind my saying so, by

Greek sophistry, men who could not have invented what they saw. I assured them that there was nothing in our gospels which is false.[31]

But Epiphanius was not finished. "As to the predictions by Jewish prophets," he said, "there are lots of those which have not turned out to be true. For example, didn't your God predict through Moses that the Jewish people were going to become rich, powerful, and fill the earth [Deuteronomy 15.6; 28.11–12; Genesis 8.17], and look what's happened to them now. So it seems impossible to claim that these things happened to Jesus just because they were foretold. Besides, if God really wanted to make men better, why wouldn't he do it by simple divine power, without sending an undistinguished special messenger?"[32]

I said quickly: "Your poets make even worse claims for your Gods. They come down to earth and seduce young girls. At least our God is morally upright and people become better by following his teachings." But Epiphanius interrupted me again with one of his poisonous glares and said: "The trouble with you Christians is that you fantasize; you imagine you know how God works, and who he is, even though you yourselves repeatedly admit that he is incomprehensible. In this, Christians are just like the Jews. They inflate their own importance in the scheme of things and laughably imagine that they are the chosen people, that only they will be saved when the rest of us are destroyed. In fact, the Jews deserve more praise, because they at least preserve their traditional laws, which the Christians have deserted. And anyhow, Christians are hopelessly divided by arguments among themselves, and in spite of their claims are not really monotheistic at all. They worship this Jesus, and the supreme God, as well as demons and angels."[33]

"We all know that demons exist," said Crispus, who was our host, and he proceeded very skillfully, I thought, to change the subject to ghost stories, which clearly gripped most people's attention more than talk about religion. Simon, the Jew, who you remember was sitting next to me, said quietly; "Don't take it to heart. None of these heathens understands our problems." And then, do you know, he had the effrontery to tell me a story he had heard recently from one of his own leaders. I suppose he was having his own back for my saying that the Jews had killed Jesus. He as good as admitted it, but turned what he should have regretted into some kind of boast. It's quite the most sacrilegious tale I have ever heard. But it does give you a good idea of the scurrilous tales those

Jews are telling about us behind our backs, not to mention cursing us three times a day in their public prayers.

Brother, I thought I had better share all this with you. They had mixed up and distorted all the ingredients of our sacred gospels. It's really disgraceful that they are allowed to get away with it. But because the others were swapping ghost stories, I didn't always quite hear exactly what Simon was saying, and I certainly didn't want to ask him to repeat any of it. This is what I think he said, or the wicked gist of it.

THE WICKED JESUS STORY

In the reign of the emperor Tiberius,[34] when all Jesus' five disciples had been executed, the Roman governor Pilate judged that both Jesus and John the Baptist, Jesus' teacher, also deserved to be put to death. When Rabbi Joshua, the leader of the Jews, heard this, he volunteered to write a letter to the emperor outlining the wickedness of all seven. The emperor Tiberius received the letter and summoned Pilate, the leaders of the Jews, Jesus, and John all to appear before him in Tiberias, the chief town of Galilee.

Under questioning, both John and Jesus claimed to be "sons of the God of heaven." And Jesus, in order to impress the emperor and to escape punishment, boasted that he was a mighty magic maker, able by spells garnered from books to heal, to resurrect the dead, to kill the living, even to make barren women fertile. Now, as chance would have it, the emperor had a daughter who had had difficulty conceiving (unsurprising this, since as we discover later, she is a virgin—but the story was hopelessly confused). With a few magic words, Jesus made the princess pregnant. Still suspicious, the emperor asked: "What sex is it?" Jesus said: "You choose; whatever you ask shall be done." The emperor was impressed but cautious; he asked for a son, and ordered Pilate to keep Jesus and John in prison for nine months.

The Jewish leaders were depressed by Jesus' success. So they wrote around and ordered a general fast, to be followed by universal prayer in all Israel, that Israel should prove triumphant over its wicked rivals in this trial of strength. And behold, the Lord God had mercy, and changed the embryo in the princess' womb into a stone.

The nine months passed; the emperor summoned the "wicked Jesus" (yes, that's actually what Simon said) and asked him why the princess had not yet given birth. Jesus, in a fix, like other prisoners in similar situations, played for time and said that among the Jews, some women take twelve months to bear children. The emperor sent him back to prison. (I personally think this is quite unrealistic; emperors are not that credulous. It's just a cheap tactic for spinning out the story.)

Three months later, the emperor again questioned Jesus: "Why has she not given birth?" Jesus said that sorcerers had been at work, and "besides, she is a virgin," and so he asks Caesar for permission to perform a cesarean. The emperor agreed, so Jesus "rent the womb of Caesar's daughter," but lo, all he brought forth was a stone. Caesar angrily commanded Jesus to make it live; after all, that was what Jesus had boasted he could do. Jesus prayed, but failed. "You see," Simon said, "he was not praying to the right God."

The emperor consulted the Jewish leaders about the appropriate punishment. They demurred politely; punishment was for the emperor and God to decide on. The emperor's judgment was that Jesus and John were sorcerers, in violation of the Law, and needed to be "uprooted from the world." They were loaded with chains, and John was crucified and buried.

"You have got it all wrong," I protested; "it's all a complete travesty. John the Baptist was killed by King Herod years before Jesus died. And it was Mary, the mother of Jesus, who was a virgin. The gospels say so quite clearly." "Well, that's your story," said Simon, cool as a cucumber. "This is my story, and it would be polite of you not to interrupt." "Yes, do let him finish," said Crispus; "there's a good fellow." And I suppose they were right. I simply had to let him get away with murder.

"Well," said Simon, "then Jesus too was prepared for crucifixion. But he escaped; by a magical trick, he flew off like a bird. So Judah, one of the Jewish leaders, after a brief consultation, uttered the name of God and flew off after Jesus in hot pursuit. When the wicked Jesus saw Judah close behind him, he hid in a cave and magically shut the cave's entrance. But Judah knew not only how to fly, but also how to open doors, for was he not 'an apostle of the the great God'? The cave door opened. Jesus the wicked, in a desperate last throw, turned himself into a cock, but Judah grabbed him by his comb, and the Jewish leaders together crucified Jesus on a cabbage stalk.

"That's not quite the end of the story," said Simon. "They crucified Jesus alive, and then stoned him.[35] But everybody knew that Jesus had told his gullible followers that if he was not on the cross on the morrow, it was because he had ascended to heaven. Now the Jewish leaders were in a quandary, because it is written in the Torah (Deuteronomy 21.23) that a body hanged upon a tree shall not remain unburied over night. If they obeyed the Law and moved the body, then they would help give credence to the myth of Jesus' resurrection. But how could they, the leaders of the Jews, disobey the Law, even for a good purpose? So they buried Jesus secretly.

"Now the followers of Jesus boasted that Jesus, in accordance with his own prophecy, had gone up to heaven. And Pilate heard this, and asked the leaders of the Jews if it was true. But they knew exactly where Jesus was buried, disinterred his body, and had it dragged through the streets of Tiberias by a rope around its legs. And people said, 'This is Jesus, the son of Pandera, the wicked one who rebelled against the great God.' And Pilate ordered the corpse to be buried in the regular cemetery. And the day of the crucifixion was the fourteenth of Nisan, and the day of the second burial was the twenty-first of Nisan. This was the judgment and retribution enacted on Jesus the wicked, and similar retribution will fall on 'everyone who forsakes the worship of God in heaven.'"

That roughly was Simon's outrageous calumny against Jesus. And of course, I would have replied, but Crispus had clearly overheard some of it, so once again he jovially tried to make peace, without at all realizing what was at issue. "Well, we all believe in one set of Gods or another," he said. And there really wasn't the time for any more discussion about religion, because someone had let in musicians and dancing girls, and I thought it was time to go home and lick my wounds. I can tell you it will be some time before I go to another dinner party like that—though you do get to realize what we are up against: heathens on one side and Jews on the other, to say nothing of the oddest heresies which claim to be Christian and give us a bad name.

WHAT I SHOULD HAVE SAID

I know I ought to stop here; my letter is really long enough. But after that dinner party, I really can't get to sleep. I began to realize slowly what

I ought to have said. So many arguments came flooding into my mind.[36] After all, we are not the cretins they take us to be just because we believe in the one true God.

I really should have emphasized the fact that in the empire, different people observe different laws and customs. No one is hindered by law or by fear of punishment from devotion to their ancestral gods. For example, the Egyptians worship cats, crocodiles, and serpents. It's ridiculous, everyone knows that, but it is allowed. The Romans afford legal toleration to all these cults. Roman law gives everyone equal rights. The whole empire enjoys the fruits of Roman peace. Only Christians are treated differently, although they are well disposed both to God and to the Roman empire.

It is contrary to the law of reason that we should be attacked by mobs and made to suffer by Roman administrators. People attack our property, take away our civil rights, torment our bodies. Thanks to our strength from God (I'm not sure I'd say precisely that to them, but you know what I mean), we accept our mistreatment with humility. We do not countersue, or pursue our rights in the law courts. Indeed, we believe that if someone smites us we should turn the other cheek, and pray even for the salvation of our enemies. But being persecuted for our virtue does seem unfair. Of course, if any of us had committed crimes, they should be punished. But we should not be attacked simply because we bear the name of Christians. We should be punished only for proven crimes. And if we can disprove the charges, we should be acquitted. If anyone in authority heard our case impartially, I'm sure we'd be acquitted. And if only we could get our case heard by the emperor himself, I'm sure he'd be generous and merciful.

I should have been more orderly in my defense, but it's difficult to think clearly in the heat of the moment. Of course, I know very well (I've experienced it enough, as I'm sure you have) that people levy three main accusations against us: atheism, cannibalism, incest. Our conduct, our teachings, our loyalty and obedience to authority and the empire as a whole all indicate that we are not guilty.

The charge of atheism is particularly absurd and hurtful. We know and preach that God is uncreated, eternal, grasped by the mind and by intelligence. He is not made of created matter. Anyone who contemplates the order and harmony of the world and its beauty can see that it was made by one God and by his ordering Reason (Logos). Philosophers through the ages (Plato, Aristotle, and the Stoics) have all speculated about the nature of God. They disagree among themselves; why cannot we therefore disagree with them? Why can't we also be allowed to think about God? Moreover, we derive our views not from individual speculation but from the holy and ancient word of the prophets. We believe that one God made the universe; God is indivisible; there is no room for a second God. Any second God would be created and noneternal and so inferior. God is therefore uncreated, eternal, invisible, incomprehensible.[37]

I wish I had put all this as clearly then as I can now in the calm of writing to you. Thank you for the comfort you bring me. Of course, they would be bound to ask how this imperceptible God could have a son. I would have answered that the Son of God is God's expressed Reason (Greek: Logos) in spiritual form. I think the best formulation is for us to see the Father and the Son as one entity; the Son is in the Father and the Father is in the Son. The Holy Spirit is an effluence of both.[38] I realize that's a bit theoretical for general consumption, but at least educated people should be able to realize that we believe in God, and in one spiritual God. We are not atheists.

I think we ought to emphasize that our ethical teachings are at least as impressive as our beliefs. For example, we tell our followers to love their enemies, to bless those who curse them, and to pray for those who persecute them. After all, the sun shines on both good and evil. OK, sophisticated logic choppers may scoff at these ideas, but none of those observant sceptics purges his heart, as we do, so as to love his enemies. Logic choppers and speechifiers aim at skill rather than at goodness. *We* aim at virtue; when *we* are robbed, we do not pursue wrongdoers. What's more, we give to those who ask. We succor the poor and welcome everyone. That is why we include among our numbers "unlettered people, tradesmen, and old women." Our openness should be admired, not criticized.

If we did not think that God ruled the universe, why would we live in such purity?[39] And so we are fully convinced that when the hour of judgment comes, we have to give an account of our lives. On this earth, we may live despised, temperate, and generous; but it is at a cost to ourselves which is small compared with the heavenly reward we hope for. Some pagans think only of today's pleasures; they regard death as but sleep. We regard death as a new beginning.

And I should have counterattacked.[40] Pagans sacrifice to idols made of stone, metal, or wood. Our creator God does not need blood, smells, flowers, or incense. He is perfect. What he needs instead is our realization of his creation. Our God is superior. Their tales about their Gods, by contrast, are unbelievable, intrinsically ridiculous, and often immoral. Their Gods were created out of mud and water, if, as some claim, there are divinities behind the idols. But as a consequence, their Gods suffer from human emotions, such as passion, wrath, lust, and sexuality. All that is just not appropriate for God.

Now, more briefly, for the two other accusations, of cannibalism and incest.[41] Calumnies like this do not affect us. We stand before God, all of us, blameless. We will not entertain even the thought of the slightest sin. We realize that God day and night witnesses our thoughts and our speech. This is not the only life. God can see into our hearts. In heaven we shall live close to God with our souls free from passion. We know that any man who looks at a woman lustfully has already committed adultery in his heart. Our eyes are made for other purposes. Because we know we are to be judged after death, we exercise self-control. We treat our fellow Christians as members of the same family. A wicked man may evade the laws of humans, but not the law of God.

We despise enjoyment. Each of us thinks of the woman he has married as his wife only for the purpose of bearing children. Many of us, both men and women, stay unmarried in the hope of being closer to God. We avoid both sexual acts and sexual thoughts. We marry either not at all or only once. A second marriage is veiled adultery. Given our behavior and beliefs, compared to their open sinfulness in public marketplaces, how could we commit murder of children, flesh eating, or incest? After all, we do have slaves; some of us have lots of them, others only few. Have they reported any such crimes? Besides, why should we eat bodies when we believe in the resurrection of the body? And incidentally, the corruption of the body does not prevent its reconstitution. In sum, we are religious, gentle, and kind in spirit. We pray for the continued authority of our imperial rulers. We should be honored rather than attacked.

I'm sorry, Clement, I got quite carried away by the power of my arguments. And I'm sure you've heard all of them before. I suppose I wanted to write down what I should have said to Celsus. Oh well. Next time I'll be better prepared.

You know, I can't get those ghost stories out of my mind. Some of them were quite upsetting. I thought you might like to hear the best one. It was told by Lucius, who in effect runs our town; he is a very witty lawyer who dabbles in magic himself, or so everyone says. He's a bit of a ladies' man too, and an expert in mystery rituals. For some reason he claimed that he had heard this tale from a wholesale cheese merchant. I can't imagine why; perhaps it's because cheese is so indigestible, so that if you eat it for dinner, it gives you nightmares. Still, I shouldn't be snobbish about its origins. The story's good, though a bit complex, like one of those Egyptian mummy cases; you strip away the outside and find another case inside. It's quite scary. Do you think it can possibly be true?

THE CHEESE MERCHANT'S TALE

I swear by the Sun, who sees everything, this is a true story.[42] It happened to me, and everyone in the next town will vouch for it. You know I'm a cheese merchant. I heard about a bargain but just missed it, and to console myself I went to the public baths. There, to my amazement, I met an old friend called Socrates, who I thought had died. He was hardly recognizable, he looked so emaciated and yellow, barely dressed in a filthy tattered cloak, like a beggar. Immediately I remonstrated with him about his disappearance, deserting his wife and children, who mourned him for dead. It was like meeting a ghost.

He groaned, blushed, and then out of shame covered his head with his threadbare cloak, only to reveal what he should have been ashamed of. Out of concern, I straightaway gave him one of the two garments I had on, took him into the private baths, scrubbed him down (God, he was filthy), took him back to my inn, plied him with food and all the news from back home. Gradually Socrates cheered up and told me his tale:

"It all began when I went out of my way to watch a gladiatorial show. I was coming home from a longish business trip, carrying a fair amount of money, when I was set upon by bandits and robbed of almost everything except my life. I just managed to get here, and went to an inn run by a woman called Meroe. She's not young exactly, but still amazingly attractive. I told her my story and about my anxiety to get back to my wife. She pretended to be sympathetic, cooked me a grand meal without charging me a penny, and then induced me to sleep with her.

"As soon as I climbed into her bed, I was lost. I was bewitched. My mind went. I began working for her. I gave her all I had or could earn. So I've come to this, and you can see the state I'm in. I daren't leave her because of her incredible magical powers. She can raise the spirits of the dead. Even here, she might just be able to overhear us talking. She has enslaved all sorts of men to love her, and if they fall for another woman and try to leave, she turns them into beavers. Why beavers? Because a beaver, when hunted, tries to decoy the hounds by biting off its own testicles. And Meroe hopes that this is what will happen to them. And that's not all. She turned a rival innkeeper into a frog, and after the wife of another of her lovers complained, Meroe kept her pregnant perpetually; and that was eight years ago, and she's getting bigger all the time. Everyone around here is terrified of her."

I was pretty skeptical at first. But Socrates had sounded convincing. It was all very worrying. We decided to leave this hellhole as fast as we could early next morning. Thanks to the wine, Socrates drifted off to sleep. I saw to it that the door of my room at the inn was safely barred and locked, and just for good measure, propped my bed against the hinges. I had some difficulty in getting off to sleep because of Socrates' scary stories, but eventually I drifted off. The next thing I knew it was the middle of the night. Suddenly the door burst open, locks and all. I was upended, with my bed on top of me, peering out like a tortoise from under its shell. It was two old hags—obviously, from what they said, the witch Meroe and an accomplice.

They began to discuss how to punish my friend Socrates for planning desertion, and me for prying and meddling. Should they dismember me bit by bit, or simply hang me up by my balls with a piece of string and castrate me? I was gutted. As for Socrates, they settled on making a large gash in his neck. Meroe carefully drained out his blood into an empty bladder she had in one hand, then put her other hand deep into the wound and pulled out his heart. With a magic spell she closed the wound. Then they turned on me. But all they did was to squat over me and piss long and hard. In a trice they were gone, magically restoring the door and its locks.

You can imagine I was in a cold sweat, caught alone with a corpse in a locked inn room. If the case ever came to trial, I'd be found guilty in a second. I panicked and tried to leave. But the porter, half asleep, simply refused to unlock the yard gates in the middle of the night; for all he knew there might be a gang of cutthroats waiting outside. And when I insisted, to my horror he even suggested that I might have strangled my companion. In despair I went back to my room, feeling suicidal. In fact, I tried to hang myself, but the rope broke. I fell to the ground on top of my murdered friend.

To my amazement, he woke up. Out of sheer relief, I gave him a hug, but he pushed me away and said that I stank like a sewer. Without further ado we paid and left. I glanced surreptitiously at Socrates' throat, but not the slightest trace of a scar. It must have been a dream, a nightmare, brought on by too much food and drink. And I had been exhausted. I said this to Socrates. He agreed about the cause, but pointed out that I actually did smell.

Besides, he said that he had had a real nightmare. He had dreamt that his throat was cut. The mere memory made us both feel weak. We sat down in the shade of a tree. By this time there were a fair number of people around. I didn't feel hungry, but Socrates ate some bread and a whole cheese. To wash it down, he walked a few yards to a brook, bent forward to drink, and at that moment the wound in his neck opened. He fell dead, and would have fallen in the water if I hadn't caught him by the leg. I buried him hurriedly by the brookside, and then ran from the scene as though I had myself been guilty of murder.

The whole experience changed my life; I never returned home to my wife and children. I settled down instead to a new life, and a new wife, in another part of the country.

DEMONS EVERYWHERE

After the ghost stories, Crispus ordered in the musicians and the dancing girls, so I made my excuses and left. Simon stayed; he said he didn't see anything wrong with having a good time.

Of course, what worries me about ghosts is the notion that wicked demons are simply everywhere. Perhaps, Clement, if you don't mind, I think I ought to go through with you what I've learned from several of the brethren here about how demons originally came into existence. This is what we Christians say here. In the beginning, God created both matter and the angels who inhabit matter.

Just as God gave men free will to choose between good and evil, so too with angels. One angel, the Prince of Darkness, or matter, became negligent in his duties and chose to be wicked. He and other angels like him were consumed with lust for human virgins and became slaves of the flesh. They had children who were giants, whom God destroyed in the flood. But the fallen angels became the demons, who mislead men and tell lies which resemble truth. These demons cause chaos, both inside humans and in the external world.[43]

These are the demons which attract men to worship idols, because the demons are hungry for the blood of sacrifice. Long ago they disguised themselves as famous humans, who in due course came to be worshiped as Gods. Yet other demons still mislead the multitude; they tempt the irrational powers of the soul to produce fantasies (which are spirit mixed

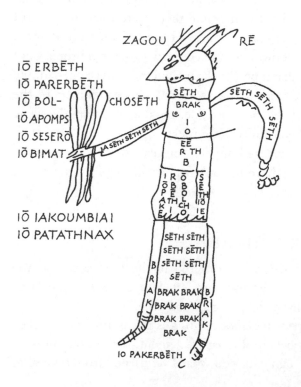

with matter), and these fantasies then lead the common folk to worship idols and to imagine that they have power.

These are the demons which our Lord Jesus Christ and his holy apostles cast out. One of my elders here explained it like this to me. Christ became man and was born by the will of God the Father for the salvation of believers and the destruction of evil spirits. And we know this to be true because of what happens in front of our own eyes. In the whole world, in our own city too, lots of people are possessed by devils and they can't be cured, especially by unbelievers, using drugs, incantations, and enchantments. But Christians, calling upon the wicked demons in the name of Jesus Christ crucified under Pontius Pilate, have cured these poor people, and still cure them even today, by mastering and expelling the evil spirits who possess them.[44] And so, as you know, it is not we who are the atheists. We worship the one and only true Creator of the universe.

But dawn is breaking, and I have a lot to do today. I'll send this letter by my trusted slave Theophilus; he is, as you know, one of us, and quite *au fait* with our faith.

INTERLUDE: OBJECTIONS

Theologische Fakultät
Heidelberg
October 22, 1996

Dear Keith,

Thank you for sending me your second piece. Of course, I enjoyed it. It's very lively. I hope you don't mind, I also sent a copy on to Avi; I thought the Jewish sections were more up his street. Have you heard from him yet? Is he prompter with his mail than I am? But then, I have been busy, not only with work, faculty politics, settling into a new house, but also with babies. Two are much more work than one—but then you know, or have you forgotten?

To be frank, I thought you took too much pleasure (almost a childish delight) in debunking Christianity. OK—I agree that these are the arguments which thinking Christians preserved, though I'm a bit torn in deciding whether they preserved them because they took the criticisms seriously or because they were arguments which could so easily be dismissed. Perhaps, as I think you would put it, Christians preserved silly arguments against themselves just in order to enhance their own sense of identity. [At least this shows that Hartmut is learning, whether from me or from early Christians, that attributing ideas to opponents is a good rhetorical tactic.]

But there are two further aspects of your piece to which I object, quite strongly. Don't worry, both are curable. First, and most important, your pro-Christian arguments should surely be put much more forcefully. So I think you need a reply from Clement (you see I'm beginning to collude with your fiction—is this the first stage of a subtle conversion? I pray not) which puts the devout Christian case convincingly. If you wanted to be fair (!!!), you'd have Clement invite a solitary pagan and perhaps a Jew (though you know that I don't consider Judaism particularly important for the *evolution* of Christianity, especially in the second century) to dinner with a whole host of Christians.

My second point is comparatively minor. I realize that the Christian arguments advanced in Macarius' letter are taken from Origen's refutation of Celsus. Even so, they really are rather naive, at least when compared with the arguments advanced by the theologically sophisticated Fathers of the Church in the fourth century, whom I study. Shouldn't you have at least a footnote explaining to the reader that these second/third-century ideas were not the very best defenses of Christianity which ancient Christians thought up?

Just to help you keep on the right track (after all, I can't bear to leave good Christian arguments to the mercies of an atheist), let me suggest that Clement's answer should follow the conventional Christian apologists' four-fold approach:

a. Attack the Jews for their murder of Jesus and claim the Hebrew moral tradition as basically, even exclusively, Christian.

b. Attack the fatuousness of pagan idol worship. However regrettable we may now think it, early Christians forged their identity partly by vigorous attacks against their religious rivals.

c. Describe the principles of simplicity and virtue according to which most Christians lived.

d. Explain the merciful beneficence of God, who offers believers salvation as a reward for their virtue. I think it was the novelty and power of this message, that God cares for and rewards human virtue, which most impressed pagans. Don't you?

Warm greetings as ever to Jennifer and the girls.
Hartmut

P.S. You know I don't agree with you about demons. You were just trying to be provocative, as usual.

Jewish Theological Seminary of America
3080 Broadway
New York NY 10027-4649   10/20/96

Dear Keith,

Hartmut sent me your dinner party piece—I hope you don't mind—but he thought I might want to comment on the Jewish wicked Jesus story. He said I should be as outspoken with you as you have been about our work. So here goes.

Of course, I *could* say, what on earth do you think a Jew was doing having a fun time with a Christian and a lot of idolaters, without a hint of a kosher caterer? Do you *really* think that they ever sat down together in those days and politely talked about religion? After all, they don't do it nowadays in Golders Green, London, or in Borough Park, New York. Somehow your piece seems more of an idealized twentieth-century Cambridge college high table than genuine second-century Antioch or Caesarea.

Rather funny, really—you try to write a genuine atmospheric piece about antiquity, and quite unconsciously, instead, you reproduce your own social world. That's the danger with empathetic imagination as a historical tool; it can be useful, but it can also turn out to be naive projection. You look into the past and see yourself. I suppose your defense is, and I can hear you saying it, that such contamination is inevitable, and besides, such attempts provide a rhetorical bridge between their world and ours. And I suppose you'd also say that fictional accounts of intellectual conversations were fashionable in the ancient world. Think of Plato's *Symposium* or Petronius' *Satyricon*—though that's more of a brawl—or Athenaeus' *Dinners with the Sophists*, which is very, very dull, or the pious chatter of Methodius' Christian women—I can't imagine you've read that, I only have because I did it at graduate school.

In spite of the difficulties, you may be roughly right, or at least plausible, in your portrayal of an educated hellenized Jew, hobnobbing a little uneasily with heathens. There always were collaborators and apostates, perhaps particularly in the propertied classes, and especially after the three dramatic rebellions and humiliating defeats of the Jews in their futile battles against the Roman state [66–73/74, 117–19, and 132–35]. Of course, by contrast, there always were other Jews who were passionately committed to detailed observance of the Law, or to their particular version of Judaism. After all, some hundreds or thousands of them, led by the prophet Theudas, marched to the river Jordan in 44 CE in the expectation (so it was said) that the waters would be parted, only to be mowed down by Roman cavalry.[45] Many others fought three rebellions for their religion against Roman rulers. And some, with similar commitment, it is difficult to know how many (a small proportion, I guess, of Jews, and a large proportion initially of early Christians), joined the Jewish renewal movement, which evolved into Christianity. Commitment, passion, sacrifice, martyrdom were repeatedly important elements in the practice of ancient Judaism.

In short, if I felt inclined to be generous, I'd say that your dinner party letter gains in dramatic confrontation but loses the standard advantages of conventional history: the presentation of variety and evolution. There was never a single representative Jew, and the tension between Jews, heathens (pagans, polytheists, idolaters—no single description does justice to how they thought of themselves), and Christians changed over time. Your single-moment dinner party confrontation can't do justice to that variety and evolution.

I wonder whether you couldn't, you certainly should, include some brief characterization of ancient Judaism. You know how much I hate it when Christians (and I include you, in spite of your intellectual agnosticism—your whole way of thinking is irremediably Christian) use Judaism just as the backdrop to Christianity, as a vague prefigurement, just as the ancient Christians used the Hebrew Bible as a prefigurement of Jesus. But even I have to admit that a vague sketch is better than complete omission. After all, Jesus was a Jew, and so were all his disciples and most of the early Christians. Ancient Jews and Christians shared the same holy writings, the same foundation myth about the origins of the world, similar liturgical practices (prayers, psalms, and songs), and a similar ethic in counterpoint to surrounding paganism. Christianity was an offshoot of Judaism.

The destruction of the temple in 70 CE was a symbolic turning point in the evolution of Judaism. It broke the power of the temple priests and of the political elite. After that, Judaism could no longer center itself on temple sacrifice. Instead, it centered on the observance of the Law, on internal piety, local

communities, apocalyptic hopes, and the growing status of rabbis as specialist interpreters of religious law. I say that the destruction of the temple was a
symbolic turning point because several of these developments started before
the destruction of the temple, while others, such as the evolution of the rab-
binate, took centuries after the destruction.

It is always difficult to explain to Christians and skeptics like you why the
observance of Torah is so important. Of course, one of its functions is that it
confirms our social identity as Jews. But religiously, each observance, even of
outwardly insignificant rules (eating kosher, wearing phylacteries), brings us,
in the course of the act, closer to God, or so we feel. Some Christians scoff,
but that's often out of narrow-minded failure to understand difference, and
because most modern Christians (except perhaps Quakers or Pennsylvania
Dutch) don't let their relations with God suffuse every daily action. Ancient
Jews and Christians were perhaps much closer (and certainly, in this respect,
different from pagans) in thinking of God as interventionist. Jews typically
thought that God minded if Jews observed or neglected their side of the covenant. Christians typically believed that God was concerned with each believer's faith and virtue, which would be rewarded either in this world or the
next.

Although observance of ritual rules was a fundamental element in ancient
Judaism, Jewish writers also often stressed the importance of pious feelings.
The ear and heart should be circumcised, not just the penis. OK, I knew that
idea would appeal to you, Keith. But this concern with internal piety recurs
in Jewish writers with particular frequency and intensity from the last two
centuries BCE. In the Psalms of Solomon, for example, written perhaps in the
middle of the last century BCE, the writer distinguishes between those who
profess piety but sin privately (Psalm 4) and the righteous, who may sin but
repent; they live in an awareness of God (Psalms 3 and 13). Christians not
only preserved such Jewish writings but took over and developed in their own
way these Jewish ideas of a concerned, forgiving, but judgmental God. But
what I would particularly want you to stress, Keith, is not so much the similarities in the Judaeo-Christian conception of God, but rather the importance
of internal piety/virtue/repentance in ancient Jewish religious thinking.

Now a very brief word on apocalypticism. In the canonical Hebrew Bible,
there were effectively no angels. In popular Jewish thought, at least from the
third century BCE, angels and demons become prominent and important.
First Enoch is the classic text—it is basically a rewrite of Genesis, and incidentally it is 1 Enoch which lies behind your story of demons and idol gods
recounted at your dinner party. The Christian Minucius Felix simply lifts a
story from a good Jewish text which only Christians bothered to preserve.
OK, enough of scholarship and polemic. My idea is that these Jewish writers
tried to incorporate the demons and angels of popular thought into stories
which were roughly speaking within the covenantal canon. The stories incorporated visions of the beginning and end of the world, and gave the faith-

ful an idea that in the end the righteous (us) would be rewarded with eternal resurrection, when the wicked (you, and the Romans) would be damned and eternally punished. This was another set of latish Jewish ideas which the early Christians took over.

One final point: domestication. When you involve your hellenized Jew, Isidorus, aka Simon, son of Judas, in your confrontational dinner party, you inevitably domesticate him into mainstream Roman or Graeco-Roman culture. You get him to talk just like all the others. And of course, there were Jews like that; Philo the philosopher and Josephus the historian are the classic examples—though you might want to take Philo's nephew, the apostate Roman governor of Egypt, Tiberius Julius Alexander, as your case in point. More generally, you could argue that in the second and third centuries Judaism was increasingly permeated with Hellenism; for example, even synagogues were decorated with human figures, in defiance of both Law and tradition. A skeptic might even say that in the aftermath of Jewish defeat and pessimism about being God's chosen people, some of the heart went out of Judaism, and it became permeated with non-Jewish symbols and lifestyles. This temporary despair within some sectors of Judaism might even have contributed to the growth of Christianity, since the bulk of early Christian converts must have been Jews.

But in the very same period rabbinical commentaries on Jewish religious practice were codified in the Mishnah. And the rabbis, a smallish group (perhaps a hundred or so in the whole Roman empire) of religious specialists descended from the Pharisees, gradually enhanced their status and developed a specifically Jewish way of arguing, which marked them off quite dramatically from both Christians and Romans. To show you what I mean, I've copied one of my favorite passages from the Talmud. Needless to say, to me it seems infinitely preferable to Christian theological dogmatism, but then, that's irrelevant. What is indisputable is the difference in intellectual style. I wish I knew why the difference occurred.

What I like particularly is its wry humor and implicit self-questioning. Each statement of a position about religious meaning implies its own contradictability. It is as though the rabbis collectively knew that no religious interpretation is, or can be, final. It seems so different from early Christians, at least in their presenting style, who repeatedly claim to have discovered the one and only true doctrine, and then seek collectively, eventually through successive councils of bishops, to impose the true faith universally. I do *not* mean, by the way, that individual rabbis were tolerant; far from it. Instead, what I mean is that tolerance of diversity evolved as a systemic property of Judaism collectively, at least in the mind frame of the sixth-century authors of the Babylonian Talmud, from which this extract comes. Of course, under pressure I might even admit that this collective agreement to disagree was a symptom not of superior Jewish virtue but of an incapacity even to imagine having the political power to impose unanimity on all Jews. But I retain a certain romantic feeling that this Jewish form of argument reflected, or has become, an important part of a specifically Jewish mind frame.

This particular scene, with a dramatic date in the early second century, portrays an intense battle of interpretation between competing rabbis, in which several solutions are found to be impressive but no one single solution is found to be final. Even miracles and the voice of God do not have overwhelming authority. Eventually, as this anonymous redactor portrays it, the majority of rabbis claim supreme authority, even over the inspired opinion of one. But what did God think of their solution? He laughed.

On that day Rabbi Eliezer used all the arguments in the world, but the others did not accept them from him. So Rabbi Eliezer said: "If the Law is as I say, this carob will prove it." The carob was uprooted from its place one hundred cubits. Some report four hundred cubits.

The other rabbis said to him: "One does not quote a carob tree as proof."

Rabbi Eliezer further said to them: "If the Law is as I say, the water pipe will prove it." The water began to flow backward.

The other rabbis said to him: "A water pipe cannot be used as proof."

Again Rabbi Eliezer said to them: "If the Law is as I say, let the walls of the study house prove it." The walls of the study house tilted over.

But Rabbi Joshua rebuked them, saying to them: "If the disciples of the wise are contending with one another about the Law, what concern is it of yours?" So the walls did not fall, out of respect for Rabbi Joshua, and did not stand straight out of respect for Rabbi Eliezer.

Rabbi Eliezer said to the [other rabbis]: "If the Law is as I say it, let heaven prove it."

A voice went out from heaven and said: "What are you next to Rabbi Eliezer? For the Law always accords with what he says."

But Rabbi Joshua rose to his feet and said: "It is not [from] heaven. . . ."

And Rabbi Jeremiah said: "Since the Torah has already been given from Mount Sinai, we do not pay attention to heavenly voices, for you have written already at Mount Sinai: 'Incline after the majority.'"

Then Rabbi Natan found [the prophet] Elijah and asked him: "What was the Holy One, blessed be He, doing at that moment?"

And Elijah said to him: "He laughed and said: 'My children have defeated me, my children have defeated me.'" (Babylonian Talmud, *Baba Mezia* 59a–b)[46]

After this, Rabbi Eliezer was outvoted by the other rabbis and excommunicated. The earlier Jerusalem Talmud gives a slightly different version of this story, and adds a touching scene at Rabbi Eliezer's deathbed. When the other rabbis hear that Eliezer is dying, they come to visit him, and sit at the ritual distance necessary between insiders and the excommunicated. He asks them why they have come, and their leader says: "To study Torah with you." The great scholar is revered by his fellows, even though he has been excommunicated. Need I say more?

By the way, as you probably know, the earliest manuscript of the wicked Jesus cycle of stories, of which you quote one version (is that the one from Sinai?) comes from the sixth century (I think). I personally regard it as more medieval than ancient, but Horbury, who is a great scholar, thinks it very much earlier. His arguments are respectable.

I hope all goes well with you, the kids, and the college. I miss the grass and the conversations, though if I have to eat one of your British dinners just to have conversation, well. This letter is far too long, but I hope of some use to you.

All the best,
Avi

CHRISTIANS AGAINST UNBELIEVERS AND JEWS

Clement Sends Greetings in Christ to Macarius, His Brother:

We have, my dear brother, received your letter, which showed much good sense and sound faith.[47] I sympathized with you in your distress— you were like Daniel in the den of lions.

I thought you were too gentle with your Jewish neighbor, Simon, son of Judas (how reminiscent that name always is). Of course, their leaders tell them not to associate with us, and some of them even let their relatives die rather than be cured in the name of Jesus Christ.[48] But I myself see no harm in discussion and confrontation, so long as it is two sided, though I wish you had stopped your ears rather than hear (and repeat) his sacrilegious and lying tales about our Lord Jesus.

We need to remember that it was the Jews who crucified him, the only righteous One, by whose stripes we are healed. It was the Jews who failed to recognize Him as the Messiah and Son of God; and though they know He had risen from the dead and ascended into heaven, as the prophets foretold, they sent emissaries out from Jerusalem to denounce the Christians as godless heretics. Even now, it is the Romans who protect us from Jewish attacks, while the Jews in their synagogues daily curse all of us who believe in Christ.[49]

Our Lord Jesus, the Word and Son of God, suffered to take on flesh, and through his teachings, death, and resurrection, destroyed the devil and his angels, and gave to us, who believe in Him, a New Covenant. The Jews slighted Him and rejected Him because "their ears are closed, their eyes are blinded." They are circumcised in the body, but not in the hardness of their hearts.[50] Our Lord God, who is the only God, had given the old law through Moses to the Jews, as a punishment for their sins. The old law was an inferior and temporary memorial to God, designed to stop the Jews slipping back, once again, into idolatry. But note, before Moses there was no need for circumcision among the ancient patriarchs. So there is no need now for circumcision among those baptized by the Holy Spirit. The everlasting law of Jesus Christ brings a circumcision not of the body but of the spirit. Through God's mercy all men and women, wherever they come from, may now obtain the blessing of baptism, equally.[51]

The New Covenant has brought the old covenant to an end. This is quite clear from the scriptures, which, to be frank, are not theirs but ours. Admittedly, some of our brethren, with misplaced generosity, consider that the scriptures [the Old Testament] are both theirs and ours. True, the Jews read the same scriptures, but they fail to capture their spirit, fail to understand how often the prophets clearly predicted the coming of Jesus as Messiah.[52] The very coming of Jesus as Messiah, his crucifixion and resurrection, all clearly predicted by the prophets, *prove* that our interpretations are true. It is the Jews' own wickedness which prevents them from discerning the scriptures' inner wisdom. I pass over the fact that they themselves have only quite recently abandoned the old, well-established translation [from the Hebrew into Greek] made long ago by wise men and have made a new translation, which omits several clear references to our Savior. To take but one example: Psalm 96 [95] states, "The Lord hath reigned from the wood," meaning the cross, but this clear prediction the Jews have now omitted.[53] Of course, the Jews hate us because we understand the very scriptures which they revere but misunderstand, though daily many of them do repent and convert. The rest fear to convert, lest they too be persecuted by our Roman rulers. But whatever their failings, we pray for the Jews, as we pray for all who hate us.[54]

As to the heathens, by whom you were so unfortunately surrounded, they will soon give up their vain worship of idols; as the scriptures say:

"The eyes of the blind shall be opened" (Isaiah 35.5). Meanwhile, we have an obligation to let them know how violent, disgusting, and immoral their myths are. Even some heathen philosophers like Euhemerus agree with us on that. Take Zeus or Hercules, for example. Zeus had intercourse with his mother, and in the shape of a serpent with his daughter. Hercules deflowered fifty virgins in a single night. And in another ridiculous myth, the Titans tore a baby limb from limb and grilled the pieces on a spit. In the mysteries of Aphrodite, initiates are still handed a lump of salt and a phallus, and for that they are required to pay an initiation fee. In short, it is the heathens who are atheists, not us. We worship the true God by righteousness and temperance, while the heathens shamelessly indulge in nighttime rituals, and worship a boy torn in pieces, or a woman's genitals.[55]

Their Gods are either, at best, vague sentiments, like Justice or Fate or the planets, which immortal God really made, or much worse, the once mortal and licentious heroes of local cults. Just think how many different Zeuses or Apollos there are now; there is one Apollo of Crete, another Apollo of Libya, yet another Apollo of Delos; one is son of Zeus, another the son of Hephaestus, or of Corybas, or of Ammon, or of countless others. Perhaps all that is merely confusing, but the worship which they demand and get is degrading. The heathen gods are insatiable demons who gloat over human slaughter, as in the arena, and demand human sacrifice. They call it sacrifice, but we know it is just butchery and murder. And I'm dealing here not just with myth but with real history. The Roman general Marius sacrificed his daughter; and the emperor Hadrian made Antinous, his beautiful dead Ganymede, into a God, replete with temple and a city named after him. Even now people honor the sacred nights of Antinous, though they must know that they are celebrating the debauchery of licentious vice.[56]

How idiotic the heathens are to worship idols, which they know mortal craftsmen have made and decorated. And then they place these senseless images everywhere, even in toilets. They consecrate pillars of shame [ithyphallic statues] in public places as well as at home, and guard them with scrupulous care, as though they were the Gods themselves. They cast or paint erect phalli, drunken satyrs, naked girls, so that their eyes commit fornication or adultery even before the rest of their bodies. They even decorate their bedrooms with paintings of the Gods having intercourse. The heathens are in bondage to demons, bound for destruction and eternal punishment by fire.[57]

But our God offers those who believe in Him freedom, salvation, and everlasting life. Awake to the Light of the Resurrection. Believe and obey. Become as children, and the Lord will waken you from the sleep of darkness, for great is the grace of his promise, and with his Love, He invites all men to the knowledge of the truth. Give Him your love and your living faith in Christ Jesus, who clothed Himself with flesh, and vanquished the serpent and enslaved the tyrant death. Through his grace you will secure salvation. The wicked, on the other hand, will receive just punishment. Let us therefore repent, pass from ignorance to knowledge, and from godlessness to God. Search no longer for wisdom in Athens or Greece. The whole world has already become the domain of the Lord.

Some of our brethren worry whether we should marry, have children, or assume public office. These are unimportant. What matters is that you should obey the Lord's teachings: "Love your neighbor as yourself," and "You shall not lust, for by lust alone have you committed adultery" (Luke 6.29; Matthew 5.28). Sin is eternal death. So let us comply with God's laws; let us render Him a thankful heart. And remember, the soldiers of Christ are the soldiers of peace. The trumpet is his gospel. Abandon pleasures and amusements; cultivate instead the blessings of self-control, that you may be counted a friend of Christ and inherit the kingdom of God. There is no room for doubt. Follow the Word. Follow God.[58]

EPILOGUE: ANTI-JUDAISM AND NUMBER

Jewish Theological Seminary of America
3080 Broadway
New York, NY 10027-4649   11/21/96

Dear Keith,

Of course, I thought your Clement's swinging attack on Judaism in poor taste, but authentic enough. I suppose what troubles me most is that blaming the Jews for the death of Jesus has been the peg on which so much destructive later anti-semitism hung. Why repeat it? The world is better without it.

And incidentally, why anyone would read your Christian's long exhortation beats me. Such stuff sends me to sleep. But I suppose that's what second-century Christian ideologues went in for, particularly when they wrote to each other—and at even greater length. But don't forget, they were even beastlier to their own heretics than they were to either Jews or pagans. It is as though they forged their own identity largely via struggles with their opponents. For all their talk of peace, they manufactured both sins and enemies.

Actually, the intellectual tack behind these Christian confrontations with Jews (of which there are several surviving, not just the one you use most, Justin's fictional *Dialogue with Trypho*) seems interestingly complicated. They are trying a quartet of complementary but not obviously compatible arguments. First, the Hebrew scriptures "properly" interpreted prefigure the arrival of Jesus as Messiah, and the total Christian message. Second, in a sense, therefore, Christianity has always existed, or at least it is as old as the original patriarchs of Israel, so that Christianity in its earliest form predated Greek wisdom. Tertullian says somewhere that Moses lived a thousand years before Priam [king of Troy] and fifteen hundred years before Homer. Christianity therefore came first, Greek wisdom later![59] Third, Christian thinkers claim that Jesus was not just the bodily savior; he is preexistent with the Father, and indeed it was Jesus who talked with Abraham at the oak of Mamre—a fine intrusion of Christianity into Jewish history. There's cultural imperialism for you. Finally, of course, Christians repeatedly claimed that they were a completely new sect, created by the life and death of Jesus. So Christianity was preexisting, prefigured, old, and new, all at the same time.

Back to real history! Here I think some relative numbers would help. By convention, if we think of the population of the Roman empire at about 50–60 million in the mid–first century, there may have been 4–5 million Jews, of whom only say half a million probably lived in Palestine. The rest were spread about the eastern Mediterranean, particularly in the cities, with a large concentration in Rome itself. So there were say 45–50 million pagans, 4–5 million Jews, and in 100 CE (what do you think?) probably less than ten thousand Christians, rising, if they were phenomenally successful, to two hundred thousand in 200 CE. Christians constituted only a tiny fraction of the total population of the Roman empire even in 200 CE. The political historian Herodian, writing in the early third century, didn't even mention Christians. Small wonder. They didn't matter.

But Christian leaders made one hell of a lot of noise (rather like the early rabbis) and thought of themselves as at the center of the universe—and the Christians even managed to change the universe, you might say, to make themselves the center of it.

By the way, I don't imagine that most of your Christians actually behaved in the way their leaders prescribed, even when Christians constituted very small communities. These were ideals, not descriptions. Shouldn't you make that clear?

We have a similar problem with how to treat Jewish observance. I like to divide Jews into three notional sets (their relative size fluctuates according to circumstances):

a. rigorists, who set the standards, and whose prescriptions survive
b. laxists, who collaborate with and are "contaminated"/softened by the surrounding culture, and
c. the inert mass, who have a more or less vague consciousness of belonging, which varies in intensity (As you like to say, religious identity is a persuasive and porous category; the rigorists like to claim that all Jews/Christians are real, true observers/believers.)

Best wishes,
Avi

P.S. Send me more; I'm having difficulty sleeping.

SEVEN

Recreating the Cosmos

INTRODUCTION

In *The Brothers Karamazov*, Dostoyevsky brilliantly portrayed Christ's fate when he returned to earth in the sixteenth century in Spain, on the day after a grand auto-da-fé in which "almost a hundred heretics had been burned for the greater glory of God . . . in the presence of the king, the nobles, the cardinals, the most charming ladies of the court, and the people of Seville." Christ by his charisma swiftly drew an admiring crowd, performed some miraculous cures, and raised a young girl from the dead.

The Grand Inquisitor, passing by, saw the crowd, recognized Jesus, immediately had him dragged off to prison, and sentenced him to death. At dead of night, before the execution, the Grand Inquisitor visited Christ in his cell and upbraided him for having resisted the three great temptations in the wilderness: worldly wealth, earthly power, and the use of magic to escape danger. In his view, Christ had in each case reached the wrong decision, and in so doing had imposed a huge burden on his followers: poverty, powerlessness, and the freedom of moral choice. The Catholic church, Dostoyevsky maliciously added, had been doing its best for centuries to repair this damage. Christ could not be allowed to endanger the social order which the church had so painfully established.[1]

Dostoyevsky's fable is disconcerting because it dramatically reaffirms how much of Christ's original teaching was lost when Christianity developed from a radical sect of believers into the universal religion of an established church, favored by emperors and in alliance with the state. The antiauthoritarian, proletarian elements of Christ's original message ("Blessed are the poor," Luke 6.20) were undermined by an increasing reluctance to upset the influential ("Blessed are the poor in spirit,"

Matthew 5.3). And Jesus' scathing comment, for example, that it was easier for a camel to pass through the eye of a needle than for a rich man to
enter the kingdom of God (Mark 10.25) was rendered socially innocuous
by allegory. One powerful and noble bishop, for example, explained Jesus' saying this way: Wealth was admittedly poison, but almsgiving,
which redeems humans from sin, was the poison's antidote. Rich sinners
could therefore redeem themselves by giving money, either to the poor
or to the Church. In this way, wealth was made acceptable and turned to
the advantage both of the rich and the Church. The rich were given the
privilege of being able to buy a place in heaven by charity.[2] This theme
of lost innocence, of a pure primitive Christianity corrupted over time by
ecclesiastical wealth, still entices committed Christians. They think that
all we have to do is to return to Jesus' original message (but see Chapter
Eight below).

But for me the most disturbing element in Dostoyevsky's story is the
suggestion that within the existing religious framework of revelation and
redemption, Christian beliefs could have been quite differently conceived. The Christian Son of God should have succumbed to temptation. And then he could have, should have, been portrayed not as
infallible, punitive to sinners and forgiving only to the good, but as himself fallible, sinning and yet forgiven. This idea is not as far-fetched as it
may at first sound.

In the Indian Siva myths, which are roughly contemporary with early
Christianity, the God himself and holy ascetics repeatedly succumbed to
temptation, often sent to them by other Gods.[3] In one story, for example, it is told that Siva once practiced asceticism for a thousand years.
The other Gods were so envious of his pious self-control that they sent
a beautiful prostitute to seduce him. Successfully.

This Siva tale suggests both similarities in moral patterning with early
Christianity, and recognizable differences. First, the prostitute who is
beneath morality reminds the ascetic who is above morality that the
spirit needs the flesh. Similarly, Mary Magdalene, in some early but noncanonical Christian writings, becomes Jesus' closest confidante, much to
the indignation of Jesus' male disciples. She provides an image of sin,
forgiveness, and eroticism to complement the purity of the Virgin Mary,
with whom she is sometimes conflated.[4] The two Marys form one composite character.

Second, the ascetic's repentance for his lapse fires his subsequent ascetic zeal. Lapses do not necessarily lead to lower standards. So Christian monks, athletes of Christ, were stimulated to greater mortification by their own lascivious thoughts and by their struggles with the demons of temptation—though perhaps the ideal ascetic, if he or she ever existed, never succumbed to, or perhaps in the end even felt, temptation.[5]

Third, Siva is God both of asceticism and of lust. He combines the opposites, which in Christianity are ideally split between God and Devil, or which in Gnosticism are split between Darkness and Light. This Indian dualism, the divine combination of good and evil, may seem alien. But the underlying problem is familiar enough. How can we live in this world enjoying earthly pleasures without being corrupted by them, and yet free the spirit, achieve immortality (which is apparently what many inhabitants of the Roman empire wanted), and acquire salvation, whether in this world or in the next?

Few early Christians, in constructing their Godhead, consciously faced up to the choice of locating God along an axis of complementary opposites, earth versus heaven, body versus spirit, pleasure versus salvation. But surprisingly, some did. Gnostic Christians, in particular, seem to have speculated repeatedly about God's nature and origins. The Gospel of Philip, for example, states: "God created man, men create God and worship their creation. . . . It would be fitting for the Gods to worship men." I too take it for granted that humans create their own God(s)—perhaps in part as an idealized projection of themselves or of their parents. The Christian Godhead, comprising God the Father, Christ as the potent but obedient Son, the Holy Spirit (she is female in Aramaic and Syriac), and eventually Mary, the sanctified but asexual and shadowy mother, was in some sense, however strange, an idealized projection of the ancient family.[6]

As Dostoyevsky implicitly suggested, these central problems of human morality and the nature of God could have evolved differently, whether inside or outside a Christian framework. After all, there was never any guarantee, and for a long period no reasonable prospect, that orthodox Christianity would win. Pagans had a huge variety of religions and philosophies to choose from, and there can be no doubt that many pagans long remained passionately committed to them (see Chapters One and Five). They ranged from traditional civic cults, like those of Zeus and Apollo, which were widespread throughout the whole Roman empire, to local cults, like those of Souchos/Sobek, the crocodile God, worshiped

only in Egypt.[7] There were mystery cults such as Isis worship
Mithraism, religious philosophies like Stoicism and Neoplatonism,
the grand rival religions such as Judaism and Manichaeism, each in various forms. And Christianity itself had many different forms, inadequately
divided by convention between orthodoxy and heresies. Retrospectively,
we can trace the pattern of religious evolution. But it was neither predictable nor foreordained. No one in the first century, or even in the third
century, knew that Christianity (of whatever form) would win.

The religious ferment of syncretism and choice which occurred in the
Roman empire during this period was by no means exceptional. In the
long millennium from about 600 BCE to 650 CE, the religious map of the
whole world changed. In different regions, humans invented Judaism,
Zoroastrianism, Buddhism, Jainism, Christianity, Manichaeism, and Is-
lam, religions which influenced and competed with one another. Some
became the world's "great religions," mostly after they had been adopted
as state religions by rulers of preindustrial empires, partly to help legitimate their exercise of power. These often exclusive alliances between
state and church constituted a key element in each religion's formation.

The focus of this chapter is on religious choice in the Roman world and
on competition between religions, as mirrored in different stories about
how the universe began. Stories about creation served as a metaphorical
map on which competing religious leaders—Jews, pagans, Christians,
Gnostics, and Manichees—drew their particular versions of belief. Understanding the origins of the world was a symbol for understanding the
nature of divinity and of humanity, and for revealing the ethical rules by
which humans should conduct their lives in order to gain salvation. Stories of creation provided critical clues for highlighting central problems
about the nature of God and humanity. If God is good and omnipotent,
how could he/she have been responsible for this corrupt and evil world?
Where did evil come from? Was God (were Gods) concerned, or unconcerned, with minor details of individual human action? Perhaps, in reality, there were two Gods, one good but essentially unconcerned with
mundane matters, the other an inferior God who created this imperfect
world. Others believed that the two Gods were more evenly matched; one
was the good God, the other the Devil; the created universe is the battleground on which the cosmic struggle between them is still being fought.

Some believers concentrated on quite different problems. Did God create the first humans as sexual? Was sexuality good, or was it a trivial and demeaning compensation for humans' loss of immortality? How should humans best behave toward one another and toward God(s) in order to optimize their own chances of salvation? Perhaps salvation was to be won by withdrawing from the contaminated world and by solitary contemplation of the divine, or perhaps, instead, through committed membership of a religious commune and by good works? What will be the reward for the virtuous, and what will be the punishment for the wicked? What are heaven and hell like?[8]

These problems of good and evil, of salvation and punishment, of God's (un)concern for humanity and of humans' proper conduct toward God were all central to early Christianities in their various forms, and to the surrounding religions in competition with Christianity. Nor did canonical writings, whether Jewish, Christian, or Manichaean, answer these questions once and for all. Rather, they provided center points around which religious debates, inside and between religions, could continuously circulate. Speculations about the origins of the world were not always, necessarily or intentionally, subversive. Even the pious, or especially the pious, needed an endless stream of reinterpretations as a token of their faith. And some, perhaps especially the Gnostics, tolerantly allowed their incompatible answers to unanswerable problems to lie next to one another, with their differences unresolved.[9]

Some interpretations were incorporated within orthodoxy, while others were eventually rejected as heresy. For example, the elaboration of the Genesis creation myth found in the grand apocalyptic visions now called 1 Enoch, dating from the third century BCE, was long regarded favorably by pious Jews (several fragments were discovered at Qumran). But later, 1 Enoch was apparently rejected by Jews and preserved only by Christians as a semisacred text, which deeply influenced the thinking of second-century Christian writers.[10]

Rewriting Genesis served as a symbolic marker which helped forge a separate identity for different religious sects or schools within, or at the margins of, Judaism or Christianity. Christian Gnostics in the second century rewrote the prehistory of the universe with fetid imagination.[11] Such stories were their trademark. And for Mani, the founder of Manichaeism in the third century, rewriting the creation story symbolized his rejection of Judaism and his adaptation of Christianity. Beliefs about creation also revealed the nature of God(s) and the ethics of sexuality. They helped show to believers the path toward salvation, back to the universe as it had been in the beginning, and as it would again be in the end.

GENESIS REVISED: THE BASIC CREATION STORY, SOME VARIANTS, AND THEIR IMPLICATIONS

The creation stories in Genesis form a core foundation myth for both the Jewish and Christian religions. In the beginning, God created heaven and earth, and then in due course Adam, and out of his rib, Eve. He allowed them to live in paradise, provided they did not eat from the tree of knowledge. One day the serpent tempted Eve. She ate, so did Adam; and God expelled them both from paradise, to live in this imperfect world of hope and tears.

Actually, the creation story in Genesis is much more complicated than this, and combines elements from several stories, which later Jewish and Christian commentators struggled to reconcile. For example, in the beginning, God said: " 'Let us make man in our image.' . . . So God created man in his own image, in his own image he created him; male and female he created them" (Genesis 1.27). He blessed the human pair and instructed them to be fruitful and multiply. Some later Jewish interpreters used this passage to legitimate their high regard for human sexuality.[12] By contrast, some Christian intellectuals concentrated instead on the words "*Let us* make man," and took them as convincing proof that God at the time of the creation was talking to and cooperating with a coeternal and preexistent Jesus.[13]

Then in Genesis 2 comes the best-known creation story, according to which God sets man in the garden of Eden, forbids him to eat from the tree of knowledge of good and evil, and creates for him a female companion out of his rib. But in Genesis 6 there is the germ of what is or became a third creation story. Wicked angels, "the sons of the Gods" (*sic;* LXX—the Septuagint, which was for centuries the standard Greek translation of the Jewish scriptures—has "sons of God"), lusted after the daughters of men, copulated with them, and bred giants, who were so immoral and disruptive that God decided to clean earth up again, brought the flood, and in this third, restorative creation, allowed only selected humans and animals to survive.[14]

Successive elaborators—Jewish, Christian, Gnostic—struggled with these rival versions in order to resolve the basic problem. How and why did a good and omnipotent Creator God allow evil and sexual desire into this world? The orthodox, ancient Jewish, and Christian answer was that God gave humans (and angels) free will, so that each, whether angel or human, could choose between virtue and vice. But the creation story was, or was made to seem, more complicated than that. Some thinkers speculated that there had in fact been a two-stage creation. As the opening of Genesis implies, God's first creation had been a spiritual androgyne (both male and female), or even a bodily androgyne, only later split into separate and complementary halves. This invented sequence was partly an apologetic attempt at reconciling apparently incompatible accounts in order to protect sacred texts from further elaboration. But the solution also had implications for the priority of male over female, and for the godliness of sexuality. Some concluded that the human, physical body and gender divide were primary (and good), others that they were a secondary (and therefore evil) creation.[15]

The children of God, according to Genesis 6, were angels; but how was it that angels felt desire for humans? Perhaps, after all, as in paradise, it was all the fault of human women, who seduced the angels? Or perhaps the angels originally came to instruct humans in the arts of civilization, and then were corrupted by desire? Either way, desire and corruption were not themselves part of God's original game plan; they were the product of angels' and humans' own free will. For others, this view was quite unsatisfactory. Desire was a good part of God's creation. Adam and Eve had had sex before the fall; the serpent was inflamed with desire because he saw them making love. Sexuality was a natural consequence of man and woman's complementary differences, and as such always blessed by God. But sex with the serpent was illicit sex, like adultery or miscegenation. It was this sin which made Eve guilty.[16]

But who was the serpent? Answers were surprisingly varied. Some Gnostics speculated that the serpent was the Creator God himself, who had fallen in love with and then raped his own creation. Or it was God, admittedly only the inferior Creator God, who had planted seductive desire in Eve, but at some cost: as soon as Adam and Eve experienced sex, they lost knowledge. Some pious, although "heretical," Christians thought that the serpent was Jesus, kindly making available to God's creatures the benefits of God's creation.[17] After all, eating the fruit of the tree made Adam and Eve, as God himself later acknowledged, "like *God*, knowing both good and evil" (Genesis 3.5, 22 LXX). Jesus wanted to protect humanity from the envious shortcomings of his Creator Father. But eventually the envious Father got his revenge on his son, in his later manifestation, through Jesus' suffering crucifixion.

And who was responsible for Adam and Eve's ejection from paradise? Once again, the answers were varied, mutually reactive, and complicated; each version bred further variants. At first sight the answer may seem simple: it was all Eve's fault. Woman was clearly responsible for man's fall. Eve succumbed to evil temptation from the Devil and then seduced Adam. God gave humanity procreation as compensation for the loss of immortality. Before the fall, there had been no sex in paradise, just as there will be none in heaven. That is a classic Christian interpretation.[18]

But is the orthodox Christian explanation satisfactory? Surely both man and woman, Adam and Eve, were jointly complicit in the fall? And given the messiness of the world, can we really be confident that the Creator God was concerned with human welfare? Some Christians, whom for convenience we call Gnostics, were convinced that the true God could not be held responsible for such an imperfect creation, and so they concluded that this world was created by mistake, perhaps by a woman's mistake, but if so, a glorious mistake, and one which men had subsequently made worse. We shall examine some of these Gnostic views in the next section. For the moment, let us note that their interpretations implied a stratified Godhead. Above, in the high heavens, there is a supreme, uniquely good God, superbly unconcerned with daily humanity. Below him, with many intermediaries, there is an inferior creator God (whom Jews and orthodox Christians mistakenly call God), and it was this inferior God who made this world.

THE FEVERISH IMAGINATION OF THE GNOSTICS

In 1945, two peasants were digging for fertilizer below a steep rock overlooking the river Nile at Nag Hammadi in southern Egypt. They discovered an ancient sealed jar. One thought it might contain a hostile djinn (the spirit of the *Arabian Nights* lives on); but then he wondered if it might contain gold. Greed beat fear. Together they cracked the jar open and discovered thirteen leather-bound volumes, and took them home. Their mother used some of the pages to light the cooking stove. But in due course, the potential value of the books was realized. And today we have over fifty tracts, the great majority of them previously unknown, several hundred pages of primarily Gnostic treasures.

These tracts were written in Coptic (native Egyptian transcribed in a predominantly Greek alphabet) but were based on and translated from much earlier Greek originals. They had been buried in the middle of the fourth century, probably by Christian monks from a nearby monastery who feared persecution by orthodox Christians. The Nag Hammadi library (as it is now called) was written, translated, collected, and read by pious Christians, though we can easily imagine the horror of orthodox bishops on reading its wilder speculations.[19] For our convenience, we label these writings under the modern collective name Gnostic, or Gnosticism. But ancient orthodox church fathers gave each of the many schools and sects within Gnosticism separate names—Valentinians, Sethians, Ophites, Borborites—perhaps in order to stress their discordant and perverse diversity. As to the Gnostics themselves, some did form distinct groups, while others were individual teachers or members of loose affiliations. Both the Gnostic groups and the gnosticizing individuals probably thought of themselves as being within, rather than at the margins of or outside, Judaism or Christianity.

Giving a simple account of Gnosticism is like presenting a hungry gourmet with the bare bones of a fish. The whole point of Gnosticism lies not in its common core or propositional frame, but in its florid and inventive variations; indeed, one orthodox Christian tactic was to reduce Gnosticism to a series of propositions, just in order to make it seem ridiculous. What united Gnostics was principally their myths and a worldview. But their myths are complex and their worldview is rather more mystical than most modern realists feel comfortable with.

The core myth of Gnosticism turns on the belief that inside humans there is a spark of divinity, put there from a supreme Divinity which is lodged in the high heavens of outer space. The divinity within each human can be awakened and discovered only through a process of contemplation and self-knowledge. This process of internal enlightenment, or illumination, can best be accomplished with the assistance of a divine mediator, or redemption figure, who has a passing interest in the fate of God's creatures. A human instructor can also sometimes help, but even when Gnostics combine in groups, they seem anticlerical ("Bishops are dry canals").[20] Salvation is primarily the individual's own responsibility.

So Gnostics search individually for personal salvation through internal experience. God lies within us. Each of us has a share of Jesus inside. Humanity has been given a wonderful gift, namely the ability to sense spirituality, to hear the celestial harmony, to understand and to penetrate the divine world. The authenticity of our perceptions of the divine is guaranteed by revelation, ecstasy, and dreams. The discovery of divinity within (by any standards an exciting and ambitious adventure) is pursued via self-knowledge, which in its turn is achieved through contemplation and through new myths which outline the complex reality, located outside this world, in the multiple heavens which surround our universe. The process of illumination involves finding a path through these complex enveloping spheres to the highest heaven.

The pursuit of this metarational knowledge of the divine is not purely intellectual but psychic, spiritual, divine. It is ideally available to us all. But only few, the chosen few, avail themselves of the opportunity to gain the key to the cosmic mystery, and so can eventually ascend to be remerged with the heavens from which their spirit came. This spiritual self-knowledge is not ethical, nor is it a mystical ecstasy which suspends individuality, nor is it like modern psychoanalytical self-knowledge, which reaches an inner ego by self-awareness. Rather it is a movement of the mind, a flicker, which brings the inner self into touch with divinity. The me inside me intuitively grasps its divine counterpart.[21]

There are three categories of humans: the *spirituals*, the *sensualists*, and the *dross*. Spiritual humans form the top level; they are the true insiders. The sensualists are ordinary Christians, flawed might-have-beens, while those completely outside the faith are mere dross, material people, weak vessels of the flesh. Only truly spiritual people can perceive, and so receive, revelations of the spirit.[22] True understanding (gnosis) puts the spark of divinity which is inside them in touch with its divine counterpart in heaven. Redemption holds out the promise of the eventual reunion of the spirit with its divine origin. But the true way of Light on earth is hard, beset by the countervailing forces of Darkness. For some, the task can be best achieved by rejecting the passions of the body. But then

again, once salvation or illumination has been achieved, the chosen elect
are immune from the corruption of the material world or flesh. Gnostic
knowledge is beyond reason. It is the lived experience of spiritual regen-
eration.

The Gnostic worldview is dualistic, an exacting balance between the
optimism of hope and the pessimism of despair. The potential for good
is balanced by the pervasiveness of evil, symbolized by the flesh and the
material world in which we are all imprisoned. Humanity's predicament
can best be understood through two mythical syndromes, the passionate
but nightmarish creation of the universe, and the merciful and beautiful
creation of a flawed humanity. Both accounts are complex, and each version is only one of several, like a set of musical variations. Each successive version makes best sense only as part of the series, and all depend on
the hearer knowing the original theme, the creation stories in Genesis.
The novel versions both subvert and depend on the Judaeo-Christian
tradition.

Three underlying elements in the Gnostic charter myth seem especially important. First, the supreme God was not responsible for creating
this inadequate world, though he/she benevolently salvaged what was
good within it and circumscribed the contamination and destruction
caused by the powers of evil. Thanks to divine mercy, spiritual humans
can also follow a similar trajectory: perseverance and insight enable some
humans to escape evil and hope for salvation. A second dominant motif
is the upstaging of the ethnocentric Judaeo-Christian foundation myth,
as set out in Genesis. The inferior Jewish Christian God (called Yaldabaoth, which means "king of chaos" or "son of shame") arrogantly and
repeatedly boasts that he is the only God, and a jealous God, a boast
which makes sense only if he also acknowledges that other Gods exist.
Once he discovers the beauty of the supreme God, who existed long before him but of whose existence he was long unaware, he is deeply
ashamed; and more to the point, we are taught to despise his ignorance
and arrogance.[23] Thirdly, God is both perfect and imperfect; he/she is
both male and female; she/he is unknowable, perhaps even to itself, and
yet divine forces and humans ambitiously struggle to understand God's
nature.

In some versions, Gnostics merge the Genesis story with the Christian Jesus tradition to make a more universalistic, transcendent myth. So,

for example, the mythical Adam and the divine, preexistent Jesus (as against the "human," historical Jesus) are merely different images of the same "true perfect man, the first revelation."[24] After all, the Roman world was too large and too diverse to have been created in a Middle Eastern garden backwater. Instead, creation really took place in the spacious magnificence of the outer heavens. And to understand its magnificence, Gnostics used a transcendental language which united the thought worlds of Judaism, Christianity, and pagan Neoplatonism. Gnostics in the second century moved Christianity out of Palestine and out of the restricted world of Judaeo-Christian myth onto a cosmic stage.

In the beginning, there was Profundity, a male, whose female partner was Silence, also known as Thought or Loveliness.[25] This original male/female pair (though Profundity was also adrogynous: "the Mother/Father of the All") together bred a first son, Intelligence, and a daughter, Truth. The first son, Intelligence, alone knew the true nature of his father, Profundity, but was kept from spreading the good news by his mother, Silence, because ignorance stimulates the desire for knowledge.

This first quartet of divine beings (Profundity, Silence, Intelligence, and Truth) then bred another quartet of godlike male and female aspects: male Reason (or Word/Reason), female Life, male Humanity, and female Church. These divine aspects then generated twenty-two virtues, each comprising male/female pairs. Some were erotic, such as Deep Mingling, Undecaying Union, Self-existent Pleasure, and Only-begotten Happiness. Others were more routinely ethicoreligious: Intercessionary Faith, Fatherly Hope, Motherly Love, Ecclesiastical Blessedness, and a final pair, Desired Wisdom.

Wisdom (the female Sophia) was the last-born child. She conceived an illicit passion for her First Father, Profundity, and in the agonizing frustration of her solitary but unrealizable and despairing love, she self-generated a son. Divinity is distinguished by achieving what we do not even dare to hope to do. But because this son was imperfectly conceived without the consent of her male partner, he was misshapen ("like a lion-faced serpent"), so that even his mother was ashamed when she first saw him. In vain she tried to hide what had happened; all her strength drained away, but finally she prayed to the First Father for forgiveness. Thanks to her prayers and the intercession of other divine emanations,

Wisdom half succeeded. Her divine image was permitted to stay in the highest heavens (the Pleroma). But her lesser image, containing her desires, was expelled to the lower heavens, together with her misbegotten son.

In order to prevent a repetition of Wisdom's error, the first son, Intelligence, created a new divine force, called Limitation. And to redeem Wisdom's error, the glorious Trinity of First Father (Profundity), the Mother (Silence or Forethought), and Intelligence, with contributions from all the other divine emanations, together created Christ and his female partner, the Holy Spirit. This was the glorious preexistent Christ, of whom the human Jesus was subsequently to be but a pale imitation. Meanwhile, the lesser image of Wisdom, exiled into darkness, suffering and repentant, remembered her divine past and strained with all her might to recover the Light which she had lost. In her grief, fear, and ignorance, she once again struggled to create, but this time managed to produce only a formless material world.

Once again in despair, the image of Wisdom prays for help to the redeemer Christ. He suitably sends down from the highest heaven only a lesser emanation of himself, which Wisdom greets with due reverence—at first she is modestly veiled, but then, more boldly, she reveals herself to him fully. Christ, in return, separates out her virtues from her vices, and together they jointly finish creating the physical world, which combines the three archetypes of existence: Spirit, Sense, and Matter. As in her first transgression, Wisdom once again creates only in the passion of contemplating Christ's dazzling perfection, but this time, because of Christ's participation, without the previous disastrous consequences. Indeed, it was this lesser image of Wisdom who, with her new Christ-given powers, created out of her formless son the Mother-made Father, the Artificer or artisanal Creator (Demiourgos) whom Jews and orthodox Christians foolishly call God. But in reality he was only an angel with a similarity to God. But since he was ignorant of the secret of his own creation (his mother had hid herself from him), he deluded himself into thinking that he alone had created this world, and boasted, "I am the Lord God, there is no God beside me" (Isaiah 45.5; 46.9 LXX).[26]

In this highly edited and purposefully critical version of the Gnostic creation story, derived from Irenaeus, the orthodox bishop of Lyon at the end of the second century, the material world is seen as the vicarious product of Wisdom's passion and tears, created in fear, perplexity, and grief. But even in this derivative account, the imaginative originality seems extraordinary. The leading role given to the female as the active if tragic heroine of creation is surprising.[27] But what seems even more amazing is that emotions of inadequacy (such as unrealized love and foolish arrogance) and sexual/erotic drives were divinized, or at least prominently projected onto the Godhead. The problem of incestuous love, necessarily implicit in any creation story which begins with an original pair, is handled directly but delicately. Wisdom creates out of consciously illicit passion.

The whole story of the creation of God, his/her divine powers, and the universe is a pre-script for the subsequent repeat tragedy of the human condition. God's failure to reveal himself, divine Wisdom's agonized and tragic failure to understand God, both mirror and predict the human search to find and know God through Christ. This is not just a story, it is a moral tragedy, with instructive lessons for believers. The creation of the Creator God, that ignorant mixture of Darkness and Light, and of humans was a mistake, but a mistake from which salvation could be salvaged. So too, the divine female Wisdom unwisely tried by herself to know the highest God but could not achieve it. Eventually she succeeded, albeit imperfectly, but only through the intermediacy of the divine Christ. Spiritual humans too can try to reach out to the divine, partly through the self-help of contemplation, but for success they too need the aid of the divine redeemer, Christ.

The intellectual problem underlying all these speculations is how and why God moved from divine singularity to the complexities of our physical and metaphysical worlds. Gnostic answers varied. Perhaps it was by a mere movement of his mind that the divine First Father created (female) Thought as an emanation of himself, and Thought then requested Incorruptibility as a further self-objectification, and so on.[28] These divine replications populated the highest heavens untroubled, until Wisdom's tragic error. Wisdom's fall set in train the creation of lower worlds, and symbolized the continuing tensions between the three levels of supreme good, flawed good, and evil, but also presaged hopes of salvation, which is a return to the divine above. In this version of the story, Wisdom's error functions in divine history roughly as Jesus' humanity and crucifixion function in the orthodox Christian version of human his-

Gnostics

tory. They are the vital fault lines, along which tragic but salvific possibilities emerge.

In these stories, in spite of all the deference which humans properly paid to the glories and trials of the divine, the real Gnostic hero is human. Whereas for orthodox Christians the mythic climax is in Christ's incarnation, death, and resurrection, for Gnostics the climax is in Wisdom's error and the creation of Adam and Eve. For Gnostics, each of God's created humans already contains the key to his/her own salvation. It was to humans that God revealed, however imperfectly, his/her complex nature. It is humanity which is at the center of every divine history. And it is humans who fancy that they understand and can capture God's nature in a net of words and emotions. God is made in humans' image. As Gnostics see it, humans are, at least in part, of the same substance as God.

Gnostic creation myths drive their main points home by repetition, variety, and mystification. Theirs is a drama in four grand acts: the creation of God, the creation of the universe, the creation of the first humans, and final salvation or damnation. Three acts belong to history; the fourth is in the future. Each historical act turns on a cycle of error, conflict, mutual misunderstanding, and redemptive forgiveness. Each act repeats the basic message: some superior creatures, whether divine or human, have flawed elements of divinity trapped inside them. By magnifying the power of the divine, and by divine mercy, the best creatures can increase their potential to be saved. But this core message is repeatedly disguised in variant forms. Just as divinities replicate aspects of themselves, so Gnostic myths create their own voluptuous variety. There seems no end to the diversity or to the ever-increasing complexity of the subordinate divinities and their stories.

Nevertheless, the basic thrust of Gnostic tales is recognizably and powerfully Christian. It is also pointedly polemical.[29] God is both unitary and multiple. For Jews and orthodox Christians (to solve a huge problem with inappropriate simplicity), God just is, ever was, and created the universe. But for Gnostics, God was both ever existent and self-evolving. The Gnostic God had a prehistory. He/She replicated herself by a repeated process of self-objectification. And there was a further difference: the Gnostic position was not coherently argued, as it came to be in orthodox Christian theology. Gnostic myths were told and retold in story and metaphor, as though to say that knowing the nature of God is a matter not of rationality but of understanding. That seems more immediately inviting. But in both systems, barriers of sophistication ensured limited access to true understanding. Orthodox Christian theology required logical coherence and fine epistemological distinctions; Gnostic visionaries (or their hearers) threaded their way, instead, through a maze of mystical elaborations.

To capture the spirit of Gnostic writings, we have to enter their thought world of metaphor, poetry, and paradox. We have to rehear the same stories in at least some of their variations. According to the Secret Book of John, for example, shortly after Wisdom/Sophia has passionately self-created a son and hidden him out of shame on a throne in the clouds, she repents and begs forgiveness. In answer to her prayers, merciful Foreknowledge, the holy and perfect Mother/Father, wishes to create mankind. So with a flicker of thought, he/she looked down onto the waters. The inferior powers of this world immediately saw this reflection, and their chief ruler, Yaldabaoth, said, "Let us create a man in the image of God and according to our likeness, so that his image may become a light for us." And each of the 365 angels and demons contributed different parts of his body and emotions: pleasure, desire, grief, and fear. But when they had finished, Adam still lay lifeless.[30]

Then Yaldabaoth, in his ignorance, but acting on divine instructions without even knowing it, breathed luminous spirit from his mother, Sophia, into Adam. Immediately, Adam's body moved and gained strength, and behold, it too was luminous. And the powers who had made him were instantaneously jealous because Adam was superior to them in intelligence and virtue. So they threw him down to earth. But the blessed Mother/Father had mercy and sent female Thought, or Life (Zoe), to enter Adam and teach him about his divine origins and the possibility of salvation. But the jealous rulers still recognized Adam's superiority and hauled him into the shadow of death, and remodeled him with the ignorance of Darkness, desire, and forgetfulness. And the powers of Darkness, "took him and placed him in paradise. And they said to him, 'Eat at leisure,' for their luxury is bitter and their beauty is depraved. Their luxury is deception, their trees are godlessness, their fruit is deadly poison, and their promise is death."

And the powers of Darkness hid the tree of knowledge from Adam, but Christ made sure that both Adam and Eve ate from it. At this point in the story, John questions the savior, "Lord, wasn't it the serpent who taught Adam to eat?" Christ smiles and says that what the serpent had taught them to eat was the wickedness of lust, so that Adam would be useful. And the powers of Darkness threw a cloud of forgetfulness (rather like a modern anesthetic) over Adam, extracted a rib, and created Eve in the image of divine Thought, whose reflection they had only dimly seen. And when Adam saw Eve, luminous Thought lifted the veil of Darkness from his mind, and Adam "recognized his counterimage, and said, 'This is indeed bone of my bones, and flesh of my flesh. For her, man will leave his father and his mother and cleave to his wife, and they will both be one flesh.'"

And Wisdom came down to Adam and Eve and brought them Life, and made sure that they both tasted perfect Knowledge. And Christ came down in the form of an eagle and woke them as from a deep sleep, in order to teach them. But Yaldabaoth, whom Jews and orthodox Christians foolishly call God, saw Eve as she was preparing herself for her husband, Adam. He recognized the luminous divine Thought within her, seduced (or raped) her, so that she produced two sons, Cain and Abel, one bad, the other good. And so, according to this story, it was the creator God who planted sexual desire in Eve. But Wisdom, ever watchful, planted Spirit in Adam and his son (by Eve) Seth, so that they and their successors might eventually be saved and regain the divinity of their origins, while sinners burn in everlasting fire.

Another Gnostic tract, On the Origins of the World, tells the same story again, but slightly differently. The economical reader may wisely want to skip it; but repetition of the familiar story with minor variations seems to have been part and parcel of the Gnostic experience. This story also describes the successive struggles between the creator God, Yaldabaoth (ignorant, arrogant, ambitious, repentant), and the supreme God, Faith/Wisdom (merciful, loving, sensual, and generous). But in addition, it triumphantly celebrates the intrinsic superiority of humanity in its varied forms over the imperfect though divine Creator. And it shows, at every stage, how the canonical story in Genesis was wrong. "Let us therefore concern ourselves with the facts of the matter."

At an early stage in creation, Forethought fell passionately in love with the reflection of man which Faith/Wisdom had projected onto the waters. She assuaged her love and lost her virginity by pouring light over the earth, and out of her virgin's blood, Desire appeared. He was "lovely in his beauty," so that all the Gods and angels, when they saw him, fell in love with him.

> And he appeared in all of them and set them on fire. And Desire became dispersed in all the created beings of Chaos. From the midpoint of Darkness and Light, Desire appeared, and at the midpoint of angels and humans, Desire was consummated, so that out of earth, primal pleasure blossomed. Woman followed earth, marriage followed woman, birth followed marriage, death followed birth.
>
> After Desire, the grapevine sprouted out of the (virgin's) blood, which had been shed over the earth. So those who drink of the grape conceive the desire of sexual union. After the grapevine, a fig tree and a pomegranate tree sprouted up from the earth, together with the rest of the trees, all species having within them their seed from the seed of the powers [of Darkness] and their angels.

Then Justice created a beautiful paradise, in the land of Wantonness. And it set Desire among the beautiful trees, and the tree of eternal life to the north of paradise. And it is the fruit of this tree which releases souls from the control of demons, and gives humans power to look down on Gods and their angels. Eating from it opened Adam's mind and enabled him to love Eve. And it is loss of virginity, this story repeatedly emphasizes, not its preservation, which is beautifully creative.[31]

The attractions of this revisionist creation story are in its poetry, its positive sexuality, and the prominence it gives to the women Wisdom and Eve, or Life (Zoe). In this version of the creation story, it is Eve/Life who is Wisdom's first creation, made out of a droplet of Light. She is the female instructor of life; her child is the snake in paradise. She is also the first virgin, who bore her first child without a husband.[32] Eve eventually saves Adam, the flawed but yet in some ways divine creation, modeled by the forces of Darkness in imitation of the image of divinity which they had only briefly glimpsed.

"After the day of rest, Sophia sent her daughter Life, being called Eve, as an instructor so that she might get Adam, who had no soul, to arise, so that those whom he would engender might become containers of Light. When Eve saw her male counterpart lying prostrate [in paradise], she had pity upon him, and said, 'Adam, become alive! Arise upon earth!'" Immediately her word became accomplished. For Adam arose and suddenly opened his eyes. And when he saw her he said, "You shall be called

Mother of the Living. For it is you who has given me Life."³³ It seems ironic that the male, as soon as he was rescued, unself-consciously took charge.

But when the powers of Darkness heard that Adam, whom they had created but had abandoned lifeless, was now alive, they came to look. But they saw Eve, luminous in the image of Forethought, and they desired to seize her, have sex with her, and contaminate her, so that she could not rise up again to the Light of heaven. In this way, they plotted that Eve and her children would be at their service. But Eve laughed at their self-deception, and escaped into the tree of knowledge, though she kindly left an image of herself with Adam. At first, the powers were bewildered, but when they saw the image of Eve with Adam, they thought it was the true Eve, and fell upon her and ravaged her foully, without realizing that it was themselves they were defiling.

In reality, the powers (whom some call God[s]) were afraid that Adam and Eve would surpass them. And they told Adam and Eve not to eat from the tree of knowledge in paradise. But the wisest of the creatures, a child of the divine Zoe/Eve, told them that God, by this prohibition, was merely serving his own interests. Eating from the tree of knowledge would make Adam and Eve like God. Eve saw that the fruit of the tree was beautiful, and ate it. She gave some to her husband, and he ate it. The light of knowledge shone on them, and they fell in love with each other. But the rulers were angry and ignorantly asked Adam: "Where are you?" They cursed the instructor and Eve, because they were powerless to do more. "And from that day the Powers realized that truly there was something mightier than they." At the very least, humans have the power to disobey God. For fear that Adam and Eve would eat from the tree of immortality as well, they were expelled from paradise to earth. But when Wisdom/Life saw how evilly the powers had behaved toward her images, she chased them too from the heavens, and turned them into evil spirits, to instruct men on earth in animal sacrifice and the worship of images.³⁴

These elaborate Gnostic creation stories do not solve the problem of the origins of evil. Intellectually, the basic two-level split between supreme divinities and the lesser creator God(s) is unsatisfying. After all, why did the supreme godhead allow Wisdom's mistaken passion? Why did he/she tolerate the compromise solution of an imperfect creation? The supreme, omnipotent, and just God cannot be let off his responsibility for this world so lightly. Of course, one answer is that mythographers begin with the imperfect world they know, and then work backward. No one knows the right answer, or knows that his answer is right.

But here God is consciously and innovatively constructed, and as inadequate. The lesser God(s) are malevolent, incompetent, cruel, jealous, and fearful, rather like, I imagine, the secular rulers of the Roman empire, after whom they are generically named (the authorities, powers, rulers). These lesser God(s) try, in vain, to keep humans down, as their slaves, and often succeed. The Gnostic stories are repeatedly polemical, without expending a lot of effort on argument and without losing track of the plot. And thanks to the merciful generosity of the supreme God, invisible in the highest heaven, truly spiritual humans with spiritual knowledge do recognize the limitations of the lesser God(s) and can rise above them; they can with effort escape to the real freedom of the highest Divinity.

As religious myths go, these stories seem magnificent in their variety and inventiveness. All the ingredients of the canonical stories are reused and controverted. As in the Siva myths, even the highest Gods cannot immediately get all that they want, and they create emotions which they cannot fully control. Even the supreme God has a satisfyingly wide range of merely human emotions. Lust and beauty are given significant parts in the process of creation. The Jewish all-male God is displaced by a whole array of males, females, and androgynes, while the undersexed Christian Trinity is replaced by an eroticized family. Even the Virgin Mary is converted, rather savagely, into the idea of virgin blood creatively spilled to produce vines and roses. At the level of religious storytelling, if what we want in the story is conflict, sex, blood, morals, and magic, these myths are well designed to be attractive.

Lovers of lost causes may wistfully regret Gnostics' gradual demise. Their chaotic inventiveness must have been an ingredient in their failure. They lacked coherence, hierarchy, and unified purpose. The sheer virtuosity of their inventions induced more conservative Christians to sharpen the boundaries of orthodoxy. Christian traditionalists insisted more rigorously on the uniqueness of the single, ever-existent Creator and his single human/divine son, Jesus. In contrast to the esoteric, mutually conflicting, and unverifiable inventions of the Gnostics, conservative Christians also increasingly insisted on a fixed canon of sacred texts, on the bodily resurrection of a historical Jesus, and on the traditions of a "known" apostolic succession.

Instead of seeking for the divine inside oneself through self-knowledge, orthodox Christians were asked to rely on a professional and hierarchically ordered priesthood, which claimed an effective monopoly of religious interpretation. Gnostics, by contrast, although they too mostly considered themselves as Christians, were committed to finding a personal redemption by uniting the spirit of the believer with the spirit of the divine. For them, the humanity of Jesus was an embarrassment which could be triumphantly denied. They needed only a spiritual messenger, who could be found and refound in their mythic revelations. The spiritual Jesus, who for Gnostics mattered most, had fought his primal battles before human history had begun.

GOD'S BEGGAR TWIN

Mani (216–76 CE) is one of the great but undervalued figures of religious history. Like Jesus he was, in effect, the founder of a world religion, Manichaeism. Unlike Jesus, according to the sacred texts, he consciously set out to found a new supergnostic religion, and during his lifetime dispatched missionaries all over the Middle East to preach and convert. But unlike Christianity, Manichaeism to all practical purposes gradually died out, although only after centuries of persecution.

When Mani was twenty-four (in 240 CE), the Living God revealed to him the hidden secrets of the origins and future of the universe, "the mystery of Light and Darkness" and the true history of the primal war which Darkness had long ago stirred up against Light. In this revelation, God instructed Mani about the mystery of the tree of knowledge from which Adam ate, and about the mystery of the apostles—Zarathustra, Buddha, Jesus—each good enough for his time, previously sent to found religions. The Living God "revealed to me all that has happened and all that shall happen, everything that the eye sees, and the ear hears, and the thought thinks. Through him I understood everything. Through him, I saw everything."[35]

Armed with this omniscience, Mani consciously set out to found his own new, universal religion. This religion, which we call Manichaeism, was not just a sect within an existing religion, but a brand new amalgam. Mani, like Muhammad later, generously acknowledged the legitimate variety of previous religious understandings—each venerable but only temporarily valid.[36] But thanks to God's revelations, Mani felt able to fuse and transcend all previous religious traditions: Zoroastrian, Buddhist, Christian, Gnostic. And just as he borrowed across cultural frontiers, so Mani worked hard with repeated missionary journeys to ensure that his new religion flowed across those same political frontiers, all the way from India through Parthia to Roman Egypt.

With a magnificent sense of his place in history, Mani produced "a great wisdom, the like of which had not hitherto been proclaimed in all earlier generations. All the writings," he declared in one of his voluminous books, "all the wisdom, the revelations, parables, and psalms of all earlier religions were gathered up and brought to my church, and were added to the wisdom which I revealed."[37] We are a far cry here from the humble crib and the oral simplicity of the Jewish carpenter Jesus of the early Christian tradition. Mani was explicitly determined to avoid replicating Zarathustra's, Buddha's, and particularly Jesus' failure to write down their own divine message.[38]

Jesus was trumped, but not ignored. Far from it. Jesus was a key character in Mani's mythology and self-identity. Jesus was imitated, borrowed, and subsumed. The recently discovered story of Mani's early life, incidentally the smallest book ever found from the ancient world, written down by his disciples, begins: "I, Mani, an apostle of Jesus Christ through the will of God, the Father of Truth, from whom I also came into being."[39] Mani, rather like Jesus, was born of/created by God, though more often Mani was envisaged as God's partner or twin *(suzugos)*. "And it is with his power that I fight greed and the Devil (Ahriman), and teach men the wisdom and knowledge which I have received from my twin."[40]

It was this conviction of divine inspiration which fired Mani to overcome his repeated sense of loneliness and despair when he first left the pious Jewish Christian baptist sect in which he had been raised and set out to preach his superior message of peace and salvation: "I am alone and poor. How shall I behave in the presence of kings, princes, and religious leaders? Then the Most High spoke to me [and said]: 'You were not sent for this sect, but to every nation, all schools, every town and region. Your message of hope will be proclaimed and explained in all countries of the world. Step forward and turn round. I am with you, your helper and protector. Therefore be not troubled.' Countless are the words which [the Father of Greatness] spoke to me, as he gave me strength and courage, and trust in his hope. I worshiped him, and my heart rejoiced at beholding the beauty of my blessed twin, the most glorious and the most high."[41] Reassurance bred increased confidence, so that although Mani still occasionally felt like a lone sheep among wolves, he could also write about the superiority of his own religion. "The religion which I have chosen is in ten respects superior to other religions. First, previous religions arose only in one country and one language. But my religion is such that it will exist in every land, and all languages, and will be taught in most distant countries."[42]

This blend of inspiration and explicit syncretism enabled Mani and his disciples to preach tirelessly and successfully for the next three decades and more (240–76 CE), not only in Mesopotamia and Iran, but as far as India in the east and Egypt in the west. Part of Mani's success lay in his willingness to adapt his message to the varied education of his listeners. He wrote his teachings both in words and pictures. "Let those who hear [my message] in words, see them also in images. Let him who is unable to learn from words, learn from pictures."[43]

Through his family connections, Mani succeeded in getting close to three successive Parthian kings. According to Mani, Shapur I (241–73 CE) gave him favor and protection, even though it is difficult for us to envisage how a radical missionizing religion led by an unwashed, unkempt, vegetarian beggar ascetic could find consistent favor at a luxurious royal court. All the more so if Mani really dressed, as he was described in one ancient though hostile description, in high-heeled boots, a multicolored coat, and trousers with one leg red and the other green. Christianity, by contrast, started in poverty and welcome obscurity, and then waited almost three centuries while it established a broad base before it confronted court politics. After Shapur, the next Parthian king, Hormizd (273–74 CE), also favored Mani, but died soon. His successor, Bahram I (274–77 CE), was hostile and reportedly under the influence of envious and traditional Zoroastrian priests.[44] He summoned Mani to the capital. Mani's last journey to court was filled with foreboding, and all his worst fears were fulfilled. The confrontation between radical religious leader and oppressive civil power could finish only one way.

According to the Manichaean story, the king kept Mani waiting while he finished his dinner, and then, on his way out to hunt, came into the audience chamber, leaning with one arm on his young daughter-in-law, and with his other arm resting on the severe Mazdaean (Zoroastrian) high priest, Kartir. The Great King said to Mani: "You are not welcome." The Lord said: "What wrong have I done?" The king said angrily: "I have sworn not to let you into this country; what are you good for, since you go neither hunting nor fighting?" But then he grudgingly conceded that Mani might be useful for curing and healing. Mani surprisingly colluded with this characterization. The Lord replied: "I have not done you any harm. Always have I done good to your family. Many are the servants of yours whom I have freed from demons and witches . . . many were at the point of death, but I revived them."[45] His pleas were of no avail. Bahram I ordered Mani's imprisonment and execution, though according to some accounts, Mani just died in prison, cruelly loaded with chains. His head, or his flayed skin stuffed with hay, was displayed at the city gate. So the emerging myth of Mani's life, now (like Jesus') had its dramatic trial and unjust ending, its hostile priests and martyr's death, which faithful Manichees celebrated annually as the key point of their liturgical calendar in March and called a crucifixion.[46]

After Mani's imprisonment and death, Manichees were severely persecuted both in the Persian and Roman empires. In the Roman empire, under pagan rule, Manichaeism was treated as an unwelcome infection from enemy Persia, and later under Christian emperors as a vicious Christian heresy; surprisingly, even knowledgeable outsiders confused Manichees with Christians.[47] In spite of, or perhaps even because of, persecution, Manichaeism spread to Spain, Gaul, Italy, and north Africa, where St. Augustine was a noted convert for some years (373–82 CE) before he became a Christian. And in the east, persecutions probably helped the further diffusion of Manichaeism from Iran throughout central Asia, where it even became the state religion in one small kingdom. Eventually, at the end of the seventh century, it reached Chinese Turkestan. Even to this day, the holy texts of Mani and his successors survive in multiple languages—Chinese, Middle Persian, Uighur, Sogdian, Greek, Syriac, Coptic, Latin.[48]

Manichaean myths move on a magnificent scale through three periods of universal history: before creation, during human history, and at the end of the world. These myths tell the story of a fundamental battle between the forces of Light and Darkness, a battle fought first when the universe began. The good God, with his numerous godly and angelic emanations, fights a long and tough battle, not always winning, with the cunning king of Darkness. The battle still goes on. But we know, or hope, that the great God and his successive helpers (the Mother of Life, Archetypal Man, the Third Messenger, the Great Sustainer, Jesus the Radiance, and of course Mani, the Luminary) will rescue and redeem those who by faith and good works make themselves worthy of salvation.

The sacred writings are sometimes strikingly beautiful and rhapsodic. Others are quite repulsive in the cruelty of their mythological imagination. Archetypal Man, for example, is sent from Light to Darkness as a decoy to capture the slimy elements of Darkness. Humans are made of disgusting matter, relieved only by trapped particles of light. Their carnal lust is seen only as repulsive, not as pleasurable or creative. So the truly committed faithful, the Elect, should be ascetically uncarnal, eating vegetables filled with light, such as gourds and cucumbers, and harming none of God's creatures. The core myths were not only a cosmic history explaining how the universe began; they also served as a sacred charter for ethical behavior.

The complexities of Manichaean creation myths are bafflingly difficult to remember (Mani's own accounts themselves differ). But then, as in other canonical religious texts, inconsistency and opacity, which are more troubling for scholars than for believers, are important ingredients in their mysterious appeal. The tortured conflicts between primal forces, which occurred long before our world began, reflect the imagined lives of the pervasive demons who populate ancient visions of the unseeable and incomprehensible worlds of heaven and hell. But more important for their longer-term appeal, they also project on to a mythical screen the internal torments of the human mind. In psalms, sermons, letters, prayers, and illustrated exegetical texts, these were the stories and images which Mani's beggar missionaries carried from China to the Atlantic Ocean, walking barefoot, hungry, and dependent for their survival and success on the alms of the faithful and the patronage or tolerance of kings.

REPRISE

Skeptical readers will have long since noticed that I have committed two sins. Like an obedient Manichee, I should confess. My first sin (as I see it) is that I have colluded with the Manichaean sources in their persuasive fiction that it was Mani himself who said and wrote all that he is reported to have said or written. Of course, given Mani's explicit claims, it seems churlish to doubt that Mani wrote several books. One of his great virtues, as he saw it, was that unlike Buddha, Zoroaster, and Jesus, he had himself written down his own teachings.⁴⁹ But by the same token it would be credulous to think that Mani really wrote all that is attributed to him, or that his books survive unrevised, unredacted. (So also it would be legitimate to *believe* but—after two generations of modern form criticism and redaction criticism—ill informed to *think* that the gospels of the New Testament or the Gospel of Thomas preserve the actual sayings of Jesus, unedited and unrevised; but more of that in the next chapter.) My general point is that there was simply no mechanism available in widely dispersed ancient religions for accurately preserving the words of charismatic leaders. Words and teachings were sensibly adapted to local circumstances and subsequent events.

For Mani, I can briefly illustrate this argument with two passages which show adaptive intrusions. The first quotation is taken from the *Kephalaia*, or main teachings, of Mani, which survive in a Coptic codex of the late fourth century. Mani says: "The world has not allowed me to write down, but if you, my children and my disciples, write down my wisdom, the questions you have asked me, and the interpretations which I have explained to you from time to time, the homilies and lessons which I have delivered to the teachers, leaders, Elect, and catechumens . . . you must remember them and write them down."⁵⁰ For me, this is a clear indication that the teachings of this lengthy book, all ostensibly delivered by Mani himself in the dramatic first person, were drawn from notes, memory, and tradition. They may capture the spirit of Mani's teaching; it is unlikely that they report his words verbatim.

The second illustrative quotation is taken from Mani's earliest work, the *Sabuhragan*, said to have been written soon after Mani's great commissioning revelation (240 CE), when he presented an overview of his beliefs to King Shapur I (242–73 CE). In it, Mani described the fate of those condemned to hell: "You have pursued and persecuted us from land to land, so do not say now, 'If we had known that it would befall us so, we would have believed what you said to us and accepted the religion.'"⁵¹ But widespread persecution of Manichees "from land to land" started only after Mani's death, and so it seems reasonable to assume that this passage is a later insertion.

My second sin is more serious. I have been content, like a naive positivist, to give a rough chronological account of Mani's career as though we have been dealing here with real rather than with symbolic events. I have ignored the story's underlying structure. My chief point is that the life of a divine, or more specifically, a divine/human redeemer, has a specific, prescripted shape. It must be *U*-shaped. By *U*-shaped I mean that the redeemer must in some way start and finish in heaven, with dramatic and miraculous descent and ascent, and so he spends only the middle portion of his supernaturally extended life on earth.

So, ideally speaking, what we should expect is the following twelve stages in a divine/human redeemer's career. These stages represent a cluster of expectations. Not all of them are necessary in any one redeemer's life. Part may stand for whole.

1. supernatural or mysterious origins
2. birth portents
3. infancy perils
4. initiation, revelation
5. voyage in search of wisdom
6. contest with demonic powers
7. miracle working such as cures, resuscitations
8. extreme ethical virtue and/or wise sayings
9. conflict with conservative/repressive/civil/religious authorities
10. dramatic final scene
11. violent, mysterious death
12. resurrection, ascension, postresurrection appearances, and the judgment of the dead

This general scheme, mutatis mutandis, applies to Buddha, Jina, Jesus, and Mani. And of course, the similarity between Jesus and Mani was not accidental. Mani and his followers consciously attempted to imitate and surpass Jesus. Similarity and rivalry were necessary in the genre because the general shape of the scheme and its interstitial points are not so much historical/chronological events, though they can be presented as such; they are more structural imperatives which ensure the authority and legitimation of the human/divine redeemer. Or put another way, Mani's biography was prescripted.

So we find ten of the twelve basic elements of this scheme in Manichaean writings. For example, Mani's divine origins are secured by his preexistence before the universe was created. His appearance on earth came about through a double paternity; he was the child of earthly parents, but also born of God, the Father of Light. He was separated from his heavenly Father and clothed in hateful flesh.[52] When he was born, his mother had a vision which showed her that baby Mani had been taken up to the sky and kept there for two days before being brought back to earth. When Mani died, there were heavenly signs, and he entered a specially prepared paradise in which he no longer perceived the face of the enemy, or heard the voice of power, but enjoyed the rest of redemption.[53] The two missing elements from the scheme are infancy perils and struggles with demonic powers.

Both omissions can be plausibly explained. Struggle between good and evil is a central pivot of the Manichaean charter myth about the creation of the cosmos. Perhaps there seemed no need to rehearse it in the story of Mani's life. As for infant dangers, Mani(chaeans), unlike orthodox Christians, had no interest in the human/divine mix of the redeemer; for him/them, the body was a despicable shell. So for the Manichaean faithful, the interesting part of Mani's worldly career began with his great revelation, his violent break from the pious sect of Jewish Christian Elchasaite baptists in which he was reared, and the beginning of his mission. But his early life was not completely overlooked.

From an early age, Mani was protected "by the might of angels and the powers of holiness," and received countless revelations and visions. While he was still living in his earthly father's pious baptist sect, he once revealed to a fellow baptist the secret pain which trees feel when their fruit is plucked. The other baptist recognized the great power in Mani, was overcome with awe, and fell at Mani's feet, saying, "I did not realize that you had this secret mystery inside you." As a result of his great revelation, when the Twin showed him the secrets of heaven, he at last acknowledged his own divinity. An angel raised him up by the right hand to heaven; "he became like unto one of the greatest angels" and traveled from heaven to heaven in a chariot of wind, until the Father "revealed to me the nature of my being before the creation of the universe."[54]

Mani's other redeemer credentials have mostly been covered, though his trip to India (which parallels Jesus' journey to Egypt), his ascension to heaven after death, and his judgment of the dead all deserve mention.[55] Of course, we cannot tell how much of the total construct was built up as a conscious imitation and revision of Jesus' life. For early Manichaeans, Jesus was a divine precursor of Mani who in his human life suffered like Mani in his holy cause. The priests of Zoroaster at the court of the Persian king are explicitly likened to the Jewish priests at the court of Pilate. "O Magians, priests of fire, you seized my God in your foul hands, impious men, mad and godless, brothers of the Jews, murderers of Christ, you murdered the righteous ambassador. . . . They all cried out with one voice to the godless judge: 'We implore thee, O king, do away with him, for he is a teacher who leads men astray.' You left your body, ascended to your kingdom, they attacked your body, cut off your head, and set it high on a gate. Your blood will be avenged. Blessed are your loved ones who weep."[56] The life of Mani the redeemer is only one segment of the total Manichaean message. The central core of the Mani myth package is set out in the grand story of creation.

THE CENTRAL STORY

In the beginning, there was only Light above and Darkness below. Neither knew each other. Light was good, Darkness was evil. But whereas Light was content with itself and harmonious, Darkness was continuously writhing in self-destructive hate. For it is in Darkness' nature to be self-absorbed and at war, even with itself. In the course of these running battles, eventually Darkness came to its own boundaries, and for the first time caught sight of the beauties of Light.

The envious forces of Darkness (or Death) view the harmony of Light (or Immortality) with ignorant greed. They even unite to attack. But Light, which is filled with peaceful good, has no weapons with which to repel the invaders, or chooses from moral virtue not to use them.[57] Implicitly here, Greek and Jewish Gods are being morally upstaged, at least for the moment; after all, in Greek myth, Zeus hurled thunderbolts against the mythical Giants and the monstrous snake-headed Typhon, and Yahweh condemned Satan to the miseries of hell. In Mani's myth, the good Father of Greatness and the evil king of Darkness are both eternal and coexistent.

But back to Mani's Father of Greatness and his successive emanations. In the second stage of cosmic evolution, the Father of Greatness in cooperation with the Mother of Life calls out a divine figure called Archetypal Man and commissions him, armed with light, wind, water, fire, and soul, to fight against Darkness. The Godhead here, as often in eastern Christianity, consists of Father, Mother, Son. But the forces of Darkness, vice, lust, greed, smoke, and scorching wind, long used to war, are too strong. They overcome Archetypal Man, bind him, blind him, and devour his armor, namely his soul (or in some accounts his sons). Sacrificing Archetypal Man as a prey to Darkness (just as a shepherd, to save his whole flock, throws a single sheep to a hungry lion) assuages Darkness' appetite and averts danger from the realm of Light.[58]

Even more significantly, Darkness now has Light trapped inside it, like a poisoned bait. And so begins a long struggle for redemption. Archetypal Man awakens in captivity, in a deep abyss of Darkness. For long generations he patiently waits for his eventual rescue and salvation; he knows he is fulfilling the will of the Father. But eventually he prays to the Father seven times, just as the Manichaean elect are meant to pray seven times each day. The myth is both history and instruction for current behavior. The Father finally hears his prayer and sends the Living Spirit to rescue him from the contamination of hell. The Living Spirit calls out to Archetypal Man, looks into the abyss of hell, stretches out his right hand, and pulls Archetypal Man free.

For Manichaeans, this myth of Archetypal Man's rescue from hell by God's messenger is the central moment in sacred history, as the crucifixion and resurrection are to normative Christianity. Man's relationship with God is of call and answer, of being saved by God from danger. "That is why the Manichaeans when they meet each other grasp their right hands in greeting as a sign that they are themselves among those who were saved from the Darkness."[59] The story seems to say that in the present world also, God will answer believers when they call, and stretch out his saving right hand. And of course, in this myth, Mani was also reworking the Christian idea of the saving Son sent by God into the world as a sacrificial figure of redemption. But Mani's emphasis (before his own death) was on God's purposefulness in sending his son, the Archetypal Man, as bait and as eventual victor, and on his being rescued after his initial defeat. Archetypal Man, Jesus, and Mani himself are all variations on the same theme. They are all intermediaries between vulnerable humanity and an omnipotent but invisible God.

The cosmic drama now turns to the creation of our world. The divine

Archetypal Man has been rescued. But at some cost. He has left behind those parts of himself which the forces of Darkness had consumed. So in the next stage of cosmic evolution, the king of Light orders the Living Spirit (or the Father of Life) to create the world as we know it from these elements of mixed Light and Darkness, a task made easier because the forces of Darkness had been weakened by their admixture with Light.

Then, in response to the prayers of the Mother of Life, the Living Spirit, and Archetypal Man, the king of Light empowers a Messenger, who sets the new world in motion. This Messenger also tries to release more particles of light from their imprisonment by the powers of Darkness. In a desperate and dramatic play, he shows off the image of his nakedness. At first his tactic is successful. The male Darknesses are lustily attracted to his female form; the female Darknesses to his male form. And the Light particles so released rise to fill the waxing moon. But here too there is a price to pay. Some of the male semen triggered by the seductive female image of Light falls to earth, and creates the vegetable world. The female demons, self-impregnated by their desire for the male image of Light, abort; the abortions fall to the ground, copulate with the buds of trees (that is, with the earlier vegetable product of the male demons), and so produce animals. The Mani story has distinct similarities to Gnostic cosmogonic myths, and like them is somewhat more complex than Genesis, but goes beyond them in arguing that our material world is made up from the debris of rejected sins.

Eventually, of course, the powers of Darkness began to realize that they were being continuously drained of Light. They planned the best possible stratagem for its (and their own) preservation. They had seen the divine Messenger's form. He/she represents what is most desirable, and yet least achievable. So they devised an imitation, which will imprison Light in the most desirable form. Demons copulate, the king of Darkness eats their aborted progeny (in order to concentrate elements of Light), and in memory of the image which he has seen of the divine Messenger, creates Adam and Eve, and pours over them all the Light which is left. By this devilish trick, the divine form (that is a variation on God's image in the Genesis creation story) is turned through satanic invention into Darkness' best form of defense.[60]

Thereafter, all the struggles between Darkness and Light turn on Adam, created in lustful concupiscence by the king of Darkness out of matter washed over with Light, and on Eve, the woman, who is not only an instrument of Adam's seduction, the stimulus to his concupiscence, but even more the tool of human reproduction. It is reproduction which ensures that the surviving particles of Light, now mixed with matter, are multiplied and diversified, so that their ultimate rescue is hindered and postponed.

Once more the Light Gods pray to the king of Light for Adam's salvation. The king of Light sends Jesus, who makes Adam eat from the tree of knowledge (by implication, as in several Gnostic myths, Jesus serves here as the snake in paradise) and so acquaints Adam through visions with the misery of his current lot and the image of the ideal world which he has lost. Jesus' revelation is both depressant and stimulant. But Jesus for Manichaeans served not only as a prime revealer and as the arch Intelligence linking Gods with humanity; he also symbolized the suffering of Archetypal Man. Indeed, in Manichaean myth, Jesus suffers every day; he is served up, bound like a prisoner, in every dish.

> I am in the midst of my enemies; the beasts surround me.
> The burden which I bear is of the powers and principalities.
> They burned in their wrath, they rose up against me. . . .
> Matter and her sons divided me up amongst them,
> They burned me in their fire, they gave me a bitter likeness.
> The strangers with whom I mixed, me they know not;
> They tasted my sweetness, they desired to keep me with them.
> I was like life to them, but they were death to me;
> I bore up beneath them, they wore me as a garment upon them.
>
> I am in everything, I bear the skies . . . I support the earth.
> I am the Light that shines forth, which gives joy to the souls.
> I am the life of the world; I am the milk that is in all the trees.
> I am the sweet water which is beneath the sons of Matter. . . .
> I bore these things until I had fulfilled the will of my Father;
> The First Man is my father, whose will I have carried out.
> Lo, the Darkness I have subdued; lo, the fires I have extinguished. . . .
> O soul, raise thy eyes to the height and contemplate thy bond. . . .
> Lo, thy fathers are calling thee. Now go aboard the ship of Light and receive
> thy garland of glory.[61]

Mani's Jesus also instructs Adam not to have sex with Eve, but Adam, after a brief obedience, relapses because she seduces him, of course with the help of demons.[62] So the reign of Darkness persists, and a further cycle of partial human revelations is necessary, through Buddha, Zoroaster, and Jesus, culminating in Mani.

THE THEN AND THE NOW

The bare bones of a complex, multilayered cosmogonic myth cannot do justice to the rich and often incompatible graphic incidental details with which the basic stories were elaborated, by Mani and by his followers in various cultures over the succeeding centuries. Besides, retelling a complex myth cycle in a simple form is probably more a device of refutation, used by a religion's enemies, than a method of instruction used for neophytes or familiars.[63] All that said, the psalms and homilies of the Manichees take up individual episodes in the cosmogonic myth cycle and fit them back—for example, into the stories of Jesus' and Mani's life and death. By implication, these cosmogonic myths are not just about how the world began; they are about the rival spiritual forces which still struggle for possession of believers' souls. Like the core Christian myths of Jesus' teaching, life, and death, the Manichaean myths are not only stories about the past; they are contemporary charters for everyday living.

The mythical past and future were fused with present practice, so that custom seemed part of cosmic nature. It was as though Mani was teaching that what the faithful do, and what makes them special, is that they act out in their lives, however imperfectly, scenes and emotions whose meaning they know only from his revelations about the cosmic past. For example, Manichees greet one another with five signs: the greeting of peace, the right-hand shake, the kiss, the obeisance, and the laying on of hands. Each of these signs and mysteries was part of cosmic history, both past and future, as well as being part of current communal practice.

The first greeting of peace was given long ago by the Gods and angels to Archetypal Man in the land of Light, as he prepared to fight against Darkness. The Gods and angels walked with him, and through their greetings gave him their peace, power, blessings, and good wishes for his victory. And it was this same peace which gave Archetypal Man strength when he was trapped in the abyss of Darkness, and which blessed him when he rose again to the land of Light. Nowadays, as Mani revealed to his disciples, Light-Intelligence (another of God's great emanations) gives peace to the Church; and he who receives that peace is a child of peace, and so can become one of the Elect, and Light/Intelligence pulls him by the right hand, and establishes him within the Church.[64]

Similarly, the right hand was first given to Archetypal Man by the Mother of Life when he wanted to enter battle. She too gave him the first Kiss, when Archetypal Man separated from her to fight the king of Darkness. So too nowadays, all the guardians of the Church kiss a believer with the kiss of love, when he leaves on a journey. And the Father of Life and the Mother of Life kissed Archetypal Man again (the second Kiss), when Archetypal Man returned from battle to the land of Light, defeated, saved, but with the prospects of eventual victory. The Manichaean godhead is familial without being sexual, demonstrative without being effusive, and more forgiving of error than triumphalist.

And nowadays, so Mani the luminary instructed his followers in the assembly of the faithful, the kiss of love is a symbol of being a son of the Church. Believers kiss when they separate or when they meet one another, in memory of the mystery which Archetypal Man first experienced before the world was created. And at the end of time, Light-Form (a female redeemer figure in the complex Manichaean godhead) calms the believer's heart with a kiss, which protects him from demons, while an angel stretches out his right hand and pulls the dead Elect up from out of the abyss of his body and receives him into the realm of Light with the kiss of love.[65]

One great strength of Mani's teaching is that it does not blame humans for their own weakness. Evil has always existed, and is engaged in a perpetual struggle with good. Right from the beginning, when evil and good became mixed up with each other, evil imprinted itself on the divine elements within the human soul. Sin constructed the human body, and in the shape of lust entered the human heart; humans by their very nature are likely to be led astray to error, idolatry, and forgetfulness. But help is at hand, both macrocosmically and in our waking lives.

According to Mani, the redemptive teaching and love of Jesus and of Mani, his successor apostle, can help believers to help themselves, by giving them insight and freedom in their souls. His religion helps believers to construct a new human, the son of righteousness, out of the old, sin-bound human, by offering intelligence, love, faith, insight, wisdom, and patience. With help from fellow believers and from the teachers of the Church, there is hope that Manichaeans can achieve purity from sin—even if this purity is occasionally disturbed by doubt, folly, lust, error, and distress. Of course, if people remain blind or stubborn in their follies, clothed in lust and pride, in spite of priests' wise and patiently repeated counsel, then they sacrifice their hopes of salvation and become the enemy of virtue, "a worldly man, like a bird without feathers."[66]

THE GRAND INQUISITOR PREFIGURED: KARTIR AND AUGUSTINE

I anathematize Mani . . . the vessel of the devil, and the instrument of all atheism, the advocate of evil.[67]

Kartir

Creation stories were the stuff of religion and politics. In the ancient world, religion and politics were necessarily intertwined. Religions were symbols of political loyalty and instruments of social control. So competing myths became a battleground on which centralized regimes fought to constrain choice and force adherence.

On a high rock face, under the horse's tail of Shapur I, King of Kings, Kartir, the Persian high priest of Zoroaster, carved out the record of his life's achievements. Indeed, both king and priest had their life's work inscribed on the same rock face outside Persepolis, and on the walls of an impressive towerlike sanctuary nearby.[68] (plate 25)

Shapur I, king of Persia (242–73 CE), boasted of his conquests. Twice he had defeated huge invading armies of Romans; once he had himself ravaged the eastern Roman empire, had taken numerous prisoners, and captured many cities, including even Antioch (253 CE). He had killed one Roman emperor (Gordian III) in battle (244); a second (Philip the Arab) immediately sued for peace and retreated; and he had captured a third (Valerian) with his entire entourage (260). Valerian was the only Roman emperor ever to have been taken prisoner. Several Iranian rock carvings commemorate this magnificent Persian triumph. One depicts three Roman emperors, the first lying dead under Shapur's horse, the second running, while the third, Valerian, bows his head in a humiliated gesture of submission. The rock relief outside Persepolis on which Shapur and Kartir inscribed their lives depicts the Roman emperor Valerian with his ankles chained and kneeling.[69]

But a good half of Shapur's inscription is devoted to thanking the Gods for their help: "By the help of the Gods we have attacked and taken so many lands."[70] In reciprocity, Shapur had established many fire shrines to the great God Ahura Mazda and conferred many benefits on Zoroastrian priests (magi). And he established this sanctuary in particular to commemorate his soul and the souls of his relatives and courtiers, in whose honor one thousand sheep would be sacrificed yearly at the state's expense. The king's triumph was also the triumph of the state's religion.

The achievements of the high priest Kartir were triumphantly set out under those of his royal master, on the rock face, in the sanctuary, and on two other rock faces. "Whoever reads this shall know that I am that Kartir, who under . . . Ormizd, King of Kings, was entitled Kartir, Ahura Mazda's magus master. . . . And may he be himself as devout and sincere as I have been." The prominence of this self-advertisement, unparalleled for a Persian priest until modern times, reflected the revolutionary changes being attempted in third-century Iran. Under four successive kings (Shapur I, 242–73; Ormizd 273–74; Bahram I, 274–77; and Bahram II, 277–93 CE), Kartir was, at least by his own account, increasingly entrusted with the establishment of a single dominant state religion, and with crushing heresies and rival religions: "I have punished heretics and reprimanded them with an eye to their improvement."[71] Iranian kings pursued this objective thirty years or so before Constantine's conversion to Christianity and the development of an exclusive alliance between Christianity and the Roman state. Under Kartir's leadership, Iran became embroiled in religious persecution, as Rome did from 303 CE. Mani was merely one among many victims.

Constantine's religious policies were not simply imitative. But it seems more than mere coincidence that Rome and Iran, two competing world powers which had fought with each other repeatedly during the previous half century (244, 253, 260, 283, 298 CE), both embarked on similar policies of religious centralization and exclusivism at roughly the same period. Perhaps both states, threatened by each other and needing to draw upon more of their subjects' resources, decided to increase political authority at the center. And to do that, both Iran and Rome needed the help and legitimation of a single (but different), all-pervasive religion.

But back to the Kartir inscriptions. At the end of a long and successful career, Kartir boasted of his influence with kings, their trust in him, and his success in having established fire temples to Ahura Mazda and in defeating rival religions. Under Bahram II, he had been promoted to be "Savior of the King's Conscience," and few people were in a position to dispute his view of history. "I, Kartir, the magus, obedient and devoted toward the Gods and King Shapur, King of Kings . . . Shapur, King of Kings, made me independent and in charge of the service of the Gods." In all regions, fire temples and altars were established, and many priests, both of high and low rank, were installed and prospered. While Ahura Mazda and the Gods benefited greatly, Ahriman (the God of evil) suffered.[72]

Shapur ordered his heir to follow the same religious policy. To judge from Kartir's inscriptions, the next two kings obeyed. No sense here of the shift recorded in Manichaean sources, that Shapur and Ormizd looked on Mani with favor. According to the Manichees, it was Bahram I alone, under priestly influence, who moved from tolerance to persecution. According to Kartir, all four successive kings supported only Ahura Mazda. Under Bahram II, Kartir reached the pinnacle of his power. A grand rock carving at Sar Masad shows the king protecting his wife and child by killing two magnificent lions with his sword. Between king and queen, as a visible index of his influence and power, stands the high priest (plates 25–26).[73] According to Kartir, Bahram II was devout, sincere, beneficent, and kept his promises. By the grace of Ahura Mazda, he promoted Kartir to a higher rank, equal in dignity to secular grandees, and holding greater power and independence than ever before. Kartir became master of ceremonies, Bahram's keeper of conscience, and Ahura Mazda's high priest.

Throughout the Iranian empire, Kartir tells us, the Mazdaean religion became supreme, the priests achieved dignity, the Gods were satisfied, the God of evil and his demons suffered humiliation, and the teachings of the Devil were banished from the empire. Jews, Buddhists, Brahmins, Nasoreans (? = Mandaeans), Christians, and Manichees were smitten, their idols destroyed, their devilish haunts deserted. "I got good priests honored, but I brought punishment, reprimand, or reform to heretics and those priests who did not obey the rules of the Mazdaean religion." In their place, many fire temples and shrines were established, magi priests became prosperous, and "I was acknowledged as Kartir, Bahram's keeper of conscience."[74]

Heretics who did not observe rules of ritual were beaten or rebuked. Many of the faithful who had become unfaithful were recalled. Many of those who had followed the teachings of the Devil "through my efforts," reverted, and many endowments were made to the religion of Ahura Mazda. Kartir has all the calm of a dictator who after a mass protest simply states that the police restored order. Bruised protesters may have viewed matters differently.

Kartir was interested primarily in the foundation of temples, in the prosperity of priests, in proper respect for his supreme religious authority, and in the performance of rituals, celebrated "in their essential features" identically throughout the Iranian kingdom. His objective was uniformity of devotion to a single God, through performance rather than belief. In striking contrast to ancient Christian ideologues and to Mani himself, Kartir revealed very few traces of dogma or theology.[75] But what mattered for dissenters—Jews, Christians, Manichees, Buddhists, and heretical Zoroastrians—was that with the support of the state, the Mazdaean authorities in Iran, like the Christian authorities in the Roman empire, embarked on a cruel and persistent campaign of religious exclusivism and persecution. The inquisition had begun.

Augustine

For nine years, throughout his twenties, Augustine (born 354 CE) was a Manichee, not one of the elect but one of the ordinary hearers. After his conversion to Christianity (386) and appointment as bishop of Hippo in north Africa (395), he wrote several treatises, notable for their repetitious length, attacking Manichaean arguments and beliefs.[76] Augustine obviously took the threat of Manichaeism seriously. One index of its influence in north Africa among the intelligent and well educated is that at the end of the fourth century, five Christian bishops there were ex-Manichees. Another indication is that Augustine's own thought about good and evil, for all his Christian protestations, was indelibly marked by his Manichaean past.

The altercation which follows is a résumé of a dialogue written by Augustine in 398 CE. His opponent, Faust, then already dead, had been in his time a leading Manichaean bishop and preacher. Faust had come to

Carthage on a much-heralded preaching tour (382–83) when Augustine (then a young teacher of rhetoric) was on the verge of breaking with Manichaeism. Faust had been unable, Augustine thought, to answer his sharp questions satisfactorily. Faust had charmingly acknowledged his own incapacity, so he and Augustine had spent some time reading classical texts together. Subsequently Faust had been tried for his faith, exiled, and then pardoned in a general amnesty. In 397 CE or so, Augustine and some of his local Christians had received a copy of a short book by Faust in effect attacking Catholic Christian beliefs. Augustine felt himself compelled to answer.[77]

Augustine reported Faust's arguments and replied at several times Faust's length. In the interests of evenhandedness (and readability) I have reduced both their arguments to their substance. Public confrontations between religious leaders of different sects were quite commonly reported at this period, although it's difficult now to tell how much the report varied from the performance. Augustine himself wrote up other public altercations with Manichees; one with Felix at Hippo in 404 took two days and ended very satisfactorily for Augustine, with Felix cursing Mani and converting to Christianity—just as well, since Felix had volunteered, if Augustine showed evil in his sacred books, to be burned alive along with them, in accordance with the savagery of Roman law.[78]

Faust: I can put my case succinctly. You are only half Christians. We are the true heirs of Jesus. You count the Jewish Bible as sacred literature, but ignore most of the Law which it contains. You eat pork, reject sacrifice and circumcision, and break the rules of sabbath observance. You select which parts of the Hebrew Bible you want to believe and do not even reject the immoral tales of ancient Jewish heroes. Isaac, for example, fornicated with a concubine and sold his wife into adultery, Lot committed incest with his daughters, while Moses was a brigand and a murderer. And you falsely claim that this Old Testament contains many predictions of Jesus' coming. But it clearly doesn't. Why should it? Jesus came for the whole world, not just for the Jews. You might just as well look for predictions of Jesus' coming in pagan literature. But Christ doesn't need the Hebrew Bible or any other ancient writing to justify him or his message. He is divine.[79]

We too worship one God, who has three manifestations: almighty Father who is the Father of Light; his son Christ, who is immortal but appeared on earth as mortal; and the Holy Spirit. God is the principle of all good things, and evil is his opposite. We also believe in the teachings of Jesus, who offered life and salvation for us all. And I, for example, obey to the letter the commandments made by Christ in the Sermon on the Mount. I have left my parents, wife, and children. I have given up gold and silver. I live a life of poverty, gentleness, and peace, and in the service of our message I am quite prepared to face hatred and persecution. I have been tried and exiled, and my religion is unjustly persecuted by Roman governors, thanks to the repressive influence of Catholic priests.

The New Testament contains the salvific message of Jesus, so it supersedes the Old Testament. But even in the New Testament we have to be careful. For example, the story of his human birth from a virgin is not genuine. Mark did not know about it when his gospel was written. In fact, there are lots of discrepancies between the gospels. The gospels were obviously not written by the apostles themselves or by those close to them. So several sayings attributed to Jesus were not really said by him; they are later interpolations. We have to be skillful in knowing which sayings attributed to Jesus are genuine. Incidentally, that is why our Lord Mani took such care to write down his own teachings, so that the blessings of his revelation from the Father of Light could be handed down faithfully.

Finally, you claim to believe in only one God, but in fact you have preserved many pagan practices. Instead of sacrifice you have the eucharist, in which you eat flesh (which is disgusting) and drink wine (which is sinful). We neither eat flesh nor drink wine, ever. Instead of worshiping idols, you pray to martyrs and placate the ghosts of the dead with offerings of food and wine. You have betrayed Jesus. We are the true Christians.

Augustine: These profane absurdities must be answered one by one. You are pseudo Christians. You pervert Christianity by your false and blasphemous teachings. You don't know what righteousness or holiness means. You are deluded or rather self-deluding prostitutes to the Devil. How dare you slander Christians, especially when your own practices and fables are so loathsome?

You reject the Old Testament only because you do not appreciate how it is to be understood, in spite of my explaining it to you repeatedly. Basically, as the prophet said, "unless you believe, you shall not understand" (Isaiah 7.9). For example, you are ignorant of the distinction between moral and symbolic commandments. "Thou shalt not covet" is a moral commandment; "thou shalt circumcise every male on the eighth day" is a symbolic commandment. The moral commandments of the Old Testament are of everlasting validity; the symbolic commandments were prefigurements of Christ to come; when Christ came, they were fulfilled, and are no longer valid. The yoke of bondage represented in the sacraments of the old Jewish law was imposed on an obstinate and carnal people. But now the righteousness of the Christian faith has been revealed, the children of God are freed; we are set free by grace. The old commandments of this symbolic type are no longer valid, and other, more effective and beneficial sacraments are in place, fewer in number and easier to perform. So, for example, Christians are not now circumcised, precisely because what was prefigured by circumcision was fulfilled in Christ. Circumcision symbolically stood for the removal of our fleshly nature, fulfilled by Christ's resurrection, and is now replaced by the sacrament of baptism, which teaches us to hope for our own resurrection. But we should still revere and study the meaning of the Old Testament, because it was for us that it was written.[80]

Your treatment of our sacred texts is arbitrary and obstinate in its error. It might make sense for you to reject all our scriptures as pagans do, or just the New Testament as Jews do, or as we ourselves reject the books of your sect and of heretics. But it is quite different to select from holy scripture only those verses which you choose to accept. So when you are asked for proof, you don't search out the original text, or the best or oldest manuscript, or the majority of manuscripts; you simply decide to accept what you like, and reject anything which goes against you. But this makes *you*, not the text itself, into the standard of truth. And this procedure leaves you powerless against an opponent with an opposing view.

The Catholic Church behaves quite differently. We are governed by the exceptional sacredness of the holy scriptures, which come to us from the apostles in a continuous line secured by a succession of bishops. Their supremacy demands the submission of all pious and faithful minds. So we cannot say that the scriptures are mistaken; it must be instead that we have not understood. More recent writings do not have the same authority and we can properly dispute them unless there is a canonical ruling that a teaching must be true. But as regards the scriptures, because they are sacred we are obliged to accept as true whatever the canon shows has been said by even one prophet, apostle, or gospel writer. If contempt for the authority of canonical books were allowed, it would undermine hierarchy, remove guidance for human error, and create chaos.

Mani uses the name of Christ in order to persuade the ignorant, but really wants to be worshiped instead of Jesus. But the authority of the Catholic Church forbids me to believe you. Jesus Christ is the one and only Son of God. He took upon himself human form to liberate us from sin. My aim here is to restore you from thoughtless heresy to the true faith, rather than just to defeat you in argument, just as the aim of God's punishment is the healing of men, not their destruction. I too was once a Manichaean, but now, thanks to the tender persuasion of the merciful physician, I have found the simple truth—in the Catholic Church, inaugurated by miracles, nurtured by hope, multiplied by love, and strengthened by time, to such an extent that all heretics want to be called Catholics.

But beware. You claim to obey Christ's commandments because you obey the gospels. But superficial virtue profits you nothing without true faith. After all, robbers practice brotherly love out of shared complicity in crime and guilt. You cannot claim virtue when your beliefs are based on a pernicious fiction. And being persecuted for your beliefs is no proof of righteousness. Besides, you hold out for most of your believers only the promise of another life on earth, whereas we promise resurrection and immortality.

You do not understand the nature of God, or the origins of good and evil. God created everything from nothing. God created light. God dwells in light inaccessible. The brightness of this light is his coeternal wisdom. Because God is quietly benevolent, all that he created was good. Evil is nothing but good corrupted. So knowledge corrupted is ignorance, justice corrupted is injustice, beauty corrupted is ugliness; corruption is not the nature which God created, but antinature.

God did not make sin. God allowed men free will. But Adam sinned voluntarily, so that we who are his descendants are also subject, by heredity, to his carnal mind and its constraints and the pernicious sweetness of pleasure. The mind of fleshy pleasure in humans struggles against the pure law of God. But thanks to God's merciful love, the grace of God frees us from the law of sin and death.

It is simply impious and ignorant to ask why God did not make us as perfect as himself. Only God is perfect. But if we say that God's creation is not good, then we do an injustice to God's goodness. We should submit to God, lest he punish us with worse. We should be thankful that God is a just judge who rewards and punishes justly. So, although corruption is an evil, it does not come from God, but it is so "ordered that it hurts only the lowest natures, for the punishment of the condemned and for the trial and instruction of the returning, that they may keep near to the incorruptible God, and remain incorrupt, which is our only good. . . . And you must not say, God did not make corruptible natures; for as far as they are natures, God made them; but as far as they are corruptible, God did not make them, for corruption cannot come from Him who is incorruptible." If you can accept this, give thanks to God; if you cannot, be quiet and do not condemn what you do not understand, but humbly wait on Him who is the light of the mind.[81]

AUGUSTINE'S NIGHTMARE

In 430 CE, when Hippo was besieged by Vandals, Augustine, aged seventy-six, lay dying, surrounded at his own request by copies of the penitential psalms attached to the walls of his cell. Augustine wrote the following confession on his deathbed, in secret, so as not to distress his closest admirers. He buried it beneath the floor of his library, which miraculously escaped being burned when the Vandals captured Hippo a few months later.[82]

Was I right, O God, to leave Floria, after twelve years of passionate love together? Or was I simply cruel, as my father so often was to me in my childhood, to desert her and keep our son? And we could have married, even as the apostle allows (Ephesians 5.25), though of course, the good in marriage lies not in the passion of desire or its gratification, but only in the propagation of children.

Now that I'm dying, in the loneliness of my monkish bed, I can't help but remember the warmth and beauty of her body, and regret my wasted years. How could I forget those sweet pleasures of the flesh? But after so many years of solitude, now I want to be alone, if only so that those who serve me so faithfully will not hear, they would not want to hear, the weakness of my faith.

But why, O my God, why did I waste my life in the desert of continence? Wouldn't it have been better to continue yielding to human love, rather than surrender to ostentatious piety? Did the rod of Christ really demand fear of sin instead of the fulfillment of love?[83]

And was I right, my Love, to insist that there is only one path to God? Petilian [a schismatic bishop of the Donatists] once asked me why I did not allow each person to follow his own free will, and choose his own way to worship you, almighty God. And I replied, in the madness of my pride, that few people have the intellect to understand my reasoning. No one had robbed them of their free will. If they were truly righteous, then their suffering would reap its due reward in heaven. But if they were being justly punished under civil law, then that was a timely warning for them to reconsider, time for them to use their free will to turn away from schism and return to the Catholic Church, and so avoid further pain in this world and the next. Indeed, in my view their present suffering was as but nothing, compared with the enormity of their crimes in disobeying God. I allowed pride in my argument to cloud my judgment. Vainly I imagined, O my God, that your infinite unknowability could be captured by a chain of clever syllogisms, and that I alone knew the right path to your salvation.

And was it right, O merciful God, for some Catholic bishops to stone Donatists, just because they belonged to another church—"the church of truth," as they deceitfully called it? Did your victory require such cruelty? Can I have been right to advise an official, when he consulted me, to burn a Donatist bishop with all his followers in his church at Timgad, since they were already condemned by you, O God, to burn in hell forever? Or had some hardening of my heart made me immune to human suffering, even though I know so well your sacred commandments that I should repay evil with good? Was it high office which made me forget mercy?[84]

I know, O God, that all that you created was good. In your infinite goodness you could not have created evil. But you gave Adam free will. Voluntarily, he committed sin. We are his heirs. By the carnal concupiscence of sexuality, we inherit his tarnished and corrupted self. That is why even infants have to be baptized, so that their sinfulness may from the beginning be forgiven. It follows with relentless logic that infants who die unbaptized will be punished in eternal fire. That is the consequence of Adam's sin, by which we are all bound. But you in your bountiful mercy, by your gift of free will, and through the perpetual infusion of your grace, encourage us to do good, but leave us free to do evil. But if it is good that we do, that is only through your grace, not through our own virtues. Our works do not bind your salvation. The few predestined by your grace will be saved; the mass will be justly punished in everlasting fire.

Lord, have pity on me. You are merciful. I need your mercy. But how, O Lord, shall I be judged before the heavenly tribunal at the end of days? Shall I too by your mercy be saved? For years I was tormented by anxious doubts and searching, until in the end I found your truth. In the courts of this world I hammered the poisonous perversions of the heretic Pelagius, so that he was justly excommunicated by councils of bishops in east and west and exiled by the sacred emperor's commands. How could he argue that humans are born without the contamination of inherited sin? Or that Adam would have died even if he had not sinned, and that Adam's single sin of disobedience was too small to merit the punishment of the whole of humanity? Or that it was far too unjust to punish unbaptized infants until eternity? Or that after you beneficently gave us the capacity to do good or evil, and once you had through Jesus Christ revealed your teachings and the hope of forgiveness of sins, then the merits of virtue or the penalties of sin were the products of individual will? How dare he denigrate your universal grace, effective in every act we do? How dare he claim the independence of humans from your pervasive power, O God, who have the wills of men more in your control than they do themselves?[85] Was I not right, O Lord?

It seems likely, of course, that in other circumstances Augustine would have written at greater length. And ideally, I imagine, he would have liked a heavenly sign of reassurance that he was one of the predestined elect. But history records only his death—and beatification.

EIGHT

Jesus and the New Testament, or, *The Construction of a Sacred Hero*

CONTEXT

Jesus was the Son of God, human and divine. We know very little about his life. Nor did the writers of the gospels, though at least two of them were alleged to have been his disciples and so, close acquaintances. But the disciples were reportedly illiterate, so they could not have been the authors of the gospels, as critics both pagan and Christian saw in antiquity. So in a narrow sense, the gospels of Matthew, John, Thomas, and Philip are religious fakes.[1] That lessens their factual but not their historical value, or their religious truth. Belief validity is quite separate from fact correctness, and religious history is more concerned with representations than with facts. The gospels tell us what some ancient Christians thought and believed about Jesus.

Jesus was a retroconstructed sacred hero. Most of the important Christian claims about him—his preexistence before his earthly life, his cocreation of the universe with God, his miraculous birth, life, teachings, miracles, arrest, trial, crucifixion, resurrection, postresurrection appearances, and reunion with God, his Father—were invented after his death. I do not mean that none of these events occurred. What I mean is that the significance of all these events was imagined, discovered, contemplated, and magnified only once Christians had come to believe that Jesus was the Messiah, the Christ, and son of God. They then set about creating Jesus' divinity, just as contemporary pagans deified their dead emperors and called the living emperor "son of God." "Son of God" was a pagan title. Exceptional pagan holy men were even called God out of respect during their lifetimes.[2]

But ancient Christians believed that Jesus Christ was truly divine, the son of the one true God. They would have forcefully resented any comparison with human emperors or holy men. Admittedly, some Christians prayed for the preservation of the Roman empire and believed it was God who had appointed the Roman emperor. Still others, in spite of Jesus' measured saying "Render unto Caesar what belongs to Caesar, and unto God what belongs to God" (Mark 12.17), saw themselves as inevitably opposed to secular powers. Christians regularly used the term "rulers" (archontes) to describe the demonic powers of darkness. But early Christians also fiercely disagreed among themselves for several centuries about the degree and nature of Jesus' divinity: Was he divine from birth, or from baptism, or only after his resurrection?[3] Was he wholly divine, or a mixture of humanity and divinity, or as pagans and Jews thought, wholly human?

In this chapter I shall explore the principles and practices by which the divine Jesus was constructed. This will involve tracking and analyzing changes in the perception of Jesus made in successive gospels and in early Christian tracts. But first a few basic facts, all of them disputed. Jesus was born, perhaps in the period loosely bounded by the death of Herod the Great, in 4 BCE, and the Roman census in Syria (but not in Galilee) held in 6 CE.[4] Jesus died apparently when Pontius Pilate was subgovernor of Judaea, between 26 and 36; persuasive precision within that period is impossible, but many guesses (some argued with acumen) center around 30 or 33. Not a great deal hangs on either date.[5]

Our earliest source for Jesus and early members of the Jesus movement is the Pharisee Paul (he is incidentally the only Pharisee whose writings survive). Paul himself wrote seven surviving letters between 50 and the early sixties (seven other letters are reckoned by many scholars to be spurious but were accredited to him within a century of his death).[6] Remarkably, Paul rarely mentions Jesus' life or sayings; he is interested, passionately interested, not in the living Jesus but in the risen Christ, in the connection between the dead Jesus and God. Outside the gospels, the earliest surviving Christian writers rarely mention details of Jesus' life, though there are some quotations and echoes of Jesus' sayings.

The New Testament gospels—the so-called synoptic gospels (Mark, Matthew, and Luke) and in a different tradition, John—were written probably between 70 and 90 CE, thirty-five to sixty years after Jesus' death. By that time, given low life expectancy in the Roman world, very few eyewitnesses of Jesus' teachings would have survived. No one knows the dates of the gospels' composition for sure, but proponents of both earlier and later dating abound; and some cling to earliest dating, as though that guaranteed a higher truth content. The Gospel of Thomas, rediscovered in its entirety only in 1946 (but first published only in 1959), contains over a hundred sayings of Jesus, many not preserved in the canonical gospels. Scholars are divided over whether it belongs to the first pregospel wave of writing about Jesus or was written much later.[7] Either way, the Gospel of Thomas only adds to our understanding about how the Jesus story was created, without fundamentally changing its character. The other writings eventually included in the canonical New Testament date probably from the late first century and the first half of the second century.

The canon of the New Testament, considered as a collective entity, was established only in the second half of the second century.[8] By canon I mean that limited set of books (gospels about Jesus' sayings and deeds, Acts of and letters by apostles, plus Revelation) which were recognized by Christians as sacred literature. As such, canonical writings were to be read aloud in church and were cited as proof texts in order to legitimate particular interpretations of correct belief. There were minor disputes about books peripheral to the canon, both inside and outside it, until much later.

Since the writings which now constitute the New Testament were for long not agreed to be sacred, they were repeatedly edited, revised, and elaborated.[9] The story of Jesus and his sayings was changed according to the context and interests of successive believers. So, different sets of believers read and transmitted variant texts. For example, when Jesus was baptized (Luke 3.22), a voice from heaven said: "You are my son, whom I have today begotten." This quotation, from Psalm 2.7, was used by some Christians to prove that Jesus' divinity began not with his birth, but with his baptism. And vegetarian Christians, by altering a couple of Greek letters, changed John the Baptist's diet from "locusts and honey" to "cakes and honey."[10]

Or again, in Mark 2.27, Jesus' famous saying "The sabbath was made for humans, not humans for the sabbath" was omitted from some later manuscripts, just as Matthew and Luke themselves omitted it from their own versions of Mark.[11] Jesus' teaching on sabbath observance was clearly a matter of dispute between some early Jewish Christians and gentile Christians, so some of them simply altered the record. For example, the following story about Jesus—"That same day, on seeing a man working on the sabbath, [Jesus] said, 'If you know what you are doing, you are blessed; but if you do not know, you are cursed and transgress the Law'"—is found in one of the earliest surviving biblical manuscripts. But it is omitted from the standard text of Luke 6.5, while a similar Jesus saying is found in a second-century papyrus but not included in the canonical gospels: "Jesus said: 'If you do not fast, you will not find the kingdom of God, and if you do not keep the sabbath, you will not see the Father.'" In its early stages, the Jesus story was changed by alteration, additions, and omissions.[12]

Some additions, revisions, and deletions to early Christian writings were on a much grander scale. The intrusion of seven spurious letters into the Pauline corpus, the helpful compression of two of Paul's letters to make 2 Corinthians, and the clumsy addition of revised endings to the gospels of Mark (16.9–20) and John (21)—both designed to include extra postresurrectional appearances of Jesus to the disciples—all illustrate the fluidity and porosity of these texts before they became canonical.

Three instances from the mid–second century drive this point home. Marcion, a dedicated and ascetic Christian, revised Luke's gospel and Paul's letters to cut out any mention of the Jewish God and the completely unacceptable (to Marcion) notion of his fatherhood of Jesus. Marcion then offered the revised and simplified texts (the first known collection of Christian gospel and letters) to the Christian priests at Rome. Unsurprisingly (as we now see it), his offer was rejected, and so Marcion founded his own, "heretical" Christian sect, which persisted for centuries. The "orthodox" Justin emended gospel texts to make them fit his arguments better and, perhaps in reaction against Marcion, neither mentioned Paul nor quoted from his letters. Justin's Christianity was Paul-free. Nor apparently did he know John. Finally, Tatian, also in the mid–second century, produced a simplified, single-gospel version of Jesus' life and sayings. He tried to combine four gospels, including John, and some noncanonical writings into a single consistent account. His version proved popular for centuries among Christians in Syria.[13]

Still other Christians, out of piety, or diversity of belief, or both, continued to write supplementary stories about Jesus and his apostles, as well as exhortatory tracts designed to supplement previous advice. Early Christians argued vigorously with one another. "Peter" (as in the New Testament letters conventionally called 1 Peter and 2 Peter) wrote to correct Paul and complained about the difficulty of understanding him. The pastoral letters attributed to Paul (1 Timothy, 2 Timothy, and Titus) were written partly to domesticate Paul's views. The later books of the New Testament repeatedly denounce false teachers. The false teachings which survive are only a fraction of what once circulated. There was no effective mechanism for ensuring conformity. Only a few of these writings became part of the canon; others survived, but most—the great mass of early Christian writings—have disappeared.[14]

The fluidity and porosity of early Christian writings about Jesus highlight two important and complementary points. First, early Christians, still without an accepted sacred literature of their own, long continued to regard the Jewish scriptures as the prime sacred legitimators of their own beliefs. The frequent direct quotations and the even more numerous echoes of and allusions to the Jewish scriptures in the New Testament illustrate the Jewish scriptures' continued significance for Christians.[15] The Jewish scriptures provide the scaffolding within which the life, sayings, and achievements of Jesus were constructed. Early Christian leaders seemed to think that they could make a stronger and more convincing appeal to their at first predominantly Jewish Christian readers/hearers if they could show that Jewish prophets of old had predicted all that came to pass in Jesus' life, and that incidents in his life repeated or echoed incidents in Israel's history. It had been predicted, it has come to pass—so they seemed to argue—therefore both the predictions and their interpretations are true.[16]

A single and trivial example illustrates the transposition from Jewish scripture to Christian story. Shortly before his death, Jesus rides, or more properly, is represented as riding into Jerusalem on an ass (Matthew 21.5; cf. John 12.15), and so fulfills a prophecy in Zechariah 9.9: "Your king is coming . . . his victory gained, humble, and mounted on an ass." It is, of course, completely possible that Jesus rode into Jerusalem on an ass. And those who think he was conscious of his destiny may think he did it on purpose in order to fulfill the prophecy.[17] But it is not the act in itself which matters most. The significance of the simple act is transformed in the story by its echo of the prophecy; Jesus is the long-predicted, and now arrived, victorious but humble king. Both the act and the prophecy are made to work together (plates 27–28).

Second, the easy alterability of the earliest writings about Jesus, by addition, omission, or redaction, indicate that for all the sacredness of their subject, the gospels themselves were not regarded as sacrosanct. Or put another way, for a century or more after Jesus' death, Christian groups existed and flourished without the New Testament. The existence of the Gospel of Mark, probably the earliest of the canonical gospels, did not prevent Matthew and Luke from changing what Mark had written, or from writing their own gospels, apparently in ignorance of each other's efforts. John probably knew Mark's miracle source, but not Mark's gospel itself or Matthew and Luke; and his knowledge did not prevent him from writing in a completely different style.[18] These written gospels circulated separately. Many Christian house cult groups probably had at best only one gospel, and throughout most of the second century, the gospels were cited in no set order. The gospels had to compete with oral traditions, with the fluid traditions of apostolic teaching, with collective unwritten memories of what Jesus had said and done, and with contemporary church concerns and evolving customs. Above all they had to compete with belief in Christ as the savior God, rather than in Jesus as the human/divine Messiah.

Only from the mid–second century do we find arguments in surviving Christian writers which are legitimated by citing the gospels. But even at this late date, there seems to have been no standard way of describing the writings about Jesus (they are called memoirs, memories, rarely gospels). Indeed, what is surprising in the small corpus of very early Christian literature which survives outside the New Testament (such as the Teaching of the Apostles, the Letter of Barnabas, the two Letters of Clement, the Shepherd of Hermas) is the infrequency with which Jesus' canonical sayings and deeds are mentioned. The closing of the canon in the second half of the second century was itself a decisive ingredient in creating for the first time a gradually standardized Christianity, in which the life and sayings of Jesus became a central pivot.

JESUS, HUMAN, DIVINE, HISTORICAL, TIMELESS

The canonical gospels, each in its own way, tell the same magnificent story of tragic triumph. God sent his Son, Jesus, down to earth in human form to offer humans who believe in him the prospect of salvation. Jesus himself, because of his combination of divinity and humanity, through the force of his moral teachings, by his miraculous deeds, and by the example of his self-sacrificing death, showed God's benevolent care for humans. And at the same time, because of his humanity, Jesus indicated that even humans, through their own virtues, or through repentance if they sin, and by their belief in Jesus as savior, could hope to overcome both sin and death.

The gospels tell a story which is based in history. Its apparently simple facticity, its location in real place and time, are important ingredients in its persuasive power: this is how it all happened, eyewitnesses saw it, it is true. But the historicity of Jesus is also a theological illusion. The bare historical facts (for example, Jesus died when Pontius Pilate governed Judaea) are interwoven with theological metaphors and beliefs, so that they mix inextricably with one another. For example, Jesus spoke in parables, he cured the sick, he said to a rich man, "You lack one thing; go, sell what you have and give to the poor, and you will have treasure in heaven" (Mark. 10.17ff). And he was a great moral teacher, he was the Son of God, he performed miracles, and he reappeared on earth after death.

The gospel writers are not simply telling a story, they are also constructing a belief system; they are seeking to reaffirm believers' faith and to persuade us that Jesus was/is the long-awaited Messiah. He has already come, he has defeated death and the Devil. Christian historicity has trumped vague Jewish millenarianism. Christians (ideally) believe their foundation story to be sacred and true and believe it to be true partly because it is grounded in history.

The gospels also tell a story which goes beyond history. Jesus is a sacred hero. He teaches with complete authority and assurance. He summons uneducated men to follow him, and they obey. He is sometimes called Rabbi, but he does not act like a stereotypical rabbi, he does not dispute like a formalist. Indeed, he repeatedly challenges the tired power of legalistic scribes. He acts with the charismatic power of a king. But at the same time he is unaffectedly simple, an ideal human who yet, like us, is baptized, eats, sleeps, and dies. He is also (as some see him) a radical reformer who inverts and subverts social conventions by his teaching and by his actions; for example, he mixes with outcast prostitutes and tax collectors (Mark 2.16). He outwits and undermines his opponents with pithy repartee, patient determination, and inner certainty, until they are forced to take refuge in the institutional violence of Rome, the alien and oppressive state. Jesus' enemies win, but we know their victory is only apparent.[19]

Christ is human, and yet more than human. He can conquer, even has conquered, death itself. He is a miracle worker who heals, raises from the dead, triumphs over the Devil, is comforted by angels, and fulfills ancient prophecies. Jesus has the awesome aura of the divine—even the demons recognize his power, though his family think him mad (Mark 3.11, 21). Faithful readers and, more important, rereaders of the gospels acknowledge his divinity more easily even than the disciples. They know already how the story ends, and its new beginning. Jesus is the Son of God.

The story of Jesus is both uniquely idiosyncratic and prestructured. Like any divine emissary sent by the supreme deity to spend time among humans (*cf.* Mani, Buddha, Zarathustra), Jesus' life curve is necessarily *U*-shaped. His divinity is secure only if he begins and ends in heaven. His entry onto and departure from earth should be miraculous and impressive, rather than quietly unnoticed. Since the divine, but now appearing to be human, emissary has a salvific and reformative purpose, he must teach or reveal ways in which the faithful can gain salvation. Complementarily, he must threaten sinners or nonbelievers with condign punishment. Both his message and divine status are clearly enhanced if he does things which normal mortals cannot do (walk on water, feed thousands, cure the incurable). His proposals for ethical reform must upset conservative authorities, both secular and religious. And his death is more likely to be memorably dramatic if it follows confrontation and unjust oppression. The only way humans can be convinced of his reunion with the divine after death is by supernatural signs. This divine aura is not just an optional extra; it infuses the whole of his ethical teaching with its powerful electric charge.

Miracles are the critical symptom of the gospels' extrahistorical character. For ancients, miracles were an intrinsic part of Jesus' message, and a powerful symbol of his divinity. I define miracles as reported and wondrous events whose explanation involves supernatural intervention. The skeptic might initially think that miracles don't happen. But he/she is wrong. Of course, they happen—but only in a special sense. Miracles occur not when someone reportedly sees them but only when we hear or read about them—and believe the story. The miracle takes place in the believer's mind. That is the miracle. And the mind, heart, imagination are, I think, the only places in which a miracle can happen. But more important, each reading or hearing by believers repeats the miracle.

How important are miracles in the Jesus story? They are fundamental. I'm not thinking here of Jesus walking on water, or feeding five thousand people with five loaves, or being taken up to the top of a mountain by the Devil and resisting temptation, or even the virgin conception and virgin birth. However impressive and significant these reports were for early or subsequent Christians, they are merely side decorations, like entry music in a royal cavalcade. They warn us and prepare us to accept that something very special (and supernatural) is happening. They are important incidentals, but not the main show.

The fundamental miracles in the Jesus story are its basic frame. The omnipotent creator God is interested in the welfare of individuals. This God sent his son, Jesus, as a pledge, or perhaps even as a metaphor, for his own and Jesus' continuing benevolent concern with individual humans' welfare. Jesus is the Son of God who came voluntarily to earth to sacrifice his life in order to save humans from sin and provide them with the chance of gaining immortality. Now all these (God's creation of the world, God's benevolent interest in individuals, his having a son in human form, and the son's voluntary self-sacrifice and resurrection with its salvific implications), all these are huge miracles. Admittedly, all of them are so deeply entrenched in western religious and cultural thought that they are not usually considered as miracles. But within the terms of my definition (reported happenings whose explanation involves the supernatural), all of them clearly are miracles. And every time believers believe any of them, the miracles are (re)performed. The story is a fundamental part of the belief, and the story performs the miracle. The story is itself performative.

Did ancient Christians (and pagans) really believe in miracles? It is tempting to say, "Yes, of course." Miracles (as I have defined them) were part and parcel of ancient religions, whether Jewish, pagan, or Christian. How else, after all, can God be shown to have interacted with humans? But perhaps we should be cautious about claiming, for ourselves by implication, a monopoly of sophisticated skepticism. Certainly some pagan intellectuals in antiquity ridiculed claims, made by both pagans and Christians, that miracles had occurred. They simply laughed at believers' credulity, and revealed the tricks by which pagan temple priests deceived (some of) their clients. It also seems reasonable to doubt that intellectuals in antiquity had a monopoly on skepticism. Christians themselves repeatedly called attention to the wisdom of the ignorant, and contrasted it with the foolishness of the wise. Or put another way, the presence of the unbeliever, or even of doubt in the believer's own mind, is fundamental to the miracle's success. The miracle must always be in some tension with the believer's own reality; it can never be taken for granted. The miracle has to be wonder-ful.[20]

Perhaps we should rephrase the initial question. Did believers believe the miracles which were celebrated in their own religion? After all, it seems probable that in a polytheistic society like the Roman empire, believers in one cult were skeptical about miracles proclaimed by another cult. But miracles in one's own religion? If frequency of mention is an index of widespread acceptance, there can be little doubt. Christian writers repeatedly describe miracles. Miracles occur in stories about Jesus, in the canonical and apocryphal Acts of the Apostles, in the Martyr Acts, and in the pious lives of saintly ascetics. Christian writers for centuries kept on finding and reporting new miracles. Miracles celebrate the terrible power of God, the awesome gap between the human and the divine, and the merciful concern which God repeatedly shows for human sinners.

These miracle stories work, I think, largely because religious discourse itself is bracketed off from the mundane world. Miracles are believed in, and happen, in sacred space and time, where everyday prosaic incredulity is suspended. They are reported in holy books and retold in the sacred space of church liturgy. They thrive on the expectant hush of religious meetings, with flickering light and special music; miracle stories are told in special language and with a special voice. In the modern world, the closest analogy (for unbelievers) is cinemas and films, where watchers accept that the unreal—for example, beautiful people, perfect love, perfect happiness—can and does repeatedly happen. We all *want* to believe, and for an illusory moment, we do actually imagine that what is happening in the film is (well, almost) happening to us. Miracles in antiquity, like films nowadays, belong to that other, imagined, desired, and almost real world of suspended disbelief.

So Jesus Christ, the Son of God, is made to be both historically human and divinely timeless. "Jesus Christ is the same yesterday, today, and forever" (Hebrews 13.8). According to John, Jesus preexisted with the Father, and was there with him at the creation of the universe. "In the beginning was the Word, the Word was with God, and the Word was God. He was with God in the beginning. . . . The Word was made flesh, he lived among us" (John 1.1–2, 14). After that, according to some Christian thinkers, Jesus had been the spirit who inspired successive Jewish prophets into predicting his life and death on earth. Jesus will also be there at the end of time, when the faithful will inherit the immortality they deserve, and all sinners, unbelievers, and the material world will be destroyed. This preexistent and ever-existing Jesus complemented the historical Jesus and bound him back into coequivalence with God the Father. The coalescence of divine God with the human/God helped protect Christian insistence that Christians believed in only one God, not in two or three.

But for all Jesus' historicity and timelessness, Christians over time *necessarily* evolved an ever-changing consciousness of the diverse meanings of Jesus and his message, and developed fresh understandings of their own religious past and its meanings. After all, the Jesus story is not only a story about Jesus, it is also a charter myth—in the special sense that believers both believe it to be true and want to use it as a privileged store of wisdom and prescription, which should be used as a guide for the conduct of their thoughts, feelings, and actions. But contexts, and with them interpretations, change. The process of evolving interpretations is already visible in the successive gospels, as we shall see in the next section. The successive gospels manufacture and incorporate their own meanings of the past in the sacred message. Jesus was, and is still, continually changing.

So there is, and always has been, a tension between the one-time-only historical Jesus and the evolving interpretation of his significance. Christians set special store by the brief period in which Jesus lived, suffered, died, and was resurrected. It was a supersacred time in human history. And to match this single, special time, Christians eventually (by the end of the second century) came to believe that there could be only one privileged set of sacred books which described and interpreted Jesus' life and revelation. But there is a tension between this reliance on a single set of sacred texts and the necessary evolution of interpretations which match changing conditions and desires.

The resolution of the problem is well known. The canonical texts came to be treated as a composite block of writings, inspired by the Holy Spirit, from which it is unproblematic to snippet sacred quotations in order to legitimate current ethical attitudes and political needs. The life of the human Jesus is transformed into a series of symbolic moments which are stitched onto one another to form an unproblematic whole. The complex and brilliantly awkward thoughts of Paul are reduced to series of memorable aphorisms. The texts are ransacked for quotations, which are then reinterpreted and allegorized: they do not necessarily mean what they overtly say; their true meaning has to be discovered by a faithful and spiritual understanding. Time is upstaged by making the sacred texts timeless.

The sacred texts may belong to the past, but they are also ours. Successive changes in interpretation are disguised by the illusion that all the interpreter is doing is getting back to the text's and Jesus' original and unique meaning. Fixation on the single special period in Christian history and on the canonical texts veils the variety of sequential meanings which different Christians in different centuries have always constructed. Concentration on credal truths (such as "I believe in the resurrection of the body") as a defining characteristic of the committed Christian militates against the simultaneous understanding of the relativity of each Christian's interpretation. But Christianity is and always has been diverse and continually changing. Right from the beginning of Christianity, the meaning of Jesus was both disputed and successfully recreated by, and within, each generation of believers.

CONSTRUCTING THE GOSPELS: BORROWED CLOTHES

The Jesus movement began as a radical revisionist sect within Judaism. Jesus himself lived and died as a Jew. Jesus, the historical man, can have had no inkling that he would become the cornerstone of a new religion.[21] It is arguable also that Paul long remained a Jew, albeit a deviant Jew, and in conflict with Jewish religious leaders. Christianity's break from Judaism was jagged and protracted; some Christians and some Christian house cult groups separated from Judaism sooner than others. But for a longish period, Jews were Christianity's primary audience, and Jews were for a long time the chief source of Christian converts.

The construction of Jesus as sacred hero therefore had to be achieved initially by fitting him into a matrix which had already been formed in the Jewish scriptures. The gospel writers, and before them the early members of the Jesus movement, tried to understand the significance of Jesus by latching on to the language, stories, and prophecies known from (what was to become) the Old Testament. So the New Testament contains over four hundred direct quotations from the Old Testament (often via its slightly divergent Greek translation the Septuagint, or LXX), and many more echoes and allusions.[22] Some of these Old Testament quotations have come to be seen as central or dramatic moments in the quintessentially Christian message (see proof texts on p. 300). The familiarity or half remembrance of stories often told made the radically different teachings of the New Testament more acceptable to the original Jewish Christians. The appeal of the new message was enhanced by its innovative use of established religious tradition. Besides, this traditional religious language was the only religious language by which the gospel writers could express the divinity and passion of Jesus.

The interplay between dependency and innovation in the gospel stories can be illustrated by taking a close look at the birth narrative of Jesus in the first two chapters of Matthew's gospel, and then very briefly at the death narratives. Matthew begins with the startling words usually translated "Book of the birth of Jesus the Messiah, son of David, son of Abraham." But the two opening words in Greek, "Book of Genesis" *(biblos geneseos)*, also powerfully echo Genesis, the first book of the Jewish scriptures. By these opening words Matthew overtly presents his gospel as a continuation of, and as a rival to, the canonical Jewish scriptures. The opening of the Old Testament prefigures the New Testament.

Matthew then presents Jesus as the descendant of both David and Abraham. To prove it, he lists a very long, forty-two-generation genealogy, presumably designed to show that Jesus both fits in with and is a fulfillment of Jewish national history. David is there because in Jewish lore, the Messiah must be of Davidic (that is, kingly) descent. And Abraham is there perhaps because God through his angel said to Abraham, "Through your seed shall all nations be blessed" (Genesis 22.18 LXX). So, allusively, Abraham is a link between Jesus and all gentiles—though to understand that we need a knowledgeable, and preferably a priestly, interpreter. The inclusion of Abraham is not the only sophisticated wrinkle; the long genealogy is mostly male, but curiously contains in addition

PROOF TEXTS: OLD TESTAMENT AND NEW TESTAMENT

Virgin conception

Mt. 1.23. "Behold a virgin shall conceive and bear a son and his name shall be Emmanuel" is a quotation from the Greek version of Isaiah 7.14, though famously, as was recognized in antiquity, the Greek version has the word for "virgin," while the Hebrew means "a young woman."

Jesus' place of birth was/had to be Bethlehem

Mt. 2.6. "For so it has been written by the prophets: And you, O Bethlehem in the land of Judah . . . for from you shall come a ruler who is to shepherd my people Israel" is a loose version of Micah 5.2.

Jesus' boyhood journey to Egypt and his sonship of God

Mt. 2.15. "This was to fulfill what the Lord had spoken by the prophet, Out of Egypt have I called my son," is from Hosea 11.1: "When Israel was a boy, I loved him. I called my son [Israel] out of Egypt."

Critical moments

a. The soldiers after the crucifixion cast lots

Mt. 27.35. "And when they had crucified him, *they divided his garments among them, by casting lots*" is mostly a quote from Psalm 22.18.

b. Jesus' final cry from the cross

Mt. 27.46. "My God, my God, why hast thou forsaken me?" is the first line of Psalm 22.

Jesus' teaching

a. Mt. 12.7. "I desire mercy not sacrifice" is from Hosea 6.6.

b. Mt. 13.13ff. "Hearing they do not hear, nor do they understand" is from Isaiah 6.9 (LXX).

c. Jesus on John the Baptist, Mt. 11.10. "Behold I send a messenger who will clear a path before me" is from Malachi 3.1.

d. Mt. 21.16. "Out of the mouths of babes and sucklings" is from Psalm 8.2.

e. Mt. 22.37. "You shall love the Lord your God with all your heart, and with all your soul, and with all your mind" is from Deuteronomy 6.5.

f. Mt. 22.39. "Love your neighbor as yourself" is selected from a short list of commandments in Leviticus 19.18.

Who is Jesus?

Mt. 24.30. "Then will appear the sign of the Son of Man in heaven" is an adaptation of Daniel 7.13: "I saw one like a Son of Man coming with the clouds of heaven."

Mt. 22.44. "The Lord said to my Lord, Sit at my right hand," is from Psalm 110.1.

Mt. 8.17. "He took our infirmities and bore our diseases" is from Isaiah 53.4.

to Mary, four women—Tamar, Rahab, Ruth, and (Bathsheba), the wife of Uriah—all of them in some sense either anomalous and/or sinners.[23] The sacred text tempts its attentive reader to delve below the surface and so to discover its half-hidden secrets. The text describes the Jewish origins of Jesus and also empowers its skilled interpreters.

The second half of Matthew's first chapter contains an amazing story. Mary has conceived, not by her human husband/fiancé but by the Holy Spirit, in fulfillment of the prophecy in Isaiah 7.14: "Behold a virgin shall conceive and bear a son and his name shall be Emmanuel (which means God with us)" (Matthew 1.23).[24] Joseph is understandably perturbed because he has not yet had sex with Mary. But a messenger from God, an angel, comes to him and persuades him not to divorce Mary, because her pregnancy and the impending birth are all part of God's plan. And the child's name will be Jesus. Already in the second century, if not before, Jews pointed out that the Hebrew text of Isaiah reads not "virgin" but "young woman"; only the standard Greek translation reads *parthenos,* "virgin."[25] So perhaps the story of the virgin birth originated among Greek-speaking Jews. But whatever the legitimating text, this claim for Jesus' divine origins, miraculous conception, and birth was a masterstroke. The birth narrative opened the way for reintroducing the feminine into the Christian Godhead.[26] The Virgin Mary became for generations of Christians a feminine intermediary between humans and God. The whole idea of human mother and divinely conceived and divinely born child, by its originality, complemented and reinforced Jesus' later miraculous resurrection. Jesus originated from and returned to God.

The brilliant inventiveness of Matthew (or his sources) was echoed in the similar but slightly different birth narrative of Luke. For Luke, Mary herself was the main recipient of God's message instead of Matthew's Joseph, and there were shepherds instead of magi; and Luke's Joseph came from Nazareth (instead of Bethlehem), and traveled to Bethlehem for a census. But for Luke there was no guiding star, no journey to Egypt, no massacre of the infants. The disagreements between Matthew and Luke are substantial, and illustrate the fluidity of the Jesus' birth stories during the first century (but then, as far as we know, Christians did not celebrate Jesus' birthday at Christmas until well into the fourth century).[27]

The differences between Matthew and Luke are minuscule when compared with Mark and John. Neither Mark nor John mentions Jesus' miraculous birth; nor does Paul; they either did not know the story of his virginal conception or did not want to include it.[28] Both Mark and John start Jesus' divine mission on earth with his baptism as an adult. Mark mentions Jesus' brothers by name and his sisters (6.3). For Mark, Jesus was the natural child of human parents. John makes Jesus unequivocally the son of Joseph, and has Jesus' brothers unable to believe in him (John 1.45; 7.5). One general implication is clear. Whole groups of early Christians believed in the virginal conception and/or virginal birth; others did not. Eventually, belief in Mary's virginity before and after birth triumphed. But variety persisted; some Christians used Matthew's gospel but simply cut out the first chapter; others thought of Jesus as wholly human in origin; still others, more wildly, believed that Jesus descended from heaven fully grown as an adult.[29]

But back to Matthew. In chapter two, the eastern magi follow a star, and tell Herod the king about the birth of the baby who is to be king of the Jews.[30] The wicked king consults the Jewish priests, who tell him that the ruler will be born in Bethlehem (cf. Micah 5.2). The magi find Jesus, worship him, and give him rich gifts, but are warned in a dream not to tell Herod. Joseph too receives a dream, telling him to escape from Judaea to Egypt, so Jesus is not killed in the slaughter of the innocents ordered by the angry king. Eventually, the king dies, Joseph receives another two dreams, which tell him to go back to Palestine, and to Nazareth in Galilee in particular; so is fulfilled the prophecy "Out of Egypt have I called my son" (Hosea 11.1).

These brief episodes—angelic visits and prophetic dreams, Joseph's kindly obedience to God's command, the traveling star, the heroic birth, the worshiping kings, the massacre of the innocents, the family's flight into Egypt/escape from persecution, to say nothing of the miraculous conception and birth—have all shaped the cultural imagination of western civilization. Thousands of pictures and stories celebrate these events, which are, or used to be, a central part of Christian children's education. It seems pedestrian and a little churlish, therefore, to analyze the origins of the individual episodes. But they do help us understand both the shape of the stories and the reasons for their initial success among Jewish Christians.

Jesus' infancy story is a revised version of the story of the birth of Moses. The Moses version is told in Exodus. Matthew follows its general sequence with specific and detailed borrowings and echoes of action and language.[31] But as usual in religious stories, the original had been often retold and changed. Three different Jewish versions from the first century survive. One version has an Egyptian scribe telling the pharaoh that a Jew (namely, Moses) would be born who would surpass all men in virtue and immortal renown. The wicked foreign king on hearing this prophecy orders the slaughter of all Jewish male babies. But a noble Jewish father prays to God, who appears to him in a dream and reassures the father that he is watching over Israel's common welfare. The child whom the Egyptians are seeking will be your savior; he will deliver the Jews from Egyptian bondage and will be remembered for ever, not only by Jews, but universally. He will be, according to the second account, "the greatest and most perfect of men." The Jesus' birth story is a compound of well-known sacred tales and their contemporary elaborations.[32] At the very least, the newborn Jesus was a second Moses.

But Jesus was more than that. God was his Father. Jesus was Son of God. In the pagan world, "son of God" was a regular title of kings and the lineage of mythical heroes. Hercules, for example, was the son of Zeus and a human mother; the twins Castor and Pollux had a human mother; one twin was also the son of Zeus, the other of a human father; so, with divine consent, they were both half human and half divine. The line dividing Gods from humans was more crossable then than it is now: in ancient stories, Gods came down to earth; and special humans, like emperors, lived after death in heaven (plate 8). The concept of God as father was well known in pagan religions and Judaism. So Israel collectively, or pious Jews, or even angels were sometimes thought of as God's sons, as was the apocalyptic Messiah who would rule at the end of days: "I will be his father, and he shall be my son."[33] But giving the title "Son of God" to a crucified criminal was bold, bordering on sacrilegious. And restricting the idea of God the Father to the special sense that he had only one son was a magnificent religious innovation, offensive to conventional Jews.

These parallels help us understand, but do not detract from, the hugely inventive leap made by early Christians in calling their dead leader *the* Son of God. Even the gospel writers struggle with the idea, or rather they cleverly create tensions between what the readers (and even more the rereaders) know and what the apparently privileged disciples and blind contemporaries, Jewish and Roman, fail to recognize, that is, Jesus' divinity. But then, Jesus was believed to be human and divine. The gospels, and believers subsequently, constantly play on the harmonics of the mixture. Jesus is human like us, and so imitable. But he is also divine, and so, out of reach and impossible for us to imitate. But then, perhaps as intermediary between mere humans and an unknowably invisible God, he is more accessible than God the patriarchal Father.

Knowledge of Jesus' divinity became widespread only after his death, resurrection, and ascension. Mark, for example, completed his gospel without the apostles ever fully realizing that Jesus is the Son of God. Of course, *we* know that Jesus is divine, but the disciples themselves have only a dim recognition of a miraculous truth, which has not yet fully dawned on them and will not until after Jesus' death; they sort of know, but their knowledge is not explicit ("They did not understand" 6.52). Symbolically, the first person in Mark's gospel (apart from God and Jesus himself, 9.1–9) who recognizes Jesus as the Son of God is an outsider, a gentile, the Roman centurion at the cross: "Truly, this man was Son of God" (15.39).

Matthew's ambiguities are more complex. He opens his gospel, as we have seen, with a royal but earthly genealogy which legitimates Jesus as the Messiah; through his human father, Joseph, Jesus is in the line of David. But then, and apparently incompatibly, Matthew has his Son of God conceived via the Holy Spirit and without human intervention, miraculously, in the womb of a virgin. At one stroke, apparently, the whole significance of the Davidic line of Joseph is castrated by the fatherhood of God. Of course, we can (and ancient exegetes did) labor to harmonize the discrepancy; accordingly Joseph was Jesus' adoptive father, as Mary was only stepmother to Jesus' brothers.[34]

But the magic of religious stories lies in their affront to common sense, in their demand that we believe. Divine wisdom is beyond human understanding. The story is all the more divine because it is difficult to understand; as Tertullian put it crisply, a century later: "It is to be believed because it makes no sense . . . this fact is certain because it is impossible."[35] And so, once again in Matthew's gospel, when Jesus embarks on his religious mission, his divine birth is forgotten; the disciples recognize his divinity only gradually and with the help of divine revelation (though, of course, we know the truth). Halfway through the gospel, Simon Peter dramatically professes, "You are the Christ, the Son of the living God," and Jesus replies, "Blessed are you, Simon ben Jona! For no human has revealed this to you, but my Father who is in heaven" (16.16; cf. 14.33: "Truly you are the Son of God").

Jesus' death, burial, and resurrection are the climax of the gospel stories. Once again, their symbolic meanings, especially to their earliest readers, were enhanced by echoes of well-known or half-remembered passages from the Jewish scriptures. One image will suffice. The murder of Jesus, God's son, who sacrificed himself to save humanity from sin, recalls and develops the story of the sacrifice of Isaac by his father, Abraham (Genesis 22). In the original story, Abraham, the father, was prepared to sacrifice even his beloved young son out of devotion to God, but in the end God stepped back from demanding human sacrifice and replaced Isaac with a ram.

Over the course of time, ancient Jewish commentators significantly altered and elaborated the Isaac story. These elaborated versions were trenchantly similar to the Jesus death stories. Early Christian writers themselves also drew direct parallels between Isaac and Jesus at his death.[36] Some modern Christians are understandably reluctant to accept that Jesus' unique and centrally symbolic death story was adapted from Jewish scriptures. But the objection is based on imagining a radical split or even opposition between Jews and Christians in the mid–first century, which is anachronistic. The gospel (and pregospel) stories about the death of the Messiah inevitably came from a Jewish milieu. The earliest Christian stories were inevitably Jewish stories.

The similarities between the elaborated Isaac stories and the death of Jesus are remarkable. Isaac is Abraham's only and beloved son. At Satan's suggestion, as a final test of Abraham's devotion, God instructs Abraham to sacrifice Isaac. Abraham obeys. But in these elaborated versions, Isaac himself is not a helpless bound boy but a mature adult who voluntarily goes to his own death, and like Jesus, at Passover. Both Isaac and Jesus are paschal lambs. A first-century Jewish writer has Isaac say: "Have I not been born into this world to be offered as a sacrifice to him who made me?" And Isaac goes on to contemplate his future renown.[37] In the original version, God stopped the sacrifice before it was finished, but in the elaborated versions, Isaac is the model martyr. By implication, his willingness to die counts as a sacrifice already made: "When he saw his father's hand holding a knife descend, he did not flinch." Or as the second-century Christian author Melito writes: "He was let up to be killed like Isaac by his Father. But Christ suffered, Isaac did not suffer. Isaac was the model of Christ's future suffering."[38]

For both religions, the story introduces and legitimates a whole gamut of liturgical practices and ethical prescriptions. For Jews, the Isaac story illustrates that animal sacrifice is a worthy replacement for human sacrifice, but it also indicates that devoted Jews, out of commitment to God, may be called upon to sacrifice even what they hold most dear. In the Christian gospels, the story of Jesus' death may in part echo the Isaac story, even be built onto it; but the ingredient is also transformed in the telling, almost beyond recognition. The sacrifice of Jesus—in effect, the horrific execution by a father of his son—goes beyond the sacrifice of Isaac.[39] This time, God does not stop the sacrifice ("My God, my God, why have you forsaken me?" Mark 15.34) but allows it to go its full course.

Usually we do not get to recognize the full horror of the Christian plot, father-kills-son, any more than committed Christians see the eucharist liturgy as cannibalism ("Take, eat; this is my body. . . . Drink all of you, for this is my blood of the covenant," Matthew 26.26–27). The Jesus death story, like other religious stories, is bracketed off from reality and so is read metaphorically, not literally. It takes place in the sacred space of holy scripture and liturgy. Besides, believers believe that Jesus is divine, immortal, so that his suffering death is not real death, but death which metaphorically conquers death itself. The Christian Father is himself disembodied. Unlike Abraham, he does not wield the knife himself. In the story, responsibility for Jesus' death is shifted from God and Jesus (though Jesus is willingly complicit) to a combination of Romans and Jews. They are the guilty agents. And finally, of course, the Isaac story within the Jewish charter myth is one event among many; while in Christianity's self-construction, the Jesus death story is a central symbolic moment.

RECONSTRUCTING THE GOSPELS:
FLOATING TEXTS, CHANGING CONTENTS

In this section I shall analyze how the gospels were constructed, how texts were moved around and changed, and how the sayings of Jesus were altered, so that reliable reconstruction of what he originally said is, I think, impossible. The historical Jesus is a theological mirage.

By the time the gospels were being written, toward the end of the first century, the context and location of early Christianity had completely changed from the time of Jesus' mission and crucifixion. In the intervening period, most eyewitnesses of Jesus' mission and death had themselves died. Jerusalem had been destroyed, huge numbers of Jews had been killed. And Christianity had spread far outside its original Palestinian homeland. Christians were now of both Jewish and gentile origin. They were scattered throughout the towns and villages of the eastern and central Mediterranean seaboard, and met, sometimes covertly, in small house cult groups. These dispersed groups were connected by a sense of common origin, by the idea of a united church (but it was as yet only an idea), by a thin stream of beggar missionaries, and by intergroup letters. But in the absence of effective local or regional control, varieties of tradition, memory, invention, belief, and practice flourished.

The canonical gospels are only a small fragment of early Christian history. In their time, they had many competitors, nearly all of them now lost. There were local traditions of teaching and practice, collective memories orally transmitted, written sources such as those which the gospel writers themselves used, and the ones which they did not use. Luke himself begins his gospel by acknowledging that many accounts of the origins of Christianity were already in existence. For almost a century after they were written, the gospels had no special sacred status; their texts were permeable to alteration and probably had only patchy circulation in the scattered house cult groups.

One trivial example drives this point home. An important group of western biblical manuscripts incorporates heretical Marcionite prologues into the Pauline letters.[40] This indicates that the communities which received and copied these texts of Paul's letters first received them only after the middle of the second century, and were then indifferent to their heretical views; but presumably there were no competing texts available against which to correct/excise the heretical prologues. Put more broadly, the implication is startling but clear: for the first century of Christianity, many/most Christian house cult groups did not use a written account of Jesus' life and teachings as a sacred text, and may not have had one available.

In order to understand how the surviving representations of Jesus were written and transmitted, we have to speculate how the gospels were interrelated. By convention, the three synoptic gospels (Mark, Matthew, and Luke) are treated together as a group because of their similarity in material and narrative style—in sum, because of their interdependency. Of these, Mark is the shortest and earliest. By the normal rule that successful prophecies are recorded after the event, because of Jesus' prediction of the temple's destruction (13.1–2), Mark is most sensibly dated after 70 CE.[41] Matthew and Luke both depend heavily on Mark.[42] They reproduce virtually all the units of Mark's narrative, and whole sections follow Mark's order, although they also change his text by omissions and expansion.

Matthew and Luke also include additional material of their own. This additional material is of two types (see the chart on p. 311). The first type is derived from an immensely important written source, by convention called Q, containing Jesus' sayings (and like the Gospel of Thomas, it contains only the sayings). Q no longer survives. Its existence is highly probable, because Matthew and Luke order their narratives similarly, and in each story about Jesus, borrow long groups of words in roughly the same order, which do not therefore derive from an oral tradition. (It seems probable that all the gospel writers depended heavily on previously written sources.)

The second, much smaller component in Matthew and Luke comprises materials individual to each; apparently each wrote using sources of which the other was unaware, or chose to omit, and in ignorance of the other's composition. For example, in their narratives about the birth of Jesus, Matthew has Joseph and Mary living in Bethlehem, being visited by magi, escaping mass murder, fleeing to Egypt, and returning to Nazareth. But Luke has Jesus' parents living in Nazareth, being summoned to Bethlehem for a census, and returning without danger to Nazareth. Because of their independence from each other, Matthew and Luke are by convention dated to the same rough period.

1.

"Shitter Beware." Jokey fresco and graffito from a Pompeian lavatory. A naked man sits where the altar should be, between two snakes (symbols of good fortune), while the Goddess Fortune towers above him.

Sexual intercourse on a tightrope. Pompeian pub scene.

2.

3.

The priests of Isis perform their rites in front of the faithful. Wall painting from the Temple of Isis at Pompeii.

Fancy wall decoration in the House of the Gilded Cupids, Pompeii.

4.

Jolly man weighs his erect penis against a bag of money in the entrance hall of the House of the Vettii, Pompeii.

5.

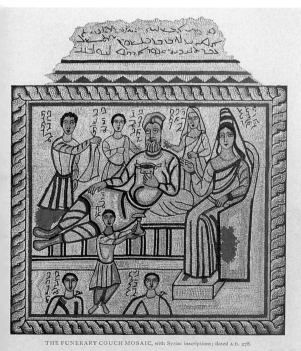

THE FUNERARY COUCH MOSAIC, with Syriac inscriptions; dated A.D. 278.

A prosperous family in Roman Syria, with four living and two dead (in front as busts) children (third-century mosaic).

6.

The beautiful Goddess Artemis (Diana), multi-breasted, marble statue (second century, Ephesus).

7.

The emperor Commodus as Demigod Hercules: inside the slaughtered lion's head (late second century, Rome).

8.

9.

Christ, naked and uncircumcised, being baptized; Ravenna, the Arian Baptistery (sixth century).

10. According to Revelation (4.6–7), the throne of God was surrounded by four winged creatures: a lion, bull, human, and eagle. All of which explains (!) this demonic representation of the gospel writer Mark as lion, from the Baptistery at S. Gennaro, Naples (fifth century).

10.

11.

Christ as lamb with halo, from St. John Lateran, Rome (fifth century).

Christ the teacher enthroned in gold from Sta. Pudenziana, Rome (fifth century).

12.

*Street scene, Pompeii;
paved streets, high curbs.*

13.

*Vulgar caricature of Rome's foundation myth: the
hero Aeneas, with grotesque face and phallus, carries his aged father from the ruins of Troy.*

14.

15.

Household altar (lararium) in the House of the Gilded Cupids, Pompeii, with statuettes of the major Gods (Jupiter, Juno, and Minerva) and household Gods (Lares).

Household Gods (Lares) from the altar of the House of the Gilded Cupids, Pompeii; bronze statuettes.

16.

Inside the House of the Gilded Cupids, Pompeii; the garden is decorated with images of Gods, and looks like a temple courtyard.

17.

Phallus as fountain: water spouts from erect phallus, in direct line of vision from entrance; House of the Vettii, Pompeii.

A grand bronze mirror back, showing a couple having sexual intercourse, on a comfortable bed, under a picture of a couple also having sex; images of gods are carved into the headboard; below, a rat, slippers, and a jug of wine (first century, now in Rome).

18.

19.

20.

Egyptian priests carrying a mummified crocodile in a sacred procession (first to second century, Theadelphia, Egypt).

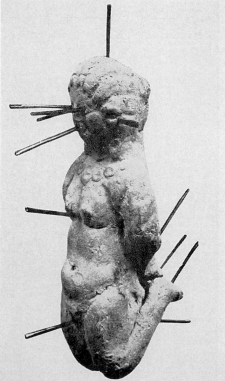

A clay doll pierced in her vital parts by thirteen bronze needles; a magical inscription was attached (third to fourth century, Roman Egypt).

21.

A satirical graffito from the Palatine at Rome; a man and a crucified donkey with the caption "Alexamenos worships his God."

22.

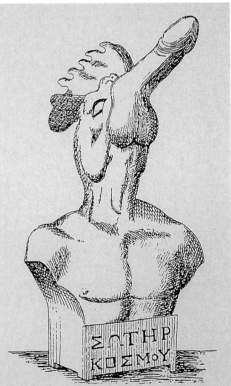

23. *A male bust, with his face modeled as a cock's; his beak is an erect penis; it is labeled in Greek "Savior of the World."*

23.

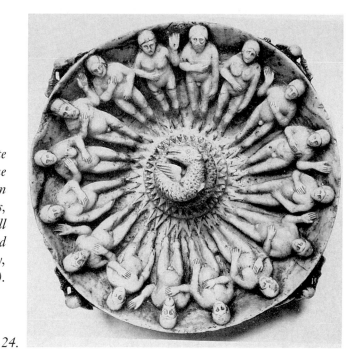

Fine, snow white alabaster bowl; nine naked women and seven men, lying in pairs, worship the serpent; all the men are infibulated (early third century, Syria).

24.

The Persian high priest Kartir stands between the King of Kings and his queen (or the Goddess Anahita); schematic drawing of a monumental rock carving beneath Kartir's autobiographical inscription (third century, Iran).

Sar Mašhad. Sasanidisches Felsrelief 1 : 20 (Schematisierte Zeichnung)

25.

A Zoroastrian priest (magus) with ebony wand (like Mani) in the shrine of Mithras at Dura-Europus, Syria (mid–third century).

26.

Jesus carried into Jerusalem on an ass; church wall painting near Verona (fifth century).

27.

28.

Amulet with ass and foal, inscribed "Our Lord Jesus Christ, the Son of God."

Fine marble statuette of Jesus seated; some think it feminized (mid–fourth century, now in Rome).

29.

Jesus crucified between robbers; the earliest surviving portrayal of the crucifixion; from the grand door of Sta. Sabina, Rome (early fifth century).

By convention also, the Gospel of John is dated latest. But the discovery of a papyrus fragment from his gospel datable to the first quarter of the second century sets a limit. The Gospel of John is radically different in tone from the other three gospels. John's Jesus is more divine than human. He is a spiritual and miracle-working redeemer sent by God. John shares some of the same traditions as the synoptic gospels. Like Mark, he begins Jesus' mission with his baptism, not with his human/miraculous birth. Like the other three gospels, John finishes with the drama of Jesus' death and postresurrection appearances (predicted but not described in Mark). Compared with the other gospels, John's is a spiritualist narrative, which transforms his information in a distinctive and poetic style from the factually mundane to the mysterious and otherworldly.

This sense of variety in the gospel traditions is enhanced once we consider three additional sources. First, Paul, the earliest surviving description of the Christian message. Notoriously, Paul mentions very few of Jesus' sayings (barely half a dozen, with echoes of a few more); Jesus' life, actions, and sayings are not the primary focus of Paul's concern.[43] In his first letter to the Corinthians (15.1–5), Paul summarizes what he apparently considered the core message of his own teaching to the new community: "Christ died for our sins in accordance with the scriptures, he was buried, raised on the third day in accordance with the scriptures, and he then appeared first to Peter," then to the disciples, then to a crowd (some of whom are still living to bear witness to the truth of the message). Paul's central concern is with Christ as salvific messenger and with their legitimation through predictions made in the Jewish scriptures. For Paul, what mattered was the dead/living Christ, not the sayings source.

Second, the Gospel of Thomas contains over one hundred sayings of Jesus, many not known from the canonical gospels.[44] In modern times, it was first published as a whole only in 1959, in a Coptic translation dating from the fourth century. But fragments of Thomas in Greek (dating from about 200 CE) have been known for a century. The close similarity (but not identity) of the Greek and Coptic texts confirms the Coptic text's basic reliability. But the Coptic version also has distinct Gnostic overtones. Thomas' Jesus repeatedly says that the kingdom of God is to be discovered by looking inside oneself. "Jesus said . . . the kingdom is inside of you, and it is outside of you. When you come to know yourselves, then you will be known, and you will realize that it is you who are the sons of the living Father" (G Th 3). This Gnosticism has understandably tempted conservative church historians to consider the Gospel of Thomas as secondary to and later than the canonicals. This is still, I think, the majority view. But close comparisons of the Thomas version of Jesus' sayings with each of the synoptics and John suggests that Thomas often preserves what could be the earliest stratum of the Jesus sayings record.[45]

Finally, we have dozens of later and supplementary records of what Jesus said and did. For example, the Infancy Gospels represent Jesus as a troublesome but amazing child. He kills fellow pupils who get in his way, and adults who rebuke him. But then in compensation he magically cures an innocent victim. For these writers and their readers, Jesus was a miracle worker but not a teacher of ethics. The First Gospel of James, from the second century, celebrates the postbirth virginity of Mary, her unconsummated marriage to an aging Joseph, and her lineage from David.[46] All these works are designed, I imagine, to fill gaps in the canonical gospels and to serve as a defensive answer to critics of the gospel birth narratives.

In addition, there are supplementary revelations about the nature of Jesus' teaching to his disciples, for example, in the Epistle to the Apostles and the Secret Book of John, dating from the second century. These derivative elaborations are not historical, in the naive sense of history as being primarily concerned with facts. But they do illustrate how the magisterial and divine figure of Jesus was continually being reinterpreted and reinvented by pious believers. I shall argue, of course, that this process of pious invention began immediately after Jesus' death (it probably began even before he died) and flourished both before and after the gospels were written.

The accompanying chart illustrates some probable lines of dependence between Mark, Q (the Jesus sayings source), Matthew, Luke, Thomas, and their other sources. In addition, scholars hypothesize a miracle book(s), common to Mark and John, though John did not use Mark directly (the order of miracles is similar, but not their description). Of course, all such diagrams are simplifications of a more complex reality.[47] Texts circulated in different versions; many circulating texts have been lost without trace. In those days, even texts about sacred subjects were not secure. Authors and copiers changed the text to suit their needs and be-

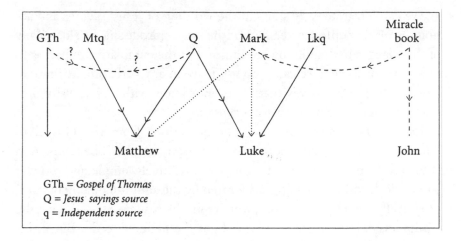

liefs, just as Mark, Matthew, Luke, and John themselves changed what they had read about Jesus. And their texts subsequently, as we shall see, were also changed. The gospel texts were not fixed like a printed book; they were malleable, at least to a degree, well into the second century.

The early Jesus movement was a dispersed, fluid set of diverse house cult groups, embattled against both internal and external enemies. In this volatile environment, early Christians used a mixture of collective memories, liturgies, catechisms, sermons, and sacred and semisacred texts. Among them, what later became the canonical gospels had no traceable primacy until the mid to late second century.[48] No single view predominated. There was no way of enforcing conformity. When Paul, James, and Peter fell out, Paul stormed off. Paul's Christian message concentrated on Christ's death, burial, and resurrection. Diotrephes refused to acknowledge John's authority, and expelled his opponents from his church (3 John 9–10). The sayings source Q and the Gospel of Thomas contain wisdom sayings, but tell us nothing of Jesus' death and resurrection. Neither Mark nor John has a birth story; Mark has no descriptions of Jesus' postresurrection appearances. John's gospel virtually ignores Jesus' trademark, the parables. Marcion's Christianity is without the Jewish God; Justin's Christianity is without John and Paul. The eventual Christianity of the four canonical gospels plus Paul and the other apostles' letters is at once a simplificatory mirage and a collusive agreement among leading Christians to allow a wide diversity of paradoxically conflicting opinions to coexist.

We can illustrate early shifts in the wording of Jesus' sayings and actions by placing different versions of the same episode side by side. Many of the changes in description are minor, but the cumulative impact is to reduce the trust that we can properly place in any verbatim attribution. The result, in my view, is that we cannot know with any security precisely, or even roughly, what Jesus said or did.

In the first examples I have put quotations from the Gospel of Thomas on the left and synoptic parallels next to them. The temptation is to read from left to right, to see how a relatively simple and pithy, if paradoxical, wisdom saying is elaborated by the addition of a theological or ethically prescriptive closure, which tells the reader precisely what the wisdom-saying means or what it obliges the believer to do. But if, instead, we choose to read the quotations right to left (on the ground that the Gospel of Thomas is later), the direction of the argument is changed, but its force is not diminished: the Jesus sayings change with each author who reports them.

That's the theory; now to the practice. For a page or three, this will mean a close grind. Let's begin, quite arbitrarily, with one of Jesus' wisdom sayings, to see how different authors changed Jesus' words.[49]

Gospel of Thomas	Luke 11.39–41	Matthew 23.25–26
Jesus said, "Why do you wash the outside of the cup? Did you not realize that he who made the inside is the same one who made the outside?"	And the Lord said to him, "Now you Pharisees cleanse the outside of the cup and the dish, but inside you are full of extortion and wickedness. You fools! Did not he who made the outside make the inside also? So give for alms those things that are within; and see, everything will be clean for you."	"Woe to you scribes and Pharisees, hypocrites! For you clean the outside of the cup and of the plate, but inside they are full of greed and self-indulgence. You blind Pharisee! First clean the inside of the cup, so that the outside also may become clean."

The Gospel of Thomas version is bare, without theological or ethical comment, and so plausibly comes from an earlier stratum of reportage. By this I by no means wish to imply that Jesus himself spoke in simple pithy aphorisms. We have simply no idea whether he did or didn't. The Luke and Matthew versions expand Jesus' saying into an attack against

Pharisees; Luke converts it into an ethical prescription, Matthew into a gnomic saying.

We can see a similar pattern in other comparisons. For example:

Gospel of Thomas 107	Luke 15.3–7	Matthew 18.10–14
Jesus said, "The kingdom is like a shepherd who had a hundred sheep. One of them, the largest, went astray. He left the ninety-nine and sought the one until he found it. After he had gone to so much trouble, he said to the sheep: I love you more than the ninety-nine."	So he told them this parable: "Which one of you, having a hundred sheep and losing one of them, does not leave the ninety-nine in the wilderness and go after the one that is lost until he finds it? When he has found it, he lays it on his shoulder and rejoices. And when he comes home, he calls together his friends and neighbors, saying to them, Rejoice with me, for I have found my sheep that was lost. Just so, I tell you, there will be more joy in heaven over one sinner who repents than over ninety-nine righteous persons who need no repentance."	"Take care that you do not despise one of these little ones; for, I tell you in heaven their angels continually see the face of my Father in heaven. What do you think? If a shepherd has a hundred sheep, and one of them goes astray, does he not leave the ninety-nine on the mountains and go in search of the one that went astray? And if he finds it, truly I tell you, he rejoices over it more than over the ninety-nine that never went astray. So it is not the will of your Father in heaven that one of these little ones should be lost."

Once again, Thomas is completely simple, if opaque, with its theological framing implicit but unexplored; its ethical implication, that love is a function of ego's effort, is quite human but not particularly Christian. Luke's Jesus is more cheerful, has an apparently informal, small religious group consisting of friends and neighbors, but greets them with the paradox that repentant sinners are more welcome than the virtuous. The paradox is easily resolved: the virtuous are necessarily sinners. Matthew's introductory and end framing are balanced and secondary theological elaborations, illustrating Jesus' special knowledge of his Father's universal concern, even for the underprivileged.

One obvious implication emerges from these successive changes made in the reportage of Jesus' sayings from gospel to gospel. We can have no confidence that any of Jesus' reported sayings record verbatim what Jesus actually said. By this logic, even Mark's gospel, the earliest of the synoptic gospels, was not immune to the editorial changes made before and by its author. Besides, some of the sayings attributed to Jesus seem like the foolish sayings of a wise man.[50] Indeed, the collection of sayings in the Gospel of Thomas suggest that at least one component in the Jesus tradition was a traditional collection of anonymous wisdom sayings, in the style of the Egyptian Ankhsheshonq or Insinger Papyrus collection (from the last century BCE/first century CE) or the Wisdom of Ben Sirach (also called Ecclesiasticus), now in the Old Testament apocrypha.[51] After all, Jesus was a wise teacher, and these were the sort of sayings which wise teachers were known to have spoken. To be acceptable (as we have already seen in our discussion of borrowings from the Old Testament), Jesus had to be, at least partly, dressed up in traditional clothes.

Three further examples illustrate how the traditional, anonymous wisdom text was changed by a gospel writer's theological interest, how the gospel writers drew upon a variety of traditions which existed previously and independently of Jesus, how apparently trivial changes in successive, parallel texts reveal specific tendencies and current concerns in different gospel writers, and finally how even within gospels, different manuscripts incorporated changes in the Jesus message, which later tradition attempted to blot out by harmonizing the record.

Gospel of Thomas 8
And [Jesus] said, "The man is like a wise fisherman who cast his net into the sea and drew it up from the sea full of small fish. Among them the wise fisherman found a fine large fish. He threw all the small fish back into the sea and chose the large fish without difficulty. Whoever has ears to hear, let him hear."

Matthew 13.47–50
"The kingdom of heaven is like a net which was thrown into the sea and gathered fish of every kind; when it was full, men drew it ashore and sat down and sorted the good into a vessel but threw away the bad. So it will be at the close of the age. The angels will come out and separate the evil from the righteous and throw them into the furnace of fire; there men will weep and gnash their teeth."

The brief image described by Thomas obviously belongs to a peasant tradition which is independent of and predates Jesus' mission. Of course, it's difficult to say what Thomas' uncontextualized parable means; its openness allows a whole variety of meanings. But to judge from the general drift of similar sayings in the Thomas collection, one recurrent idea is that the truly wise man concentrates on finding and consuming a single great treasure, namely knowledge of the divine, which can be achieved through selective and inspired, but solitary, self-knowledge.[52]

Matthew 16.15	Mark 8.29	Luke 9.20
He said to them, "But who do you say that I am?" Simon Peter answered, "You are the Christ, the Son of the living God." And Jesus answered him, "Blessed are you, Simon Son of Jonah. For flesh and blood has not revealed this to you, but my Father in heaven. And I tell you, you are Peter, and on this rock will I build my church." . . . Then he sternly ordered the disciples not to tell anyone that he was the Christ. From that time on, Jesus began to show his disciples that he must go to Jerusalem and suffer greatly from the elders and the chief priests and scribes, and on the third day, be raised. And Peter took him aside and began to rebuke him, saying, "God forbid it, Lord. This must not happen to you." But [Jesus] turned and said to Peter, "Get behind me, Satan; you offend me. You are thinking not of God, but of men."	He asked them, "But who do you say that I am?" Peter answered him, "You are the Christ." And he sternly ordered them not to tell anyone about him. Then he began to teach them that the Son of Man must suffer greatly, and be rejected by the elders and the chief priests and scribes, and after three days, rise again. He said this openly. And Peter took him aside and began to rebuke him. But [Jesus] turned and looked at his disciples, and rebuked Peter and said, "Get behind me, Satan. You are thinking not of God, but of men."	He said to them, "But who do you say that I am?" Peter answered, "The Christ of God." He sternly ordered and commanded them not to tell anyone, saying the son of man must suffer greatly, and be rejected by the elders and the chief priests and scribes, and be killed, and on the third day, be raised.

Matthew restricts the range of possible meanings, and tailors Jesus' saying into a comment about the imminent last judgment, in which the righteous will be sorted out and the evil will be burned. Neither Mark nor Luke reports this saying.

The gospels were written when the Jesus movement was split into rival factions, which followed the tradition of particular apostles. Their reports of Jesus' relations with the disciples sometimes reflect these earlier and ongoing conflicts. For example, Mark 10.35 shows up the disciples James and John as crudely ambitious: they want to sit on either side of Jesus in heaven. Matthew in the parallel passage (20.20) exonerates them by attributing these ambitions to their mother; Luke helps make peace by omitting the incident. When Jesus asks the disciples who they think he is, Mark 8.29–33 has Peter recognize Jesus as the Christ, but then he rebukes Jesus, who in turn compares Peter to Satan.

Matthew, in the same incident (16.13ff.), rescues Peter by having him make the much more challenging acknowledgment that Jesus is not only the Christ but "the Son of the living God." And Jesus rewards Peter for this revelation with the reciprocal elevation of Peter into the rock on whom the future church would be built; and then when Peter rebukes Jesus, it is only because Peter is on Jesus' side, and doesn't want Jesus to die; he is like Satan only because of his inferior understanding. Luke, again the peacemaker (9.18), typically truncates the whole passage and omits any mention of a quarrel between Jesus and Peter. In the gospel of John, the favorite disciple is not Peter but the anonymous disciple "whom Jesus loved"; John demotes Peter from favorite disciple to a secondary hanger-on who is repeatedly shown up as inadequate and as making clumsy mistakes (13.8ff.; 18.10ff.; 21.7; 21.23).[53]

My final example is the Lord's Prayer. Matthew has Jesus tell his followers to distinguish themselves from hypocritical Jews who pray ostentatiously and from pagans who splutter endlessly. Jesus said:

Matthew 6.9ff.	Mark 11.25–26	Luke 11.2–4
"Pray then in this way: Our Father in heaven, hallowed be your name, your kingdom come. Your will be done on earth as it is in heaven.	"Whenever you stand praying, forgive, if you have anything against anyone, so that your Father in heaven may also forgive you your tres-	"When you pray, say: Father, hallowed be your name, your kingdom come. Give us each day our daily bread. And forgive us our sins, for we

Give us this day our daily bread. And forgive us our debts, as we also have forgiven our debtors. And do not bring us to trial/temptation, but rescue us from the devil/evil. *For the power and the glory are yours for ever, Amen.* For if you forgive others their trespasses, your heavenly Father will also forgive you."

passes. *But if you do not forgive, neither will your Father who is in heaven forgive your trespasses."*

ourselves forgive everyone indebted to us. And do not bring us to trial/temptation."

The emphasized text comes from ancient manuscripts of the gospels which incorporate what modern scholars now agree to be later (pre-fourth-century) additions to the gospel texts. The traditional English Lord's Prayer is a mixture of Matthew and Luke, because it is a translation of the text of an ancient Greek manuscript which has a longer version of Luke (a version that harmonized the text of Luke and Matthew). Even in antiquity, the texts of the gospels were open to emendations and additions.[54] The text that we have, and translate, is not necessarily the original text, but the closest scholars can get to it. The variants reflect the diversity of ancient Christianities.

But surely, a believer might say, in spite of all these minor changes from gospel to gospel in what Jesus is reported to have said and done, overall we have a reasonably good, general sense of Jesus' main teaching and message. Jesus was a new-style prophet with an inspirational vision of an imminent heavenly kingdom in which only the virtuous could share, or an inspired teacher who taught a simple but powerful message in parables, so that he could be understood.[55] Jesus was a healer, a miracle worker, a man learned in the law, a radical who fell foul of conservative priests and oppressive Romans, a holy man, a drunkard, a peasant.

There are as many portrayals as there are books. Given the plethora, why not admit that no one knows? We are in a hall of mirrors, with hundreds of competing representations, part real, part invented, and part only projections of ourselves. It was always so. The gospels do not settle the question as to who Jesus was, or what he taught; they invite further inquiry, as do the answers. The sacralization of four complementary and discrepant gospels was both a compromise between competing local traditions and a masterstroke. The collection of different gospels and the opaque letters of Paul offered believers the reassurance that their beliefs were firmly based in history, a history which or from which they could learn, and at the same time a history which ensured the continuation of the mystery: Jesus could be what you believed him to be.

CAN A NONBELIEVER EVER REALLY UNDERSTAND?

The Parsonage
Hungerford

My dear Keith,

Thanks for your typescript on Jesus, which I read with a mixture of pleasure and dismay. I admit that an unbeliever like you is completely at liberty to write about Jesus and the New Testament. But what comes out is so bloodless, all reason and innuendo—no passion, no commitment, no faith, no realization of the humility and majesty of God's incarnation and self-sacrificing death. No hope, no belief. And without all these, I think you can't understand early Christianity or convey an understanding, whether to believers or nonbelievers. The whole enterprise of an unbeliever's guide to a living religion is misconceived.

I don't want to come over as a soppily sentimental country vicar. That's not at all how I feel. But I do know from experience that Jesus represents (not just for believers, but I suspect for our whole culture) all that's best in human nature; a capacity to be kind, generous, and unselfish. Academics in their ivory towers can scoff, but they shouldn't. When you fall ill, it is exactly that kind of selfless care that you hope to find. A culture needs ideals, and a symbol to represent those ideals of hope and purpose; people need the best inside themselves acknowledged and encouraged; they even need the worst accepted for what it is, and to be given some incentive for improvement, by confession and repentance. No, as you know, I'm not a crypto Catholic; I'm not into wooden confessional stalls; I mean confession and repentance as an internal process of self-control; and I think belief in Christ is one way (in our culture, the way) to get the best out of humans. I concede that in this country the institutional church is not succeeding in getting its message across. But even so, I insist, Jesus stands for all that's best in humans and western culture.

So you see, all your clever technical arguments leave me a bit cold, even when I find them persuasive. For me personally—but don't tell my bishop (he's a bit cautious), and it's not what I'd stand up in the pulpit and say (it's not worth the fuss)—miracles, the virgin birth, the literal truth of the gospels don't matter too much to me. It's not even the ethical precepts of the gospels which matter most, though I see no reason to disregard them; it's the spiritual drive, "the electric charge" you call it, which makes the gospel message so timeless and relevant. And it's belief—so different from thinking—which gives us a humbling glimpse of the divine.

And besides, I find that reading the gospels is like reexperiencing Jesus' own growing sense of his mission and revelation. Of course, this is a subjective understanding. And I realize that you had to select; but why select the similarities between Jesus and Isaac, rather than the sheer beauty of Jesus' own humility and love for his father and those who believe in him: "Come to me all who labor and are heavy-laden and I will give you rest . . . for I am gentle and lowly in heart, and you will find rest for your souls" (Matthew 11.28–29)? Surely you admit that's beautiful, humbling, and consoling.

Now I've said all that, I can make a few technical points, which you'd better check up with a specialist at the Divinity School in Cambridge. I feel you go too far in doubting the basic historical truth of the synoptic gospels. Surely Jesus made a huge impact on his immediate followers, so that they treasured a collective memory of his teachings, not necessarily word for word (you've convinced me of that), but in broad outline. For all their minor disagreements, the gospels collectively present a broadly concordant, almost symphonic picture of Jesus as teacher, healer, leader, and inspirer. They agree with each other.

But that's not all. The gospels also preserve some of Jesus' sayings which were awkward for later generations of Christians; for example, when Jesus says he's interested only in Jews, not in gentiles, or that he's teaching a message of violence as well as peace. These are probably genuine sayings of Jesus, neither invented by the gospel writers nor purposefully edited out by later scribes. The gospels are more varied and genuine than you imply. Finally, I personally feel that Jesus' outbursts in Aramaic come from the earliest and most genuine level of the apostles' personal memories. Of course, this method of testing the Jesus record has to be used cautiously and cannot be 100 percent reliable. It won't convince the precommitted sceptic. But as you would surely be the first to admit, history is about speculative and imaginative reconstruction, not just facts.

Of course, in the final analysis, my belief in Jesus as our saviour is a matter of belief. I think* his incarnation, his willingness to die for our sins to save us

---

*Andrea is slipping effortlessly here (as believers do) from believing to thinking, as though there were no difference. In my view, believing begins where thinking stops, where explanations involve the supernatural, though of course we can think about beliefs to make them explicit and coherent. But then she would probably say that the separation of belief from thought is self-serving, as though the atheist/agnostic position did not have an a priori base.

from the worst in ourselves and give us a chance to do better, did happen in real time. But debate over the fine points of historical truth cannot be the essence of good Christianity. What matters is to believe and to act in a Christian way on the basis of those beliefs.

I am sorry for my long letter. I did not have the time to make it shorter. I need a new sermon for Sunday. Any ideas?

Yours ever,

Andrea

IN THE HALL OF MIRRORS

Jesus met a man and asked him, *What are you doing?*
    The man replied, *I am devoting myself to God.*
    And Jesus asked, *Who is looking after you?*
    My brother, said the man.
    And Jesus said, *Your brother is more devoted to God than you are.* (From *The Muslim Jesus*[5])[6]

The historical Jesus is an illusion. Almost a century ago, a famous German scholar showed convincingly how successive modern portrayals of Jesus reflected changing contemporary concerns.[57] Scholars and believers looked long and hard at historical sources and saw principally a reflection of themselves. So far in this chapter I have illustrated how this process of changing the image of Jesus started already in the first century. By implication, as so often in history writing, I think we get more out of tracing changing representations than from chasing the uncatchable shadows of a real, onetime Jesus. The important Jesus is the Jesus in believers' minds.

And for Christians, Jesus Christ was far too important a symbol to be left alone. Paul's letters and the gospels did not settle questions about the nature of his humanity and divinity, the purpose of God's creation, the prospects of salvation, the place of evil and suffering, obedience and virtue. Christian writings, both before and after they became canonical, just served as a platform for further pious speculations. And in particular, one central problem recurs: what was the relationship between the earthly Jesus, and the risen Christ, and the original God of the Old Testament? Could God really suffer? Was he beyond human understanding? Did Jesus merely appear to be human? If he was completely human and imitable, he was not God, but if he was spiritually divine, he could not be imitated. Or was Jesus perhaps a second God, created by the Super God? All these views and many more were advanced by early Christians, and contributed by their rejection to the gradual creation of "orthodoxy." Orthodoxy changed to incorporate its own defenses against heresies. It is this orthodoxy which has partly veiled early Christianity's extraordinary variety.

Some pious Christians even rejected the notion that Jesus had come down to earth just once. Why waste such a good idea? So they made Jesus repeatedly reappear back on earth, either in the flesh or spiritually, in visions. One third-century visionary tract, called *Faith Wisdom (Pistis Sophia)*, has Jesus come back after his resurrection to instruct his disciples for eleven years, and still they don't fully understand his teachings.[58] And unlike Jesus himself, the disciples are resentful, jealous, and hostile toward Jesus' female followers. Of course, religious stories do not necessarily just reflect external realities; they can be, often are, fantasy. But they also suggest what some contemporary concerns were, and allow us to imagine that the role of women in some early Christian groups was much more open and disputed than male-dominated orthodoxy allowed. In some "heretical" groups women officiated at baptism and took turns to hold office.[59]

It cannot be accidental that in this long book, Mary Magdalene was by far the best disciple. She repeatedly questions Jesus with persistence and insight. In fact, moved by the Spirit (as though what counts in this Christian group is personal inspiration, not authority), she asks twice as many questions as all the male disciples put together. She interprets Jesus' answers; she has privileged, semiprivate dialogues with Jesus in the disciples' presence; and once even, with Jesus' permission, she answers a question put to him. Jesus duly praises her assurance and understanding. "She had become pure Spirit . . . blessed beyond all women upon earth. Jesus answered and said to Maria: 'Excellent, Maria. You ask well with an excellent question, and you inquire with certainty and accuracy. . . . Hear now, Maria, and listen all you disciples.'" It was more than Peter could bear: "We cannot abide this woman who does not allow us to speak, but speaks often." He finally asked Jesus to keep the women (Mary Magdalene; Jesus' mother, Mary; Martha; Salome) quiet, so that the men too could have a chance to ask Jesus questions.[60]

Mary Magdalene's closeness to Jesus gives her special status. In the second-century Gospel of Mary, when the disciples were frightened after Jesus' death and depressed about the apparently insuperable difficulties of their apostolic mission, it was Mary Magdalene who stood up among the apostles and encouraged them to be resolute. In effect, she took on Jesus' leadership role. Peter reciprocated by acknowledging that Jesus loved Mary, though here only "more than other women." He then asked her to reveal to them what she had heard from Jesus privately.

Mary Magdalene obliges by recounting an astounding vision which she had had, and Jesus' revelations to her during it. Andrew and Peter are both skeptical that Jesus could have said all this to her alone, a woman. Mary weeps at their disbelief. "Do you think I am lying about the savior?" And Levi rebukes Peter for his jealousy. Jesus, he says, knew Mary well; "that is why he loved her more than us." All of them should seek to perfect themselves like her, "without laying down any law beyond what the savior said."[61] The writer's appeal (as it so often is in Christianity) is to the original Jesus message, uncluttered with subsequent and false traditions. Through Jesus, women too can be saved.

In the male-centerd, female-phobic world of some early Christian groups, Mary needed Jesus in order to secure the privilege of equal treatment. These Gnostic writings repeatedly represent females in important roles, but they also often conceptualize "male" as the ideal image of perfection, while "female" by contrast is sensual and inadequate. So in the Gospel of Thomas, when Peter wants a male-only conversation with Jesus, Jesus supports Mary. But he then says what every modern feminist must hate to read: he will himself make her male, so that she too may be saved. Jesus said, "For every woman who makes herself male will enter the kingdom of heaven."[62]

The familiarity of Mary Magdalene with Jesus was troubling in its implied sexuality. The second-century Gospel of Philip again privileges Mary as Jesus' partner: "He loved her more than all the disciples, and used to kiss her often on the mouth."[63] This closeness provoked anger and jealousy among the disciples. They asked: "Why do you love her more than all of us?" And Jesus answered enigmatically: "Why do I not love you like her?" But was his kissing only the asexual Christian kiss of peace, just the spiritual kiss of the elect, who have risen above the prison of corrupting flesh?[64] The disciples clearly feared that it was not, and by their very questioning displayed their own inadequacy. We too cannot know the answer and perhaps even we should not ask. Even if we spiritualize Jesus' sexuality into holy asexuality, the success of the image with the reader depends completely on the pull of its ambiguity. Did Jesus really kiss Mary often in public on the mouth? We, like the disciples, are left with the uncomfortable feeling that after all, perhaps he did, and it was for real.

But Jesus is meant to be asexual. This is so well established as to be self-evident and unquestioned. But then, very occasionally, as in the Gnostic Gospel of Mary, Jesus' potential sexuality is hinted at; in the Arian baptistery in Ravenna, Jesus is depicted on a stunning mosaic as naked and uncircumcised (plate 9). Very occasionally, early Christian texts leak a forgotten consciousness that the gender of the godhead is problematic. So we get hints in passing that God the Father had milk-yielding breasts, or that Jesus could turn into a woman, and there are even some statues of Jesus which faintly suggest a hidden female form (plate 29).[65] And occasionally we are reminded that the Holy Spirit in Aramaic and Syriac was female, so that the Trinity was (?originally) constituted as a respectable family of Father/Mother/Son. So the Gospel of Philip mockingly rejects the idea that Mary, Jesus' mother, conceived by the Holy Spirit: "When did a woman ever conceive by a woman?"[66] Valentinian Gnostics (see Chapter Seven) eroticized the whole pre-Jesus godhead and had the female/androgyne Wisdom self-impregnate through unfulfilled passion for her cosmic father; so she became the real mother of God. But in general, especially in contrast with pagan Gods and Goddesses, who frequently frolicked with immoral lust both above and among their worshipers, the early Christian God and Jesus are determinedly asexual, even antisexual.

But the sexuality of Jesus was too powerful a symbol to ignore. To be sure, only "heretics" and marginals celebrated it with gusto, but their subversions and the shrill, horrified objections of the "orthodox" helped keep Jesus' normative asexuality on track. The center needs its rejected margins. Jesus once went with Mary Magdalene up the Mount of Olives; he prayed, and from his ribs produced a woman; Jesus began to have intercourse with this woman, and then swallowed his own semen, saying,

"We must do this, so we may live." Mary was understandably horrified, fainted, and when Jesus raised her up, he upbraided her for her lack of faith.[67] By implication, this Jesus is rejigging the paradise scene in Genesis 3; here he is both God and the second Adam; Mary (or her sexual substitute) is his second Eve; but this time, in contrast to the original, they celebrate together not sinful sex but sex without reproduction. And their act together, Jesus' words imply, is a life-giving sacrament.

The sacralization of Christ's sperm in the eucharist seems shocking. Some Christian groups (from second to fourth century, so it is alleged) even mixed male sperm with menstrual blood and lentils (as an optional extra) to make a eucharistic wafer. Still others made love in a special ritual space, the mirrored wedding chamber, or spiritually simulated lovemaking (it's hotly disputed by modern scholars which) in order to cease being mere Christians and to become themselves Christ. They wanted, and believed they had achieved, resurrection now: "While we are in this world, it is fitting for us to acquire the resurrection," so that when we die, we may already be at rest. "Jesus came to crucify the world."[68]

Yet other Christians (males) allegedly hoped to gain salvation by having sex 730 times (2 x 365) promiscuously with sect-devoted females, in puzzling imitation of an ascent to and descent from heaven. Each sexual act was dedicated to a different ruling spirit; and when one of the sect had completed the required number, he proudly proclaimed: "I am Christ." Epiphanius, future bishop, confessed that as a youth he had himself been sorely tempted and nearly seduced by the prettiest women of this sect, from whom he learned their secrets. But quite properly, he had reported them to his bishop, who had expelled all eighty of them from the local town.[69] Allegorically, we can easily make sense of their liturgy. Sperm and blood are the essence of God's creation; both are liberated by emission from the corruption of the material body. Their mixture puts together what had been wrongly separated in the abortive creation by Wisdom, or after the fall in the sexual separation of Adam and Eve.

Transgression, inversion, and overperformance are primary, though not sufficient, markers of the sacred. Christ, for example, was a crucified criminal (plate 30); the eucharist is the sacred consumption of blood and flesh; baptism was egalitarian nakedness in a steeply hierarchical society. Once the sacred ceases to be shocking, it too becomes part of the unproblematically normal. The boundaries of the sacred are then stretched and reconstructed by further transgressions: so, for example, in early Christian history, martyrs suffer torture and death willingly; holy virgins become brides of Christ; ascetics in search of holiness forgo sex in a society in which everyone else marries, go voluntarily without food in a society which is hungry, and live in a desert in a society where towns are equated with culture; and gospel writers become wild beasts (plate 10).

What matters here is image and story, more than reality. And stories about ever more marginal and easily rejectable transgressions, such as becoming Christ oneself, eating sperm, or having sex as part of the eucharist, are boundary markers for the acceptably orthodox. They educate us in what we should never do, or would only dream about doing. But such images and stories are no more marginal than criminals are marginal to bourgeois property owners and the legal system. Or rather, they are both marginal and essential. But they are more than that; the stories about Jesus' sexuality operate (like modern crime stories) as a fantasy field for risk-free adventure in the unacceptable, undertaken in the complete security that the writer (and proper readers) are cozily wrapped up in orthodoxy. Orthodoxy without rejectable and objectionable heresies cannot be orthodoxy.

Some orthodox projections of Jesus are almost equally strange, if less disturbing (plate 11). The second-century Letter of Barnabas, the apostle, was much respected by orthodox Christians; some even considered it genuinely apostolic. But it treats Jesus, inter alia, as a combination of the two goats sacrificed by Jews at Yom Kippur, the Feast of the Atonement. At this annual festival, the Jews offered God two beautiful he-goats, one of which is chosen by lot to be sacrificed and consumed by the priests; the other is beaten and derided, but with a scarlet thread on its head is chased away and murdered near a bush of thorns. Both are offerings to atone for the iniquities and sins of the people, just as Jesus took upon himself the sins of the world. Jesus, as seen by Barnabas, is a combination of both goats, the sacrificial goat and the scapegoat, because he comes into the world twice. He is derided and murdered, like the scapegoat; the scarlet thread and the thorns recall the scarlet cloak which Jesus was made to wear at the crucifixion in mockery of his kingly pretensions (Matthew 27.28); the thorns recall Jesus' crown of thorns and the "pain and suffering of those who would attain my kingdom." Jesus is also the beautiful sacrificial goat, whose flesh Christians consume at the eucharist. But Barnabas also envisages that one day Jesus will return in a scarlet robe of glory, and people will say: "Is this not he whom we once crucified and spat upon?" And did he not say that he was the Son of God?[70]

Some devout and orthodox Christians completely recast the Jesus story by stitching Old and New Testament traditions together. Jesus here is the last and best in a cast of prophets, whose suffering for their faith prefigured the sufferings and glory of Christ. The following tale, called the Martyrdom and Ascension of Isaiah, was written probably between 50 and 150 CE in Christian circles, which valued the Jewish scriptures and prophetic inspiration rather than the gospels and episcopal authority. The story includes the hostility of father and son, the suffering death of the good Jew Isaiah (Jesus is not alone), the persecution and retreat of the righteous to asceticism in the desert (echoes of Qumran?), a Judaslike traitor, the early corruption of Christian leaders, the death of inspired prophecy, and a cosmic Christ who himself worships the supreme God.[71]

Once upon a time, in the reign of the good King Hezekiah, the great prophet Isaiah predicted his own tortured death at the hands of a wicked prince, Manasseh, in whose heart Satan dwells. The good king proposes to kill his own son, but Isaiah tells him that Christ will prevent it. Instead, it is fated for Isaiah to die. The good king dies and Manasseh inherits his father's kingdom. Satan and sin flourish. The righteous are persecuted. Isaiah retreats to Bethlehem, but even there sin prospers, so he takes refuge in the desert with a few faithful and frugal followers. A traitor denounces Isaiah at the king's court for making sacrilegious prophecies about Jesus' forthcoming incarnation, crucifixion, and resurrection, and the miraculous early growth of Christianity. Isaiah also predicts that the Christian leaders will soon abandon apostolic teaching of faith, love, and purity. Instead, they will seek offices in the church out of greed for money, ambition, and vainglory. No longer will there be prophets, only mutual hatred, discord, and indiscipline. Already.

Isaiah prophesies that Satan will descend on the world in the guise of a Roman emperor (Nero) and persecute Christians. All will obey him and sacrifice to him, including most Christians.[72] Only a few of the faithful will remain. But then, at the end of time, the Lord will come, eject Satan to hell, and enliven the pious. After judgment, the impious will be consumed utterly by fire. Because of these predictions, Satan is enraged against Isaiah and dwells in the heart of the wicked King Manasseh, who orders Isaiah to be slowly sawed in two, while the false prophets stand around laughing derisively. Satan tempts Isaiah to recant with false hopes of his own reform. But Isaiah curses Satan, the king, and all his court (did the audience immediately think of the Roman emperor and court?). And all the time during his protracted death, Isaiah did not once cry out, but his mouth spoke only of the Holy Spirit. In reality and representation, the willingness of martyrs to die bravely for their faith was a Jewish-Christian creation.

Now, years before all this, Isaiah had come to the court of the good King Hezekiah, and surrounded by forty prophets (those were the days when prophecy still flourished), he went into a deathlike trance and was taken up by an angel to the seventh heaven, and had a vision. The first heaven is filled with the discordant hordes of Satan; the next four heavens are filled with choirs of angels. In the sixth heaven, with one voice they all sing the praises of the Father, his beloved Christ, and the Holy Spirit. Only in the seventh heaven does Isaiah hear the prophecy that the Lord will descend to earth to be called Christ, and "they will *think* that he is flesh and a man" (a docetist heresy), so that they will not know who he really is. The God of that world (the Devil? but *not* the Jews) will kill him. Christ will die, plunder the angel of death, rise on the third day, but remain in the world for 545 days, then will ascend again with many of the righteous to the seventh heaven.

When he has heard this divine prophecy, Isaiah and the righteous worship the Lord and the angel (*sic*) of the Holy Spirit; and then all of them, including the Lord Jesus and the angel of the Holy Spirit, worship the invisible Most High God (this was seen later as a heresy of subordination of Christ to God). And the Most High instructed Jesus to descend from the seventh heaven, disguising himself as he went so that he was not recognized by the lower angels, because he was like them. The dream ends with a vision of Mary of the house of David, and her virgin pregnancy and virgin birth. But when he had finished telling this vision to the good King Hezekiah, Isaiah asked him that it be kept secret from the Jews. Isaiah and Jesus were in the same holy tradition, the story seems to say, of the righteous prophet whose inspired teachings the wicked at their own peril stupidly ignored. This pious story was preserved, and often translated, by Christians, who were clearly not affronted by its variations from the canon.

Marcion, by contrast, was determined to sever all links between Christianity and Judaism. To understand Jesus, he argued, we need also to understand God. Ignore the gospels. They are stuffed with lies implanted by Judaizers trying to implicate Jesus with the God of the Old Testament. But the God of the Old Testament is an inferior God, of doubtful morality, the inadequate creator of this material world. At best, Marcion argued, he is a just God; at worst, warlike, foolish, mean, and contemptible. His religion is beset with irresolvable contradictions. How can the creator of a world filled with demons be a good God? How can Jesus, the new redeeming savior, teaching wonderful new doctrines, be constrained by, predicted by, legitimated by temporary and outdated laws, whose validity his very presence brings to an end? Christ has redeemed us from the curse of the Jewish law. We should be honest and interpret the Old Testament literally. And taken literally, of course, it did not prophesy Jesus as the future Christ. The Old Testament should therefore be rejected by Christians. The God of the Old Testament cannot be, is not worthy to be, the Father of Christ. Indeed the whole idea of God begetting a divine redeemer is disgusting, inappropriate, and unnecessary.[73]

Marcion's solution was simple and radically brilliant. He believed that the inferior God of Creation, and creation generally, have nothing to do with the good God and future salvation, which he first offered through Jesus. This good God, a God to be loved not feared, was unknown before Jesus. God's single act of care for humans was to send Jesus, as an adult made of angelic flesh, to earth as a beneficent savior; Jesus' self-sacrificing death was the price paid for releasing humanity from the clutches of the inferior creator God. Those who believe in the divine mercy of Christ should have confidence in their faith and pursue love by a strict renunciation of the material world and sexuality. The Christian priests at Rome understandably rejected Marcion's revisions to conventional Christianity. So Marcion founded his own church, which flourished for centuries as a separate entity. It was built on one gospel, the gospel of Luke (carefully edited to remove the Judaizing interpolations, which incorrectly referred to the God of the Old Testament as Jesus' Father), and on the ten "genuine" letters of Paul, also duly emended. His followers engagingly conceded that there might be some inconsistencies in Marcionite beliefs and that proof was sometimes difficult, but true Christianity depended only on belief in the crucified Christ and on good works.[74]

Justin, in contrast to Marcion, was determined to preserve the Old Testament as the fundamental legitimator of Christian belief and antiquity. He also etherealized Jesus into a universal creative force. Justin envisaged Jesus as ever-existent Reason (Logos/Word), preexistent with the Father, begotten before all creation.[75] It was Jesus who was with the Father at the time of creation; so when God said, "Let us make man in our image," he was talking to Jesus; and it was Jesus who appeared in the form of an angel to Moses at the burning bush (Exodus 3.14–15). Reason can appear as the Holy Spirit, as the glory of the Lord, as Wisdom, as an angel, and as the Son of God. For example, it was Jesus as prophetic Reason who inspired the prophets of the Old Testament to predict his own coming and crucifixion; and in turn it was these predictions, properly understood, which prove the truth of the Christian revelation. Because of their sins, the Jews failed to understand the true meaning of the predictions, so clearly recorded in their scriptures. It was Jesus, as "seed-sowing Reason," who gave Socrates his inspired but imperfect understanding, and informed Plato, who in turn had plagiarized Moses. At that stage, Jesus' revelation was incomplete; even so, it enabled Justin to consider holy men like Abraham, Moses, and Socrates as Christian. And finally, it was Jesus who, as the Power and Reason of God and Holy Spirit combined, became incarnate in Mary; so according to Justin, Jesus begot himself.[76]

For Justin, Jesus is the Reason of God made human, and as such the prime mediator of Christian revelation. By this characterization, Justin wanted to show that worshiping Jesus does not dilute monotheism. Jesus is part, though only a secondary part, of God. Above all, in an audacious act of intellectual empire building, Justin wanted to subordinate Judaism and pagan philosophy, and incorporate them both into Christian revelation: "Our religion is clearly more sublime than any human teaching because the Christ who has appeared for us represents the principle of Reason in its totality: body, Reason, and soul." Anything which previous philosophers or rulers did correctly was by virtue of the seeds of Reason which they were given. "But they did not know the whole of Reason, which is Christ."[77]

Jesus, for Justin, was the principle of world order, humanity's great revealer and savior. His incarnation, teaching, and death constituted a key stage in God's grand creative plan, an end to the power of demons, who are the Gods of the Romans. Jesus' second coming will herald the bodily resurrection of the just and the eternal punishment of the wicked. Justin acknowledges that in memory of Jesus' incarnation and death, believers seek salvation through weekly worship and the rituals of baptism and eucharist, and by prayer, obedience to the commandments, and mutual help.[78] But his main objective was to show that Christianity was predicted by and had superseded Judaism—though the Old Testament was still vital as proof of Christianity's antiquity and inevitable triumph—and that Christianity was superior to and incorporates pagan philosophy. Christianity is the true philosophy. Jesus' humanity is neglected, or at least etherealized. In pursuit of intellectual respectability and victory, Justin's Christianity had moved upscale, and a long way from the simply expressed central message of the gospels.[79]

The variety of early Jesuses was amazing. So far, I have barely scratched the surface. One breakaway cult in late–second-century Rome, for example, founded by a cobbler, Theodotus, considered that Jesus was just a man. His humanity mattered more than his divinity. The sect's membership must have been significant, because it managed to pay its bishop an (admittedly modest) monthly salary; it is the earliest such arrangement we know about among Christians. Paul, a third-century bishop of Antioch, who had significant local support and made a fortune out of his bishopric, also stressed Jesus' humanity; like Melito, bishop of Sardis, he believed that Jesus was infused with the Holy Spirit only at the time of his baptism. Yet others, also eventually branded heretics, thought that God the Father and Jesus were identical. It was God the Father himself who had put on human flesh and had been crucified. They accused the orthodox of believing in two Gods.[80]

But surely most early Christians cannot have appreciated the sophistics of these theological arguments. Tertullian admitted that simple folk, "who always constitute the majority of believers," found it difficult to accept the orthodoxy of the Trinity. They thought it bordered on the polytheism which they had rejected. Orthodox Christian ideologues fought vigorously against heretical ideas with proof texts and inventive, if incomprehensible, arguments. Bishop Hippolytus, for example, proclaimed:

Yet there is the flesh which was presented by the Father's Reason as an offering—the flesh that came by the Spirit and the Virgin, which was shown to be
the perfect Son of God. It is clear, therefore, that he offered himself to the
Father. Before, there was no flesh in heaven. Who then was in heaven except
Reason incarnate, who was sent to show that he was on earth and also in
heaven? For he was the Word, the Spirit, and the power.[81]

At first sight, it does seem that such abstract arguments, however log-
ically coherent some Christian thinkers managed to make them, must
have bored most parishioners stiff. But in the hierarchies of Roman society, sophisticated language both illustrated and enhanced status. Priests
were not immune from the struggle for social prestige. As the church
grew larger, and especially in the fourth century, when it entered into alliance with the Roman state, sophistication and incomprehensibility
were essential weapons in putting over the Christian message. Church
audiences colluded, I imagine, because they too were part of the public
performance, on show almost as much as the officiating priest. At least
some of them needed to imagine that the priest's elaborate rhetoric convinced them. And in the empire as a whole, theological sophistics created
a symbolic politics, which the Roman state otherwise lacked. Its utility as
a unifying force was enhanced in a poor society by the very fact that passionate discussions about the nature of Jesus and God had no or few material implications for the redistribution of resources. As the bishops in
synod argued interminably, the savant emperors must have smiled.
Christ was the heavenly ruler, and the emperor his glorious representative on earth (plate 12).

But for the vast majority of early Christians, I suspect, what mattered
most was the dramatic narrative of Jesus' passion and resurrection, and
the hopes which that story fostered for their own salvation. Their faith
and commitment were enhanced not by Christological debates, however
involved they occasionally became, nor by the hectic pursuit of alien
heretics, but by the regular round of rituals. What fostered church membership, surely, was the weekly church meetings, whether in private
houses or on the spacious floors of new churches. What gave Christians
a sense of common identity was the hymn singing and prayers, the mor-
alizing sermons explaining half-familiar texts, and the eucharist of bread
and wine for the elect; plus, every year, the humbling initiation of new
Christians through repeated exorcisms and naked baptism.[82] These routine experiences were supplemented by the minor dramas of giving char-

ity to the poor and their visible (if insufficient) gratitude, the outing of the proud in public confessions, and the protracted self-humiliation of the penitent, who were excluded from the congregation of the baptized, sometimes for years. And then there were the major dramas of local persecutions—rumored, threatened, remembered, and commemorated in the annual feasts of the martyrs. For most, *being* a Christian may have mattered even more than believing.

Notes

NHL: Nag Hammadi Library (a fourth-century collection of mostly gnostic texts, written in Coptic). See J. M. Robinson, ed., *The Nag Hammadi Library in English* (Leiden³, 1988).

ONE: *A World Full of Gods*

1. Cicero, *Against Verres* 5.27.

2. The bronze statue is in the Museo Nazionale in Naples. It is conventionally thought to represent Caligula, but the attribution is uncertain. Typically for practical Romans, the arch was also used as a water tower. Clay pipes brought the water down to a public tap at the base. L. Richardson, *Pompeii: An Architectural History* (Baltimore, 1988) 208–9.

3. *Corpus Inscriptionum Latinarum* (hereafter *CIL*) 4.149 and 202 for election posters, and 1265–1365 for other graffiti in Mercury Street.

4. On kissing hands to Gods on passing sacred places or statues see Apuleius, *Apology* 56; Minucius Felix, *Octavius* 2.4.

5. Actually three of them were temples: the Temple of Apollo, the Temple to the Public Lares, and the Temple to the Genius of Augustus (later Vespasian). And in the other buildings, the Market Hall, the Hall of Eumachia, and the basilica, there were statues to Gods and altars at which people could worship. So Martha's general impression seems understandable.

6. *CIL* 10.808–13. On the Eumachia building and in general, see W. Jongman, *The Economy and Society of Pompeii* (Amsterdam, 1988), 179ff.; in general, see A. Mau, *Pompeii, Its Life and Art* (London, 1899), and R. Laurence, *Roman Pompeii* (London, 1994).

7. G. K. Galinsky, *Aeneas, Sicily and Rome* (Princeton, 1969), 32 and plate 30. The serious version of the Aeneas legend is above the shop of Fabius Multitremulus in the main shopping street, the Via dell' Abbondanza.

8. *Bulletin de correspondance hellénique* 110 (1986), 513–30: on Aulus Caprilius Timotheus, *somatemporos* (slave trader). His tombstone depicts eight slaves chained together, followed by two women and two small children. For a grisly portrait of slaves in a bakery, branded on their foreheads, chained by the ankles, backs whipped, and thinly clad in rags, see Apuleius, *Metamorphoses* (hereafter *The Golden Ass*) 9.12.

9. H. Dessau, ed., *Inscriptiones Latinae Selectae* (hereafter *ILS*) (Berlin, 1892), 8726–33, gives examples of bronze tags attached to these iron slave collars; "I have escaped; grab me, bring me back to my master, Zonius, and you'll receive a reward" (*ILS*, 8731).

10. L. Daly, *Aesop Without Morals* (New York, 1961), and *Life of Aesop* 15.

11. A bit of poetic licence from Martha here. The known cookie molds in the shape of emperors, from Britain and the Danubian provinces, date from the second century and

later. See A. Lengyel, ed., *The Archaeology of Roman Pannonia* (Budapest, 1980), 184 and plate 122.

12. L. Jacobelli, *Le pitture erotiche delle terme suburbane di Pompei* (Rome, 1995).

13. In standard works on Roman art, such as D. E. Strong, *Roman Art* (London, 1976), and R. Ling, *Roman Painting* (Cambridge, 1991), Roman erotic art does not exist, or if it does it is disguised as mythology. But see J. P. Hallett, *Roman Sexualities* (Princeton, 1997), for sophisticated discussion and fashionable views, or J. R. Clarke, *Looking at Love-Making in Roman Art* (Berkeley, 1998).

14. These sexual scenes in the suburban baths, just outside the Porta Marina, were themselves whitewashed over in antiquity shortly before the eruption of Vesuvius, and this was the only wall of the changing room repainted. Apparently, the paintings, exceptional in their explicitness and variety, did not appeal to all the baths' owners or customers. So Jacobelli, *Pitture erotiche*, 28 and 78ff.

15. On the baths, see L. Jacobelli, "Die suburbanen Thermen in Pompei," *Archäologisches Korrespondenzblatt* 23 (1993), 327ff. On Roman bathing in general, see I. Nielsen, *Thermae et balnea* (Århus, 1990), esp. 119ff. Jacobelli and Nielsen correctly insist on the normalcy of nakedness in baths for men and women, sometimes separately, but from the early first century CE increasingly together. Cf. Clement, *Paidagogus* 3.32: "The baths are open for men and women; there they strip for lust"; and *The Teachings of the Apostles (Didascalia Apostolorum)* 3 (ed. Connolly, pp. 14–17). And for Christian reactions, A. Berger, *Das Bad in byzantischer Zeit* (Munich, 1982), 34ff. and 148. For Jewish reactions to gods in baths, see the Palestinian Talmud, Avoda Zara 3.8.

16. *Scriptores Historiae Augustae, Elagabalus* 12.2; cf. 5.4 and 8.6; Cassius Dio 80.16.

17. See *CIL* 6.29,848b for the graffito painted in large letters on the outside walls of the baths of Titus, near Trajan's market in Rome. R. Meiggs, *Ostia* (Oxford, 1960), 143.

18. In general, see R. Neudecker, *Die Pracht der Latrine* (Munich, 1994); for an excellent catalogue raisonné, cf. V. M. Strocka, *Die Wandmalerei der Hanghaeuser, Forschungen in Ephesus* 8.1 (Vienna, 1977), 88–89. The painting of Fortuna, with Isis' rudder in her right hand, is in the latrine of a bar at 9.7.21–22 (these conventional numbers give the precise location within Pompeii, by district, block, and room).

19. James and Martha were clearly staying at the inn of Hermes (1.1.6–9). See best James Packer, "Inns at Pompeii," *Cronache pompeiane* 4 (1978), 5ff. In the inn of the Seven Sages at Ostia, seven finely painted philosophers give salutary maxims on constipation: "Thales advised hard shitters to shove hard; shit well and bugger the doctors," *Année épigraphique* (1939), 162.

20. These particular graffiti (*CIL* 4.2146 and 2145) come from an inn (7.12.34–35) which James looked at first but thought too squalid.

21. *CIL* 9.6089 and 11.6728; and N. Purcell, "Literate Games," *Past and Present* 147 (1995), 3ff. On *spintriae*, see J. D. Bateson, "Roman Spintriae," in *E. A. Arslan Studia Dicata* (Milan, 1991), vol. 2, 385ff., or B. Simonetta and R. Riva, *Le tessere erotiche romane* (Lugano, 1981), and J. Ward-Perkins, *Pompeii AD 79* (London, 1976), 239b.

22. Reproduced in Jacobelli, *Pitture erotiche*, 93 (6.10.1).

23. A sculpted sign shaped like a gravestone, from central Italy, advertises an inn's services; the innkeeper is called Lover Boy, and his wife is called Joy; the jokey bill of fare includes food, stabling, and a girl (*CIL* 9.2689). Roman law presumed the sexual accessibility of women serving customers in inns (*Digest* 3.2.4; 23.2.43). Ps. Vergil, *Copa* 1–3: innkeepers' wives "trained to sway their hips to castanets, tipsily dancing lascivious steps in a smoky tavern."

24. These stories were also told by the court doctor Galen (ed. Kuehn: 12.254) and by Augustine, *City of God* 18.18, but they apparently circulated earlier. For the nightmarish story of a cheese merchant, see Chapter Six.

25. We have an account of a journey by a middle-ranking civil servant from Alexandria to Antioch, who lists all the expenses of his slaves buying food to be cooked at each stopping point; see *P. Ryl.* 627–38 (c. 317 CE).

26. What follows is Martha's informal version of Apuleius, *The Golden Ass* 11.21ff. and 6, with special attention to the notes of J. Gwyn Griffiths, *The Isis-Book* (Leiden, 1975), and the exquisite analysis by J. Winkler, *Auctor & Actor* (Berkeley, 1985).

27. See Gwyn Griffiths, *Isis-Book*, 222ff., for commentary on Apuleius, *Metamorphoses* 11.11.The relevant speculations are Clement of Alexandria *(Protreptikos) Exhortation* 2.19.4 (Loeb, pp. 44–47), plus Hippolytus, *Refutation* 5.7.21–22: on the Christian heretic Justin, who believed that the good God was an erect phallus. Griffiths declares firmly that there wasn't a phallus inside the sacred casket, but clearly some ancients thought there was.

28. Apuleius, *The Golden Ass* 11.15.

29. The story is told by Josephus, *Jewish Antiquities* 18.65–80. In Josephus' account, the devotee submits willingly to Anubis' advances; Martha understandably changes the story into one of rape.

30. Josephus, *Jewish War* 7.123–24.

31. These bars were at 6.10.1, 6.14.35–36, and 9.11.2 (Packer, "Inns at Pompeii," 48, 33, and 46).

32. *CIL* 4.3494 and Accademia dei Lincei, *Memorie* 1 (1876), 108; see Jacobelli, *Pitture erotiche*, 74.

33. C. Dionosotti, from "Ausonius' Schooldays," *Journal of Roman Studies* 72 (1982), 104.

34. James is not kidding. Pompeian inns really did serve wine from glass cups and jars (Packer, "Inns at Pompeii," 48, on 9.11.2) and have statues or paintings of gods (5.2.13 and 5.1.13). Cnaeus' account is based on Apuleius, *The Golden Ass* 11.6.

35. Based on Apuleius, *The Golden Ass* 11.23, plus Griffiths, *Isis-Book*, notes *ad loc.*, Dio Chrysostom, *Speeches* 12.33, and Plotinus, *Enneads* 1.6.7. Cf. Plutarch, *On Isis* 3 and 25.

36. This is based on Apuleius, *The Golden Ass* 11.6.

37. *Inscriptiones Graecae* 14.641 and Apuleius, *The Golden Ass* 11.24–25.

38. In Italy, during the first century CE, freed slaves were particularly prominent in the emperor cult; Lares were household Gods. On Poppaea's unpopularity in Rome, see Seneca, *Octavia* 794ff.

39. The best introductions to houses in Pompeii are A. Wallace-Hadrill, *Houses and Society in Pompeii and Herculaneum* (Princeton, 1994), J. R. Clarke, *The Houses of Roman Italy* (Berkeley, 1991), and Richardson, *Pompeii*.

40. The house is therefore known as Casa degli amorini dorati (the House of the Gilded Cupids = 6.16.7–38), on which see best the exemplary monograph of F. Seiler, *Casa degli amorini dorati* (Munich, 1992), which I largely follow here. I am very grateful to Prof. Seiler for showing me round the house. If James and Martha slept there now, they would risk having rainwater pour down over their heads, such is its disrepair. The room next to the dining room is decorated with mildly erotic pictures of pretty girls.

41. Convention has it that Cnaeus Poppaeus Habitus was the owner of this house. Actually the name of the owner is unknown, but I saw no harm in following tradition here, in spite of Seiler's *(Casa degli amorini dorati*, 136) well-based doubts.

42. Seiler, *Casa degli amorini dorati*, 131–33: an inner circle of Gods look inward, while a protective outer circle of Demigods look outward. See also W. F. Jashemski, *The Gardens of Pompeii* (New Rochelle, 1979–93), vol. 1, 32ff.; cf. E. J. Dwyer, *Pompeian Domestic Sculpture* (Rome, 1982), 38ff.

43. The best description of Roman wedding etiquette I have found is H. Blümner, *Die römischen Privataltbertümer* (Munich, 1911), 341ff. A convenient modern summary with literature is S. Treggiari, *Roman Marriage* (Oxford, 1991), 161ff.

44. Apuleius, *Apology* 87: his wife had given 50,000 HS on the occasion of her son's wedding.

45. Festus, ed. Lindsey, 55, s.v. *calibari hasta*, suggests various competing interpretations: just as the spear has been conjoined with the body of the gladiator, so should she be with her husband; or it was a sign that she might give birth to brave men; or by the rites of marriage a wife is subject to the commands of her husband. None seems to make much sense.

46. On the house of the Vettii, see best still A. Mau, "Scavi di Pompei," *Römische Mitteilungen* 11 (1896), 3ff., and A. Sogliano, *Monumenti Antichi* 8 (1898), 234ff., and D. Fredrick, "Beyond the Atrium," *Classical Antiquity* 14 (1985), 266ff.

47. The silver mirror left in the house of the Vettii: see A. Sogliano in *Monumenti Antichi*, 235.The sexy bronze mirror is in the Antiquarium Comunale on the Celio, and admirably discussed by A. Ferrea, "Uno specchio in bronzo," *Bolletino dei musei comunali di Roma* 9 (1995), 133ff. Or see conveniently C. Johns, *Sex or Symbol* (London, 1982), 137, plate 35; cf. 116. I am grateful to Dr. Ferrea for showing me the mirror. For a Christian objection to such self-reflecting erotic pictures, see Clement of Alexandria, *Paidagogus* 3.27.

48. Seneca, *On Benefits* 3.16, and Soranus, *On Gynecology* 2.44 (113): women in Rome have sexual intercourse often, and when drunk, and neglect their children.

49. On pictures of Roman weddings nearly all on sarcophagi, the sacrifice and the joining of right hands by groom and bride, with Concord blessing and Hymen crouching below waist height, see L. Reekmans, "La dextrarum iunctio . . . ," *Bulletin de l'institut historique de Belge* 31 (1958), 23ff. See also I. Scott Ryberg, "Rites of the State Religion in Roman Art," *Memoirs of the American Academy at Rome* (1955), 166 and figure 94.The only surviving Roman painting of a marriage has a large wedding bed at its center, with a seemingly reluctant veiled bride sitting on it, being advised by a seminude Aphrodite; see F. G. J. M. Mueller, *The Aldobrandini Marriage* (Amsterdam, 1994).

50. Romans were quite fond of the connection between pleasure and death. One touching tombstone from a mistress to her dead lover goes: baths, wine, love rot our bodies, but make life; *ILS* 8157. On silver cups, see L. P. B. Stefanelli, *L'argento dei romani* (Rome, 1991), 139 and 157.

51. On libations to the emperor ordered by the senate at private and public banquets in 30 BC, see Dio 51.19.7; they were apparently still in vogue in the sixties CE; see Petronius, *Satyricon* 60.

52. D. A. Russell and N. G. Wilson eds., *Menander Rhetor* (Oxford, 1981) 2.6, gives a model wedding speech.

53. It is difficult to tell which room Martha and James ate in. It could have been either the Ixion or the Theban room; both have pictures showing mythological scenes of punishment and death, of and by the hands of women: Dirce being forced by her stepsons to have sex with a bull as punishment for mistreating their mother; Pentheus the king who banned the Dionysiac cult being torn to bits by his mother, etc. See R. Brilliant, *Visual Narratives* (Ithaca, 1984), 71ff.

54. Of course, I have no idea if she was telling the truth.

55. In the late second century, newly married couples were all expected to say a prayer celebrating the *concordia* of the emperor's family. On the known evolution of the idea, see Reekmans, "La dextrarum iunctio." This married couple were doing it earlier than any previously known couple.

56. On the House of M. Lucretius, see P. Zanker, "Die Villa als Vorbild," *Jahrbuch des deutschen archälogischen Instituts* 9 (1979), 496–97; E. J. Dwyer, *Pompeian Domestic Sculpture* (Rome, 1982), 19ff.

57. He had. See Menander Rhetor 2.7. But thanks to Martha, this is a shortened version.

58. On dedication of toys and girlish clothes to Venus, see Persius 2.70 and Blümner, *Privataltertümer,* 343.

59. Shouting for blood: Augustine, *Confessions* 6.8. Unevenly matched: Ps. Quintilian, *Rhetorical Exercises* 9.6; Crescens: *CIL* 4.4353. Bleeding, shield on ground: V. Spinazzola, *Pompei alla luce degli scavi nuovi* (Rome, 1953), vol. 1, fig. 212. Nemesis: *CIL* 5.3466; she is the Goddess of merciless retribution, but also much worshiped by gladiators, who presumably saw in her other virtues.

60. On the cost of gladiatorial games in a small town, see *CIL* 11.6377, where a donor allots the interest on 600,000 HS to provide games every four years; at 6 percent p.a., this would provide 150,000 HS, probably for four days' fighting. Popidius was providing games for only one day here, but had probably spent the rest of the money on some public building, much needed in Pompeii after the earthquake of 62 CE.

61. For what the whole world wants: *CIL* 4.1184; "pro salute Augusti [Tiberi] sine ulla dilatione": *CIL* 4.1180. Crescens: *CIL* 4.4356. Hercules: *CIL* 4.1513. Celadus = Crowd's Roar: *CIL* 4.4289, 4342. Baby's bottle: Mau, *Pompeii,* 366.

62. Gods in the games: Tertullian, *(On the Games) De spectaculis* 5–6 and 12.7, and Novatian, *De spectaculis* 4: "Idolatry is the mother of all games."

63. Toast: *CIL* 4.7990, cf. 4499. Meals before games: Aulus Gellius, *Attic Nights* 2.24, and *CIL* 10.114. Betting: Ovid, *The Art of Love (Ars Amatoria)* 1.168. Written programmes: *CIL* 4.2508.

64. Scattering tokens: *CIL* 10.5849 (=*ILS* 6269) and 5853.

65. L. Bruit Zaidman and P. Schmitt Pantel, *Religion in the Ancient Greek City* (Cambridge, 1992); although it's about Greek religion, it is amazingly informative and thoughtful about paganism and much of what they think is transferable to Roman religion. The two-volume work of selected sources and analysis by M. Beard, J. A. North, and S. Price, *Religions of Rome* (Cambridge, 1998) is groundbreaking.

TWO: *Jews and Christians,* or, *How the Dead Sea Scrolls Were Found and Lost*

1. On the Jewishness of Jesus, see both G. Vermes, *Jesus the Jew* (London, 1983), and E. P. Sanders, *Jesus and Judaism* (London, 1985); on James, see Acts 15.12; Paul, Galatians 2 and Josephus, *Jewish Antiquities* 20.200.

2. On the Qumran community, see G. Vermes, *The Dead Sea Scrolls in English* (Sheffield[4], 1995); L. H. Schiffman, *Reclaiming the Dead Sea Scrolls* (Philadelphia, 1994); for a stimulating essay on the history of Qumran scholarship, see H. Stegeman, "The Qumran Essenes," in J. Trebolle Barrera, ed., *The Madrid Qumran Congress* (Leiden, 1992), vol. 1, 83–166.

3. The Essenes were a pious Jewish sect scattered throughout Israel. Josephus reports that there were four thousand of them, compared with six thousand Pharisees *(Jewish Antiquities* 18.21 and 17.42). But such figures are notoriously unreliable. See the

excellent summary in E. Schuerer, *The History of the Jewish People in the Age of Jesus Christ* (Edinburgh, 1975), vol. 2, 550ff. The tie between Essenes and Qumranites is disputed by some; see for example, the nice arguments of A. Baumgarten, *The Flourishing of Jewish Sects in the Maccabean Era* (Leiden, 1997), 1ff., and M. Goodman, *Journal of Jewish Studies* 46 (1995), 161ff.

4. The population of the Qumran commune must have fluctuated, but its average size can be estimated from the size of the nearby cemeteries. The main cemetery, only fifty meters from the central buildings, contained 1,100 corpses in regular rows, oriented north/south. All the corpses examined were of adult males, though a handful of female and child corpses have been found in small peripheral cemeteries. A total in all the cemeteries of 1,200 corpses produced over 150 years suggests an average death rate of over eight persons per year, which, at probable mortality levels, would have been produced by 150 adult males. Much depends, of course, on how many entrants left/were expelled before death; we do not know, but if their numbers were negligible, we can imagine an average annual intake and exit of about eight adult males per year. For mortality levels, see A. J. Coale and P. Demeny, *Regional Model Life Tables* (New York², 1983), level West 3. The main assembly hall apparently had a maximum seating capacity of 120–50 persons. See M. Broshi, "The Archaeology of Qumran," in D. Dimant and U. Rappaport, eds., *The Dead Sea Scrolls* (Leiden, 1992), 113–14.

5. See, for example, *The Community Rule*, or *Manual of Discipline* = 1 QS 3.4–6. References to the Dead Sea Scrolls by convention give first the number of the cave, so 1 Q = cave 1 at Qumran, then sometimes a mnemonic letter: 1 QS = *The Community Rule*, 1 QH = *Thanksgiving Hymns*. A section number follows if necessary.

6. For a brief guide to what surviving classical authors wrote about Essenes, see Schuerer, *History of the Jewish People*, vol. 2, 562ff.

7. Isaiah 40.3, cited in 1 QS 8.13–14.

8. See the *Commentary on Habakkuk* = 1 QHp 7, plus 1 QM on end of world.

9. The ancient commentaries often interpret the scriptures and at the same time tie them into the sect's own history: for example, the commentary on Micah 1.5 ("And what is the high place of Judah? Is it not Jerusalem?") runs: "Interpreted this concerns the Teacher of Righteousness who expounded the law to his Council and to all who freely pledged themselves to join the elect of God to keep the Law . . ." (1 Q 14). The Messianic collections are 4 Q 174-.5. See also note 11 below.

10. Catholics keep these books in the canonical Old Testament. Protestants know them as the Old Testament apocrypha. Jubilees, the Wisdom of Ben Sirach (Ecclesiasticus), the Testaments of the Patriarchs, and 1 Enoch also figured largely in what the Qumran sectarians copied, and presumably studied. For these texts, see J. H. Charlesworth, ed., *The Old Testament Pseudepigrapha*, 2 vols. (London, 1983).

11. 4 Q 258 1.10 (men of perfect holiness). Messianic hopes are expressed in the Messianic Rule (1 Q 28a) 2.11ff. and in 1 Q 28b, in *The Blessing of the Prince of the Congregation* (1 Q 28b) 5, as well as in 4 Q 161 and 4 Q 252: "until the Messiah of righteousness comes." N.B. 11 Q 13, which combines Isaiah 52.7 ("How beautiful are the feet of the messenger who proclaims peace") with Daniel 9.25 and Isaiah 61.2 ("until the appearance of one anointed, a prince, who brings good news"). The birth of the Messiah is predicted in 4 Q 534: "His wisdom shall reach all peoples." 4 Q 246 dreams of "The son of God he will be proclaimed and the son of the Most High they will call him." See also note 9 above.

12. 1 QS 6.7 and CD 13.8ff.

13. 1 QS 5.20ff. and 6.13ff.

14. 1 QS 5.1; 8.13; quotations from 1 QS 9.22; 1.2; 4 Q 258 2.7; 1 QS 1.7; and CD 6.20.

15. 1 QS 5.4: "They shall practise truth and humility in common, and justice, uprightness, charity and modesty in all their ways"; and 4.3. For detailed rules: 1 QS 6.25ff. and 4 Q 266 and 270.

16. 1 QS 4 and 8–9.

17. 1 QS 9.4–5: "They shall atone for guilty rebellion and for sins of unfaithfulness that they may obtain loving-kindness . . . without the flesh of holocausts and the fat of sacrifice. Prayer rightly offered shall be an acceptable fragrance of righteousness, and perfection of way a delectable free-will offering."

18. 1 QS 5.6: "Circumcise the foreskin of evil inclination."

19. CD 14.12 for contributions, on which see also Schiffman, *Reclaiming*, 107.

20. 1 QS 3.22–24: "The Angel of Darkness leads all the children of righteousness astray, and until his end, all their sins, iniquities, wickedness . . . are caused by his dominion, in accordance with the mysteries of God." Cf. CD 4.15–18.

21. 4 Q 270: "Whoever has approached his wife, not according to the rules, thus fornicating, he shall leave and not return again."

22. 4 Q 266/270.

23. Josephus (*Jewish War* 2.8) tells us that Essenes expelled from a commune suffered because the expelled thought they had to go on obeying the commune rules which they had sworn; they could not gain a livelihood, so they starved, and were sometimes readmitted on the point of death out of pity. This sounds like a myth, with perhaps a slight base in reality.

24. See 4 Q 266/270 15, and CD 9.

25. Some similar texts to those at Qumran have also been discovered at Masada (Schiffman, *Reclaiming*, 49), which has led some scholars to speculate that a number of Qumran sectarians joined the Zealots in Masada. But then there's also a fragment of Virgil's *Aeneid* at Masada. On mixing with the ejected and on immediate accusations with witness, see 4 Q 266.15, and 1 QS 6.1.

26. The Qumran text which is most hostile to the Romans (called Kittim) is the *Commentary on Habakkuk* (1 Q pHab 3ff.); it also envisages the role of the new Covenanters in God's final vengeance against the unfaithful Jews. For millenarian dreams, see the War Scroll, 1 QM 7.5ff.

27. 4 Q 534.

28. Beggar wrapped in mat, contrasted with the luxury at Rome: see M. Freedman, ed., *Midrash Rabba* (London, 1939), *Genesis Rabba* 33.1; on the destruction of Jerusalem, see, for example, 2 Baruch 5 and 13–14; the quotation is from 2 Baruch 5 and 13.4. Hilary and his family have rejected the rulings of the Law, have forgotten the sabbath, and are following the festivals of the pagans; cf. 4 Q 166–67 and 1 Q 22.

29. For the opinions cited here on Jewish reactions to Rome, see 4 Ezra 11.40ff.; *Genesis Rabba* 1.1.5 and 65.1; *Leviticus Rabba* 13.5; Babylonian Talmud, Pesahim 118b: on Rome's fabulous wealth and power; Abodah Zarah 17b–18a: on being closely cross-questioned by a Roman judge; and *Sybilline Oracles* 5.155ff. There is a general discussion in M. Hadas-Lebel, *Jerusalem contre Rome* (Paris, 1990), and more briefly in the brilliant article by S. Lieberman, "Roman Legal Institutions in Early Rabbinics and in the Acta Martyrum," *Jewish Quarterly Review* 35 (1944), 1ff., and N. de Lange, "Jewish Attitudes to the Roman Empire," in P. D. A. Garnsey, ed., *Imperialism in the Ancient World* (Cambridge, 1978), 255ff.

30. Jerusalem Talmud, Ta'anith 1: "Where is your God? . . . In the city of Rome" (M. Schwab, ed. [Paris, 1933], vol. 6, 144).

31. The words, slightly jumbled (as Hilary heard them), are from 1 QH Hymn 4.

32. The quotations are from the beautiful hymn 1 QH Hymn 22: "I thank thee O Lord, as befits the greatness of thy power . . . thou art a merciful God, pardoning those who repent of their sin." I have tried to convey some sense also of the implicit reciprocity between the faithful and God, and the hope of immortal salvation, for which see also 1 QH Hymns 10 and 17, 4 Q 521, and 11 Q 5 (Apocryphal Psalm 19): "For no worm thanks thee, nor a maggot recounts thy loving-kindness. . . . I belonged to death because of my sins, and my iniquities had sold me to Sheol. But thou didst save me, O Lord, according to the greatness of thy mercies." On curses collectively pronounced in the commune against the wicked and their punishment in hell, see 4 Q 280 and 286–87. On the Army of God and other victorious slogans, see 1 QM 3.

33. Isaac's memory was not quite as good as he thought. The quotations are a jumble of extracts from 1 QS 1 1–11. In fact, if you, dear reader, actually read all that stuff, including this note, congratulations. Quotations from the ancient texts are meant to give the genuine ancient experience. They don't? Well.

34. 4 Q 159.

35. 4 Q 186: according to Qumran lore, Mike's features place him irredeemably in the category of the unsaved: eight parts darkness, and only one part light. When Isaac sees Mike, he automatically shivers.

36. The mythical camera (like sources, according to the historians' charter myth) never lies.

37. The arrival of the TV crew is of course the miracle for which Isaac had been praying, but not expecting. It symbolizes the rediscovery of the Dead Sea Scrolls, which more people read or know about now than ever did in antiquity. My first account of the Dead Sea Scrolls and the Qumran Covenanters was analytically objectivist, the second a fictional narrative. The next three scenes are at different stages of editing, designed to show how the raw material of history is changed by the process of re-presentation (cf. Chapter Eight).

38. Josephus, *Jewish War* 2.123–29, 137, and 148, and 4 Q 169.2.5ff.

39. For Jewish Christian attacks against Roman immorality, see, for example, *Sibylline Oracles* 5.386ff. and Revelation 17. The Babylon of Revelation is commonly interpreted to mean Rome.

40. This is a loose amalgam of ideas in 1 QH 2, CD 1 and 3, 1 QS 9, 4 Q 171, CD B2 and 3.

41. 4 Q 186.

42. Isaac's speech here is a mosaic of fragments from CD 5 and 8, 4 Q 504, and 1 QS1–3.

43. Isaac's anti-Roman and antiauthority speech with visions of God's vengeance is based successively on 1 Q pHab 3 and 7; 4 Q 162, 166–67, 390, and 169.

44. This quotation is from 4 Q Mess. Ar., translated by F. García Martinez, *Qumran and Apocalyptic* (Leiden, 1992), 4.

45. CD 1–2 combined.

46. Quotations are from 1 Q 27, 4 Q 246 and 521; cf. 1 QH Hymn 17: "Bodies gnawed by worms may be raised from the dust."

47. 1 QH Hymn 4, plus 1 QSa = 1 Q28a2: "begotten of God."

48. For the two Messiahs, see 1 QS 9, and 1 QSa = 1 Q28a for the priest Messiah, discussed briefly in Schuerer, *History of the Jewish People*, vol. 2, 550ff. The priests blow the

trumpets of massacre, the enemy are destroyed for ever, the hordes of Satan are vanquished, whereas the elect dwell with the angels in heaven (1 QM 9 and 12): "There shall be eternal deliverance for the company of God, but destruction for all nations of wickedness" (1 QM 15).

49. 1 Q pHab 7; the quotation is from Habakkuk 2.2.

50. For example, Isaac interpreted Psalm 37.20, "Like smoke they shall vanish away," to mean: "The princes of wickedness who have oppressed his holy people shall perish like smoke blown away like the wind" (4 Q 171). And his version of Psalms differed slightly from the canonical version.

51. This story of the origins of evil via angels who exercised their free will is from 1 Enoch, the Book of the Watchers, which recurs often in the Dead Sea Scrolls and in early Christian writings.

52. 1 QH Hymn 7: "Shaking and trembling seize me . . . my heart dissolves like wax before fire. . . . For I remember my sins. . . . But calling to mind . . . the greatness of thy compassion." For the triumph of the poor, see 1 QH Hymn 9; for the new, heavenly Jerusalem, see 4 Q 554–55 and Vermes, *Dead Sea Scrolls*, 324; for the cycle of sin, confession, and repentance, see CD B2 and 1 QH Hymn 22. For God's mercy and loving-kindness, see CD 2 and 4 Q 448: "Great is his mercy to those who glorify him. He redeems the poor from the hands of their oppressors."

53. The quotation (slightly simplified, and with the omission of quotations from the Greek) is from the opening page of the published version of a public lecture given by J. Pelikan, *Christianity and Classical Culture* (New Haven, 1993), 3–4. Professor Pelikan is a distinguished and respected scholar.

54. The quotation is from 4 Q 512; the other texts drawn on are 4 Q 448 and 504, 1 Q 34, and 1 Enoch 93, 94, and 96. 1 Enoch was much copied at Qumran; in fact Qumran provides us with our earliest known texts. Previously, it was known principally from the fifteenth-century Ethiopic version, preserved by Christians, though second-century Christian writers were greatly influenced by it.

55. 1 Enoch 98 and 4 Q 286–87. This powerful passage (1 Enoch 98), from the Epistle of Enoch, blames humans themselves for the invention of sin, and so strongly contradicts the message in the Book of the Watchers (earlier in 1 Enoch) that angels, freely choosing evil instead of good, brought evil to humanity.

56. It's time for confession. I've taken a bit of a liberty with strict chronology, which is bound to get me into trouble with purists. Justin martyr lived in the mid–second century, but Isaac must have died before the end of the first century. Structurally, I think, as Ben explains later, there was probably a consistency as well as evolution in Judaeo-Christian interactions. The quotation is from Justin, *Dialogue with Trypho* 12.

57. Justin, *Dialogue with Trypho* 11. The metaphor of the circumcised heart recurs in ancient Jewish scriptures (Deuteronomy 10.16; Leviticus 26.40; Jeremiah 4.3) but was taken over by Christian writers to imply that only Christians believed in spiritual, as opposed to bodily, purity. Justin puts forward another reason against circumcision of the penis as a sign of grace: its unavailability to women *(Dialogue with Trypho* 18–19, 23, and 43).

58. 4 Q 184.

59. 1 Q pHab 5 and 10; 1 Q 22 and 1 Q pHab 9.9 and 2.

60. Justin, *Dialogue with Trypho* 16–17, 35, 96, and 133.

61. Justin, *Dialogue with Trypho* 31–32.

62. Justin, *Dialogue with Trypho* 29 and 34; some Christians, with misplaced generosity, according to Justin, were too willing to compromise, and considered that the Old Testament belonged to both Jews and Christians. Some of the famous proof texts from the

Old Testament cited by Justin (30–41) have long since become part of Christian self-perception (for example, in Handel's *Messiah)*: "Who is this King of Glory?" (Psalm 24); "My name has been glorified among the gentiles" (Malachi 1.10); "A voice of one crying in the wilderness: prepare the ways of the Lord" (Isaiah 39.8); "Thy king shall come right-eous, bringing salvation, meek and lowly, riding on an ass" (Zechariah 9.9).

63. "I will not grapple with the men of perdition until the day of revenge" (1 QS 10.19); and Justin, *Dialogue with Trypho* 38. Jews outside Qumran were later advised not to discuss religion with Christians; see Justin, *Dialogue with Trypho* 38. For similarly hostile Jewish stories, of how merely hearing a Christian give a pleasing opinion was polluting, see Babylonian Talmud, Aboda Zara 16b and Tosefta, Hullin 2.24; for the story that a rabbi preferred to let his nephew die rather than be cured in the name of Jesus, see Tosefta, Hullin 2.22–23 and Aboda Zara 27b. See D. Boyarin, "Martyrdom and the Making of Christianity and Judaism," *Journal of Early Christian Studies* 6 (1998), 577ff.

64. Justin, *Dialogue with Trypho* 39–40, 64, and 45.

65. Justin, *Dialogue with Trypho* 68 and 49.

66. In the early second century, a new and more literal translation from Hebrew to Greek was made by the Jewish convert Aquila. The motive may have been partly to give Jews a more literal rendering and a rendering different from the Septuagint, which was the third/second-century Greek translation used by Christians. Justin, *Dialogue with Trypho* 71–72, accuses Jews of cutting two other passages (besides Psalm 96) from Esdras and Jeremiah, which do refer to Christ allusively, but which are also apparently Christian interpolations into the Jewish text, not Jewish cuts. Justin also accuses Jews of cutting Jeremiah 11.19, "I was like a lamb brought to the slaughter . . . they were hatching plots against me," at least in some synagogues. The passage is still there in standard Jewish/Christian texts. These arguments reveal how sacred texts in antiquity could be cut, amended, revised, or accusations about cuts made, regardless.

67. Justin, *Dialogue with Trypho* 46–47.

68. Justin, *Dialogue with Trypho* 80 and 35.

69. Justin, *Dialogue with Trypho* 85.

70. Justin, *Dialogue with Trypho* 62–63 and 56.

71. H. Musurillo, ed., *Acts of the Christian Martyrs* (Oxford, 1954), 42ff.: *The Martyr-dom of Justin* B3.

72. This final detail is omitted by our surviving sources, but occurs with a twist in the true history of the Nazi hero Horst Wessel, though omitted also from his official martyrology; see T. Oertel, *Horst Wessel, Untersuchung einer Legende* (Cologne, 1988), 83ff.

73. This modern ending was devised by Tom Noad, who cleverly directed a highly reedited, live performance of these scenes for the Corpus Christi College Classical Society at Cambridge.

74. This final twist is, of course, a version of Origen's generous hope, later thought heretical, that God would eventually give salvation even to the Devil. Presumably, though it is not recorded, the Devil, like Meg, also had his/her own ambitions.

THREE: *The Christian Revolution*

1. Quoted in the wonderful book by W. Hinton, *Fanshen* (New York, 1966), 139. Its publication was long delayed because Hinton's notes were confiscated by U.S. Customs as subversive.

2. Pagan intellectuals in the late second century ridiculed the idea that God would have chosen such an obscure corner of the earth, would have waited so long to act, and still left millions hungry, to be saved only at the end of days (Origen, *Against Celsus* 6.78;

Minucius Felix, *Octavius* 12). Hierocles, a Roman provincial governor and persecutor of Christians in the early fourth century, thought that if Jesus had really been divine, he would have miraculously evaded execution, like the pagan wise man Apollonius of Tyana, who when brought to trial by an angry emperor, simply disappeared (Philostratus, *Life of Apollonius* 8.5, and Lactantius, *Divine Institutes* 5.2–3; cf. Eusebius, *Against the Life of Apollonius of Tyana* 1 and 34–35; Origen, *Against Celsus* 2.68). Some Christians believed that because Jesus was truly divine, that's exactly what he had done instead of being crucified; see *The Second Treatise of the Great Seth* 7.2.55–56 (*NHL*, 365).

3. A modern equivalent might be a new religious sect with an electric chair as its logo. In brutal bad taste? Precisely. Romans once lined the road from Capua to Rome with six thousand crucified rebel slaves. Early Christians made the sign of the cross over their heart or head at critical times of the day, long before they used it as a visible icon of worship (Tertullian, *On the Crown* 3).

4. By revolution I mean here principally a revolution in the sense that Mao implies, such as the Russian and Chinese revolutions. But the term is used conventionally by extension to cover the incomplete revolutions in France and the United States, and metaphorically to cover radical but partial changes, such as the industrial or demographic revolution. See helpfully, T. Skoçpol, *States and Social Revolutions* (Cambridge, 1979), and the brilliant essay by J. Dunn, "Understanding Revolutions," in his *Rethinking Modern Political Theory* (Cambridge, 1985), 68ff.

5. The Christianization of major Roman towns is splendidly illustrated by R. Krautheimer, *Three Christian Capitals* (Berkeley, 1983).

6. I cannot tell how much this nonviolent gradualism is an idealizing mirage, the product of selective and purposeful reportage, especially by fifth-century church historians constructing a trouble-free Christian triumphalism. See P. Brown, *Power and Persuasion in Late Antiquity* (Madison, 1992), and G. Fowden, "Bishops and Temples in the Eastern Roman Empire," *Journal of Theological Studies* 29 (1978), 53ff.

7. Conversion as a blinding flash of revelation is an attractive and romantic trope. But it seems to have taken Constantine longer than his biographer Bishop Eusebius allowed; see his *Life of Constantine* 1.27ff.; but for a different account, see Lactantius, *On the Deaths of Persecutors* 44.The emperor was still issuing coins of the Sun God until 322, and Christian emperors were known as chief priest of pagan cults until 381.What's critical here is not the sincerity or intentions of Constantine personally, but his and his successors' consistently pro-Christian policies. See best still, A. H. M. Jones, *Constantine and the Conversion of Europe* (London, 1965); and on coins, P. Bruun, "The Disappearance of Sol from the Coins of Constantine," *Arctos* 2 (1958), 15ff.

8. C. Pharr, ed., *The Theodosian Code* (Princeton, 1952), 16.10.11 (391 CE); 16.10 contains successive laws against pagan rites. But N.B., there was no effective state mechanism for securing widespread or thorough enforcement of laws.

9. On Christian asceticism, see particularly P. Brown, *The Body and Society* (New York, 1988), S. Elm, *Virgins of God* (Oxford, 1994), V. L. Wimbush, ed., *Ascetic Behavior in Greco-Roman Antiquity* (Minneapolis, 1990), E. A. Clark, *Ascetic Piety and Women's Faith* (Lewiston, 1986). I regret wholeheartedly that I do not deal with Christian asceticism in this book. On bishops' power and the execution of heretics, see the section "The Growth of Episcopal Power" of this chapter.

10. This fundamental aggressiveness in the ancient Christian message is visible in tracts overtly written to persuade pagans. See, for example, the *Apologies* of Justin and Tertullian, or the *Exhortation (Protrepticus)* of Clement of Alexandria.

11. In a huge field, E. P. Sanders, *Paul* (Oxford, 1991), is the best introduction I know.

See also his *Paul and Palestinian Judaism* (London, 1977), K. Stendahl, *Paul Among Jews and Gentiles* (Philadelphia, 1976), G. Theissen, *The Social Setting of Pauline Christianity* (Philadelphia, 1982), and for a Jewish view, A. F. Segal, *Paul the Convert* (New Haven, 1990); for Paul's afterlife, see E. Pagels, *The Gnostic Paul* (Philadelphia, 1975), 157ff.

12. For example, 2 Peter 1.4: "He has granted to us his precious . . . promises, so that through these you may escape from worldly corruption . . . and share in divine nature." Or Clement, *Exhortation* 1.8 (Loeb, p. 22): "The Reason (Logos) of God became human, so that you could learn from a human, how a human could become a God." Cf. the Platonic ideal of "becoming as like a God as possible" through justice and purity, Plato, *Theaetetus* 176b.

13. On confession and penance, see B. Pöschmann, *Penance and the Anointing of the Sick* (London, 1964). On eternal punishment, see for example, the words attributed to Jesus: "If your eye causes you to stumble, tear it out; it is better for you to enter the kingdom of God with one eye, than to be thrown into hell, where the worm (inside) them never dies and the fire is never quenched" (Mark 9.47–48; cf. Matthew 23.33). On Christians as the elect, see, for example, Matthew 22.14: "Many are called, few are chosen," and 1 Peter 1.2: "chosen and destined by God the Father." The idea that Christians were the elect became common in early Christian writings, until it was replaced by the idea that only some Christians were the chosen few.

14. For example, Paul's recapitulation (1 Corinthians 15.3), "Christ died for our sins in accordance with the scriptures, he was buried, raised on the third day," became part of a credal formula, of which there were many versions. The creed was not "finally" formulated until the late fourth century; see J. N. D. Kelly, *Early Christian Creeds* (London[3], 1972), 94, 167ff., 254ff. M. Goodman, *Mission and Conversion* (Oxford, 1994), is not in detail persuasive, but his general point seems plausible, namely that in the aftermath of successive Jewish defeats after 66, Judaism did not have many converts.

15. For the complexities of pagan religious practice, see M. Beard, J. North, and S. Price, *Religions of Rome* (Cambridge, 1998), 2 vols., and Chapters One and Five above, and J. North, "The Development of Religious Pluralism," in J. Lieu, ed., *The Jews Among Pagans and Christians* (London, 1992), 174ff.

16. The rabbinic quotation is from the Babylonian Talmud, Niddah 3b (trans. J. Neusner [Atlanta, 1990], 22, slightly altered). For unity, see Irenaeus, *Against Heresies* 3.3. The term "church" expresses the sense that Christian groups were, like Israel, a unity in spite of geographical separation. Acts 9.31, "So the church throughout all Judaea, Galilee and Samaria had peace and was built up." On false teachers: 2 Corinthians 11.13: "false apostles, disguising themselves as apostles of Christ"; Matthew 24.24: "False messiahs and false prophets will appear, and produce great miracles and wonders, to lead astray possibly even the elect"; Matthew 24.10–12: "Then many will fall away, and they will betray one another, and hate one another. And many false prophets will arise, and lead many astray"; 2 Peter 2.1: "There will be false teachers among you, who will covertly teach destructive heresies."

17. See helpfully W. Meeks, *The Origins of Christian Morality* (New Haven, 1993), and J. D. G. Dunn, *Unity and Diversity in the New Testament* (London[2], 1990). A. Le Boulluec, *La notion d'hérésie* (Paris, 1985), is fundamental.

18. K. Hopkins, "Early Christian Number and its Implications," *Journal of Early Christian Studies* 6 (1998), 185ff., and R. Stark, *The Rise of Early Christianity* (Princeton, 1996). A. von Harnack, *The Expansion of Christianity* (London, 1904), 2 vols., is monumental. W. Meeks, *The First Urban Christians* (New Haven, 1983), describes the social background.

19. Only at the end of the second century did leading Christians write in the sophisticated language of the Roman elite. Of the so-called apologists, surely only Tertullian rates highly as a thinker. Clement and Origen were the first surviving Christian writers to quote numerous pagan sources. Earlier claims that elite Romans became Christian are both sporadic and without firm basis. The Latin word *lautus* means both washed and socially respectable.

20. See Meeks, *First Urban Christians*, 51ff.

21. Hopkins, "Early Christian Number," 207ff., for some speculative reasoning.

22. Tertullian, *Apology* 50; on numbers, Harnack, *Expansion of Christianity*, vol. 2, 248, and Hopkins, "Early Christian Number," 192.We have no idea how few Christian women could read fluently, but their general influence in primitive Christianity is often considered to have been considerable. See, for example, the excellent study by E. A. Castelli, "Gender, Theory and the Rise of Christianity," *Journal of Early Christian Studies* 6 (1998), 227ff.

23. Gifts of money and privileges to the church: Eusebius, *History of the Church* 10.5–7; *Theodosian Code* 16.2; *Book of Pontiffs (Liber Pontificalis)* 34: rich gifts of decorative gold and silver, and rent-producing lands to the church in Italy.

24. Marcion was excommunicated in Rome in 144; see Chapter 8, pp. 328–29, and especially A. von Harnack, *Marcion: The Gospel of the Alien God* (Durham, N.C., 1990), and J. Knox, *Marcion and the New Testament* (Chicago, 1942).

25. For Gnostics, see H. Jonas, *The Gnostic Religion* (Boston, 1958), K. Rudolph, *Gnosis* (Edinburgh, 1983), and G. Filoramo, *A History of Gnosticism* (Oxford, 1990), and Chapter Seven, p. 249ff. Surviving Gnostic texts tend to ignore clerics and bishops, rather than overtly attack them; but Tertullian, *On Modesty* 21, wrote: "This is the church of the Spirit, not a church of bishops," but by then he was (in the eyes of the orthodox) a heretical Montanist.

26. The writings of Justin, from the mid–second century, and a bit later of Irenaeus, bishop of Lyon, and Tertullian (until his deviation into heresy) are a good guide to this orthodoxy. For example, Tertullian, *Against Heretics (De praescriptione haereticorum)* 13: "The rule of faith prescribes the belief that there is only one God . . . the creator of the world, who produced everything out of nothing through his own Word; . . . this Word is called his Son, who under the name of God was seen in various images by the patriarchs, spoke through the prophets, and was at last brought down to earth by the spirit and power of the Father into the Virgin Mary, was made flesh in her womb, and being born of her, came forth as Jesus Christ." For the apostolic succession, church unity, and the rule of faith, see ibidem, 26ff. On the canonical scriptures, Irenaeus, *Against Heresies* 2.35.4ff. Occasionally, these three pillars were supplemented by custom; see Tertullian, *On the Crown* 2–3.

27. The first universal council, of about three hundred bishops from all over the Roman empire, convened by the emperor Constantine, was held at Nicaea in 325. It dealt primarily with orderly promotion and control within the church, as well as with the Arian heresy. There had been smaller, local councils of bishops before that; after Nicaea they became frequent. For the decrees, see A. Hefele, *A History of the Christian Councils* (Edinburgh, 1871), with extracts conveniently in J. Stevenson, *A New Eusebius* (London², 1987), 338ff., cf. 290ff.; and his *Creeds, Councils and Controversies* (London², 1989), passim. P. Garnsey, "Religious Toleration in Classical Antiquity," *Church History* 21 (1984), 1ff., offers a succinct analysis. R. P. C. Hanson, *The Search for the Christian Doctrine of God* (Edinburgh, 1988), is useful but long.

28. On the Jewishness of Jesus, see splendidly G. Vermes, *Jesus the Jew* (London², 1983), E. P. Sanders, *Jesus and Judaism* (London, 1985). For the Jewishness of early Chris-

tians, see J. D. G. Dunn, *The Parting of the Ways* (London, 1991), and J. Daniélou, *The Theology of Jewish Christianity* (London, 1964).

29. For James, see Acts 15; Paul, Galatians 1.18ff., and Josephus, *Jewish Antiquities* 20.200. The acknowledged leadership of James, Jesus' brother, and after his death of Symeon, Jesus' cousin, suggests that Jesus and his family were not simple folk. For Paul's attendance at the temple on his return to Jerusalem after preaching the Christian message, see Acts 21.17ff.

30. Dunn, *Unity and Diversity*, 235ff.; Epiphanius, *Panarion* 29–30 on Nazoreans and Ebionites; cf. A. F. J. Klijn and G. S. Reinink, *Patristic Evidence for Jewish Christian Sects* (Leiden, 1973).

31. W. Horbury, *Jewish Messianism and the Cult of Christ* (London, 1998), with characteristic sophistication. On Judaism in this period, see most helpfully S. J. D. Cohen, *From Maccabees to the Mishnah* (Philadelphia, 1987), M. Simon, *Verus Israel* (Oxford, 1986), C. Heszer, *The Social Structure of the Rabbinic Movement in Roman Palestine* (Tübingen, 1997). The metaphor of the religious marketplace may be misleading. By no means all ancient Jews or pagans went out shopping.

32. This is obviously only a guess. Besides, the categories Jew/Christian were not as mutually exclusive as the committed might wish. But Justin in the mid–second century *(1 Apology* 53) stated that Christians were then more ex-pagans than ex-Jews. There was no mechanism by which he could have known.

33. See, for example, *Shepherd of Hermas*, Vision 1. And for a recording angel, see, for example, Apocalypse of Paul 17.

34. Tertullian, *Apology* 19, and Clement, *Miscellanies (Stromateis)* 1.17.87: "Greek philosophers . . . took from the Hebrew prophets parts of the truth, without fully understanding them, and claimed them as their own"; cf. Justin, *1 Apology* 59, and Tatian, *Oration to the Greeks* 31, cf. 40. Christian apologists treated early Christian history imaginatively. Tertullian, for example, claimed that the emperor Tiberius (14–37 CE) had been informed of and had personally supported the truth of Christ's divinity; he had even proposed it to the Roman senate, which had rejected the emperor's recommendation: "Consult your history books" *(Apology* 5).

35. These points and those in the following paragraph are argued at length by Justin, in his *Dialogue with Trypho*, for which see also Chapter Two above, Scene 3. See also J. Gager, *The Origins of Anti-Semitism* (Oxford, 1985).

36. Ignatius, *Letter to the Ephesians* 19.

37. 1 Clement 1–3, 11–19.

38. Apocalypse of Paul 17.

39. Aristides, *Apology* 15–16; Athenagoras, *Plea* 11–12; Tertullian, *Apology* 39 and 45–46.

40. See, for example, Tertullian, *On the Crown* 3; *Apology* 30–31, 35; and for Christians as God's people, 1 Peter 2.10.

41. Pagan Gods as demons: 1 Timothy 4.1 and Clement of Alexandria, *Exhortation* (Loeb edition), 19: "the bitter slavery of tyrannizing demons"; Tertullian, *Apology* 22–23; Christian women downdressing: 1 Timothy 2.11 and Tertullian, *On Female Dress* 11. On charity: "You buy immortality with money, and exchange mundane perishables for eternity in heaven," so Clement of Alexandria, *Can the Rich Be Saved?* 32, on which see L. W. Countryman, *The Rich Christian in the Church of the Early Empire* (New York, 1980). On social inversion: 1 Timothy 6.17.

42. On inspiration, see 1 Corinthians 12 and 14.2; see in general H. von Campenhausen, *Ecclesiastical Authority and Spiritual Authority in the Church of the First Three Cen-*

turies (London, 1969); beggar missionaries and the quotation: *Teaching of the Apostles (Didache)* 13; in general, G. Theissen, *The Social Setting of Pauline Christianity* (Edinburgh, 1982), 28ff. and 40ff. On baptism: Romans 6.3 and G. W. H. Lampe, *The Seal of the Spirit* (London, 1951).

43. The concepts hypocrisy and ambivalence were tactically valuable, since they allowed preachers to criticize, sow doubt in, and demand more, even/especially from those who presented themselves as committed, virtuous, or charitable; see, for example, *Shepherd of Hermas*, Commandment 9, and John Chrysostom, *Homilies on Philippians* 15.3: "It is not by money that immortality can be bought, but by the state of [the giver's] mind, which the money exhibits." For the two-day rule, *Teaching of the Apostles (Didache)* 11.7–12: "No prophet who orders a dinner when inspired shall eat of it." Gnostics (see Chapter Seven) even hypostasized the church into the spiritual cosmos; it preexisted the creation, just as Jesus was eternal Reason (the Word); but see also *2 Clement* 14: "the first church, the spiritual church constructed before the sun and moon . . . the living church is the body of Christ"; cf. *Shepherd of Hermas*, Parable 18.

44. Sins as communal possessions: see, for example, *Doctrine of the Apostles (Didascalia Apostolorum)* 5–6 (trans. Connolly, pp. 40 and 50ff.): Sinners should be too ashamed to enter the congregation, or should weep visibly so that the other sinners would fear for their own eternal damnation. But penitents after fasting and publicly pleading for two to seven weeks could be readmitted. Quotation from Tertullian, *On Repentance* 9.General amnesty imminent: *Shepherd of Hermas*, Vision 2.2. For multiple baptisms and forgiveness, see (not perhaps reliably) Epiphanius, *Panarion* 42.3.6.

45. The repeated stress in early Christian tracts on believers' obedience and on their being children is quite striking. See for example, Ephesians 5.1: "Be imitators of God, as beloved children"; 1 Peter 2.2: "Like newborn babes, long for the pure, spiritual milk"; or 1 John 2.1: "My little children, I write this to you so that you may not sin"; *1 Clement* 63: "We should bow the neck and adopt an attitude of obedience."

46. The list of vices is part of the routine characterization of Roman culture by Christians, and of pagan culture by Jews. Pagan moral teachers themselves had similar stock lists. In general, see W. Meeks, *The Moral World of the First Christians* (London, 1987).

47. For example, James 5.16: "Confess your sins to one another, and pray for one another"; 2.14–18: "What benefit is it, if someone claims to have faith but not deeds? Can faith save? . . . Faith without (charitable) deeds is sterile. But if someone says, 'I have faith, you do deeds'; then show me your faith without deeds, and I by my actions will show you my faith." James beats Paul.

48. *Shepherd of Hermas*, Vision 1.1. The Shepherd's final test of virtue was to spend a night praying chastely with beautiful naked virgins, and then once proved, he lived with them in virtue (Parables 9.11 and 10.3–4). Monk: B. Ward, *The Wisdom of the Desert Fathers* (London, 1986), Saying 22.

49. For "Kneel, pray, repent, confess," see, for example, James 5.16, *1 Clement* 54, *Shepherd of Hermas*, Vision 1.1, and *Exegesis on the Soul* 2.6.135 *(NHL*, 196). For other slogans, see Dunn, *Unity and Diversity*, 33ff.

50. Cf. Gospel of Thomas, Sayings 54 and 69b, which preserve what may be an earlier version. Luke's text was changed in several manuscripts to conform with Matthew's reformulation; see B. and K. Aland, eds., *Novum Testamentum Graece* (Stuttgart[26], 1993); Origen, *Against Celsus* 7.23, considered that Jesus meant not simply the rich, but those rich in lying thoughts! But see *Shepherd of Hermas*, Vision 1.1.8–9.

51. The stylistic simplicity of the gospels was itself a Christian commonplace, though Matthew and John are in fact sophisticated compositions, and Paul is idiosyncratically inimitable. From the mid–second century, many/most surviving Christian writers were more keen to show their sophistication than populist readability. Martyr Acts, saints' lives, and sayings of monks represent the populist fringe, but N.B. even so, well less than 10 percent of adult males (even fewer females) in the Roman empire could have read them.

52. This is my résumé of Ignatius, *Letter to the Ephesians*, with fragments from *Magnesians* 6, *Trallians* 4 and 9, *Romans* 4 and 7, *Smyrnaeans* 6–7.

53. John's gospel, for example, was attacked as spurious and as heretical, partly perhaps because it had been favored by the Gnostic Valentinians in the second century. See Eusebius, *History of the Church* 3.39.17 and 6.22.

54. I follow H. von Campenhausen, *The Formation of the Christian Bible* (London, 1972), and H. Koester, *Ancient Christian Gospels* (London, 1990). See also on oral tradition, 2 John 1.12; and Eusebius, *History of the Church* 3.39, citing Papias (c. 130): "To me writings seem of less value than what began as and remains living speech." And on the supreme authority of the Old Testament, Ignatius, *Letter to the Philadelphians* 8: (his opponents said) "If I do not find it in the ancient writings, I do not trust the gospel, and when I said: It is written, they replied: That is the question." The baronial bishop had disputative clients.

55. M. Smith, *Clement of Alexandria and a Secret Gospel of Mark* (Cambridge, Mass., 1973). Marcion's liking for Paul temporarily diminished his reputation among some of the orthodox. On Tatian, see conveniently W. L. Petersen in Koester, *Ancient Christian Gospels*, 403ff., or T. Baarda, *Essays on the Diatessaron* (Kampen, 1994), 29ff.

56. Irenaeus, *Against Heresies* 3.1–4; the quotation is from 3.3.

57. Irenaeus, *Against Heresies* 3.1–4; Tertullian, *Against Heretics (De praescriptione haereticorum)* 32ff. For truth, see *On the Veiling of Virgins* 1: "This observance is demanded by truth." For scathing criticism of bishops' inadequacy, see Tertullian, *On Modesty* 21: "a church of the spirit, not a church of bishops." A. Brent, *Hippolytus and the Roman Church in the Third Century* (Leiden, 1995), 398ff., has argued persuasively that the Christian churches in Rome even at the beginning of the third century were governed by separate parish priests, none of whom had episcopal control of the entirety. So too in Alexandria, until much later. Eusebius, and many modern church historians, retrojected fourth-century episcopal powers into the second century or further.

58. Tertullian, *On the Veiling of Virgins* 1. Of course, it might be that Tertullian's apparent orthodoxy is exactly the best disguise for a heretic.

59. The so-called Nicene creed still used widely by Christians in the liturgy was actually devised not at the Council of Nicaea in 325 but at the Council of Constantinople of 381. It begins: "We believe in one God, the Father Almighty, maker of heaven and earth, of all things visible and invisible, and in one Lord Jesus Christ, the only begotten Son of God, begotten from the Father before all ages, light from light, true God from true God. . . ." See Kelly, *Early Christian Creeds*, 215ff. Independently of meaning, believers presumably gain a ritual pleasure from the incantation of such familiar but mysterious words.

60. This is my drastic abbreviation of Irenaeus, *Demonstration of the Apostolic Preaching*, trans. J. A. Robinson (London, 1920). The original runs to some eighty smallish pages, roughly half of which are given over to a history of the Jewish people and Old Testament proof texts, predicting Jesus' coming, divine status, and suffering.

61. Tertullian, *Against Heretics (De praescriptione haereticorum)* 7. In general, on Chris-

tian acculturation, see P. Brown's brilliant *Power and Persuasion* (Madison, 1992), and J. Pelikan, *The Christian Tradition* (Chicago, 1971), vol. 1.

62. Eusebius quoted by Theodoret, *Church History* 1.12; see R. P. C. Hanson, *The Search for the Christian Doctrine of God* (Edinburgh, 1988), 165. See also for background R. Williams, *Arius* (London, 1987); F. M. Young, *From Nicaea to Chalcedon* (London, 1983).

63. The first two questions were central to the initial Arian controversy. The third, about the father's cosuffering with the son, was initially posed by Patripassians, and was still a live issue in the fourth century; cf. M. Vinzent, *Asterius von Kappadokien* (Leiden, 1993), 158, and frags. 5 and 76.The fourth is from Eudoxius, *Rule of Faith* (ed. Hahn) 261. For background, see best R. Williams, *Arius* (London, 1987), 48ff. The extract from the Sirmian creed is from Athanasius, *On Synods* 8, and Socrates, *Church History* 2.37.

64. Just as Conservative and Labor in England, Democrats and Republicans in the United States are united by opposition; they need each other to provide a spectacle of opposition.

65. N. B. McLynn, *Ambrose of Milan* (Berkeley, 1994), 315ff. The Arian emperor Constantius exiled both Athanasius, bishop of Alexandria, and Lucifer, bishop of Cagliari in Sardinia. Both objected vitriolically in pamphlets. Athanasius denied that the emperor had the right to judge bishops *(History of the Arians* 52.3), and Lucifer, *On Not Sparing* 33 (p. 255), imagined looking down from heaven at the sufferings of the emperor in hell. For Constantius' insistence, see Athanasius, *History of the Arians* 33; cf. Lucifer, *On Not Making Agreements with Heretics* 3 (p. 170): (the emperor said): "I desire peace in my empire."

66. This is a bold statement, which is difficult to justify in detail. On Constantine's considerable gifts to the church at Rome, see *Book of Pontiffs (Liber Pontificalis)* 34. His gifts of a silver canopy and silver statues weighed more than one tonne, plus over three hundred kilograms of gold. On transferring money from pagan temples, see Anon., *On Matters of War* 2.1; Eusebius, *Life of Constantine* 3.54; Sozomen, *Church History* 2.5; Socrates, *Church History* 1.3. But how could the ample gold coinage of the fourth century have been floated and the new capital, Constantinople, founded without raiding temple treasures? See also the excellent discussion by D. Metzler, "Die Enteignung der heidnischen Tempel seit Konstantin," *Hephaistos* 3 (1981), 27ff.

67. The standard work is W. H. C. Frend, *Martyrdom and Persecution in the Early Church* (Oxford, 1965), which is long and learned, but credulous. A. J. Droge and J. D. Tabor, *A Noble Death* (San Francisco, 1991), is a useful introduction; the discussion by R. Lane Fox, *Pagans and Christians* (New York, 1986), 419ff., is rich in examples, though he trusts ancient sources more than I think sensible.

68. On Jews dying for their religion, see Josephus, *Jewish War,* passim, and for example, 1.148 and 4.315, plus 2 and 4 Maccabees and the Ascension of Isaiah for martyr glorification. G. W. Bowersock, *Martyrdom and Rome* (Cambridge, 1995), 1ff., argues interestingly (but too forcefully, I think) for the Christian invention of martyrdom in the second century.

69. For the Edict of Milan, see Lactantius, *On the Deaths of Persecutors* 48: "Our objective is to grant to Christians and all others full permission to pursue whatever worship each person wishes." Among Constantine's successors, only Julian (361–63) was pagan.

70. The conversion of the Indian king Misdaeus, by the dust of the martyred Judas Thomas (his bones had been removed by pious Christians) and his ghost, forms the grand finale of the Acts of Thomas 170 (see also Chapter Four). Tertullian, *Apology* 39: "We pray for the emperors, for their ministers and those in authority, for the preservation of society and for peace."

71. Tertullian, *To Scapula* 2.2; cf. *Apology* 24; Justin, *1 Apology* 10.4, and 57.4; *2 Apology* 1.2; Tertullian, *Apology* 27 and 30.

72. Martyrs direct to heaven: Cyprian, *On the Unity of the Church* 14; *Letters* 55.17 and 58.3.

73. The standard and very convenient collection of so-called historical Martyr Acts is H. Musurillo, ed., *Acts of the Christian Martyrs* (Oxford, 1972). His selection is based on the fiction that fictional accounts lack historical value. Female martyrs are rarer than male martyrs, with some striking exceptions; see a bit idealistically, B. Shaw, "The Passion of Perpetua," *Past and Present* 139 (1993), 3ff.

74. K. Parlasca, *Repertorio d'arte dell Egitto greco-romano* (Palermo, 1969–70), 2 vols., reproduces nearly five hundred mummy portraits; for a brief introduction, A. F. Shore, *Portrait Painting from Roman Egypt* (London, 1972).

75. G. A. Bisbee, *Pre-Decian Acts of the Martyrs and Commentarii* (Philadelphia, 1989), is completely persuasive on the differences between Martyr Acts and trial records. That said, some Martyr Acts do a better job of disguise than others, and of course some claim to be verbatim copies of court records; see, for example, E. A. E. Reymond and J. W. B. Barns, eds., *Four Martyrdoms from the Pierpoint Morgan Coptic Codices* (Oxford, 1973), 220–22.

76. H. Musurillo, *Acts of the Christian Martyrs*, 2ff.; *Martyrdom of Polycarp* 1–3.

77. *Martyrdom of Polycarp* 5 and 8.

78. Polycarp, *Letter to the Philippians* 12, prays for the saints, emperors, persecutors, and enemies. Extraordinary. Herod and entrance: *Martyrdom of Polycarp* 6–8.

79. Tosefta, Hullin 2.24; discussed by J. Neusner, *Eliezer ben Hyrcanus* (Leiden, 1973), vol. 1, 401ff., and D. Boyarin, "Martyrdom and the Making of Christianity and Judaism," *Journal of Early Christian Studies* 6 (1998), 577ff. A similar joke is recorded in the trial of the pagan hero Apollonius; Philostratus, *Life of Apollonius of Tyana* 8.4.

80. *Martyrdom of Polycarp* 9–15; the prayer is ibidem 14. The only crucified corpse so far discovered in Palestine was nailed at the heels, but had his arms tied over the crosspiece, as a prolongation of torture. See J. Zias and F. Sekeles, "The Crucified Man from Givát ha Mivtar,—A Reappraisal," *Israel Exploration Journal* 35 (1985), 22ff.

81. *Martyrdom of Polycarp* 6; cf. Eusebius, *History of the Church* 4.15.4, and Musurillo, ed., *Acts of the Christian Martyrs* 15.

82. *Martyrdom of Polycarp* 17.This reads like a later interpolation about the cult of martyrs' relics. But if it is genuine, it is interesting that sacralizing the remains of martyrs' corpses began in the second century. In general, see the innovative book by P. Brown, *The Cult of the Saints* (London, 1981).

83. *Martyrdom of Polycarp* 22–23.

84. There is a whole series of pagan, often anti-Jewish, and always anti-Roman pamphlets from the late second century (though some are set earlier) which describe outrageous and scurrilous confrontations between Greek civic leaders from Alexandrian and Roman emperors. See H. Musurillo, ed., *Acts of the Pagan Martyrs* (Oxford, 1954).

85. What follows is my abbreviation of *The Martyrdom of Anatolius the Persian* in I. Balestri and H. Hyvernat, eds., *Scriptores Coptici, Acta Martyrum* (Paris, 1908), 24–29.

86. Cf. *The Martyrdom of Paese and Thecla* in Reymond and Barns, *Four Martyrdoms*, 179. Some of these Christian stories empowered women to rebel, and to act openly, like men. Their faith enabled them to step outside the normal roles of demure modesty and silence, and allowed them, required them even, to confront male power holders with their powerlessness. The affront to legitimate authority was all the starker because it was delivered in public by a woman. "She stood with great fortitude in the presence of the gover-

nor and said to him: 'These are your tortures; the Lord Jesus Christ shames you and your lawless emperor too.' " The governor was outraged at his public humiliation, but when he got home after a hard day of ineffectual torturing, and in a bilious temper, his wife unhelpfully asked why he was not eating and expressed sympathy for the Christians (ibidem 173–79).

87. Clement of Alexandria, *Miscellanies (Stromateis)* 4.26.165.

88. Clement of Alexandria, *Stromateis* 4.4.17 and 2.2.104; cf. Tertullian, *Against Valentinians* 30.

89. Crowds of pagans: Cyprian, *On the Lapsed* 8; many Christians recanted, ibid. 7–9, *Letter* 11.1; whole communities: Cyprian, *Letter* 55.11; apostasy of bishops, cursing Christ: Cyprian, *Letters* 67.6 and 65.1, *Acts of Pionius* 15–16. Conditions in prison: Cyprian, *Letter* 22. Several dozen certificates of sacrifice survive from Roman Egypt, but we simply do not know how widespread registration was in other provinces; see J. H. Knipfing, "The Libelli of the Decian Persecution," *Harvard Theological Review* 16 (1923), 345ff. On jeering at Christians: Tertullian, *On the Garland (De Corona)* 1.

90. For one version of the debate, see Tertullian, *On Flight*; jump: Tertullian, *To Scapula* 5; avoid confrontation: Cyprian, *Letter* 20.

91. The quotation is from Cyprian, *Letter* 20.2. On martyrs' and confessors' capacity to forgive, see the condescending letters by confessors included in Cyprian's correspondence as *Letters* 22–23.

92. The startling non sequiturs in this paragraph reflect the arguments (or my reading) of Christian apologetics. See, for example, at greater length: Tertullian, *On Flight*, passim, *On the Garland* 12.5, *To Scapula* 1–5, *On the Games* 1; and Cyprian, *On the Lapsed* 6, and *Letter* 11. The quotation is from Ignatius, *Romans* 4. The ideals preserved for posterity by monkish scribes presumably influenced rigorists and their rhetoric for centuries.

93. Excuse for flight, Cyprian, *Letters* 5–6, 20, and 43, best consulted with the extremely helpful commentary by G. W. Clarke, *The Letters of St. Cyprian of Carthage* (New York, 1984–89), 4 vols; on the clergy's reaction: *Letters* 8–9.

94. Drunk, adulterous confessors: Cyprian, *Letter* 11.1; *On the Lapsed* 16; *On Unity* 20. If the lapsed were genuinely repentant, they should get martyred; so Cyprian, *Letter* 19.2; for delay and collective decision, *Letter* 19.1–2; divine visions: *Letter* 15.3. Quotations are from Cyprian, *Letters* 43.5 and 2.

95. Proper procedures: Cyprian, *Letter* 15.3. Fine differences, *Letter* 30.3. Penance: "shudder together in sackcloth and ashes," "Groan, lament, pray, kneel," so Tertullian, *On Modesty* 5; and Cyprian, *Letter* 19.1: penance makes the faithful "meek, patient and obedient to the bishops of God."

96. Baptism and unforgivable sins: Hebrews 10.26; 1 John 5.16; but some priests wrongly forgive them, so Origen, *On Prayer* 17. On early baptism, disagreeing: Tertullian, *On Baptism* 18; Cyprian, *Letter* 64.2. Chastity as requirement: R. Murray, *Symbols of Church and Kingdom* (London, 1975), 11ff.

97. *Shepherd of Hermas*, Vision 2.2. Vituperatively indignant Tertullian, *On Modesty* 1.6ff., and Hippolytus, *Refutation* 9.12.20ff., ably discussed by A. Brent, *Hippolytus and the Roman Church in the Third Century* (Leiden, 1995), 501ff.

98. Tough talk: Cyprian, *Letter* 30.2. His two retrospective tracts, *On the Unity of the Church* and *On the Lapsed*, written immediately after the persecution of 250–51, are particularly important. The encouragement to give money is quite forceful at the end of each tract: *On Unity* 26, *On the Lapsed* 35.

99. There is something crudely reductionist about this argument. But by my reading

of Cyprian's *On the Unity of the Church* and *On the Lapsed*, it is justified. See too, Clement, *Will the Rich be Saved?* and especially Countryman, *Rich Christian* 47ff.

100. Julian, *Letter* 49 (quoted in Sozomen, *Church History* 5.16), thought his restoration of paganism would not succeed unless pagan priests imitated Christians in their considerable generosity to the poor and in their overt piety. On increasing church wealth, see D. Janes, *God and Gold in Late Antiquity* (Cambridge, 1998), Jerome, *Letter* 22.32.

101. Cyprian, *Letters* 43.5; 66.1; cf. 3.3.

102. On visions see Cyprian, *Letters* 11.4–5, 16.4, and 66.10: "The revelation made to me, or to put it better, what the Lord God has enjoined on his obedient and fearful slave." Ignatius' repeated insistence on the closeness of a bishop to God ("Obey your bishop so that God may heed you"; *To Polycarp* 6), if really an early–second-century view, which is disputed, stands out as necessarily exceptional. Consider the maverick independence of Paul of Samosata, bishop of Antioch in the late third century; he was eventually deposed by a gang of local bishops, allegedly with the emperor's help (Eusebius, *History of the Church* 7.27ff.). Is this evidence of individual, or collective, episcopal power? Both. Donatists: Optatus, *Against the Donatists* 1.16–19.

103. On councils of bishops, see, for example, Cyprian, *Letters* 55, 64, and 72. The first reports the discussion and decisions of two councils of bishops, held in north Africa and Italy, immediately after the end of the Decian persecutions. But his correspondent, probably a north African bishop, clearly thinks of himself as having the right of independent judgment. Cyprian puts the squeeze, while in another context *(Letter* 72.3), when writing to the bishop of Rome, he proclaims exactly the same episcopal independence: "Every appointed leader has in his government of the church the freedom to exercise his own will and judgment." *Letter* 64 simply reports the decision of sixty-six north African bishops who met probably in 252. This battle between individual power and collectivism persisted.

104. P. Brown, *The Cult of the Saints* (London, 1981), analyzes the evolution of the martyr rites. On the beginnings of Donatism: Optatus, *Against the Donatists* 1.16; on Christian repression of drunken feasts for the dead, see, for example, Augustine, *Letter* 22.6: "Fleshly and ignorant folk actually believe that their drinking and feasting in the cemeteries honors the martyrs." Cf. F. van der Meer, *Augustine the Bishop* (London, 1961), 498ff.

105. H. Lietzmann, *Die drei ältesten Martyrologien* (Bonn, 1903), 1–16; a third martyr list from Carthage, dated to the early sixth century, has only seventy-eight martyr days in the year; there must have been regional variation. J. Toynbee and J. Ward Perkins, *The Shrine of St. Peter* (London, 1956), 135ff. In general, Krautheimer, *Three Christian Capitals*.

106. On this transition, see helpfully R. A. Markus, *The End of Ancient Christianity* (Cambridge, 1990), and P. Chuvin, *A Chronicle of the Last Pagans* (Cambridge, Mass., 1990), and more formally, A. H. M. Jones, *The Later Roman Empire* (Oxford, 1964), 873ff.

107. R. MacMullen, "Judicial Savagery," in his *Changes in the Roman Empire* (Princeton, 1990), 212–13. But N.B., there are grounds for caution: twice as much evidence survives from the fourth century as from the four previous centuries; there is a danger of regarding what is first attested in the fourth century as happening then for the first time. Childlessness: *Theodosian Code* 8.16 (320); divorce: *Theodosian Code* 3.16.1 (331 CE).

108. *Canons of the Council of Nicaea* 1–11 (Hefele, 1871: vol. 1, 375ff.).

109. *Canons of the Council of Nicaea* (Hefele, 1871: vol. 1, 375–435.).

110. *Canons of the Council of Elvira* 1–5 (Hefele, 1871: vol. 1, 138–40.).

111. *Synodal Letter* and *Canons of the Council of Gangra* 1–10 (Hefele, 1871: vol. 2, 325.).

112. See the innovative discussion by J. R. Elsner, *Imperial Rome and Christian Triumph* (Oxford, 1998), on the fusion of classical traditions in Christian art. On the destruction of pagan temples, see Fowden, "Bishops and Temples in the Eastern Roman Empire," *Journal of Theological Studies* 29 (1978).

113. The quivering sensitivities of Augustine in his *Confessions* constitute a radical breakthrough within European culture in the art of self-examination.

114. R. MacMullen, *Christianizing the Roman Empire* (New Haven, 1984), presents a sensibly skeptical view. The classic work of A. D. Nock, *Conversion* (Oxford, 1933), sets the classical background admirably.

115. The prime source here is S. Vanderlinden, ed., "Revelatio sancti Stephani," *Revue des études byzantines* 4 (1946), 191ff., recension B; see also Orosius, *Liber apologeticus* 3–6. An excellent account is given in S. Bradbury, ed., *Severus of Minorca* (Oxford, 1996), whose letter is the main source for the next paragraphs. The quotation in the next paragraph is from Severus, *Letter* 5.

116. D. W. Johnson, ed., *A Panegyric on Macarius, Bishop of Tkow* (Louvain, 1980), 5.

117. At least that is the image promoted in the texts. P. Rousseau, *Basil of Caesarea* (Berkeley, 1994), 140ff. and 170ff.

118. Perhaps I've ended on too optimistic a note. Christian leaders also preached against simple pleasures. According to Gregory Nazianzen, bishop of Constantinople in the late fourth century, Christmas should be celebrated without dancing, without music, without wines, fine cooking, luxuries, or sex. But then, perhaps no more Christians listened to the condemnation of pleasure than to the benefits of virtue *(Oration* 38.5).

FOUR: *Jesus and His Twin Brother*

1. For this argument, see R. Gordon, "Reality, Evocation and Boundary in the Mysteries of Mithras," *Journal of Mithraic Studies* 3 (1980), 19–23.

2. Christian storytellers or myth makers were not necessarily conscious of their transgressiveness (though their former coreligionists probably objected swiftly and powerfully enough). Rather, I suspect, by believing that they were the righteous bearers of the true faith, they hid their transgressions against tradition from themselves.

3. Other movements in first-century Palestine, for example, were the Essenes, the followers of Judas of Galilee, of Theudas, and of Dositheus, who also claimed to be the Messiah and the Son of God. His followers two centuries later were still reading books Dositheus wrote, and claimed that he was immortal. See Origen, *Against Celsus* 1.57 and 6.11, and *Commentary on John* 13.27. Christianity gained advantage perhaps by telling Jewish-style stories without requiring rigorous obedience to the Jewish Law.

4. Acts of John 97–8.

5. Acts of John 99.

6. The quotation is from the Apocalypse of Peter 7.81.4 *(NHL*, 377). The other account is the Second Treatise of the Great Seth 55–6 *(NHL*, 365), of which I think this is the most convincing interpretation. But it is possible to argue that here too the story is making a distinction between the real, spiritual Jesus and the lesser, bodily Jesus: "For my death, which they think happened, happened to them in their ignorance and blindness. They punished me. It was another, their father, who drank the gall and the vinegar; it was not I. They struck me with the reed; it was another, Simon, who bore the cross on his shoulder" (p. 365).

7. Clement of Alexandria, *Paidagogus* 3.29; cf. Basil, *Letter* 22: Christians ought not

to laugh or even to tolerate those who aroused laughter; discussed by S. Goldhill, *Foucault's Virginity* (Cambridge, 1995), 111. See also, M. Douglas, *Implicit Meanings* (London, 1975), 90ff.

8. By myths here I mean a set of stories which unbelievers regard as intrinsically improbable but which believers believe to be true, and to which they repeatedly refer as a standard for ethical or political prescription. I follow here the arguments of E. Leach, *Genesis as Myth* (London, 1969), 7–23.

9. Acts of John 88–89; and for a similar transformation, see the Secret Gospel (Apocryphon) of John 2.1.1 (*NHL*, 105), and of course the transfiguration in the canonical gospels: Matthew 17.1ff. and parallels.

10. One message here, of course, might be: Do not put your trust in outward appearances. It is the internal state of the soul which matters more. In Luke 8.9, Jesus is reported as saying that he talks in parables *in order that* others (nondisciples) may hear and not understand. On which see the brilliant essay by F. Kermode, "Why are Narratives Obscure?" in *The Genesis of Secrecy* (Cambridge, Mass., 1979), 23ff. The quotation from the Gospel of Thomas is Saying 2 in *NHL*, 126.

11. I have blended the translations of J. H. Charlesworth, ed., *The Old Testament Pseudepigrapha* (London, 1983), vol. 2., 752, with that of H. J. W. Drijvers, *East of Antioch* (London, 1984), 339–40. Drijvers convincingly dates the Odes of Solomon to the early third century as against Charlesworth's and others' date of the early second century.

12. Secret Book (Apocryphon) of John 2.1.2 (*NHL*, 105). Some of the early surviving pictures of Jesus surprisingly display a similar ambiguity of gender; Jesus is shown as bearded, as beardless, and sometimes as suggestively feminine, with the distinct suggestion of having female breasts. In the fifth-century Arian baptistery at Ravenna, Christ is portrayed naked, with penis and, according to T. F. Mathews, *The Clash of Gods* (Princeton, 1993), 133, with female breasts. But few will share his interpretation. And in any case, early depictions of Jesus are rare. Some leading Christians objected to any representation, since it smacked of pagan idol worship. The Acts of John explicitly object to pictorial representation (26ff.), and were used as proof texts by the iconoclasts in the eighth century; when the iconoclasts were defeated, the whole work was condemned as heresy. The arguments of Mathews, *Clash of Gods*, 117ff., are an interesting introduction to the topic, though overcommitted to a single view.

13. There are two recent editions of the Acts of Andrew: J. M. Prieur, *Acta Andreae, Corpus Christianorum Series Apocryphorum* 5 and 6 (Turnhout, 1989), and D. R. MacDonald, *The Acts of Andrew and the Acts of Andrew and Matthias in the City of the Cannibals* [=*AAMt*] (Atlanta, 1990). One basic difference between them is that MacDonald includes, whereas Prieur omits, the Acts of Andrew and Matthew, which describe a trip to the land of the cannibals. I side with Prieur, whose edition and discussions are exemplary. I am much indebted to his discussion throughout. Several versions of the Acts of Andrew survive from antiquity. I have concentrated on the second-century Greek text, which describes Andrew's last days and martyrdom in Greece. This is but one section of the original, lengthy Acts of Andrew, and has itself been cut. The outline of the whole work is visible in another edited and cut version by Gregory of Tours, written in the sixth century: *The Book of Miracles of the Blessed Apostle Andrew* (*MGH SRM* 1.2.826ff.). Gregory probably maintains the basic outline of the missing episodes of the original Acts of Andrew, but his revisions make his text awkward to use as evidence for attitudes in early Christianity. When I do use details from other versions (including Gregory and an even later Armenian translation, which surprisingly includes some apparently early material omitted from the Greek text by later copyists), I have noted it.

14. These miraculous adventures are set out in Gregory's *Book of Miracles*. K. Cooper, *The Virgin and the Bride* (Cambridge, Mass., 1996), 45ff., discusses the Acts of Andrew suggestively.

15. For the cure, see Gregory, *Book of Miracles* 30; the location of the governor's seat in Patras is implausible. The Roman governor resided in Corinth in the second century. This mistake suggests that the author probably did not live in Greece; modern scholars therefore favor Egypt or Asia Minor as the place of composition; there are no convincing clues either way.

16. The governor's brother is ironically called Stratokles (Famed in War), but what we learn about him first is that he has petitioned the emperor asking to be excused from service in the army in order to devote himself to philosophy (Acts of Andrew 1).

17. There is an echo here perhaps of Plato, with Socrates/Andrew as midwife; see *Theaetetus* 143e–151b. Several pointers indicate that the text is more cultured and more carefully constructed than is obvious on a casual glance. On the similarities between the Acts of Andrew and Homer's *Odyssey* and other ancient classical Greek texts, see D. R. MacDonald, *Christianizing Homer* (New York, 1994), 211ff., perhaps a little overargued but in broad brush convincing. But the two arguments *(a)* that the author was echoing and transforming classical motifs in a new Christian ethical narrative, and *(b)* that the average reader recognized these echoes and transformations, are quite separable.

18. The venue is surprising, even shocking. The Greek *koiton* means intercourse room; the emphasis is therefore sexual. There is no parallel for such a meeting in a bedroom in other Christian apocryphal literature.

19. Gregory, *Book of Miracles* 35, says that the governor has been to northern Greece. Another version says that he has been to Rome (M. Bonnet, ed., "Acta Andreae apostoli," *Analecta bollandiana* 13 (1894), 342.

20. Cf. Lactantius, *On the Deaths of Persecutors* 33, 42, and 49.

21. It was once briefly fashionable to interpret these apocryphal stories as broadly prowoman, or even as written by women for women. I agree completely that the role accorded to women in these texts is pivotal. But male writers can use women as a reflection/projection of their own fantasies, without much reference to the real world. So it seems impractical to use these texts as evidence for real, as against imagined, life (though in my view the imagined is part of the real). But for different views see, for example: S. L. Davies, *The Revolt of the Widows* (New York, 1980), V. Burrus, *Chastity as Autonomy* (New York, 1987), and for a vigorously convincing reply, J.-D. Kaestli, "Response," *Semeia* 38 (1986), 119–31, and "Fiction littéraire et réalité sociale," *Apocrypha* 1 (1990), 279–302.

22. Her spiritual success is marked by a sudden and brief change of gender. Andrew at the very end addresses her as a man *(andros phronimou)*, as though the pinnacle of spiritual achievement is to change from woman to man! See similarly the Gospel of Thomas, Saying 114; when Peter is being disparaging about Mary Magdalen, Jesus says he will make her like a male, and, "For every woman who makes herself male will enter the kingdom of God" *(NHL, 138).*

23. The quotation is from Acts of Andrew 47. In another version of the Acts, the wife's cover during her absence is provided by a beautiful young boy, who is said to be an angel, or even Jesus himself. He imitates the governor's wife's voice, complaining about her period pains, and so realistically that the governor, who is listening outside the room, is convinced that his wife is safely at home. Presumably, the idea that an angel or Jesus mimicked period pains was later thought to be infra dig and was excised from most versions.

24. Acts of Andrew 57–58. D. R. MacDonald, *Christianizing Homer*, suggests that the Acts of Andrew here and in many other places mirror Homer. The Christian author is consciously rewriting Homeric tales with a new Christian set of values: for example, poverty replaces wealth, passivity replaces violence; chastity replaces sex and seduction. The verbal parallels between Homer and the Christian text (particularly in AAMt, not discussed here), in the voyages to the cannibals and the Myrmidons, are quite impressive. For example, in the Acts of Andrew proper, the location of Andrew on the cross by the sea may be an echo of *Odyssey* 23.266ff., while Andrew being tied to the cross reflects Odysseus tied to the mast when he was tempted by the Sirens; and his sailors (= Andrew's uncomprehending crowd) are deaf to the Sirens' message. In general, I find MacDonald's thoughtful arguments persuasive. Nevertheless, the original author's clever craftsmanship was obviously ignored by the great majority of superficial readers, or hearers.

25. The Acts of Pilate also tell of the emperor Tiberius' fury at Pilate's execution of Jesus, and how he was favorably impressed by everything he had heard about Jesus. See J. K. Elliott, *The Apocryphal New Testament* (Oxford, 1993), 164–225; W. Schneemelcher, ed., *New Testament Apocrypha* (Cambridge³, 1991), vol. 1, 501ff.

26. Gospel of Philip 2.3.71–72 (*NHL*, 152); the quotation in the previous paragraph is from the Acts of Andrew 149.

27. Hartmut seems overinfluenced by the leading Roman historian at Heidelberg, G. Alföldy, whose inclinations are positivistic but who discusses the problems of opposing (or complementary) historiographical methods judiciously in his *Die römische Gesellschaft, Ausgewählte Beiträge* (Stuttgart, 1986), 12ff. Surprisingly, P. Veyne, *Writing History* (Manchester, 1984), 11–12, forthrightly claims: "History is the relating of true events . . . a fact must fulfill a single condition to be worthy of history: it must really have taken place." How unimaginative!

28. Hartmut is being a little unfair to Peter Brown here. Brown is the most distinguished later Roman historian in the world, imaginative and artful in style, bold and influential in his choice of subjects and methods. See, for example, *The World of Late Antiquity* (London, 1971); *The Making of Late Antiquity* (Cambridge, Mass., 1978); *The Cult of the Saints* (Chicago, 1981); *The Body and Society* (London, 1989); *Power and Persuasion in Late Antiquity* (Madison, 1992).

29. E. Junod and J.-D. Kaestli, *Acta Iohannis* (Turnhout, 1983), 2 vols; J. M. Prieur, *Acta Andreae, Corpus Christianorum Series Apocryphorum* 5 and 6 (Turnhout, 1989); W. Schneemelcher, *New Testament Apocrypha* (Cambridge³, 1991), 2 vols.

30. Eventually I plucked up courage and told Hartmut that I wanted to publish our correspondence. He agreed willingly, but on condition that I did not reveal his name. He also commented that just in case I thought the idea original, a similar tactic had been used by Gerd Theissen, in *Der Schatten des Galiläers, historische Jesusforschung in erzählender Form* (Munich, 1986), translated as *The Shadow of the Galilean* (London, 1987), although the correspondence on method published there was invented by the author, and briefer.

31. A group of five Acts, the Acts of John, the Acts of Andrew, the Acts of Paul (including the Acts of Paul and Thecla), the Acts of Peter, and the Acts of Thomas, seem to form a series, probably in that chronological order, with some obvious successive influences. Crudely put, all five are strongly antisexual and dualistic, in the sense that they stress the opposition between corrupt body and pure spirit.

32. Orthodox writers varied in their attitudes to the apocryphal Acts. Some, such as Eusebius, regarded them as unequivocally impious, written by and for heretics (*History of the Church* 3.25; cf. Amphilochius, *On Heretical Writings*, frag. 10.2: "written by demons" (*CCSG* 3.235). Others, such as Philastrius of Brescia, thought of the Acts as genuinely

written by the apostles' disciples, but subsequently edited by heretics, so that they had to be read by the knowledgeable only and with care *(Diversarum hereseon liber* 88). Perhaps the Acts of Paul were the most widely accepted (Augustine, *Against Faustus* 30). The other apocryphal Acts were collectively condemned by popes in 405 and 447 (Innocent, *Letters* 6.7, and Leo, *Letters* 15.15). But, for example, the summary of the Acts of Andrew by Bishop Gregory of Tours in the sixth century illustrates that explicit rejection by the great was not uniformly heeded; similarly, Epiphanius the Monk reedited the Acts of Andrew in the east in the ninth century.

33. S. Schama, *Dead Certainties* (London, 1992), C. Ginzburg, *The Cheese and the Worms* (London, 1992), R. Darnton, *The Great Cat Massacre* (London, 1984).

34. See best A. F. J. Klijn, *The Acts of Thomas* (Leiden, 1962).

35. So Klijn, *Acts of Thomas*, 34–37.

36. "These are the secret sayings which the living Jesus spoke and which Judas Thomas the twin wrote down"; so runs the prologue to the Gospel of Thomas *(NHL,* 126ff.). See also John 20–24: "Thomas, one of the twelve, called the Twin."

37. The so-called Syrian Christians of south India still exist. In the middle of the twentieth century, they celebrated the 1,900th anniversary of St. Thomas' arrival in south India, on December 21, 52. And Jesus' brother's last recorded appearance on earth, as far as I know, was as the spiritual leader and messiah of the Taiping rebellion, in mid–nineteenth-century China; see L. Bianco, *Origins of the Chinese Revolution* (Stanford, 1971), 5. For the cult of Thomas in India, see S. Bayly, *Saints, Goddesses and Kings* (Cambridge, 1989), esp. 243ff., and L. W. Brown, *The Indian Christians of St. Thomas* (Cambridge, 1956), 43ff. The tomb of Thomas in Edessa is mentioned in the late fourth century by Ephraim, *Carmina Nisibena* 43.

38. First Gospel (Protevangelium) of James 19–20.

39. This was the belief of the followers of the Syrian Christian Bardesanes, according to Ephraem, *Commentary on Paul* 118 (Venice, 1893). The Greek text of the Acts of Thomas skirts round the question of virgin birth, and says that Jesus *"was called* the son of the virgin Mary" (AT 143); the later and more Catholic Syriac text states more conventionally that "he became visible through the Virgin Mary" (143).

40. On the children of Joseph and the competing ancient views, see conveniently, R. Bauckham, *Jude and the Relatives of Jesus* (Edinburgh, 1990), Chapter 1. See profitably still, H. von Campenhausen, *The Virgin Birth in the Theology of the Ancient Church* (London, 1964).

41. The idea that Jesus was both human and divine is quite close to the idea that he was half human, half divine. The idea of twins, one more, the other less divine, is akin; so too with the pagan twin Gods Castor and Pollux, of whom Pollux was immortal, Castor mortal. J. R. Harris, *The Cult of the Heavenly Twins* (Cambridge, 1906), makes much of the alleged worship of Castor and Pollux at Edessa; but it is unnecessary to see Jesus and Thomas as a direct borrowing. What is important is that humans repeatedly need intermediaries between heaven and earth.

42. I have used the translations of Klijn, Drijvers, and Elliott, and have occasionally translated from the Greek text myself. See Klijn, *Acts of Thomas*, Han J. W. Drijvers in W. Schneemelcher, ed., *The New Testament Apocrypha*, vol. 2, 322ff., J. K. Elliott, *The Apocryphal New Testament* (Oxford, 1993), 439–511. For commentary on this fascinating text, I have found most useful G. Bornkamm, *Mythos und Legende in den apokryphen Thomasakten* (Göttingen, 1933), and J. M. Lafargue, *Language and Gnosis: The Opening Scenes of the Acts of Thomas* (Philadelphia, 1985).

43. "I Jesus, the son of Joseph the carpenter, from the village of Bethlehem, which is

in Judaea, acknowledge that I have sold my slave Judas Thomas to Habban, the merchant of King Gudnaphar" (AT 2).

44. See Tertullian, *On the Crown* 3.

45. Acts of Thomas 10. This blessing is similar in tone to the blessing offered by St. Peter in the apocryphal Acts of Peter to a peasant's daughter. She immediately dropped dead. The father in dismay begged Peter to raise her from the dead. He obliged, though unwillingly. Some days later, a visitor to the peasant's hut seduces the girl and they elope. Peter was right. The text is in Ps. Titus, *De dispositione sanctimonii*, ed. D. de Bruyne, *Revue bénédictine* 25 (1908), 151ff. The translation is given by Elliott, *Apocryphal New Testament*, 398–99; Schneemelcher, *New Testament Apocrypha*, vol. 2, 287.

46. In Jerome's Vulgate, or Latin translation, of Tobit 8 (treated as noncanonical by Jews, accepted as canonical by the Catholic church, but treated as apocryphal by Protestants), the newly married hero and heroine, Tobit and Sarah, are described as praying after their wedding for three whole days and nights. Admittedly her previous seven husbands had died on their wedding night, so there was something to pray for. The original Greek text has them praying only briefly. Jerome's text was used as part of the wedding service for Pennsylvania Dutch in the eighteenth century. See B. Metzger, *An Introduction to the Apocrypha* (Oxford, 1957), 40–41.

47. The bridal chamber is repeatedly mentioned in the Gospel of Philip. Its meaning seems to range from a metaphor for spiritual fulfilment in this world and in life eternal (see Gospel of Philip 2.3.70 [*NHL*, 151] and *Exegesis of the Soul* 2.6.132 [*NHL*, 195]) to a general term for successive gnostic rituals, such as baptism, anointing, eucharist, redemption, and the final union of the bridal chamber (Gospel of Philip 67; *NHL* 150). Cf. Irenaeus, *Refutation of Heresies* 1.13.3 and 1.6.3.

48. The triangular pattern is so embedded in the Acts of Andrew that the author can have fun, as in a Mozart sonata, by inverting the theme tune. In the version of the Acts of Andrew preserved in Gregory of Tours, *Book of Miracles*, the triangle is recurrent; but once (4), the wife is unchaste and her son, wrongly accused of incest, is chaste, while in another triangular story (22), the wife remains pagan, while her husband, the governor, converts to Christianity. But as I have explained (see note 13 above), I think it safer not to use details from this late-sixth-century version as evidence of early Christian thought.

49. E. K. Sedgwick, *Between Men* (New York, 1985), 21ff., has a good discussion of asymmetrical erotic triangles.

50. In an imaginative article which advances recent discussion, K. Cooper, "Insinuations of Womanly Influence," *Journal of Roman Studies* 82 (1992), especially at 152–53 and 162–63, argues that imputation of womanly influence is a rhetorical gambit between influential and competitive men, who were ideally wholly committed to public life. Too great an interest in sexuality, or lack of self-control, involved putting private pleasure before public duty. Cooper sees a battle in the church triumphant during the fourth century between married men holding civic office and celibate men claiming a privileged understanding of what was involved in being a true Christian. These apocryphal Acts show that the rhetorical ploys in this battle emerged much earlier.

51. S. B. Ortner, *High Religion* (Princeton, 1989), 172ff.

52. For a different type of analysis, see G. Theissen, *The Miracle Stories of the Early Christian Tradition* (Edinburgh, 1983), 47ff. Theissen isolated thirty-three different motifs in New Testament miracle stories. I find such work, exemplarily intelligent of its kind, both informative and depressing. It is no more reproducible than stories.

53. See, for example, AT 52, 84, and 88.

54. Lafargue, *Language and Gnosis*, 14–36, shows that the narratives, hymns, prayers, and speeches are also interwoven by the repeated use of key words in the different forms. This implies greater care in composition than some modern readers have appreciated.

55. See J. D. Turner, *The Book of Thomas the Contender* (Missoula, 1975); the text is in *NHL*. J. J. Gunther, "The Meaning and Origins of the name Judas Thomas," *Le Muséon* 93 (1980), 113ff., compares the various Thomas writings.

56. This train of speculations is reasonably unproblematic. On literacy rates, see W. V. Harris, *Ancient Literacy* (Cambridge, Mass., 1989). On Edessa as the place of composition, see Klijn, *Acts of Thomas*, 30ff. On the size of age groups in ancient populations see A. J. Coale and J. Demeny, *Regional Model Life Tables* (New York², 1983), Level 3 West.

57. So Lucian, *On the Syrian Goddess* 49ff.

58. See the beautiful psalms in C. R. C. Allberry, *The Manichaean Psalm Book* (Stuttgart, 1938).

59. On the importance of participation, as against belief, in religions, see S. J. Tambiah, *Magic, Science, Religion and the Scope of Rationality* (Cambridge, 1990), 109.

60. See Junod and Kaestli, *Acta Johannis*, 621ff., for a typically perceptive discussion.

61. See, for example, John Gager, *Curse Tablets and Binding Spells from the Ancient World* (New York, 1992), 54–55.

FIVE: *Magic, Temple Tales, and Oppressive Power*

1. On the "famous temple" of the "great, greatest God" Sobek, see P. Tebt. 298ff. and 383. D. Frankfurter, *Religion in Roman Egypt* (Princeton, 1998) is now the best general guide. S. Morenz, *Egyptian Religion* (London, 1973), gives the ancient Egyptian background.

2. On Roman hostility to animal-headed gods, see K. A. D. Smelik and E. A. Hemelrijk, "Egyptian Animal Worship," *ANRW* 2.17.4 (1984), 1852ff.

3. On the terrible state of ancient Egyptian teeth, worn down, almost dropping out of abscessed cavities, and painful, see F. F. Leek, "The Practice of Dentistry in Ancient Egypt," *Journal of Egyptian Archaeology* 53 (1967), 57, and M. Ruffer, *Studies in the Palaeopathology of Egypt* (Chicago, 1921), 314.

4. The remains of the temple of Souchos at Tebtunis, excavated in the 1930s, are described by G. Botti, "Gli scavi di Tebtunis," *Bolletino d'arte* 4 (1935), 376ff.; C. Anti, *Aegyptus* 11 (1930), 389; and G. Bagnani, *Aegyptus* 14 (1934), 7. But it has long since been covered over again with sand. Village contributions: P. Tebt. 298 (107–8 CE). The painted slab is now in the Phoebe Hearst Museum in Berkeley, California: 6.20301.

5. G. Bastianini and C. Gallazi, "Un' epigrafe scomparsa di Tebtynis," *Tyche* 3 (1988), 25ff., and *Tyche* 4 (1989), 1ff. For other dedications, including crocodiles in wood, plaster, and stone, and statues of youths and Gods, one by a Roman knight, see Phoebe Hearst Museum 6:20306–7, 20313–4.

6. A letter survives warning local dignitaries at Tebtunis of the impending visit of a Roman senator; he was to be well looked after (P. Tebt. 33 of 112 BCE). On the spectacular discovery of a thousand papyri from the temple library, hidden in jars in a house just inside the temple sanctuary, see G. Botti, "I papiri ieratici e demotici degli scavi di Tebtynis," *Atti del congresso internazionale di papirilogia* (Florence, 1935), 217ff.

7. Salt sellers' guild: P. Mich. 245 (46 CE). F. de Cénival, "Les associations religieuses en Egypte," esp. 45ff.

8. See K. Hopkins, "Brother-Sister Marriage in Roman Egypt," *Comparative Studies in Society and History* 22 (1980), 303ff.; for better statistics, R. Bagnall and B. Frier, *De-*

mography of Roman Egypt (Cambridge, 1994), 127ff. On colors of clothes, see painted panels from Tebtunis in the Phoebe Hearst Museum at Berkeley (6.21374–85).

9. A second-century Greek physician commented: "If we did not know about the custom of brother-sister marriage among the Egyptians, we would have asserted that it was universally agreed that men ought not to marry their sisters"; so Sextus Empiricus, *Outlines of Pyrrhonism* 3.234. For hymns celebrating passion between Osiris and Isis, husband/wife, brother/sister, see, for example, P. Bremner Rhind 1, trans. R. O. Faulkner, *Journal of Egyptian Archaeology* 22 (1936), 121ff.

10. P. Oxy. 1477 (late third century) records the following numbered questions: "77 Am I to be reconciled with my children? 78 Am I to get leave? 79 Shall I get the money? 80 He went away, is he still alive? 81 Will my transaction be profitable?" The God, through his priests, signified yes or no. N.B. These are age-old problems, not the symptom of short-term social malaise. For similar texts, cf. P. Oxy. 2832–33 and 3330, and G. M. Browne, *Sortes Astrampsychi* (Leipzig, 1983).

11. Temple taxed and accounts inspected: P. Tebt. 306 (162 CE) and 315 (second century); priesthood auctioned: P. Tebt. 295–96 (123–26 CE); ordinary priesthoods cost very much less: P. Tebt. 298 (107–8 CE). On pervasive ordinary taxes, see for example, C. Gallazzi, *Ostraka da Tebtynis* (Milan, 1979), and for other temples at Tebtunis, idem, "Fouilles anciennes et nouvelles sur le site de Tebtynis," *Bulletin de l'institut français d'archéologie orientale* 89 (1989), 179ff.

12. A. Bowman, *Egypt After the Pharaohs* (London², 1996), 67ff., gives a skillful summary of Roman administration. W. Otto, *Priester und Tempel im hellenistischen Ägypten* (Leipzig, 1905–8), is the classic work.

13. L. Koenen, "Die Prophezeiung des Töpfers," *Zeitschrift für Papyrologie und Epigraphik* 2 (1968), 178ff.; for anti-Roman pamphlets, see H. Musurillo, ed., *Acts of the Pagan Martyrs* (Oxford, 1954); all these circulated long after they were written.

14. P. W. van der Horst, ed., *Chaeremon* (Leiden, 1987), frag. 10. I have edited Chaeremon's account, and have turned it occasionally from the third to the first person. Chaeremon's preoccupation with purity and asexuality is similar to that of Christian monks. Chaeremon was one of Nero's teachers.

15. Chaeremon, frag. 11.

16. On the price of buying the top job as temple prophet at Tebtunis: P. Tebt. 298 (107–8 CE), enough to feed half a dozen families for a year. Candidate priests were tested on their knowledge of "hieratic and Egyptian writings," at least sometimes; see P. Tebt. 291 (162 CE).

17. For school arithmetic exercises see P. Carlsberg 30, from Tebtunis, second century, in R. A. Parker, *Demotic Mathematical Papyri* (Providence, 1972), 73. The beautiful prayer is reproduced by G. Botti, *La glorificazione di Sobk e del Fayum in un papiro hieratico da Tebtynis* (Copenhagen, 1958).

18. For oracle slips from Tebtunis (such as: Is it good for me to go on living with my wife?), see P. Flor. Dem. 8700 in G. Botti, *Studi in memoria di I. Rosellini* (Pisa, 1955), vol. 2, 13. More generally, Frankfurter, *Religion in Roman Egypt*, esp. 145ff.

19. P. Oxy. 1381 (second century) contains a striking account of a curing sleepover and book-finishing visions brought by Imhotep (Asclepius).

20. For the stress on purity as a precondition of weaving magical spells, see for example *PGM* 4.735ff. and 13.343ff. (the sacred book of Moses), conveniently in H. D. Betz, ed., *The Greek Magical Papyri in Translation* (Chicago, 1986), and Thessalos of Tralles (see note 23 below). For nagging, squabbling, etc., see *PGM* 14.366.

21. The demotic Wisdom Book (P. Carlsberg 2), which reproduces some of the homespun advice from the more famous Insinger Papyrus, was written in a cramped hand on reused papyrus, which corroborates Marsisouchos' need for papyrus money; see A. Volten, *Analecta aegyptiaca* 1 (Copenhagen, 1940), 4.

22. See Philostratus, *Life of Apollonius of Tyana* 1.18 (cf. 8) for walking to India in search of wisdom.

23. This story is told in Thessalos of Tralles; see H-V. Friederich, ed., *Thessalos von Tralles* (Meisenheim, 1968) = *CCAG* 8. (Brussels, 1912) 3.135–37; and Ps. Cyprian, *Confessio* 12; the spell is cast in *PGM* 4.486ff. The best book I know on Roman magic is F. Graf, *Magic in the Ancient World* (Cambridge, Mass., 1998); but see also now R. Gordon, "Imagining Greek and Roman Magic," in S. Clarke, ed., *The Athlone History of Witchcraft and Magic* (London, 1999), vol. 2; and J. Gager, *Curse-Tablets and Binding Spells from the Ancient World* (New York, 1992).

24. The best short description of what goes on inside an Egyptian temple is by H. W. Fairman, "Worship and Festivals in an Egyptian temple," *Bulletin of the John Rylands Library* 37 (1954), 165ff. For more detail, see M. Alliott, *Le culte d'Horus à Edfou* (Cairo, 1954). On whole burned offerings to king and Sobek at Tebtunis, see P. Dem. Cair. 30606 (second century BCE) in Cénival "Les associations religeuses," 47; cf. 65.

25. The picture of the priest officiating is in V. Bartoletti, ed., *Papiri greci e latini* (Florence, 1957), vol. 14, 1452, from Tebtunis (second century).

26. For temple liturgy, see Fairman, "Worship and Festivals," 180; Frankfurter, "Religion in Roman Egypt," 52ff.

27. This extract is from two prayers to the crocodile God at Kom Ombo; the opening is late Roman, the body of the prayer was originally Hellenistic; see H. Junker, "Ein Doppelhymnus aus Kom Ombo," *Zeitschrift für ägyptischen Sprache* 67 (1931), 54, and P. Bucher, "Les hymnes à Sobk Ra," *Kemi* 3 (1930), 1–19.

28. The oath is in P. BM. Eg. 10622 (second century BCE), translated by H. Thompson, "Two Demotic Self-Dedications," *Journal of Egyptian Archaeology* 26 (1940), 68ff. For religious feelings casually expressed in a private letter, see, for example, P. Oxy. 1070.

29. The demotic papyri found in Tebtunis, most from the temple library, are listed in W. Helck, *Lexikon für Ägyptologie*, s.v. "Tebtynis." On the circumstances of the most spectacular find, see G. Botti, "I papiri ieratici e demotici degli scavi di Tebtynis," *Atti del congresso internazionale di papirilogia* (Florence, 1935), 217ff. Since then many of the papyri have been forgotten, to be enthusiastically rediscovered: G. Avezzu, "Nuovi papiri da Tebtynis," *Bolletino d'istituto di filologia greca*, no. 4 (1977/8), 192ff. See specifically P. Oslo 77, P. Tebt. 274, and P. Carlsberg 9 (145 CE) in O. Neugebauer and R. A. Parker, *Egyptian Astronomical Texts* (Providence, 1969), vol. 3, 223, and E. Iversen, "Fragments of a Hieroglyphic Dictionary" (P. Carlsberg 7), *Det kongelige Videnskabernes Selskab, Hist. filol. Skifter* 3. 2 (Copenhagen, 1958).

30. On the interior decoration of a house in Tebtunis and the wood-framed picture, see O. Rubensohn, "Aus griechisch-römischen Haüsern des Fayum," *Jahrbuch des deutschen archäologischen Instituts* 20 (1905), 1ff. and plate 1. For figurines, see C. Dolzani, "Il dio Sobk," *Atti della Accademia nazionale dei Lincei, Memorie* 10 (1961), 163ff.

31. This invocation is from *PGM* 13.39ff., 13.63ff.

32. On the clay figurine pierced with needles, see P. du Bourguet, *Mémoires de l'institut français d'archéologie orientale* 104 (1980), 225ff., and *PGM* 4.296ff.

33. The spell is a composite from *PGM* 7.880, 36.134ff., 4.296ff., and 2471, and R. W. Daniel and F. Maltomini, *Supplementum Magicum* (Opladen, 1990), vol. 1, nos 45–47.

The basic formula is given in *PGM* 4.335–433 and surviving exemplars follow a standard pattern, with variations. See also D. G. Martinez, *A Greek Love Charm from Egypt* (Atlanta, 1991), and J. J. Winkler, *The Constraints of Desire* (New York, 1990), 71ff.

34. Recipe for potency: gall of boar, rock salt, and Attic honey; *PGM* 7.191.

35. See D. Frankfurter, "Stylites and *Phallobates*," *Vigiliae Christianae* 44 (1990), 168ff.

36. In essence what follows is a very loose rendering of Lucian, *On the Syrian Goddess*. I have particularly benefited from the translation by H. W. Attridge and R. A. Dean, *The Syrian Goddess* (Missoula, 1976). The archaeological details come from the excellent book by G. Goossens, *Hierapolis de Syrie* (Louvain, 1943), 106ff.

37. *Liber Pontificalis (Book of Pontiffs*, trans. R. Davis [Liverpool, 1989]) 34 (Davis p. 16) records the construction of a silver baldachin in St. John Lateran in the beginning of the fourth century; it consisted of a decorated silver canopy with carved figures, over almost-life-size statues of Jesus, his twelve apostles, and four angels (total weight over one tonne of silver), lit by a fine golden lantern decorated with fifty dolphins, and a gilded ceiling. I doubt the temple at Hierapolis was as grand as that.

38. After what he reckons as analytical interpretation, James is back with Lucian, *On the Syrian Goddess* (see note 36 above).

39. Not eating fish and doves has already occurred as a theme in Chaeremon's account of the diet of Egyptian priests.

40. Myrmex's story is from Apuleius, *The Golden Ass* 8.24ff.

41. Roman towns apparently contracted out burial and punishment; either a magistrate or any private citizen could hand over a convicted criminal or slave to the contractor for punishment or torture, for a standard fee. The contractor's staff were pariahs, had to wear special clothes, and bathe after everyone else. See *Année épigraphique* (1971), 88, for the text, translated by J. F. Gardner and T. Wiedemann, *The Roman Household* (London, 1991), 24–26.

42. On castration, see L. E. Roller, "The Ideology of the Eunuch Priest," *Gender & History* 9 (1997), 542ff., or M. Beard, "The Roman and the Foreign; the Cult of the Great Mother in Imperial Rome," in N. Thomas and C. Humphrey, eds., *Shamanism, History and the State* (Ann Arbor, Mich., 1994), 164ff., and the literature cited there. For modern castrated priests in India, the hijras, see the perceptive account by S. Nanda, *Neither Man nor Woman* (Belmont, Calif., 1990), 41.

43. We're back with Lucian, *On the Syrian Goddess*.

44. Cf. the temple building story by Thomas, Jesus' twin brother, in Chapter Four.

45. *Tabula of Cebes* 1, J. T. Fitzgerald and L. M. White, eds. (Chico, 1983).

46. Clearly some pagans in central Asia Minor had caught the Judaeo-Christian syndrome of sin, guilt, repentance, forgiveness, without any obvious dependence on either Judaism or Christianity. More than a hundred of these confessional inscriptions dating from the late first century CE onward, but with no sign of Christian influence, are collected by G. Petzl, "Die Beicht-Inschriften Westkleinasiens," *Epigraphica anatolica* 22 (1994), 1ff.

47. L. R. Lidonnici, *The Epidaurian Miracle Inscriptions* (Atlanta, 1995), 85–86.

48. The best guide is P. Scherrer, *Ephesos, der neue Führer* (Vienna, 1996), but J. Keil, *Ephesos* (Vienna, 1957), has impressive, but no longer fashionable, hypothetical reconstructions. *PW. RE.* s.v. "Ephesos," Supplementband 12 (1970), 1592ff., provides a clear and concise archaeological summary. S. F. Friesen, *Twice Neokoros* (Leiden, 1993), G. Rogers, *The Sacred Identity of Ephesos* (London, 1991), and H. Koester, ed., *Ephesos* (Valley

Forge, 1995), together provide an overview. Details from *IEphesos* 2.430 and 4.1351, Koester, *Ephesos*, 18–19.

49. S. R. F. Price, *Rituals and Power* (Cambridge, 1984), 140ff., is brief but good on this.

50. For "free city" inscriptions honoring the emperor, see, for example, *IEphesos* 2.240 and Friesen, *Twice Neokoros*, 29ff. This is the main argument of G. M. Rogers, *The Sacred Identity of Ephesus* (London, 1991), 80ff., on the foundation of C. Vibius Salutaris in 104 CE.

51. R. K. Sherk, *Documents from the Greek East* (Baltimore, 1969), no. 69, ll. 5 and 10 from the governor's letter, ll. 40–41 from the council's decision. Various copies have been found, none yet in Ephesus, but one must have been set up there.

52. O. Dittenberger, *Sylloge Inscriptionum Graecarum* (Leipzig³, 1915), 985, from the first century BCE, found in Philadelphia, so it's a bit of a cheat, but Philadelphia is not far from Ephesus. Cf. A. D. Nock, *Conversion* (Oxford, 1933), 216–17.

53. The altercation is my mosaic from texts used to teach children Latin or Greek, or both: G. Goetz, ed., *Corpus Glossariorum Latinorum* (Leipzig, 1892), vol. 3, 641–43.

54. The advantage of having an influential patron and character witnesses in a trial, see C. Dionisotti, "From Ausonius' Schooldays," *Journal of Roman Studies* 72 (1982), 105; on C. Terentius Flavianus, cf. *Inschriften von Ephesos* 4.1032.

55. For a discussion, see P. Grierson, "The Roman Law of Counterfeiting," in R. A. G. Carson, ed., *Essays in Roman Coinage* (Oxford, 1956), 240ff. The critical texts are Paul, *Sententiae* 5.25.1, and Digest 48.10.9. I am not confident in Grierson's argument from silence, that there was no Roman law against counterfeiting bronze coins. Certainly C. Julius Alexander took it very seriously, to James' disadvantage.

56. On the Seven Sleepers of Ephesus, see E. Honigmann, *Patristic Studies = Studi e testi* 173 (Rome 1953), 125–26. Isis coins, see A. Alföldi, *A Festival of Isis in Rome Under the Christian Emperors* (Budapest, 1937).

57. For C. Julius Alexander, proconsular governor of Asia in 132/3?, see D. Magie, *Roman Rule in Asia Minor* (Princeton, 1950), 1479. For this description of a trial, see Dionisotti, "From Ausonius' Schooldays," 105. In general, see the great article by S. Lieberman, "Roman Legal Institutions in Early Rabbinics," *Jewish Quarterly Review* 35 (1944–45), 1ff., esp. 13ff., *Genesis Rabba* 37.2, and Ephrem, *Opera Omnia Graece et Latine*, vol. 3, p. 27b: "Tell me the truth before you are put to torture; how did you commit the murder?"

58. Dionisotti, "From Ausonius' Schooldays," 105; cf. P. Oslo 17.

59. P. Flor. 61 of 86/8 CE, slightly abridged. I am boldly assuming that justice was administered by the senatorial governor in Asia roughly as by the equestrian prefect in Egypt.

60. P. Ant. 87 (third century).

61. James' carelessly blasphemous remark may be referring to Jesus' sudden appearances in locked rooms (John 20.19, 26), or the sudden physical disappearance of Apollonius of Tyana, when he was being tried by the tyrant Domitian (Philostratus, *Life of Apollonius* 8.5). Some pagans thought Jesus should have disappeared in the same way; see, for example, Porphyry in Macarius Magnes, *Apocriticus* 3.1. Some Christians believed he had. See the *Second Treatise of the Great Seth* 7.2.55–56 (*NHL*, 365).

SIX: *Pagans vs. Christians vs. Jews*

1. The second-century Christian apologists which Macarius' letter imitates here are Justin, Athenagoras, the anonymous letter to Diognetus, and particularly Celsus and Minucius Felix; he also relies heavily on Origen's third-century retort to Celsus, *Against Celsus*; his arguments also seem similar to the early-fourth-century criticisms of Christianity made by Hierocles and Porphyry. The anti-Christian work of Porphyry was publicly burned by order of the emperor Constantine (*Theodosian Code* 15.5.66; 324 CE), but survives fragmentarily, though not perhaps accurately, in the work of Christian apologists, notably Macarius Magnes, *Response (Apocriticus)*.

2. This was the curse against Christians (*Birkat ha minim*) said by some Jews in their thrice-daily prayers, probably from the end of the first century CE. The extent, date, and interpretation of the practice are all disputed.

3. Paul, Romans 14.2: "One believes that he may eat anything, while the weak man eats only vegetables." Clement, *Paedagogus* 2.8 and 10, suggests that a Christian guest who accepts pagan hospitality should eat what is put before him, to avoid upsetting the social atmosphere. But if attention is drawn to the fact that it is idol meat, he should leave it untouched. The Jew Trypho in Justin's *Dialogue with Trypho* 35 alleges that many Christians eat meat from animals which have been offered to idols.

4. This is a direct borrowing of the aggressive accusations made against the Christians by the Christian writer Minucius Felix at the beginning of the third century in his dialogue, *Octavius* 8.

5. Minucius Felix, *Octavius* 9. At first sight, this attack seems fairly wild, but a drawing was found on the Palatine in Rome of a man worshiping a crucified ass-headed figure, with the graffito "Alexamenos worships his god"; cf. Tertullian, *Apology* 16: "You fantasize that our God is an ass head." And an amazing figure now in the Vatican and rarely reproduced, in which a bronze figure of a chicken ends in a human phallus, engraved with the Greek words *soter kosmou* = savior of the world, indicates either that some Christians did worship the genitals of their founder or were thought to do so by others (plates 22–23).

6. Minucius Felix, *Octavius* 9; cf. Tertullian, *Apology* 7; Justin, *1 Apology* 26; Athenagoras, *Plea (Legatio)* 3; Origen, *Against Celsus*, 6.27: "a rumor spread by Jews."

7. Clement of Alexandria makes these very same accusations against Gnostics: see his *Miscellanies (Stromateis)* 3.2.10, against Carpocratians; cf. Epiphanius, *Panarion* 26.5.5 and 48.14.5.

8. G. W. Bowersock, *Fiction as History* (Berkeley 1994), 104ff., suggests the influence of the Christian gospel narratives on Greek erotic fiction of the first and second centuries. I do not think that plausible. But he has drawn attention to their coexistence within the same social thought world. See Achilles Tatius, *Leucippe and Clitophon* 3.15, in B. P. Reardon, *Collected Ancient Greek Novels* (Berkeley, 1989), 216, and the excellent discussion of accusations of ritual murder against Christians by A. Henrichs, "Pagan Ritual and the Alleged Crimes of the Early Christians," in *Festschrift J. Quasten, Kyriakon* (Münster, 1970), vol. 1, 18ff.

9. Origen, *Against Celsus* 1.27, 8.55; 8.65 and 8.75.

10. Origen, *Against Celsus* 8.54 and 65; cf. against Christians serving in the army, while accepting that they do: Tertullian, *On the Crown* 11, and Synod of Elvira, *Canons* 2-4, on Christians holding municipal office and sacrificing.

11. Tertullian, *Apology* 40.

12. Origen, *Against Celsus* 8.56 and 73.

13. Origen, *Against Celsus* 8.65.

14. Origen, *Against Celsus* 3.55, cf. 3.18, 3.44, and 4.10.

15. Origen, *Against Celsus* 6.10–14.

16. Origen, *Against Celsus* 3.9 and 3.15; cf. Tertullian, *Apology* 10–12, 17, and 24.

17. Origen, *Against Celsus* 3.56, 3.51, and 4.26; cf. 6.1, 6.10, 6.14.

18. Origen, *Against Celsus* 3.62–67, 3.16, 5.14, and 7.9.

19. Tertullian, *Apology* 18.

20. Origen, *Against Celsus* 7.9–11.

21. Origen, *Against Celsus* 6.27–28; cf. 3.13 and 7.40.

22. We do know of Jewish town councilors in Palestine; indeed, the Jewish town councilors of Sepphoris in the second century, in an act of loyalty to the Roman regime, changed their city's name to Diocaesarea = "Zeus-Emperor Town."

23. A similar incident is reported by Lucian, *Lapiths* 8ff., especially at 15.

24. Origen, *Against Celsus* 1.57 and 6.11; Origen, *Commentary on John* 13.27; Macarius Magnes (supposedly reporting Porphyry), *The Response (Apocriticus)* 3.1; cf. *Against Celsus* 2.68. On prophetic and magic-making contemporaries of Jesus, such as Hanina ben Dosa and Honi the Circle Drawer, see G. Vermes, *Jesus the Jew* (London², 1983), 58ff.

25. Origen, *Against Celsus* 1.28–32; 1.38; 1.61 and 1.68; 6.75.

26. Minucius Felix, *Octavius* 10–13.

27. Origen, *Against Celsus* 2.8–9; 2.39; 2.47–48; 3.33; 6.47.

28. Origen, *Against Celsus* 2.48; 2.23–24; 2.33 and 5.32. Cf. Tertullian, *Apology* 24 and 30.

29. Ps. Aristides, *Oration 35, To the Emperor* (ed. J. Keil) 21; translated by L. J. Swift, "The Anonymous Encomium to Philip the Arab [244–49 CE]," *Greek, Roman and Byzantine Studies* 7 (1966), 277.

30. Origen, *Against Celsus* 2.34 and 43; 2.56–63, and 3.39.

31. Origen, *Against Celsus* 2.27, 2.15, and 3.23.

32. Origen, *Against Celsus* 7.18 and 2.19.

33. Origen, *Against Celsus* 6.66; 4.30, 5.41; 3.10; 4.32 and 65.

34. This is taken from a ninth-century Aramaic manuscript from the Yemen (edited by L. Ginzberg, *Ginze Schechter* 1 (New York, 1928), 329ff., with Horbury's supplement in E. Bammel, ed., *The Trial of Jesus* (London, 1970), 116ff., translated into English by William Horbury, as part of his systematic revision of the narratives belonging to the *Toldoth Jeshu* cycle. See originally, S. Krauss, *Das Leben Jesu nach jüdischen Quellen* (Berlin, 1902); a different version of the same story is published there, pp. 122–28. But see now S. Krauss and W. Horbury, *The Jewish Christian Controversy* (Tübingen, 1995), vol. 1; a further volume is in prospect. I am most grateful to Professor Horbury for allowing me to use his manuscript and for generously sharing some of his knowledge with me. A still different version of the Jesus story is also conveniently given in M. Goldstein, *Jesus in the Jewish Tradition* (New York, 1950), 167ff.

35. This neatly combines Jewish religious and Roman criminal punishments. The inversion of the normal Christian time order heightens the dramatic effect and serves a useful theological purpose; the disciples, so troublesome for Judaism, are all killed off before Jesus' death. Jesus the arch-Christian is first subordinated as a pupil to John the Baptist, then equated with him to form a pair, and only at the very end, left to die by himself. Understandably for events of this importance, the emperor has to be involved, however unrealistically. Given a choice of taking the whole palaver to Rome or bringing the imperial court to Palestine, the Jewish storyteller takes the stronger option: Rome comes to Palestine, though not to Jerusalem, soon to be destroyed and probably, by the time this version

is told, in the hands of Christians. Instead, the court comes but to the aptly named Tiberias.

36. What follows is a rough pastiche of the arguments put forward by Athenagoras, *Plea for Christians (Legatio)* 1–2, written about 177, and ostensibly addressed to the two reigning emperors, Marcus Aurelius and his son Commodus. This framing as a written petition or speech to be delivered at court is a rhetorical flourish. There was no chance, I think, that either emperor would have seen it. At this period, Christians were a socially and politically insignificant sect. But the distinguished addressees do signal that Athenagoras is culturally upmarket; in presenting his case, he mentions several classical authors, including Plato, Aristotle, Herodotus, and Homer. The level of argument is primitive, but the wrapping is getting posher.

37. Athenagoras, *Plea* 4–6 and 9.

38. Athenagoras, *Plea* 10.

39. Athenagoras, *Plea* 11–12.

40. Athenagoras, *Plea* 12–13. But see the powerful reply of Porphyry, or another defender of pagan religion against Christianity, as recorded in Macarius Magnes, *Response* 4.21: "Those who make an object suitable for worship of a God do not think that the God is in the wood, bronze or marble, nor do they think that if an arm breaks off, the power of the God is lessened."

41. Athenagoras, *Plea* 31–37.

42. This is my abbreviated version of Apuleius, *The Golden Ass* 1.

43. Here Athenagoras, *Plea* 24–26, seems to be repeating the creation story set out in 1 Enoch 6ff., a Jewish apocalypse written in the third century BCE, but preserved, and as we can see here highly regarded, by intellectual Christians in the second century CE (cf. Chapter Seven). This is a typical early Christian explanation and expansion of the Genesis creation story. Some early Christians regarded all *matter* as intrinsically evil. Macarius is taking a carefully neutral line.

44. Justin, *2 Apology* 6.5.

45. The reference is at Josephus, *Jewish Antiquities* 20.97–98.

46. In general, but at length, see J. Neusner, *Eliezer ben Hyrcanus* (Leiden, 1973), vol. 1, 424ff., and for further accounts of Eliezer, see Jerusalem Talmud, Mo'ed Qatan 3.1, plus Babylonian Talmud, Sanhedrin 68a.

47. This is the second previously unpublished third-century letter, sent presumably in reply to Macarius' account of the dinner party. Nothing about this Clement's life or location is known, but he probably was a minor bishop or priest, of modest talent and education.

48. Jews were advised not to discuss religion with Christians; see Justin, *Dialogue with Trypho* 38. For complementary Jewish stories, of how merely hearing a Christian give a pleasing opinion was polluting, see Babylonian Talmud, Aboda Zara 16b, and Tosefta, Hullin 2.24; for the story that a rabbi preferred to let his nephew die rather than be cured in the name of Jesus, see Tosefta, Hullin 2.22–23 and Babylonian Talmud, Aboda Zara 27b.

49. Justin, *Dialogue with Trypho* 16–17.

50. Justin, *Dialogue with Trypho* 12, cites Jeremiah for this quotation, which is not in our texts. The metaphor of circumcision of heart recurs in ancient Jewish literature (Deuteronomy 10.16; Leviticus 26.40; Jeremiah 4.3), but is taken over by early Christians as though they alone believed in spiritual, as opposed to bodily, purity.

51. Justin, *Dialogue with Trypho* 18–30 and 43. One additional reason Justin puts for-

ward against circumcision among the Jews being a sign of grace is its unavailability to women.

52. Justin, *Dialogue with Trypho* 29 and 30–41; and see Chapter Two above, note 62.

53. In the early second century, a new and more literal translation from Hebrew to Greek was made by the Jewish convert Aquila among others. The motive may have been partly to give Jews a more literal rendering and a rendering different from the Septuagint, which was the third/second-century BCE Greek translation used by Christians. Justin, *Dialogue with Trypho* 71–72, accuses Jews of cutting two other passages (besides Psalm 96) from Esdras and Jeremiah, which do refer to Christ allusively, but which are also apparently Christian interpolations into the Jewish text, not Jewish cuts. He also accuses them of cutting Jeremiah 11.19: "I was like a lamb brought to the slaughter . . . they were hatching plots against me," at least in some synagogues. The passage is still there in standard texts. The arguments reveal how texts could be cut, amended, revised, or accusations about cuts made, regardless. On Jewish wickedness as a cause of their misunderstanding see Justin, *Dialogue with Trypho* 55.

54. Justin, *Dialogue with Trypho* 39, 35, and 133.

55. Clement, *Exhortation*, pp. 26–49 and 68–71 (Loeb edition).

56. Clement, *Exhortation*, pp. 56–60, 90–92, and 110–12; and Plutarch, *Life of Marius* 20.

57. Clement, *Exhortation*, pp. 100–43.

58. Clement, *Exhortation*, pp. 224–47.

59. Tertullian, *Apology* 19.

SEVEN: *Recreating the Cosmos*

1. F. Dostoyevsky, *The Brothers Karamazov*, Book 5.5.

2. Ambrose, *De Helia et ieiunio* 76; see also Clement, *How Can a Rich Man Be Saved (Quis dives salvetur?)*, insisting on an allegorical interpretation; and similarly, Cyprian, *On Alms*. But some church fathers insisted that money could not buy a place in heaven; instead it was the (unknowable) state of the giver's mind which mattered: John Chrysostom, *Homilies on the Letter to the Philippians* 15.3. See in general, L. W. Countryman, *The Rich Christian in the Church of the Early Empire* (New York, 1980), and the astute comments of G. E. M. de Ste. Croix, *The Class Struggle in the Ancient Greek World* (London, 1981), 431ff.; cf. J. Z. Smith, *Drudgery Divine* (Chicago, 1990).

3. Wendy Doniger O'Flaherty, *Asceticism and Eroticism in the Mythology of Siva* (Oxford, 1977), 5ff. and 52ff.

4. See particularly, the Gospel of Mary (*NHL*, 523ff.), the Gospel of Philip (*NHL*, 139ff.), and Pistis Sophia (Faith/Wisdom) discussed in Chapter Eight. On the confusion of Mary the mother with Mary Magdalene, see R. Murray, *Symbols of Church and Kingdom* (Cambridge, 1975), 146ff. and 329ff.

5. "Our ideal is not to experience desire at all," so Clement, *Miscellanies (Stromateis)* 3.57. Theologically, this must be a moot point. Virtue is best exhibited by resisting temptation, rather than by its suppression. That is presumably why Christian purists were against ascetics castrating themselves, or chaining themselves to rocks.

6. Gospel of Philip 2.3.71–72 (*NHL*, 152). S. Freud, *Civilization and its Discontents* (London, 1982), especially 11–22.

7. The best introduction to this varied religious world is M. Beard, J. North, and S. Price, *Religions at Rome* (Cambridge, 1998), 2 vols.

8. On prerabbinical and Talmudic attitudes to sexuality, see, provocatively, D. Boyarin,

Carnal Israel (Berkeley, 1993), 31ff., though for my taste he sees too radical a periodic divide between earlier and later Jewish attitudes. On hell, theoretically, J. L. Kvanvig, *The Problem of Hell* (New York, 1993); descriptively, M. Himmelfarb, *Tours of Hell* (Philadelphia, 1983), and complementarily, *Ascent to Heaven* (New York, 1993).

9. I write "especially the Gnostics" with some hesitation, because we know so little about their actual practice. And besides, the Nag Hammadi Library, if it came from a Christian monastery, is itself a token of syncretistic tolerance. Its burial less so, but we can hardly complain.

10. See, for example, Athenagoras, *Plea (Legatio)* 24–26; 1 Peter 3.19–20, 2 Peter 2.4, and Jude 14 all quote from 1 Enoch, on which see quixotically J. Magne, *From Christianity to Gnosis* (Atlanta, 1992), 90–91.

11. The best introductory guide to Gnosticism is still, I think, E. Pagels, *The Gnostic Gospels* (New York, 1980). Further reading: E. Pagels, *Adam, Eve and the Serpent* (New York, 1988); K. Rudolph, *Gnosis* (San Francisco, 1987); G. Filoramo, *A History of Gnosticism* (Oxford, 1990); C. Pétrement, *A Separate God* (London, 1991); and A. H. B. Logan, *Gnostic Truth and Christian Heresy* (Edinburgh, 1996).

12. Boyarin, *Carnal Israel*, 42ff., citing *Genesis Rabba* (on 2.20): a man "who has no wife remains without good, without help, without joy."

13. Justin, *Dialogue with Trypho* 62.

14. In 1 Enoch 6–8, the angels' motives varied from lust for human women to the desire to divulge to humans divine secrets of magic, agriculture, and craftsmanship. In Jubilees 4.15 and 22, the angels came down to earth to teach humans wisdom and uprightness, but fell victim to polluting sexuality.

15. Boyarin, *Carnal Israel*, 31ff., and D. R. MacDonald, *There Is No Male and Female* (Philadelphia, 1987). Contrast Philo, *The Giants* 29, "The chief cause of ignorance is the flesh. . . . Marriage and the rearing of children, the provision of necessities . . . wilt the flower of wisdom, before it blooms," with Babylonian Talmud, Avoda Zara 5a: "Let us be grateful to our ancestors, for if they had not sinned, we would not have come into this world."

16. Philo, *On Creation* 152 on Eve: "Desire begat bodily pleasure, that pleasure which is the beginning of wrong and the violation of law, the pleasure for the sake of which humans bring on themselves mortality." On Adam and Eve's sexuality, see *Genesis Rabba* 18.6 and 19.3, discussed by Boyarin, *Carnal Israel*, 77ff., and cf. Pagels, *Adam, Eve and the Serpent*, 57ff.

17. Hippolytus, *Refutation* 5.(12)17: "the Son is the serpent," a view attributed to the heretical Peratae; cf. Secret Book (Apocryphon) of John 2.1.22 (*NHL*, 117, and parallels).

18. Augustine, for example, knows that the sexual urge, if it existed in paradise, would not have been as it is now; there was then no tension between flesh and spirit, only perfect peace; see *Letter* *6.5. Cf. John Chrysostom, *Homilies on Genesis* 18.4.

19. J. M. Robinson, ed., *The Nag Hammadi Library in English* (Leiden³, 1988), is the standard edition. M. A. Williams, *Rethinking Gnosticism* (Princeton, 1996), doubts that the categories Gnostics, Gnosticism are useful. They seem too well established to be changed; but he is right, of course; each is an omnibus, with diverse passengers.

20. One orthodox Christian tactic was to reduce Gnosticism to a series of propositions in order to make it seem ridiculous. It was a procedure which backfired when non-Christians like Celsus and Porphyry applied similar critical techniques to some effect against Christian dogma; see Origen, *Against Celsus*, and Porphyry (or other anti-Christians) reported by Macarius Magnes, *Response (Apocriticus)*.

21. On the Gnostic imagination, see Filoramo, *History of Gnosticism*, 38ff.; cf. H. Jonas, *The Gnostic Religion* (London, 1992), 48ff.

22. Spirituals *(pneumatikoi)*, sensualists *(psychikoi)*, and dross, or literally, materialists *(hylikoi)* are common Gnostic names for three strata of humans; cf. Irenaeus, *Against Heresies* 1.6.

23. "It is I who am God; no other one exists. . . . He had been afraid that they might know that another one existed before him . . . being devoid of understanding, he scoffed . . . recklessly and said: 'If anything has existed before me, let it appear.' . . . And immediately behold, Light came out of the eighth heaven . . . it was beautiful. . . . And he was greatly ashamed." On the Origins of the World 2.5.107–8 *(NHL,* 177).

24. M. Tardieu, *Ecrits gnostiques, Codex de Berlin [8502]* (Paris, 1984), 103; cf. Secret Book (Apocryphon) of John 2.1.9 *(NHL,* 109).

25. What follows is my shortened version of the account of the teachings of Valentinus and his followers given by Irenaeus, orthodox bishop of Lyon at the end of the second century, *Against Heresies* 1.1–5, with one small borrowing from the Apocryphon of John 2.1.10 *(NHL,* 110). But there are numerous variants, such as Hippolytus, *Refutation* 6.24–32. For a detailed account see A. H. B. Logan, *Gnostic Truth and Christian Heresy* (Edinburgh, 1996), 71ff.

26. Yaldabaoth, by declaring himself to be a jealous God, implied that other Gods did really exist; why else would he be jealous? So the Apocryphon of John 2.1.13 *(NHL,* 112). On God's envy of Adam, see Genesis 3.5 and 23, and the numerous accusations levied against God in the *Clementine Homilies* 2.43–44 and 3.39ff.

27. It is tempting to think that the high profile of the female in Gnostic creation stories reflected some liturgical or social prominence of women in the real life of Gnostic sectarians; but there is precious little empirical support for succumbing. See the discussions in K. L. King, ed., *Images of the Feminine in Gnosticism* (Philadelphia, 1988).

28. The Apocryphon of John 2.1.5 *(NHL,* 107).

29. For example, Profundity, Silence, Intelligence, and Truth were all created well before the Word! How could the Word reasonably come at the beginning? "On the Origin of the World" begins: "Everyone, Gods of the world and humans, says that nothing exists before chaos, (but) I shall demonstrate that they are all mistaken" *(NHL,* 171–72).

30. This and what follows is from the Apocryphon of John 2.1.14ff. *(NHL,* 112ff.), much abridged with minor details from the *Hypostasis of the Archons* 2.4.87 *(NHL,* 163).

31. "On the Origin of the World" 2.5.109–10 *(NHL,* 178–79, slightly changed and cut). The blood of virginity creates roses, and other "beautiful, good-smelling flowers."

32. "It is I who am the mother. It is I who am the wife. It is I who am the virgin. It is I who am pregnant. It is I who am the midwife, who comforts pains of travail. It is my husband who bore me. It is I who am his mother." From "On the Origin of the World" 2.5.114 *(NHL,* 181); for a similarly startling set of contradictions, see The Thunder, Perfect Mind 6.2.13 *(NHL,* 297–98): the God is first/last, whore/holy, wife/virgin, mother/daughter, bride/bridegroom. "It is my husband who begot me, I am the mother of my father, the sister of my husband and he is my son . . . I am the silence which is incomprehensible." Wow!

33. "On the Origin of the World" 2.5.115–16 *(NHL,* 182).

34. "On the Origin of the World" 2.5.116ff. *(NHL,* 182ff.).

35. *Kephalaia (The Quintessence)* 15. Kephalaia literally means "chief points," or "headings"; *The Quintessence* perhaps captures its persuasive spirit better. See conveniently, I. Gardner, *The Kephalaia of the Teacher* (Leiden, 1995); my translations were orig-

inally from the German of H-J. Polotsky and A. Boehlig, *Kephalaia* (Stuttgart, 1940 and 1966), later checked against Gardner. In general, see S. N. C. Lieu, *Manichaeism in the Later Roman Empire and Medieval China* (Tübingen², 1992), or for a brief introduction, H. Jonas, *The Gnostic Religion* (Boston, 1958), 206ff.

36. *Kephalaia* 7–8 and 12.

37. Cited as *Kephalaia* 154 by C. Schmidt and H-J. Polotsky, "Ein Mani-Fund in Aegypten," *Sitzungsberichte der preussischen Akademie der Wissenschaften (Phil-hist. Kl) (=SPAW)* (1933), 42 and 86.

38. *Kephalaia* 8–9.

39. A. Henrichs and L. Koenen, *Der Kölner Mani-Kodex* (Opladen 1988); the first part is translated into English by R. Cameron and A. J. Dewey, *The Cologne Mani Codex* (Missoula, 1979), 66. See also Hegemonius, *Acta Archelai* 5, where Mani's letter opens with the words "Manichaios, apostle of Jesus Christ."

40. F. C. Andreas and W. B. Henning, "Mitteliranische Manichaica aus Chinesisch-Turkestan II," *SPAW* (1933), 307–8. Of course, Jesus was begotten, not made, while Mani was created, not begotten. For specialists, the difference was critical.

41. The quotation (with omissions) is from *The Cologne Mani Codex* 103–5 = Henrichs, Mani-Kodex: 72–75.

42. Andreas and Henning, "Mitteliranische Manichaica II," 295–96.

43. C. W. Mitchell, ed., Ephraem, *Discourses to Hypatius* 5 (Oxford, 1912), 93.

44. On dress, Hegemonius, *Acta Archelai* 14. On successive kings, C. R. C. Allberry, *A Manichaean Psalm Book* (Stuttgart, 1938), Psalm 241, p. 43, on whose beautiful translations I rely and refer to in this section as psalms.

45. W. B. Henning, "Mani's Last Journey," *Bulletin of the School of Oriental and African Studies* 10 (1939–42), 950–52. Zoroastrianism, the worship of the fire god, Mazda, was the traditional and dominant religion of the Persian empire under the Sassanid kings.

46. Psalms 225, 226, and 241; flayed skin: Epiphanius, *Panarion* 66.12.2.

47. Alexander of Lycopolis, *Against the Manichees* 2. Alexander, a Neoplatonist writing about 300 CE, clearly thought of Mani as a Christian heretic. See P. W. van der Horst and J. Mansfield, *An Alexandrian Platonist Against Dualism* (Leiden, 1974). For the Roman imperial decrees against the Manichees, see *Comparison of Mosaic and Roman Laws* 15.3 (302 CE) and *Theodosian Code* 16.5.9ff.

48. On the westward spread of Manichaeism, see S. N. C. Lieu, *Manichaeism in Mesopotamia and the Roman East* (Leiden, 1994), 22ff.; and for its eastern spread his *Manichaeism in the Late Roman Empire and Medieval China* (Tübingen², 1992), 219ff.

49. *Kephalaia* 7–8.

50. *Kephalaia* 6.

51. D. N. MacKenzie, "Mani's Sabuhragan," *Bulletin of the School of Oriental and African Studies* 42 (1979), 517–19; it was originally written in Persian for the king Sabuhr (Shapur): "When those evildoers writhe in the conflagration, and say to the faithful, Give us a lifeline to pull us up and save us from burning." Similar postmortem intrusions of persecution are found in *Kephalaia* 187.

52. *The Cologne Mani Codex* 65 and 22–23. Cf. Theodore bar Koni in A. V. W. Jackson, *Researches in Manichaeism* (New York, 1932), 253: Adam looked at his body and said, "Woe, woe to the maker of my body and the jailer of my soul."

53. B. Dodge, ed., *The Fihrist of al-Nadim* (New York, 1970), vol. 2., 774; and F. C. Andreas and W. Henning, "Mitteliranische Manichaica aus Chinesisch-Turkestan III," *SPAW* (1934), 860–61.

54. *The Cologne Mani Codex* 3–4, 7, 23–25, 51, and 65.

55. "Journey to India," *Kephalaia* 15; Ascension, Psalm 241, p. 44; Judgment of sinners, Psalm 230, p. 26.

56. Psalms 225, p. 15, and 241, p. 44 (with omissions).

57. So, for example, Alexander of Lycopolis, *Against the Manichees* 3.

58. Versions vary. Psalm 219.25 makes it clear that the First Man of Glory was also seen as warrior, while other accounts envisage Light's tactic of sending out First Man as an enticing sacrifice. So Psalm 223.31: "Like unto a shepherd," and Psalm 246, p. 54.

59. Epiphanius, *Panarion* 66.25.8; cf. 66.47.6.

60. *Kephalaia* 38–39; Augustine, *On the Nature of Good* 44; Theodore bar Koni: Jackson, *Researches in Manichaeism*, 236ff.; Epiphanius, *Panarion* 66.27ff. The Manichaean anthropogony seems to owe a lot to the Gnostic myths discussed in the previous section of this chapter.

61. Psalm 246 (translated by Allberry), p. 54.

62. *The Fihrist of al-Nadim* (ed. Dodge), vol. 2, 784.

63. The truncated accounts we have from Alexander of Lycopolis, Hegemonius, Epiphanius, Severus of Antioch *(Homily* 123), Ephraim, *Prose Refutations of Mani*, and Titus of Bostra are all hostile.

64. *Kephalaia* 38–40.

65. *Kephalaia* 38–41.

66. *Kephalaia* 99; cf. for these ideas in general, *Kephalaia* 95–99.

67. S. N. C. Lieu, *Manichaeism in Mesopotamia and the Roman East* (Leiden, 1994), 203ff., has a longish discussion of formulas used for renouncing Manichaeism by converts to Christianity.

68. Shapur's achievements on the rock face are replicated in Parthian, Middle Persian, and Greek on the walls of the impressive nearby sanctuary (the Kabar of Zoroaster). The trilingual texts of Shapur's inscriptions and three Middle Persian texts of Kartir's achievements are given with translation and learned commentary by M. Sprengling, *Third Century Iran, Sapor and Kartir* (Chicago, 1953). The fourth Kartir text is given by P. Gignoux, "L'inscription de Kartir à Sar Mashad," *Journal Asiatique* 256 (1968), 390ff; cf. M. L. Chaumont in *JA* 248 (1960), 345ff. The Greek text of Shapur is also grandly edited by E. Honigman and A. Maricq, *Recherches sur les Res gesta divi Saporis* (Brussels, 1953).

69. F. Sarre and E. Herzfeld, *Iranische Felsreliefs* (Berlin, 1910), 77, and plate 7.

70. Sprengling, *Third-Century Iran*, 17, on Naqsh-i-Rustem.

71. Sprengling, *Third-Century Iran*, 53, and Gignoux, *L'inscription*, 397.

72. This is an amalgam of Sprengling, *Third-Century Iran*, 14ff., and Gignoux, *L'inscription*, 390ff.

73. L. Trümpelmann, *Iranische Denkmäler* (Berlin, 1975), plate 7.

74. Sprengling, *Third-Century Iran*, 50–52, and Gignoux, *L'inscription*, 397ff. For the intensification of religious centralization in Iran in the fourth century under Shapur II, see R. C. Zaehner, *The Dawn and Twilight of Zoroastrianism* (New York, 1961), 176ff.

75. In a fourth inscription (at Naqsh-i-Rajab), Kartir made the brief assertion that there is a heaven and there is a hell, but this is a rare clue about the substance of his beliefs; Sprengling, *Third-Century Iran*, 66–67; but cf. the vision by Kartir or one of his followers, Gignoux, *L'inscription*, 401ff.

76. Augustine wrote a dozen anti-Manichaean tracts (see principally *Against Fortunatus, Against Faustus, Against Felix*, and *Against the Letter Which Manichaeans Call Fundamental*, and *Confessions* 5.8ff. and 24); they are very wordy, but not as long-winded as his later anti-Pelagian tracts. See best, the insightful biography by P. Brown, *Augustine of Hippo* (Berkeley, 1967).

77. P. Monceaux, *Mémoires de l'institut national de France* 43 (1933), 41ff., argues convincingly that the chapters of Faust's original had become disarranged before Augustine received them. In Monceaux's rearrangement, they cluster around four main themes: the falsity of Catholic views on Christ's incarnation, interpolations in the New Testament, the rejectability of the Old Testament, and rival conceptions of God.

78. R. Lim, *Public Disputations in Late Antiquity* (Berkeley, 1995). On the burning of Manichees, according to a law of Diocletian of 302 CE, see *Comparison of Mosaic and Roman Law* 15.3: leaders were to be burned with their books, their followers executed, unless they were of high status, in which case they were to be sent to the mines. See also *Theodosian Code* 16.5.9ff. (382 CE onward) for a dozen laws directed with increasing ferocity against Manichees.

79. This brief statement of the essentials of Faust's arguments is a selective summary of the points which Augustine attributed to Faust in the opening sections of books 1–33 of *Against Faust the Manichee*, with special reference to 1.2; 2.1; 4.1; 5.1; 17.1; 22.2.

80. The previous and following paragraphs are taken from Augustine, *Against Faust the Manichee*, 1.3; 22.6; 15.5; 4.2; 6.2; 19.13 and 8; 11.2 and 5.

81. The preceding paragraphs are a combination from various of Augustine's anti-Manichaean tracts: *Against the Letter Which the Manichaeans Call Fundamental* (LMF), *Against Fortunatus* (CFo), as well as *Against Faustus* (CF): LMF 9.6.5 and CFo 9; LMF 1.3 and 5; CF 5.5, 5.8, and 5.10; CFo 15 and 22; LMF 42–44.

82. Possidius, *Life of Augustine* 28–31.What follows is my invented reconstruction of what Augustine should have thought if he wondered that he was wrong, and took the accusations of his opponents more seriously than the defensive stance in his polemical writings allowed. See E. A. Clark, "On Augustine's Manichean Past," in *Ascetic Piety and Women's Faith* (Lewiston, N.Y., 1986), 291ff., and *The Origenist Controversy* (Princeton, 1992), 194ff.

83. The name of Augustine's mistress, otherwise unattested, is now confirmed by the Norwegian novelist J. Gaarder, *Vita Brevis* (London, 1997), 11. Augustine's son by Floria, Adeodatus (God-given), died in 390. The remembered cruelty of Augustine's father leaks out repeatedly in his writings; see B. Shaw, "The Family in Late Antiquity," *Past and Present* 115 (1987), 18 and 24. Augustine projected this cruel father, who "shows kindness by beating" *(Sermon* 13.9), onto his image of a demanding and punitive, if just, God. At least, that's what I imagine.

84. Donatists were a schismatic Christian church, with a significant membership and organization in north Africa throughout the fourth century, and beyond. The previous two paragraphs are mainly from Augustine, *Answer to the Letters of Petilian the Donatist* 2.185–86; *Acts of the Council at Carthage of 411*, 1.133.85; 2.10 and 12; Augustine, *Letter* 204.3; *Confessions* 3.10; Pelagius, *On Riches* 6.3.

85. Augustine's thought is a quagmire; see helpfully P. Brown, *Augustine of Hippo* (London, 1967); G. R. Evans, *Augustine on Evil* (Cambridge, 1982); B. R. Rees, *Pelagius* (Woodbridge, 1988), and *The Letters of Pelagius* (Woodbridge, 1991). My text here is a mosaic from Augustine, *Confessions* 7.7 and 27, and 10.39; *Sermon* 294.10; *On the Grace of Christ* 3, 8, 13–14; *On Rebuke and Grace* 45; *On the Proceedings of Pelagius* 57 and 65; *On Original Sin* 23.

EIGHT: *Jesus and the New Testament*, or, *The Construction of a Sacred Hero*

1. Even at the beginning of the twentieth century, the Roman Catholic Pontifical Biblical Commission was insisting that the gospels of Matthew and John (!) were substantially eyewitness accounts. So R. E. Brown, *The Birth of the Messiah* (London, 1993), 27.

The Christian heretic Marcion in the second century was more realistic, and knew that the gospels were fakes: if the apostles were illiterate, they couldn't have written the gospels. Some Christian thinkers turned the disciples' illiteracy to their advantage: the success of their teaching was proof of their divine inspiration. So Origen, *Against Celsus* 1.62; John Chrysostom, *Homilies on 1 Corinthians* 3.10. Celsus thought that the gospels were "fictitious tales" *(plasmata)* whose text Christians altered at will in order to win arguments with one another *(Against Celsus* 2.26–27).

2. The title "son of God" occurs in hundreds of surviving Greek inscriptions from all over the eastern empire. But for the sensitively republican Roman elite, Augustus was only *divi filius* (in Greek: *theiou huios)*, which means son of the divine, or godlike, as distinct from son of God *(deus, theos)*. Augustus was the (adopted) son of his deified father, Julius Caesar, whose ascent to heaven had been marked by the appearance of a comet. As with Jesus, his divinity was confimed only after death. After Augustus, "son of God" became a regular imperial title, with which Christians would have been familiar. On the title "God" for pagan holy men, see Philostratus, *Life of Apollonius of Tyana* 8.5 (allegedly said in his own defense before the emperor Domitian): "Every man who is considered good is honored with the title God."

3. On Christians' prayers for the emperor, "for the empire's stability and prosperity," see Tertullian, *Apology* 30–32. On *archontes* as evil, see, for example, *The Hypostasis of the Archons* 2.4.92–96 *(NHL,* 166–69) on "the arrogant rulers of unrighteousness" and "the unrighteousness of the kingdom of absolute power."

4. The date of Jesus' birth is not known. After Herod's death, Galilee was separated from Judaea and ruled by one of Herod's sons, Antipas. In 6 CE, Rome deposed the local ruler, another of Herod's sons, Archelaus, and imposed direct Roman rule under a subgovernor. So Judaea, but not Galilee (pace Luke), was included in the census of 6 CE, to which there was considerable resistance by rural Jews, which the Roman army crushed. See Josephus, *Jewish Antiquities* 18.1, and the thorough discussion in E. Schuerer, *The History of the Jewish People in the Age of Jesus Christ* (Edinburgh, 1973), vol. 1, 399ff.

5. R. E. Brown, *The Death of the Messiah* (London, 1994), 1373ff., has a neat summary of the problems.

6. The account of Paul's teaching and journeys given by Luke in the Acts of the Apostles is theologically purposeful, and treacherous if mined for facts, rather than for representations. See R. I. Pervo, *Profit with Delight* (Philadelphia, 1987). Romans, 1 and 2 Corinthians, Galatians, Colossians, and 1 Thessalonians are genuine, albeit interpolated.

7. I have found H. Koester, *Ancient Christian Gospels* (London, 1990), persuasively impressive. G. Theissen, *The Historical Jesus* (London, 1998) is comprehensive, clear, and has up-to-date bibliography, but is rather positivist.

8. H. von Campenhausen, *The Formation of the Christian Bible* (London, 1972), is fundamental.

9. H. Koester puts this case with clarity in W. L. Petersen, ed., *Gospel Traditions in the Second Century* (Notre Dame, 1989), 19–38; F. Wisse, ibid., 39–54, disagrees.

10. The canonical text has instead: "You are my beloved son, in whom I am well pleased." The variant text is given in a third-century papyrus codex (P⁴) and is the one quoted in the mid–second century by Justin, *Dialogue with Trypho* 88. The vegetarian text change from *akrides* to *enkrides* is noted by Epiphanius, *Panarion* 30.13.4.

11. The parallel passages are at Matthew 12.1ff. and Luke 6.1ff. The omission of the saying in Markan manuscripts may have been caused by the scribe's lack of interest in the sabbath issue, or as part of a general process of harmonizing the differing gospel texts with one another, or both.

12. The extra Jesus saying is in Codex Bezae; it seems to hold a careful balance between Jewish-Christians, who should observe the law, and gentile Christians, who should break it only with forethought. The additional Jesus saying about the sabbath is from P. Oxy. 1, Saying 2, also found in the Gospel of Thomas, Saying 27 (*NHL*, 129). See, in general, D. C. Parker, *The Living Text of the Gospels* (Cambridge, 1997), 33ff.

13. A. Harnack, *Marcion: The Gospel of the Alien God* (Durham, N.C., 1990), is both idealizing and fundamental. On Justin, see Koester, *Ancient Christian Gospels*, 360ff.; Justin consciously harmonizes Matthew and Luke, but also makes cuts and additions. On Tatian, see W. L. Petersen in Koester, *Ancient Christian Gospels*, 403ff., and T. Baarda, *Essays on the Diatessaron* (Kampen, 1994), 29ff.

14. 2 Peter 3.16: of Paul's letters, "There are some things in them difficult to understand, which the ignorant and unbalanced twist to their own destruction." For false teachers, see, for example, 1 John 2.18; 2 John 7; 3 John 10. Luke 1.1 states that already by his time, many written Christian accounts existed. See also helpfully, J. D. G. Dunn, *Unity and Diversity in the New Testament* (London², 1990).

15. M. J. Mulder, ed., *Mikra, Text, Tradition, Translation, Reading and Interpretation of the Hebrew Bible in Ancient Judaism and Early Christianity* (Assen, 1988).

16. See, for example, Justin, *1 Apology* 12: "It is God's work to announce something before it happens and then to demonstrate that it happened as predicted." Cf. Tertullian, *Apology* 20.

17. Jesus' consciousness of his own divinity is theologically problematic; if Jesus was conscious of his divinity, then he could not have had a completely human experience, and so is less of a model for humans' capacity to rise above human limitations.

18. On John's knowledge of Mark's miracle source and independence from the synoptics, see Koester, *Ancient Christian Gospels*, 253ff.

19. I am much indebted here to H. von Campenhausen, *Ecclesiastical Authority and Spiritual Power* (London, 1969), 1ff. On Jesus and Rabbis, see C. Hezser, *The Social Structure of the Rabbinic Movement in Roman Palestine* (Tübingen, 1997), 55ff.

20. Tertullian captures this contrast between unbelievers' incredulity and believers' wonder: "We wonder because we believe"; God places "the physical basis of his operations in impossibility" *(On Baptism* 2). The frame myths of God's creation and Jesus' incarnation are juxtaposed with Jesus' miracles on earth in the opening of the second-century Epistle of the Apostles 3–5.

21. In 1835, K. Gutzkow in his appalling novel *Wally die Zweiflerin (Wally the Skeptic)*, originally published in Mannheim in 1835 (trans. Bern, 1974), p. 100, wrote: "Jesus was a Jew who had no idea of establishing a new religion"; he was arrested and thrown into prison in Mannheim for attacking Christianity. His books, past, present, and future, were banned. His publisher, who claimed not to have read the novel, was freed.

22. G. L. Archer and G. Chirichigno, *Old Testament Quotations in the New Testament* (Chicago, 1983), xi. The New Testament writers mostly used the then standard Greek translation of the Hebrew Bible, the Septuagint, rather than the Hebrew Bible itself. The boundaries between what counts as a quotation and what an echo are disputed. So B. and K. Aland, *Novum Testamentum Graece* (Stuttgart²⁷, 1993), 770ff., list 160 quotations and 2,600 echoes of the Old Testament in the New Testament.

23. In general, see Brown, *The Birth of the Messiah*, 71ff. The four women are variously thought to be sinners, gentiles, or a demonstration of God's reliance on women to fulfill his purpose. Ancient commentators such as John Chrysostom *(Homilies on Matthew* 3) and Jerome *(On Matthew* 9) saw them as sinners, and connected that to Jesus' need for

some sin in his origins, since he was to live among sinful humans. Cf. Origen, *Homilies on Luke* 28.2, on the genealogy of Jesus.

24. This meaning, "God with us," is artfully paralleled by Jesus' closing words in the last chapter of Matthew: "and lo, I am with you always to the end of times" (Matthew 28.20). The shape of the annunciation is mirrored in the angel's speech to Hagar: "You are with child and will bear a son. You shall name him Ishmael [meaning: "God hears"] because the Lord has heard of your ill treatment" (Genesis 16.11). Matthew writes with more art than is sometimes allowed.

25. See, for example, Justin, *Dialogue with Trypho* 43. All this happens, according to Matthew, in Bethlehem. But Luke has Joseph and Mary travel for the census and birth from Nazareth to Bethlehem; Matthew has Joseph travel from the birth at Bethlehem, after an interval, back to Nazareth via Egypt.

26. Miraculous births were well known in antiquity. The emperor Augustus was begotten by the union of his mother with a snake in a temple. But the virgin birth seems to have been an original idea. See H. von Campenhausen, *The Virgin Birth in the Theology of the Ancient Church* (London, 1964), and T. Boslooper, *The Virgin Birth* (London, 1962).

27. A. A. MacArthur, *The Evolution of the Christian Year* (London, 1953), 32ff. The first attested celebration of Christmas was in 336 in Rome; see T. Mommsen, ed., *Chronica Minora (The Calendar of 354)* (Berlin, 1892), 71. In the east, the birthday and baptism of Jesus were both celebrated on January 6 until well into the fourth century. But a separate Christmas was celebrated in Antioch in the 370s and is attested a little later in Constantinople. See John Chrysostom, *Sermon on Christmas Day*; Gregory Nazianzen, *Oration 38 (On the Birthday of Christ*; 381 CE).

28. Paul links the godhead of Jesus only to the resurrection: "descended from David according to the flesh, but designated son of God in power according to the holy spirit by his resurrection from the dead, Jesus the Messiah our Lord" (Romans 1.3–4).

29. There is no mention of the virgin birth in Barnabas and the *Shepherd of Hermas*; Justin recognizes that some Christians do not believe in the virgin birth *(Dialogue with Trypho* 48 and 68; cf. *1 Apology* 33). For Jesus' normal human birth, see Irenaeus, *Heresies* 1.26; for his descent like an angel when adult, see Hippolytus, *Refutation* 7.31; Epiphanius, *Panarion* 41.1.7; born of a virgin, but took none of her human nature, "like water through a tube," see Irenaeus, *Heresies* 3.11.3.

30. The three-magi story is an elaboration of the story of Balaam in Numbers 22–24; Balaam is a man from the east, a magus (so Philo, *Life of Moses* 1.276), has two comrades (Numbers 22.22) and makes a prophecy: "A star will rise from Jacob, and a man will stand forth from Israel" (Numbers 24.17 LXX); the star is also a king (see Targum Ps. Jonathan on the passage; cf. note 36 below).

31. For example, Matthew 2.13–14 = Exodus 2.15; Matthew 2.16 = Exodus 1.22; Matthew 2.19 = Exodus 2.23; Matthew 2.19–20 = Exodus 4.19; Matthew 2.21 = Exodus 4.20.

32. The fullest account is from Josephus, *Jewish Antiquities* 2.205–16, published in 93/4, after Matthew, but independent of it. The last quotation is from Philo, *Life of Moses* 1.1 (pre-Matthew). See also Miriam's prediction of Moses' greatness in the first century, Ps. Philo, *Biblical Antiquities* 9.10ff.: "The spirit of God came upon Miriam, and she saw a dream." The much later *Midrash Rabbah* on Exodus 1.22 has Miriam prophesy that "her mother will give birth to a son who will save Israel."

33. The quotation is from 2 Samuel 7.14; this ruler will be "the son of God, and the son of the Most High will they call him" in Dead Sea Scrolls, 4 Q 246; for Israel collec-

tively, see Exodus 4.22, Hosea 11.1; for angels, Psalm 29.1; for the pious, Ben Sirach 4.10; discussed by Brown, *The Birth of the Messiah*, 136.

34. Joseph's other children came from a previous marriage; so (Protoevangelium) First Gospel of James 9 and Origen, *Commentary on Matthew* 10.17. In the late fourth century, Helvidius argued that Jesus' brothers and sisters were the natural children of Joseph and Mary born after Jesus, but was savagely attacked for his views by Jerome, who believed the siblings of Jesus mentioned in the gospels were really cousins; see his *Against Helvidius*.

35. Tertullian, *On the Flesh of Christ* 5, is commenting on Christ's death and resurrection: "The Son of God died. This is to be believed, because it makes no sense. And he was buried and rose again. This fact is certain, because it is impossible."

36. *1 Clement* 31.3 and Barnabas 7.2, but above all, S. G. Hall, ed., *Melito of Sardis* (Oxford, 1979), frags. 9–11; cf. *On Pascha* 59 and 69. For first-century Jewish texts, see Josephus, *Jewish Antiquities* 1.227, and Ps. Philo, *Biblical Antiquities* 32.3; cf. Jubilees 17.54. The much later (sixth- or seventh-century) elaborations (targums) of Genesis incorporated or magnified the tradition; see M. McNamara, ed., *The Aramaic Bible* (Edinburgh, 1992) vols. 1A and 1B, on Genesis 22.10ff.

37. Ps. Philo, *Biblical Antiquities* 32.3; according to Jubilees 17.15ff. the idea to test Abraham's faith came from Satan. Isaac's age was twenty-five, according to Josephus, *Jewish Antiquities* 1.227.

38. 4 Maccabees 16.20; the final quotation is from S. G. Hall, ed., *Melito of Sardis* (Oxford, 1979), frag., 9, pp. 74–75.

39. The hostility of father toward Jesus is implicitly recognized in the Gnostic Gospel of Philip: Joseph the carpenter makes the cross on which Jesus was crucified (2.3.73; *NHL*, 153).

40. D. de Bruyn, "Prologues bibliques d'origine marcionite," *Revue bénédictine* 24 (1907), 11.

41. This argument is obviously insecure. Josephus, *Jewish War* 6.300ff., records that Jesus, son of Ananias, went round Jerusalem in 61 repeatedly prophesying the destruction of Jerusalem and the temple. He was arrested and beaten by the leading Jews, but persisted in his prophecies; he was arrested again and brought before the Roman governor; he refused to answer questions, was flogged mercilessly, and was then dismissed as a madman.

42. This dating of Mark is little more than a guess. *Per contra*, dependency of Mark on Matthew and Luke is unlikely, because Mark leaves out both nativity and postresurrection appearances; Mark 16.9–20 is a later addition, which does not appear in some good ancient manuscripts. All this is standard stuff; see, for example, the commentary by E. P. Sanders and M. Davies, *Studying the Synoptic Gospels* (London, 1989).

43. Listed for example by Koester, *Ancient Christian Gospels*, 53, which is fundamental. I am much indebted to him in this section.

44. The literature is substantial. See helpfully, S. J. Patterson, *The Gospel of Thomas and Jesus* (Sonoma, Calif., 1993).

45. Koester, *Ancient Christian Gospels*, 75ff., puts these arguments very persuasively.

46. Protoevangelium (First Gospel) of James 9–10, 16, and 19–20 confirms the old age of Joseph, a prosperous builder, Mary's postconception and postbirth virginity, and her Davidic descent, and harmonizes the Matthew and Luke birth narratives. For this and the Infancy Gospel of Thomas, see conveniently J. K. Elliott, *The Apocryphal New Testament* (Oxford, 1993), 48ff.

47. J. S. Kloppenborg, *The Formation of Q* (Philadelphia, 1987), and more generally, B. Mack, *Who Wrote the New Testament?* (San Francisco, 1995), as well as Koester, *Ancient Christian Gospels*, make detailed and ingenious suggestions about the timing of the different levels of composition.

48. J. D. G. Dunn, *Unity and Diversity in the New Testament* (London², 1990), provides a useful introduction to the earliest levels. G. Vermes, *Jesus the Jew* (London², 1983), sets Jesus helpfully in his Jewish context, as does E. P. Sanders, *Jesus and Judaism* (London, 1985).

49. Again I follow here the convincing and innovative arguments of H. Koester, *Ancient Christian Gospels*, 75ff.

50. For example, Gospel of Thomas, Sayings 75ff., and see Koester, *Ancient Christian Gospels*, 104.

51. See M. Lichtheim, *Ancient Egyptian Literature* (Berkeley, 1990), vol. 3, 159 and 184ff.: "I have not burned to do evil . . . the God knows it; I have not taken vengeance on another, another has not suffered on my account. The sin which I have committed unwittingly, I beg forgiveness for it. I call to the God to have mercy on me and give me sweetness" (p. 213).

52. "The disciples said to him: 'When will the kingdom come?' Jesus said: 'It will not come by waiting for it. It will not be a matter of saying "here it is" or "there it is." Rather the kingdom of the Father is spread out upon the earth, and people do not see it' " (Gospel of Thomas, Saying 113 (*NHL*, 138); cf. Luke 17.20–21 and Gospel of Thomas, Sayings 50 and 90).

53. I follow the argument here of M. Goulder, *A Tale of Two Missions* (London, 1994), 16ff. John 21 was probably added on later by a different author, who has Peter play a bigger part than in the rest of John, but even so Peter is in the end rejected by Jesus and told not to interfere (21.22).

54. Parker, *Living Text of the Gospels*, 49ff., has a learned discussion of the problems with the ancient versions of the texts.

55. This is a common but mistaken view. Luke's Jesus says explicitly (8.10) that he taught in parables in order not (*hina me*) to be understood; on which see brilliantly F. Kermode, *The Genesis of Secrecy* (Cambridge, Mass., 1979), 23ff. Theissen, *The Historical Jesus*, 109, is sure that Jesus taught in parables, but John clearly did not know, since there are virtually none in his gospel.

56. Ibn Qutayba, *Uyun al-Akhbar* (Cairo, 1925), vol. 1, 327. See also T. Khalidi, *The Muslim Jesus* (Cambridge, Mass., in press).

57. A. Schweitzer, *The Quest for the Historical Jesus* (London, 1910).

58. The third-century Coptic *Pistis Sophia (Faith Wisdom)*, trans. V. MacDermot (Leiden, 1978), 1.1 and 4.136, has Jesus reappear twice after his resurrection to teach his disciples, once for eleven years, the second time more briefly. The Apocryphon (Secret Book) of James has Jesus appear back on earth 550 days after the resurrection, and teach only James and Peter (and so by implication, not the majority of Christians) to believe in the cross and to seek death by suffering martyrdom (*NHL* 1.2.6, p. 32).

59. Tertullian, *On Baptism* 17, and Epiphanius, *Panarion* 49.2 and 79 (by implication); cf. E. Castelli, "Gender, Theory and the Rise of Early Christianity," *Journal of Early Christian Studies* 6 (1998), 227ff., for an excellent survey of the literature and problems of women in the early church; and within Gnostic sects, see the excellent essays in K. L. King, ed., *Images of the Feminine in Gnosticism* (Philadelphia, 1988).

60. The quotations are from *Pistis Sophia* 2.86–87; 1.19.25 and 36; 4.146 successively.

Complementarily, other Christian texts attacked clergy for overclaiming, "as if they received authority from God" (Apocalypse of Peter 7.2.79, *NHL*, 379).

61. Gospel of Mary in *NHL*, 524–27. A. Marjanen, *The Woman Jesus Loved* (Leiden, 1996), presents a thorough review of the ten Gnostic texts in which Mary Magdalene appears. My analysis is much indebted to his.

62. Gospel of Thomas, Saying 114 (*NHL*, 138).

63. Gospel of Philip 2.3.63–64 (*NHL*, 148). Marjanen, 151ff., thinks the word used for partner here, *koinonos*, can mean partner/spouse/spiritual consort, any or all of these three; presumably the ambiguity is intentional. *Mouth* is Schenke's plausible conjecture.

64. *The Exegesis on the Soul* 2.6.131–33 (*NHL*, 194–95) tells the sad/joyful story of a woman raped who then prostitutes herself, repents, is saved, baptized, cleansed, and unites with her brother, sent specially by God, in the ritual, uncarnal marriage of the bridal chamber. In this story, sexuality is desexualized; but can it be?

65. The baptistery at Ravenna dates from the sixth century. On God with breasts, see Odes of Solomon 19; for Jesus transfigured, Acts of John 88–90; on statues, see T. Mathews, *Clash of the Gods* (Princeton, 1993), who overstates his case; Jesus, when not male, is androgyne/angelic more than hermaphrodite; see best the critical review by P. Brown in *Art Bulletin* 77 (1995), 499ff.

66. Family Trinity, see Gospel of Truth 1.3.23 (*NHL*, 43); Gospel of Philip 2.3.55 (*NHL*, 143).

67. The *Great Questions of Mary*, unknown except for their excerption by Epiphanius, *Panarion* 26.8.

68. On semen and menstrual blood, see Epiphanius, *Panarion* 25–26; V. MacDermot, ed., *The Books of Jeu* (Leiden, 1978) 2.43 (p. 100), and V. MacDermot, ed., *Pistis Sophia* 4.146. Gospel of Philip 2.3.61, 66, and 82ff. (*NHL*, 148–49 and 158–60), on which see best, E. H. Pagels, "The Mystery of Marriage in the Gospel of Philip," in B. A. Pearson, ed., *The Future of Early Christianity* (Minneapolis, 1990), 442ff. She stresses the purposeful ambiguities of the text.

69. Epiphanius, *Panarion* 26.9–17.

70. See helpfully, J. Carleton Paget, *The Epistle of Barnabas* (Tübingen, 1994), 134ff., and W. Horbury, *Jews and Christians* (Edinburgh, 1998), 127ff. The Epistle of Barnabas, early second century, was much respected subsequently by orthodox Christians, and was for long treated by some as genuinely apostolic. The scapegoat comparison is in Chapter Seven, which is also where the quotations come from. The basic text on Yom Kippur is Leviticus 16; but Barnabas here, as Justin, *Dialogue with Trypho* 40, and Tertullian, *Against Marcion* 3.7 (all similar), depends on later Jewish elaborations of Leviticus, which we also find in the Mishnah, Yoma 3.8ff.; cf. Tosefta, Kippurim 4.

71. E. Norelli, *L'ascensione di Isaia* (Bologna, 1994), 66ff., J. Knight, *The Ascension of Isaiah* (Sheffield, 1995), and J. H. Charlesworth, ed., *The Old Testament Pseudepigrapha* (London, 1983), vol. 2, 143ff.

72. This view is complementary to Revelation 20.4: "And I saw the souls of those who had been executed for their witness to Jesus and to the Word of God, and who did not bow down to worship the beast [Nero] or his image."

73. This is my summary of Marcion's arguments, which survive only in the work of his critics, principally Tertullian, *Against Marcion*, Irenaeus, *Heresies* 1.27, and Epiphanius, *Panarion* 42. A. Harnack, *Marcion: The Gospel of an Alien God* (Durham N.C., 1990), itself a partial translation of *Marcion, Evangelium des fremden Gottes* (Leipzig, 1924), is an inspiring if idealistic guide.

74. J. Pelikan, *The Emergence of the Catholic Tradition* (Chicago, 1971), 71ff., is a clear guide. Besides the sources cited in the previous note, see Eusebius, *History of the Church* 5.13. One obvious objection was that the Good God allowed the Creator God to be inferior; so Tertullian, *Against Marcion* 2.28.

75. The common English translation of *Logos* as "Word" is too prosaic. "Reason" captures its abstract sense better. Reason is a masculine form of its feminine synonym Wisdom, *Sophia*. In Ecclesiasticus 24.3, Wisdom says: "I am the word which was spoken by the Most High [God]." It clearly suits John and Justin to have God's messenger as male, in contrast to the Gnostic female Wisdom. So too Theophilus *(To Autolycus* 2.10): "With his Wisdom, God produced Reason, which he bore within himself, and produced it before all things."

76. These views are scattered throughout Justin's writings; see especially *Dialogue with Trypho* 59–62; *1 Apology* 5, 10, 33, 46, 59, and 63. Jesus as Reason, Wisdom, and even as the angel Gabriel becoming flesh in Mary, occurs also in the second-century Epistle of the Apostles 14. See helpfully, A. Grillmeier, *Christ in Christian Tradition* (London, 1975), vol. 1, 45ff., and J. Daniélou, *Theology of Jewish Christianity* (London, 1964), chapter 4.

77. Justin, *1 Apology* 13, and *2 Apology* 10. We are a long way here from the sophistications of fourth-century Christology; Justin works sometimes with a twofold God: God the Father/God the Son = Reason and Holy Spirit, and sometimes in liturgical passages with a threefold God, God the Father, Son, and Holy Spirit: *1 Apology* 61 and 65. He doesn't seem fussed about their interrelationship.

78. Justin, *1 Apology* 14, 39–40, 52, and 61ff.

79. Or we could say that Justin was just beginning to explore the tension expressed, but left unresolved, in the whole idea of God's incarnation in Jesus.

80. Eusebius, *History of the Church* 5.28 and 7.30; *Melito*, frag. 6: Jesus spent on earth thirty years as a man, three years as God. The Monarchians, who believed that God was one, even had support, so it was alleged, from Victorinus, bishop of Rome; so Hippolytus, *Refutation of All Heresies* 9.11; cf. 9.7, and *Against Noetus* 1.

81. Tertullian, *Against Praxeas* 3, and Hippolytus, *Against Noetus* 4.

82. No doubt rituals of baptism differed widely, but we can get a notion of one ideal, a journey through death to rebirth; see *The Apostolic Tradition* 16–23, John Chrysostom, *Baptismal Homilies*, and above all, Romans 6.3: "All of us who have been baptized into Jesus Christ were baptized into his death. We were buried therefore with him by baptism, so that [like Christ] . . . we too might walk in the newness of life."

Select Bibliography

Aland, B. and K., eds. *Novum Testamentum Graece* (Stuttgart[26], 1993).

Alföldi, A. *A Festival of Isis in Rome Under the Christian Emperors* (Budapest, 1937).

Alföldy, G. *Ausgewählte Beiträge* (Stuttgart, 1986).

Allberry, C. R. C. *A Manichaean Psalm Book* (Stuttgart, 1938).

Alliott, M. *Le culte d'Horus à Edfou* (Cairo, 1954).

Andreas, F. C., and W. B. Henning. "Mitteliranische Manichaica aus chinesisch-Turkestan II," *Sitzungsberichte der preussischen Akademie der Wissenschaften (Phil-hist. Kl)* = *SPAW* (1933).

Andreas, F. C. "Mitteliranische Manichaica aus chinesisch-Turkestan III," *SPAW* (1934) 295ff.

Andreas, F. C., and W. Henning. "Mitteliranische Manichaica aus chinesisch-Turkestan III," *SPAW* (1934) 861ff.

Archer, G. L., and G. Chirichigno. *Old Testament Quotations in the New Testament* (Chicago, 1983).

Attridge, H. W., and R. A. Dean. *The Syrian Goddess* (Missoula, 1976).

Avezzu, G. "Nuovi papiri da Tebtynis," *Bolletino d'istituto di filologia greca* 4 (1977/8).

Baarda, T. *Essays on the Diatessaron* (Kampen, 1994).

Bagnall, R., and B. W. Frier. *Demography of Roman Egypt* (Cambridge, 1994).

Bastianini, G., and C. Gallazi. "Un' epigrafe scomparsa di Tebtynis," *Tyche 3* (1988), 25ff., and *Tyche* 4 (1989), 1ff.

Bauckham, R. *Jude and the Relatives of Jesus* (Edinburgh, 1990).

Baumgarten, A. *The Flourishing of Jewish Sects in the Maccabean Era* (Leiden, 1997).

Bayly, S. *Saints, Goddesses and Kings* (Cambridge, 1989).

Beard, M. "The Roman and the Foreign," in N. Thomas and C. Humphrey, eds., *Shamanism, History and the State* (Ann Arbor, 1994).

Beard, M., J. North, and S. Price. *Religions of Rome* (Cambridge, 1998), 2 vols.

Berger, A. *Das Bad in byzantischer Zeit* (Munich, 1982).

Betz, H. D., ed. *The Greek Magical Papyri in Translation* (Chicago, 1986).

Bianco, L. *Origins of the Chinese Revolution* (Stanford, 1971).

Bisbee, G. *Pre-Decian Acts of the Martyrs and Commentarii* (Philadelphia, 1989).

Blümner, H. *Die römischen Privataltherümer* (Munich, 1911).

Bornkamm, G. *Mythos und Legende in den apokryphen Thomasakten* (Göttingen, 1933).

Boslooper, T. *The Virgin Birth* (London, 1962).

Botti, G. "Gli scavi di Tebtunis," *Bolletino d'arte* 4 (1935), 376ff.

———. "I papiri ieratici e demotici degli scavi di Tebtynis," *Atti del congresso internazionale di papirilogia* (Florence, 1935), 217ff.

————. *La glorificazione di Sobk e del Fayum in un papiro hieratico da Tebtynis* (Copenhagen, 1958).

Bowersock, G. W. *Fiction as History* (Berkeley, 1994).

————. *Martyrdom and Rome* (Cambridge, 1995).

Bowman, A. *Egypt after the Pharaohs* (London², 1996).

Boyarin, D. *Carnal Israel* (Berkeley, 1993).

————. "Martyrdom and the Making of Christianity and Judaism," *Journal of Early Christian Studies* 6 (1998), 577ff.

Bradbury, S., ed. *Severus of Minorca* (Oxford, 1996).

Brent, A. *Hippolytus and the Roman Church in the Third Century* (Leiden, 1995).

Brilliant, R. *Visual Narratives* (Ithaca, 1984).

Brown, L. W. *The Indian Christians of St. Thomas* (Cambridge, 1956).

Brown, P. *Augustine of Hippo* (Berkeley, 1967).

————. *The World of Late Antiquity* (London, 1971).

————. *The Making of Late Antiquity* (Cambridge, Mass., 1978).

————. *The Cult of the Saints* (London, 1981).

————. *The Body and Society* (London, 1989).

————. *Power and Persuasion in Late Antiquity* (Madison, 1992).

Brown, R. E. *The Birth of the Messiah* (London, 1993).

————. *The Death of the Messiah* (London, 1994).

Browne, G. M. *Sortes Astrampsychi* (Leipzig, 1983).

Bruit Zaidman, L., and P. Schmitt Pantel. *Religion in the Ancient Greek City* (Cambridge, 1992).

Bruun, P. "The Disappearance of Sol from the Coins of Constantine," *Arctos* 2 (1958), 15ff.

de Bruyn, D. "Prologues bibliques d'origine marcionite," *Revue bénédictine* 24 (1907).

Bucher, P. "Les hymnes à Sobk Ra," *Kemi* 3 (1930), 1ff.

Burkitt, F. C. *The Religion of the Manichees* (Cambridge, 1925).

Burrus, V. *Chastity as Autonomy* (New York, 1987).

Cameron, R., and A. J. Dewey. *The Cologne Mani Codex* (Missoula, 1979).

von Campenhausen, H. *Ecclesiastical Authority and Spiritual Power in the Church of the First Three Centuries* (London, 1969).

————. *The Formation of the Christian Bible* (London, 1972).

————. *The Virgin Birth in the Theology of the Ancient Church* (London, 1964).

Carleton Paget, J. *The Epistle of Barnabas* (Tübingen, 1994).

Castelli, E. A. "Gender, Theory and the Rise of Christianity," *Journal of Early Christian Studies* 6 (1998), 227ff.

de Cénival, F. "Les associations réligieuses en Egypte," *Bulletin de l'institut français de l'archéologie* 46 (1972).

Charlesworth, J. H., ed. *The Old Testament Pseudepigrapha* (London, 1983), 2 vols.

Chuvin, P. *A Chronicle of the Last Pagans* (Cambridge, Mass., 1990).

Clark, E. A. *Ascetic Piety and Women's Faith* (Lewiston, 1986).

————. *The Origenist Controversy* (Princeton, 1992).

Clarke, G. W. *The Letters of St. Cyprian* (New York, 1984–89), 4 vols.

Clarke, J. R. *Looking at Love-Making in Roman Art* (Berkeley, 1998).

————. *The Houses of Roman Italy* (Berkeley, 1991).

Clarke, S., ed. *Athlone History of Witchcraft and Magic* (London, 1999), vol. 2.

Coale, A. J., and P. Demeny. *Regional Model Life Tables* (New York², 1983).

Cohen, S. J. D. *From Maccabees to the Mishnah* (Philadelphia, 1987).

Connolly, R. H. *Didascalia Apostolorum* (Oxford, 1929).

Cooper, K. "Insinuations of Womanly Influence," *Journal of Roman Studies* 82 (1992), 150ff.

———. *The Virgin and the Bride* (Cambridge, Mass., 1996).

Countryman, L. W. *The Rich Christian in the Church of the Early Empire* (New York, 1980).

Daly, L. *Aesop Without Morals* (New York, 1961).

Daniel, R. W., and F. Maltomini. *Supplementum Magicum* (Opladen, 1990), vol. 1.

Daniélou, J. *The Theology of Jewish Christianity* (London, 1964).

Darnton, R. *The Great Cat Massacre* (London, 1984).

Davies, S. L. *The Revolt of the Widows* (New York, 1980).

Dionisotti, C. "From Ausonius' Schooldays? A Schoolbook and its Relatives," *Journal of Roman Studies* 72 (1982), 83ff.

Dodge, B., ed. *The Fihrist of al-Nadim* (New York, 1970), vol. 2.

Dolzani, C. "Il dio Sobk," *Atti della Accademia Nazionale dei Lincei, Memorie* 10 (1961).

Doniger O'Flaherty, W. *The Origins of Evil in Hindu Mythology* (Berkeley, 1976).

Douglas, M. *Implicit Meanings* (London, 1975).

Drijvers, H. J. W. *East of Antioch* (London, 1984).

Droge, A. J., and J. D. Tabor. *A Noble Death* (San Francisco, 1991).

Dunn, J. *Rethinking Modern Political Theory* (Cambridge, 1985).

Dunn, J. D. G. *The Parting of the Ways* (London, 1991).

———. *Unity and Diversity in the New Testament* (London², 1990).

Dwyer, E. J. *Pompeian Domestic Sculpture* (Rome, 1982).

Elliott, J. K. *The Apocryphal New Testament* (Oxford, 1993).

Elm, S. *Virgins of God* (Oxford, 1994).

Elsner, J. R. *Imperial Rome and Christian Triumph* (Oxford, 1998).

Evans, G. R. *Augustine on Evil* (Cambridge, 1982).

Fairman, H. W. "Worship and Festivals in an Egyptian Temple," *Bulletin of the John Rylands Library* 37 (1954), 165ff.

Ferrea, A. "Uno specchio in bronzo," *Bolletino dei musei comunali di Roma* 9 (1995), 133ff.

Filoramo, G. *A History of Gnosticism* (Oxford, 1990).

Fitzgerald, J. T., and L. M. White, eds. *The Tabula of Cebes* (Chico, 1983).

Fowden, G. "Bishops and Temples in the Eastern Roman Empire," *Journal of Theological Studies* 29 (1978), 53ff.

Frankfurter, D. *Religion in Roman Egypt* (Princeton, 1998).

———. "Stylites and Phallobates," *Vigiliae Christianae* 44 (1990), 168ff.

Fredrick, D. "Beyond the Atrium," *Classical Antiquity* 14 (1985), 266ff.

Freedman, M., ed. *Midrash Rabba* (London, 1939).

Frend, W. H. C. *Martyrdom and Persecution in the Early Church* (Oxford, 1965).

Freud, S. *Civilization and Its Discontents* (London, 1982).

Friesen, S. F. *Twice Neokoros* (Leiden, 1993).

Gaarder, J. *Vita Brevis* (London, 1997).

Gager, J. *Curse-Tablets and Binding Spells from the Ancient World* (New York, 1992).

———. *The Origins of Anti-Semitism* (Oxford, 1985).

Galinsky, G. K. *Aeneas, Sicily and Rome* (Princeton, 1969).

Gallazzi, C. *Ostraka da Tebtynis* (Milan, 1979).

———. "Fouilles anciennes et nouvelles sur le site de Tebtynis," *BIFAO* 89 (1989), 179ff.

Garcia Martinez, F. *Qumran and Apocalyptic* (Leiden, 1992).

Gardner, I. *The Kephalaia of the Teacher* (Leiden, 1995).

Gardner, J. F., and T. Wiedemann. *The Roman Household* (London, 1991).

Garnsey, P. D. A., ed. *Imperialism in the Ancient World* (Cambridge, 1978).

———. "Religious Toleration in Classical Antiquity," *Church History* 21 (1984), 1ff.

Gignoux, P. "L'inscription de Kartir à Sar Mashad," *Journal asiatique* 256 (1968), 390ff.

Ginzburg, C. *The Cheese and the Worms* (London, 1992).

Goetz, G. *Corpus Glossariorum Latinorum* (Leipzig, 1892), vol. 3.

Goldhill, S. *Foucault's Virginity* (Cambridge, 1995).

Goldstein, M. *Jesus in the Jewish Tradition* (New York, 1950).

Goodman, M. *Mission and Conversion* (Oxford, 1994).

Goossens, G. *Hierapolis de Syrie* (Louvain, 1943).

Gordon, R. "Reality, Evocation and Boundary in the Mysteries of Mithras," *Journal of Mithraic Studies* 3 (1980), 19ff.

———. "Imagining Greek and Roman Magic," in S. Clarke, ed., *The Athlone History of Witchcraft and Magic* (London, 1999), vol. 2.

Goulder, M. *A Tale of Two Missions* (London, 1994).

Graf, F. *Magic in the Ancient World* (Cambridge, Mass., 1998).

Grierson, P. "The Roman Law of Counterfeiting," in R. A. G. Carson, ed., *Essays in Roman Coinage* (Oxford, 1956), 240ff.

Grillmeier, A. *Christ in Christian Tradition* (London, 1975), vol. 1.

Gwyn Griffiths, J. *The Isis-Book* (Leiden, 1975).

Gunther, J. J. "The Meaning and Origins of the Name Judas Thomas," *Le Muséon* 93 (1980).

Gutzkow, K. *Wally the Skeptic* (Bern, 1974).

Hadas-Lebel, M. *Jerusalem Contre Rome* (Paris, 1990).

Hall, S. G., ed. *Melito of Sardis* (Oxford, 1979).

Hallett, J. P. *Roman Sexualities* (Princeton, 1997).

Hanson, R. P. C. *The Search for the Christian Doctrine of God* (Edinburgh, 1988).

Harnack, A. von *The Expansion of Christianity* (London, 1904), 2 vols.

———. *Marcion: The Gospel of the Alien God* (Durham, N. C., 1990).

Harris, J. R. *The Cult of the Heavenly Twins* (Cambridge, 1906).

Harris, W. V. *Ancient Literacy* (Cambridge, Mass., 1989).

Hefele, A. *A History of the Christian Councils* (Edinburgh, 1871).

Helck, W. *Lexikon für Ägyptologie* (Wiesbaden, 1972–92), 7 vols.

Henning, W. B. "Mani's Last Journey," *Bulletin of the School of Oriental and African Studies* 10 (1939–42), 941ff.

Henrichs, A., and L. Koenen. *Der Kölner Mani-Kodex* (Opladen, 1988).

Henrichs, A. "Pagan Ritual and the Alleged Crimes of the Early Christians," *Festschrift J. Quasten, Kyriakon* (Münster, 1970), vol. 1, 18ff.

Heszer, C. *The Social Structure of the Rabbinic Movement in Roman Palestine* (Tübingen, 1997).

Himmelfarb, M. *Tours of Hell* (Philadelphia, 1983).

———. *Ascent to Heaven* (New York, 1993).

Hinton, W. *Fanshen* (New York, 1966).

Honigmann, E., and A. Maricq. *Recherches sur les Res gestae divi Saporis* (Brussels, 1953).

Hopkins, K. "Brother-Sister Marriage in Roman Egypt," *Comparative Studies in Society and History* 22 (1980), 303ff.

———. "Early Christian Number and Its Implications," *Journal of Early Christian Studies* 6 (1998).

Horbury, W. *Jews and Christians* (Edinburgh, 1998).

——. *Jewish Messianism and the Cult of Christ* (London, 1998).

Horst, P. W. van der, and J. Mansfield. *An Alexandrian Platonist Against Dualism* (Leiden, 1974).

Horst, P. W. van der, ed. *Chaeremon* (Leiden, 1987).

Ibn Qutayba, *Uyun al-Akhbar* (Cairo, 1925), vol. 1.

Iversen, E. "Fragments of a Hieroglyphic Dictionary (P. Carlsberg 7)," *Det kongelige Videnskabernes Selskab, Hist. filol. Skifter* 3.2 (Copenhagen, 1958).

Jackson, A. V. W. *Researches in Manichaeism* (New York, 1932).

Jacobelli, L. "Die suburbanen Thermen in Pompei," *Archaeologisches Korrespondenzblatt* 23 (1993).

——. *Le pitture erotiche delle terme suburbane di Pompei* (Rome, 1995).

Janes, D. *God and Gold in Late Antiquity* (Cambridge, 1998).

Jashemski, W. F. *The Gardens of Pompeii* (New Rochelle, N.Y., 1979–93), 2 vols.

Johns, C. *Sex or Symbol* (London, 1982).

Johnson, D. W., ed. *A Panegyric on Macarius, Bishop of Tkow* (Louvain, 1980).

Jonas, H. *The Gnostic Religion* (Boston, 1958).

Jones, A. H. M. *Constantine and the Conversion of Europe* (London, 1965).

——. *The Later Roman Empire* (Oxford, 1964), 3 vols.

Jongman, W. *The Economy and Society of Pompeii* (Amsterdam, 1988).

Junker, H. "Ein Doppelhymnus aus Kom Ombo," *Zeitschrift für ägyptischen Sprache* 67 (1931), 54ff.

Junod, E., and J.-D. Kaestli. *Acta Johannis* (Turnhout, 1983), 2 vols.

Kaestli, J.-D. "Fiction littéraire et réalité sociale," *Apocrypha* 1 (1990), 279–302.

Keil, J. *Ephesos* (Vienna, 1957).

Kelly, J. N. D. *Early Christian Creeds* (London³, 1972).

Kermode, F. *The Genesis of Secrecy* (Cambridge, Mass., 1979).

Khalidi, T. *The Muslim Jesus* (Cambridge, Mass., in press).

King, K. L., ed. *Images of the Feminine in Gnosticism* (Philadelphia, 1988).

Klijn, A. F. J. *The Acts of Thomas* (Leiden, 1962).

Klijn, A. F. J., and G. S. Reinink. *Patristic Evidence for Jewish Christian Sects* (Leiden, 1973).

Kloppenborg, J. S. *The Formation of Q* (Philadelphia, 1987).

Knight, J. *The Ascension of Isaiah* (Sheffield, 1995).

Knipfing, J. H. "The Libelli of the Decian Persecution," *Harvard Theological Review* 16 (1923), 345ff.

Knox, J. *Marcion and the New Testament* (Chicago, 1942).

Koenen, L. "Die Prophezeiung des Töpfers," *Zeitschrift für Papyrologie und Epigraphik* 2 (1968), 255ff.

Koester, H. *Ancient Christian Gospels* (London, 1990).

——, ed., *Ephesos* (Valley Forge, 1995).

Krauss, S. *Das Leben Jesu nach jüdischen Quellen* (Berlin, 1902).

Krauss, S., and W. Horbury. *The Jewish Christian Controversy* (Tübingen, 1995).

Krautheimer, R. *Three Christian Capitals* (Berkeley, 1983).

Kvanvig, J. L. *The Problem of Hell* (Philadelphia, 1983).

Lafargue, J. M. *Language and Gnosis: The Opening Scenes of the Acts of Thomas* (Philadelphia, 1985).

Lampe, G. W. H. *The Seal of the Spirit* (London, 1951).

Lane Fox, R. *Pagans and Christians* (New York, 1986).

Laurence, R. *Roman Pompeii* (London, 1994).

Leach, E. *Genesis as Myth* (London, 1969).

Le Boulluec, A. *La notion d'hérésie* (Paris, 1985).

Leek, F. F. "The Practice of Dentistry in Ancient Egypt," *Journal of Egyptian Archaeology* 53 (1967).

Lengyel, A., ed. *The Archaeology of Roman Pannonia* (Budapest, 1980).

Lichtheim, M. *Ancient Egyptian Literature* (Berkeley, 1990), vol. 3.

Lidonnici, L. R. *The Epidaurian Miracle Inscriptions* (Atlanta, 1995).

Lieberman, S. "Roman Legal Institutions in Early Rabbinics and the Acta Martyrum," *Jewish Quarterly Review* 35 (1944–45), 1ff.

Lietzmann, H. *Die drei ältesten Martyrologien* (Bonn, 1903).

Lieu, J., ed. *The Jews Among Pagans and Christians* (London, 1992).

Lieu, S. N. C. *Manichaeism in the Later Roman Empire and Medieval China* (Tübingen[2], 1992).

———. *Manichaeism in Mesopotamia and the Roman East* (Leiden, 1994).

Lim, R. *Public Disputation, Power and Social Order in Late Antiquity* (Berkeley, 1995).

Ling, R. *Roman Painting* (Cambridge, 1991).

Logan, A. H. B. *Gnostic Truth and Christian Heresy* (Edinburgh, 1996).

MacArthur, A. A. *The Evolution of the Christian Year* (London, 1953).

MacDermot, V., ed. *The Books of Jeu* (Leiden, 1978).

———. ed., *Pistis Sophia* (Leiden, 1978).

MacDonald, D. R. *The Acts of Andrew and the Acts of Andrew and Matthias in the City of the Cannibals* (Atlanta, 1990).

———. *There Is No Male and Female* (Philadelphia, 1985).

———. *Christianizing Homer* (Oxford, 1994).

Mack, B. *Who Wrote the New Testament?* (San Francisco, 1995).

MacKenzie, D. N. "Mani's Sabuhragan," *Bulletin of the School of Oriental and African Studies* 42 (1979), 288ff.

MacMullen, R. *Changes in the Roman Empire* (Princeton, 1990).

———. *Christianizing the Roman Empire* (New Haven, 1984).

Magne, J. *From Christianity to Gnosis* (Atlanta, 1992).

Marjanen, A. *The Woman Jesus Loved* (Leiden, 1996).

Markus, R. A. *The End of Ancient Christianity* (Cambridge, 1990).

Martinez, D. G. *A Greek Love Charm from Egypt* (Atlanta, 1991).

Mathews, T. F. *The Clash of Gods* (Princeton, 1993).

Mau, A. *Pompeii, Its Life and Art* (London, 1899).

———. "Scavi di Pompei," *Römische Mitteilungen* (1896).

McLynn, N. B. *Ambrose of Milan* (Berkeley, 1994).

Meeks, W. *The First Urban Christians* (New Haven, 1983).

———. *The Moral World of the First Christians* (London, 1987).

———. *The Origins of Christian Morality* (New Haven, 1993).

Meiggs, R. *Ostia* (Oxford[2], 1960).

Metzger, B. *An Introduction to the Apocrypha* (Oxford, 1957).

Metzler, D. "Die Enteignung der heidnischen Tempel seit Konstantin," *Hephaistos* 3 (1981), 27ff.

Mond, R. H., and O. H. Myers. *The Bucheum* (London, 1934), vol. 3.

Morenz, S. *Egyptian Religion* (London, 1973).

Mueller, F. G. J. M. *The Aldobrandini Marriage* (Amsterdam, 1994).

Mulder, M. J., ed. *Mikra, Text, Tradition, Translation* (Assen, 1988).

Murray, R. *Symbols of Church and Kingdom* (Cambridge, 1975).

Musurillo, H., ed. *Acts of the Pagan Martyrs* (Oxford, 1954).

———, ed. *Acts of the Christian Martyrs* (Oxford, 1972).

Nanda, S. *Neither Man nor Woman* (Belmont, Calif., 1990).

Neudecker, R. *Die Pracht der Latrine* (Munich, 1994).

Neugebauer, O., and R. A. Parker. *Egyptian Astronomical Texts* (Providence, 1969).

Neusner, J. *Eliezer ben Hyrcanus* (Leiden, 1973), vol. 1.

Nielsen, I. *Thermae et Balnea* (Åarhus, 1990).

Nock, A. D. *Conversion* (Oxford, 1933).

Norelli, E. *L'ascensione di Isaia* (Bologna, 1994).

North, J. "The Development of Religious Pluralism," in J. Lieu, ed., *The Jews Among Pagans and Christians* (London, 1992), 174ff.

Oertel, T. *Horst Wessel, Untersuchung einer Legende* (Cologne, 1988).

Ortner, S. B. *High Religion* (Princeton, 1989).

Otto, W. *Priester und Tempel im hellenistischen Ägypten* (Leipzig, 1905–8).

Packer, J. "Inns at Pompeii," *Cronache pompeiane* 4 (1978).

Pagels, E. *The Gnostic Paul* (Philadelphia, 1975).

———. *The Gnostic Gospels* (New York, 1980).

———. *Adam, Eve and the Serpent* (New York, 1988).

Parker, D. C. *The Living Text of the Gospels* (Cambridge, 1997).

Parker, R. A. *Demotic Mathematical Papyri* (Providence, 1972).

Parlasca, K. *Repertorio d'arte dell Egitto greco-romano* (Palermo, 1969–70), 2 vols.

Patterson, S. J. *The Gospel of Thomas and Jesus* (Sonoma, Calif., 1993).

Pearson, B. A., ed. *The Future of Early Christianity* (Minneapolis, 1990).

Pelikan, J. *Christianity and Classical Culture* (New Haven, 1993).

———. *The Christian Tradition* (Chicago, 1971).

———. *The Emergence of the Catholic Tradition* (Chicago, 1971).

Pervo, R. I. *Profit with Delight* (Philadelphia, 1987).

Petersen, W. L., ed. *Gospel Traditions in the Second Century* (Notre Dame, 1989).

Pétrement, C. *A Separate God* (London, 1991).

Petzl, G. "Die Beicht-Inschriften Westkleinasiens," *Epigraphica Anatolica* 22 (1994), 1ff.

Pharr, C., ed. *The Theodosian Code* (Princeton, 1952).

Polotsky, H.-J., and A. Boehlig. *Kephalaia* (Stuttgart, 1940–66), 2 vols.

Pöschmann, B. *Penance and the Anointing of the Sick* (London, 1964).

Price, S. R. F. *Rituals and Power* (Cambridge, 1984).

Prieur, J. M. "Acta Andreae," *Corpus Christianorum Series Apocryphorum* 5 and 6 (Turnhout, 1989).

Purcell, N. "Literate Games," *Past and Present* 147 (1995).

Rappaport, U. *The Dead Sea Scrolls* (Leiden, 1992).

Reardon, B. P. *Collected Ancient Greek Novels* (Berkeley, 1989).

Reekmans, L. "La dextrarum iunctio . . . ," *Bulletin de l'institut historique de Belge* 31 (1958), 23ff.

Rees, B. R. *Pelagius* (Woodbridge, 1988).

———. *The Letters of Pelagius* (Woodbridge, 1991).

Régnault, L. *Apopthegmata Patrum* (Solmes, 1976–77).

Reymond, A. E., and J. B. Barns. *Four Martyrdoms from the Pierpoint Morgan Coptic Codices* (Oxford, 1973).

Richardson, L. *Pompeii: An Architectural History* (Baltimore, 1988).

Robinson, J. M., ed. *The Nag Hammadi Library in English* (Leiden[3], 1988).

Rogers, G. *The Sacred Identity of Ephesus* (London, 1991).

Roller, L. E. "The Ideology of the Eunuch Priest," *Gender & History* 9 (1997), 542ff.

Rousseau, P. *Basil of Caesarea* (Berkeley, 1994).

Rubensohn, O. "Aus griechisch-römischen Haüsern des Fayum," *Jahrbuch des deutschen archäologischen Instituts* 20 (1905).

Rudolph, K. *Gnosis* (Edinburgh, 1983).

Ruffer, M. *Studies in the Palaeopathology of Egypt* (Chicago, 1921).

Russell, D. A., and N. G. Wilson. *Menander Rhetor* (Oxford, 1981).

Ryberg, I. Scott "Rites of the State Religion in Roman Art," *Memoirs of the American Academy at Rome* (1955).

Sanders, E. P. *Jesus and Judaism* (London, 1985).

———. *Paul* (Oxford, 1991).

———. *Paul and Palestinian Judaism* (London, 1977).

Sanders, E. P., and M. Davies. *Studying the Synoptic Gospels* (London, 1989).

Sarre, F., and E. Herzfeld. *Iranische Felsreliefs* (Berlin, 1910).

Schama, S. *Dead Certainties* (London, 1992).

Scherrer, P. *Ephesos, der neue Führer* (Vienna, 1996).

Schiffman, L. H. *Reclaiming the Dead Sea Scrolls* (Philadelphia, 1994).

Schmidt C., and H.-J. Polotsky. "Ein Mani-Fund in Ägypten," *Sitzungsberichte der preussischen Akademie der Wissenschaften (Phil-hist. Kl)* (1933).

Schneemelcher, W., ed. *New Testament Apocrypha* (Cambridge[3], 1991).

Schuerer, E. *The History of the Jewish People in the Age of Jesus Christ* (Edinburgh, 1973, 1975).

Schweitzer, A. *The Quest for the Historical Jesus* (London, 1910).

Sedgwick, E. K. *Between Men* (New York, 1985).

Segal, A. F. *Paul the Convert* (New Haven, 1990).

Segal, J. B. *Edessa, the Blessed City* (Oxford, 1970).

Seiler, F. *Casa degli amorini dorati* (Munich, 1992).

Shaw, B. "The Family in Late Antiquity," *Past and Present* 115 (1987), 3ff.

———. "The Passion of Perpetua," *Past and Present* 139 (1993).

Sherk, R. K. *Documents from the Greek East* (Baltimore, 1969).

Shore, A. F. *Portrait Painting from Roman Egypt* (London, 1972).

Simon, M. *Verus Israel* (Oxford, 1986).

Simonetta, B., and R. Riva. *Le tessere erotiche romane* (Lugano, 1981).

Skoçpol, T. *States and Social Revolutions* (Cambridge, 1979).

Smelik, K. A. D., and E. A. Hemelrijk. "Egyptian Animal Worship," *ANRW* 2.17.4 (1984), 1852ff.

Smith, J. Z. *Drudgery Divine* (Chicago, 1990).

Smith, M. *Clement of Alexandria and a Secret Gospel of Mark* (Cambridge, Mass., 1973).

Sogliano, A. *Monumenti antichi* 8 (1898), 234ff.

Spinazzola, V. *Pompei ala luce degli scavi nuovi* (Rome, 1953), 2 vols.

Sprengling, M. *Third-Century Iran, Sapor and Kartir* (Chicago, 1953).

Stark, R. *The Rise of Early Christianity* (Princeton, 1996).

Ste. Croix, G. E. M. de. *The Class Struggle in the Ancient Greek World* (London, 1981).

Stefanelli, L. P. B. *L'argento dei romani* (Rome, 1991).

Stegeman, H. "The Qumran Essenes," in J. Trebolla Barrera, ed., *The Madrid Qumran Congress* (Leiden, 1972), vol. 1, 83ff.

Stendahl, K. *Paul Among Jews and Gentiles* (Philadelphia, 1976).

Stevenson, J. *A New Eusebius* (London², 1987).

———. *Creeds, Councils and Controversies* (London², 1989).

Strocka, V. M. *Die Wandmalerei der Hanghäuser, Forschungen in Ephesus* 8.1 (Vienna, 1977).

Strong, D. E. *Roman Art* (London, 1976).

Tambiah, S. J. *Magic, Science, Religion and the Scope of Rationality* (Cambridge, 1990).

Tardieu, M. *Écrits Gnostiques* (Paris, 1984).

Theissen, G. *Der Schatten des Galiläers, historische Jesusforschung in erzählender Form* (Munich, 1986), translated as *The Shadow of the Galilean* (London, 1987).

———. *The Historical Jesus* (London, 1998).

———. *The Social Setting of Pauline Christianity* (Edinburgh, 1982).

———. *The Miracle Stories of the Early Christian Tradition* (Edinburgh, 1983).

Thomas, N., and C. Humphrey, eds. *Shamanism, History and the State* (Ann Arbor, 1994).

Thompson, H., trans. "Two Demotic Self-Dedications," *Journal of Egyptian Archaeology* 26 (1940), 68ff.

Toynbee, J., and J. Ward Perkins. *The Shrine of St. Peter* (London, 1956).

Treggiari, S. *Roman Marriage* (Oxford, 1991).

Trümpelmann, L. *Iranische Denkmäler* (Berlin, 1975).

Turner, J. D. *The Book of Thomas the Contender* (Missoula, 1975).

Vanderlinden, S., ed. "Revelatio sancti Stephani," *Revue des études byzantines* 4 (1946), 191ff.

Vermes, G. *Jesus the Jew* (London², 1983).

———. *The Dead Sea Scrolls in English* (Sheffield⁴, 1995).

Veyne, P. *Writing History* (Manchester, 1984).

Vinzent, M. *Asterius von Kappadokien* (Leiden, 1993).

Wallace-Hadrill, A. *Houses and Society in Pompeii and Herculaneum* (Princeton, 1994).

Ward, B. *The Wisdom of the Desert Fathers* (London, 1986).

Williams, M. A. *Rethinking Gnosticism* (Princeton, 1996).

Williams, R. *Arius* (London, 1987).

Wimbush, V. L., ed. *Ascetic Behavior in Greco-Roman Antiquity* (Minneapolis, 1990).

Winkler, J. J. *Auctor & Actor* (Berkeley, 1985).

———. *The Constraints of Desire* (New York, 1990).

Young, F. M. *From Nicaea to Chalcedon* (London, 1983).

Zaehner, C. *The Dawn and Twilight of Zoroastrianism* (New York, 1961).

Zanker, P. "Die Villa als Vorbild," *Jahrbuch des deutsches archäologischen Instituts* 9 (1979), 496ff.

Zias, J., and F. Sekeles. "The Crucified Man from Giv'at ha Mivtar—A Reappraisal," *Israel Exploration Journal* 35 (1985), 22ff.

Credits

My thanks to the following for illustrations: Faculty of Classics, University of Cambridge, photograph collection; The Ancient Art and Architecture Collection, Pinner, Middlesex, for color plate 7; Istituto Archeologico Germanico for plates 4, 14–17, and 30; D. Frederick, "Erotic Pleasure and Visual Pleasure in the Roman House," *Classical Antiquity* 14 (1995), figure 15, p. 283, and the University of California Press for plate 18; Museo Comunale di Roma, for plate 19; Y. Yadin, *Tefillin from Qumran* (1969), plate XII, and the Israel Exploration Society for illustration on page 55; E. Breccia, *Monuments de l'Egypte gréco-romaine* (Bergamo, 1926), 1.2 for plate 20; S. Kambitsis, "Une nouvelle tablette magique d'Egypte," *Bulletin de l'institut français de l'archéologie orientale* 76 (1976), plate XXX, for plate 21; R. Stark, *The Rise of Christianity* (1996), 146 and Princeton University Press for plate 22; R. P. Knight, *A Discourse on the Worship of Priapus* (London, 1865), plate 2.3, for plate 23; *Journal of Hellenic Studies* 54 (1934), plate III, for plate 24; Yale University Art Gallery, *Yale-French Excavations at Dura-Europas*, photograph Z-118, for plate 26; W. Dorigo, *Pittura tardoromana* (Milan, 1966), plate 211, for plate 27.

Subject Index

Selective Index of Proper Names